I0823033

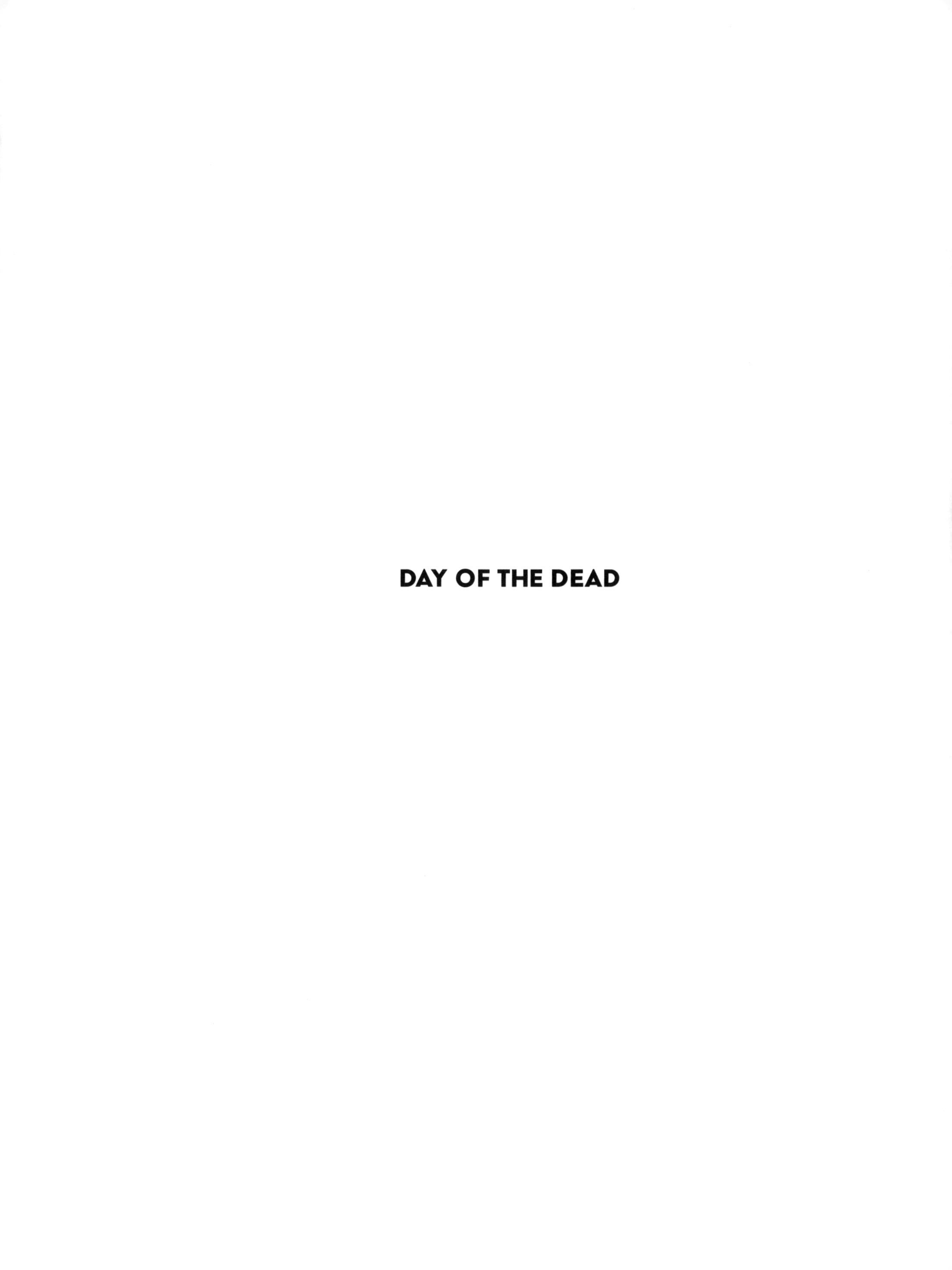

DAY OF THE DEAD

Artes de México is a publishing house with more than twenty-eight years of experience. Our goal is to promote and disseminate the cultural diversity of Mexico in all its creative manifestations. We seek to transform the knowledge of Mexican culture into unprecedented reading material of exceptional quality. We create books for a wide variety of readers, including children. Since the project was conceived, it has been linked to the most important writers, researchers, creators, opinion leaders, and entrepreneurs of Mexico. Our publishing endeavor has been recognized with more than 150 national and international awards.

Artes de México es una editorial con más de 28 años de experiencia. Nuestro propósito es promover y difundir la diversidad cultural de México en todas sus manifestaciones creativas. Transforma los saberes de nuestra cultura en material de lectura sin precedente y con calidad excepcional. Creamos libros para un público adulto e infantil. Desde sus inicios, ha estado vinculada con los escritores, investigadores, creadores, líderes de opinión y empresarios más importantes de México. Nuestra labor editorial ha sido reconocida con más de 150 premios nacionales e internacionales.

DAY OF THE DEAD

THE HISTORY OF A CELEBRATION

Artes de México

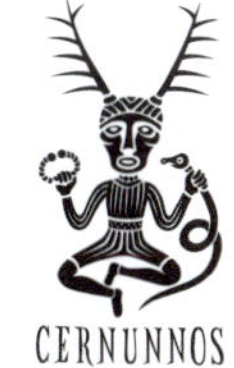

DÍA DE MUERTOS

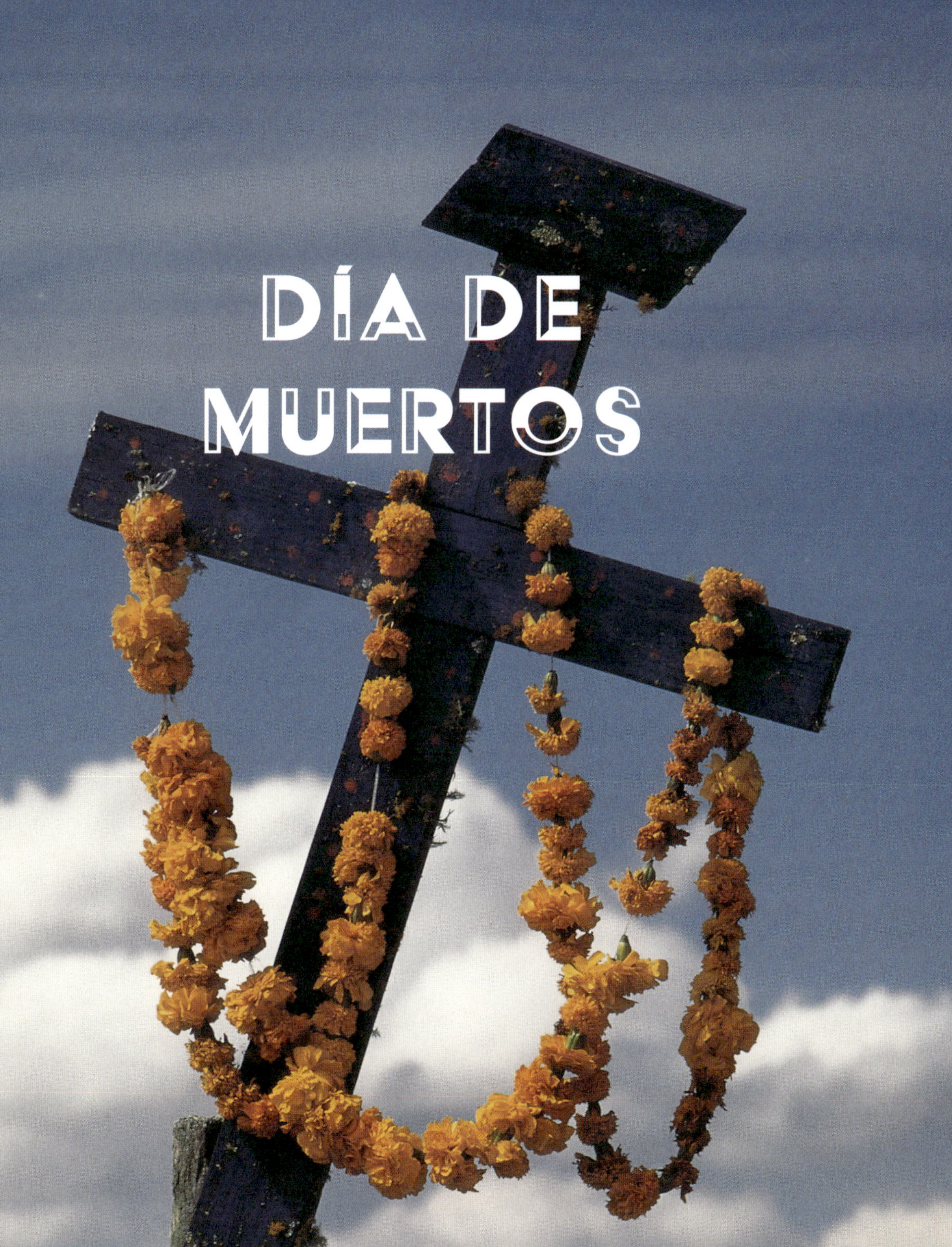

CONTENTS

CONTENIDO

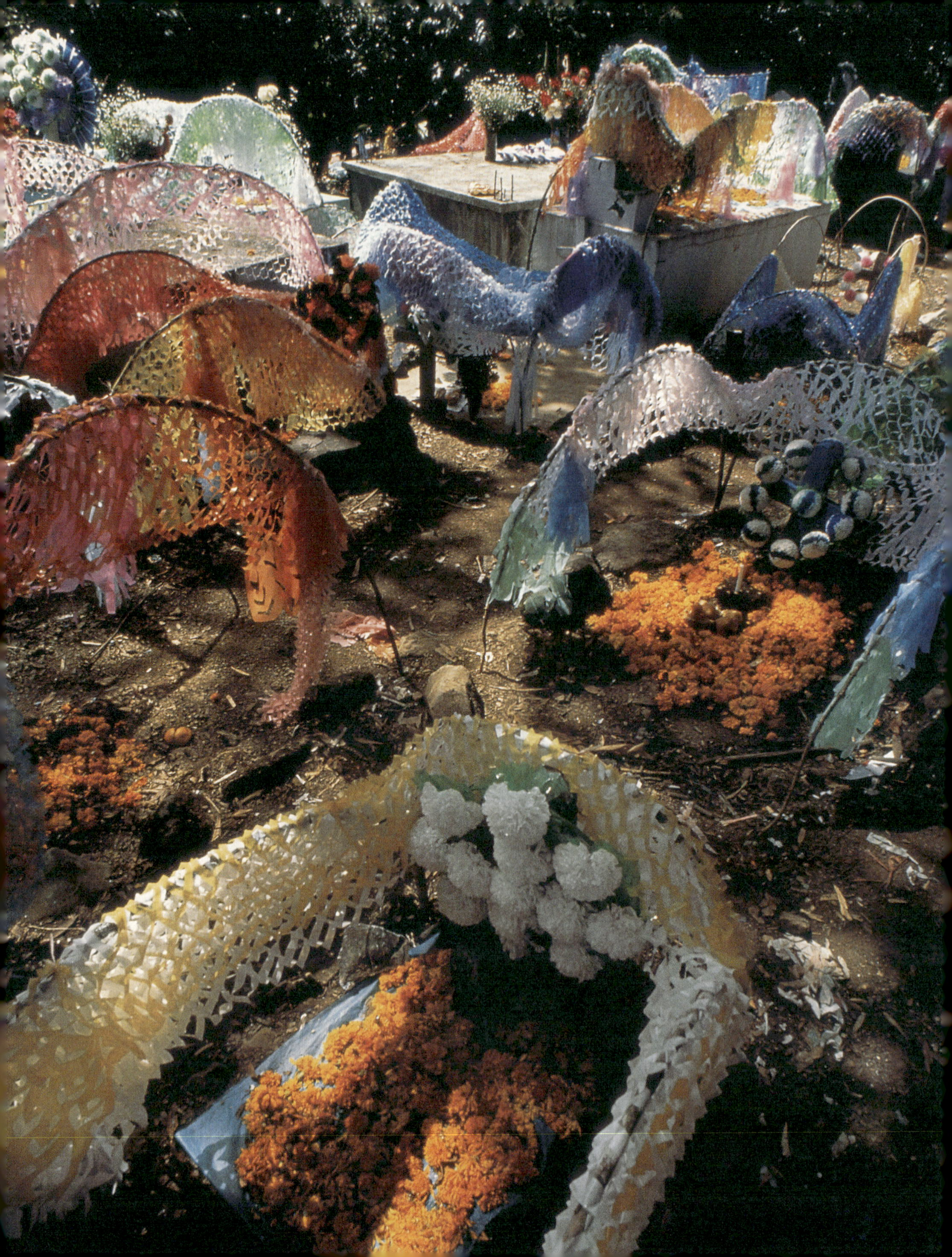

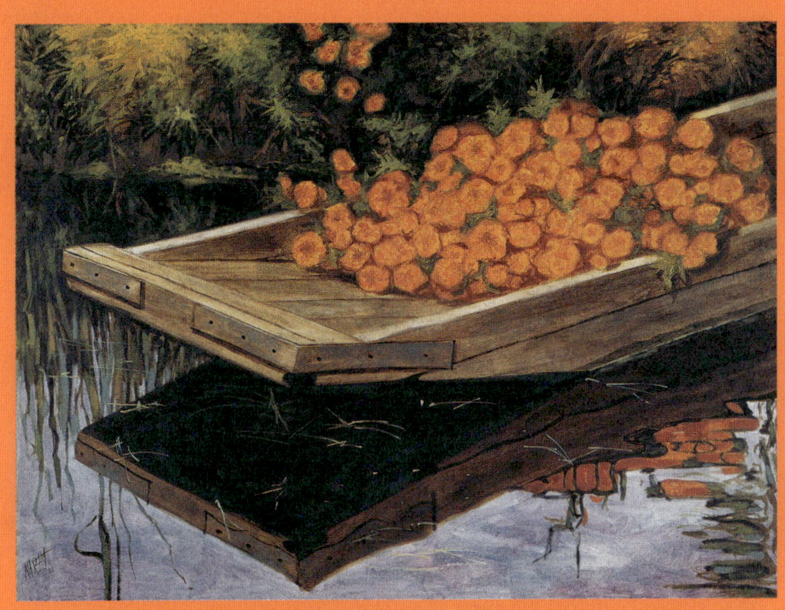

PART I

RITUAL SERENITY

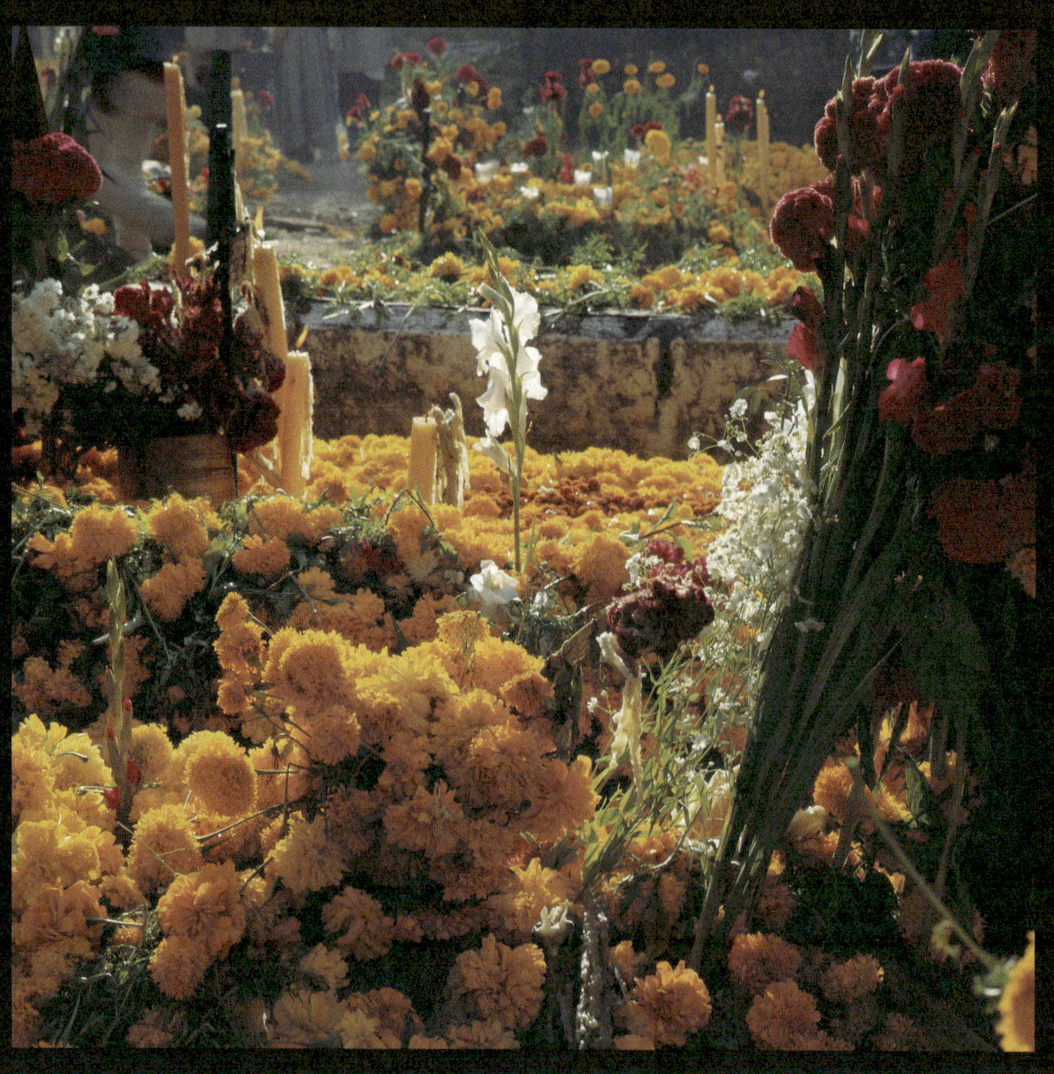

Paul Czitrom. *Pantéon de Tetelcingo*, Puebla, on the Day of the Dead. 1999. • **PAGE 10:** George O. Jackson. *Cementerio en Guadalupe Victoria*, Chiapas. 2000. • **PREVIOUS PAGE:** Nareth. *Ofrenda*. 1995. Acrylic on fibercel. 50 × 66 cm.

QUESTIONS ABOUT THE DAY OF THE DEAD AND DEATH'S GRIN

Margarita de Orellana

◆◆◆◆◆

"Urban Mexicans encounter death with fun and games, while rural Indians encounter it with absolute tranquility."

Frances Toor

Curiosity, wonder, and fascination are the emotions impregnating this volume. Unlike those who believe that Mexico's culture of death has already been thoroughly explored, we are more inclined to think it comprehends a richer universe than what is widely claimed, and that there is much to be learned about it.

When we began to research the topic of the Day of the Dead, we were first struck by a fact that contradicts all the preconceived notions most people have of this celebration: the rural and the urban experience of the Day of the Dead are two very different things. In the city, the Day of the Dead is indeed noted for its explosion of colors and forms, but they lack any religious significance and possess a more uninhibited, playful, festive air.

How and when did the rural and the urban celebrations begin to diverge? Why was the ritual nature of the celebration abandoned in the city,

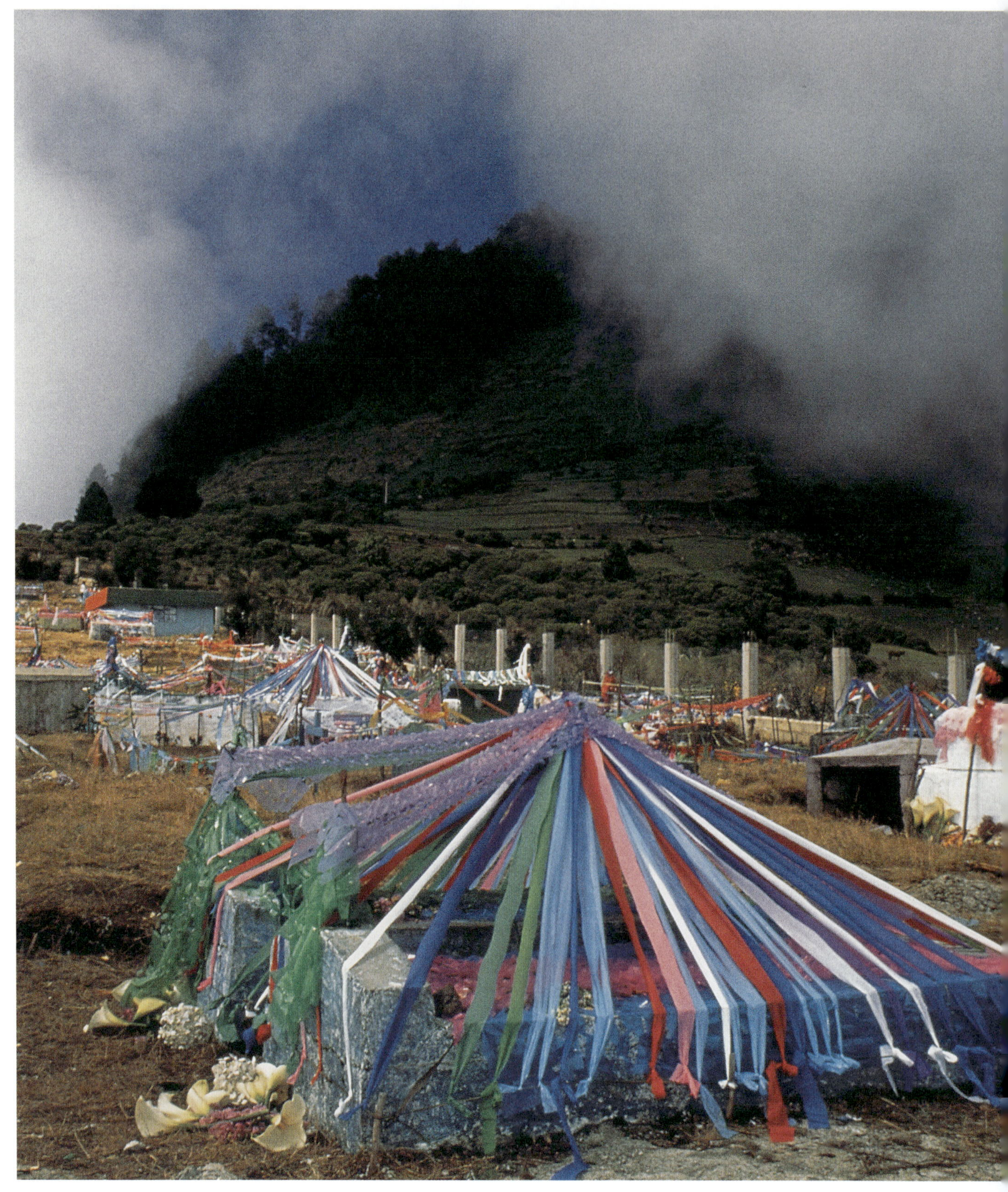

George O. Jackson. *Cementerio en El Malé*, Chiapas. 2000.

converting it into an impassioned and defiant experience? Why do many Mexicans believe that the Day of the Dead is celebrated in the same way throughout the country?

Some have thought that the urban Day of the Dead is a secular holiday due to the influence of the Mexican Revolution. Many post-revolutionary intellectuals were obsessed with lessening the importance of Catholicism and the Spanish legacy here, in hopes of emphasizing the pre-Hispanic past and thus strengthening our cultural roots. People's notions of the Day of the Dead followed that lead. However, this distancing between rural and urban Mexico had already begun in the late nineteenth century. In a society aspiring toward modernity and to join the ranks of other modern nations, this kind of festivity seemed to be an atavism, an obstacle to progress. Some individuals (especially in the educated middle classes) expressed their repudiation of these demonstrations of "backwardness." Other more traditionalist souls lamented the fact that this day, dedicated for centuries to sorrow and nostalgia, had been tainted by frivolity. According to this particular point of view, the dead no longer came to share the food of the living, but to observe "massive feasts, with gluttons ingesting food and alcohol without restraint." In the graveyards, loud voices and even peals of laughter were heard instead of prayers.

Every year, Mexico City and places such as Toluca, with its Alfeñique Market, are inundated with colors and flavors, embodied in their pastries and sweetmeats, in particular the sugar skulls. We do not observe such a proliferation of sugar in rural areas, but rather the preparation of traditional dishes that were favorites of the deceased. And sugar skulls are nowhere to be seen on the altars to the dead.

Skeletons and Grim Reapers are very familiar figures to us in the city. They express our defiant attitude before death that apparently forms part of our idiosyncrasy. It is curious how much emphasis was given in twentieth-century Mexico to a representation whose origins lie in medieval Europe, to the point where it came to be thought of as a national characteristic. The *calavera*, in all its incarnations—sugar skull, cartoon skeleton, satirical poem—becomes part of the community on this day, and like the candy skulls we all love, a kind of communion with death. Authors Luis Cardoza y Aragón and Paul Westheim were both intrigued by this phenomenon on their arrival in Mexico, and offer their reflections on diverse aspects of the visual arts as related to the *calaveras*. Cardoza y Aragón focuses on José

Guadalupe Posada's illustrations, while Westheim explores how these skeletal representations speak more of the anguish of life than any rapport with death.

Ruth Lechuga points out the fact that skeletons not only dance and play a comic role in our celebration of Day of the Dead. The pale emaciated *calaca*—the Grim Reaper, Death incarnate—is endlessly invented and reinvented in Mexico on a daily basis. And we could not leave out the tradition's exportation across the northern border. What significance has the Day of the Dead had among Chicanos? Tomás Ybarra Frausto defines it as a struggle against forgetfulness that permits a confrontation with—and perhaps a transformation of—the emigrant's new reality. This is followed by writer Ana García Bergua who offers us a literary altar of the dead that will take the reader by surprise.

Alfonso Alfaro's brilliant essay answers many of the questions that we posed when we began working on this issue. How did the Day of the Dead and the urban *calaveras* serve as a symbolic tool in the post-revolutionary strategy for creating a national identity? How has the idea that Mexicans have a privileged relationship with death been gradually interiorized in our society? This author also analyzes the urban upper classes' attitude before death—so similar to that of their counterparts in Europe and the United States. And finally, he invokes the death that appears in our country day after day, to the sound of shots fired from an AK-47. And he proposes one certainty as regards death: "our country does not have the slightest idea what to do with it." The subject of death is inexhaustible, so we will continue our exploration in hopes of arousing in our readers more questions than those addressed here.

In rural areas, most of which house largely indigenous populations, the Day of the Dead is still closely linked to ancestral beliefs. Its ritual form of expressing creativity is impregnated with an inflexible solemnity and a strict code of behavior, accompanied by the extravagant use of color, composition and texture. During this holiday period, most normal activities are suspended. Homes and cemeteries are transformed, taking on a new guise and an entire range of meanings. The living expectantly await the annual visit of the souls with whom they will interact, establishing an intense dialogue with them. The dead come to life in the memory of the living, who evoke their particular customs, tastes, virtues, and defects. There is no room for rejection here, but perhaps for a certain degree of reproach.

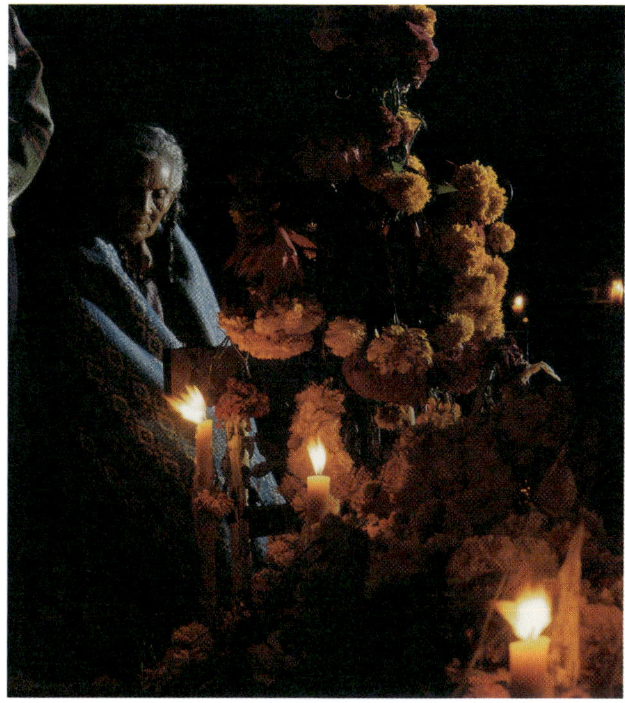

Paul Czitrom. Tetelcingo, Puebla. 1999.

In each community, this dialogue takes on a specific form: strict standards of hospitality and millenary codes of conduct that each participant understands entirely, because the laws governing that interaction are the laws of life. In communities that celebrate the Day of the Dead there are no surprises. But for those who have an outsider's view of these celebrations, the surprises are many. In this dialogue between the living and the dead, incarnated in altars and offerings, we note one surprising common denominator: their strong aesthetic sense. In ephemeral compositions made of earth, flowers, candles, baskets, colored paper, wooden or iron crosses and even plastic ornaments, we recognize one of the more fertile dimensions of folk art. In each of these majestic offerings, we discover a transcendent and vital art form, as well as an unburdening of the soul that detonates in an explosion of forms and colors.

There are some offerings that, with a handful of marigold petals and two or three candles, form a composition of great simplicity and harmony in tones of deep ocher. Others are more baroque, and reveal an aesthetic dimension that satisfies by demonstrating a natural adeptness at creating beauty. More than a celebration of the dead, are the creators of these works not celebrating life? Might these rituals not be an intense prolongation of life in the midst of death?

It would be impossible to mention the thousands of Day of the Dead rituals that are carried out every year in Mexico. The small sample we present on these pages is eloquent enough. The authors have indicated the pre-Hispanic echoes in some of these rituals, but also the direct influence our Hispanic history has had on them.

Dominique Dufétel shows us certain similarities in the customs and beliefs of both cultural sources. Given the fact that at the time of the Spanish conquest, a Mexica celebration of death happened to coincide with the European All Saints' Day, he suggests that these two holidays merged to give rise to the grandiloquence and fervor with which the Day of the Dead is currently received.

Ruth D. Lechuga outlines some of the characteristics of the ceremonies as celebrated among the Huastecs, Totonacs, Nahuas and Chatinos, discovering some of them to be reminiscent of certain pre-Hispanic practices. However, she clarifies that while Christians "pray for the souls of the dead, indigenous people pray to them." Five centuries after evangelization, this kind of religiosity has remained valid.

During the time she spent with the Huaves of San Mateo del Mar in the 1950s, Laurette Séjourné realized that in this community on the Isthmus of Tehuantepec, altars to the dead were not dedicated to any one person in particular. All souls were welcomed on the Day of the Dead, and were free to visit any home they pleased. However, those who met their death outside of town are turned away, as they are considered unwanted strangers.

Teotitlán del Valle in the state of Oaxaca is a community of extraordinary weavers who hold onto their traditions with extreme passion. Mary Jane Gagnier has formed part of that community for over fifteen years. She possesses a profound understanding of the unseen details and meanings of the Day of the Dead ritual, and generously shares them with us here. Her story reveals the deep interpersonal ties that exist in that community, and how these rituals bring people even closer together. Her testimony is both enlightening and astounding.

From Fernando Benítez, we receive several stories told to him by a Mazatec Indian from the Sierra of Oaxaca, dire warnings of the punishment awaiting anyone who does not receive the dead as ordained.

Then, Marta Turok describes how in Central Mexico and urban areas, the market has generated a demand for objects that in the past were used for offerings, eventually converting them into a decorative art form far removed from their original usage. It is clear that many woodcarvers, potters, and other artisans have found economic benefits in the spectacular aspect of this ritual.

Gabriela Olmos undertakes a symbolic reading of the Day of the Dead based on the ideas of renowned religious historian Mircea Eliade. This article hypothetically remits us to ancient agricultural ceremonies "linking death and the possibility of renewal."

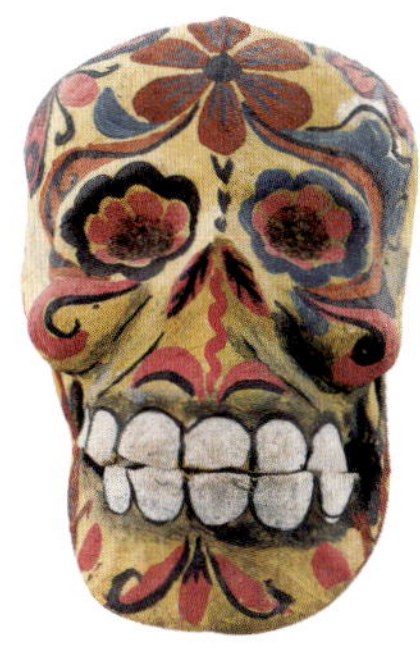
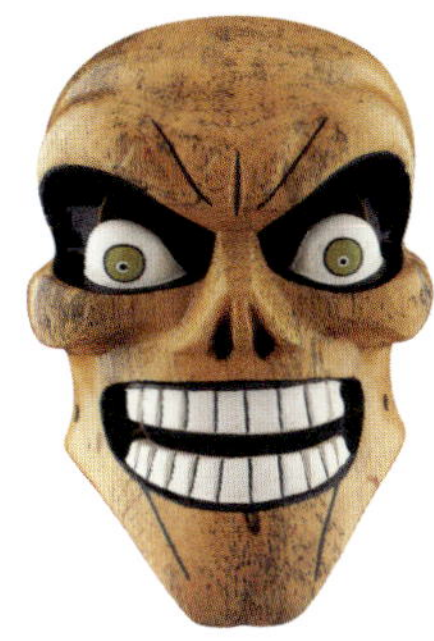
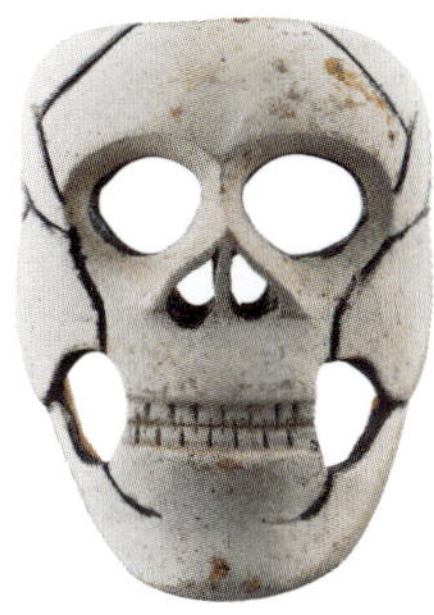

Masks from the Ruth D. Lechuga Collection of Popular Art/Franz Mayer Museum.

Skulls are an important part of the urban celebration of Day of the Dead, but they have little or no presence in rural festivities. This symbol contributes to the tendency to believe that the Mexican identity is based on a specific relationship with death. It also represents another type of relationship linked to defiance and laughter. The urban fiesta has lost virtually all trace of religious significance, but that does not imply that artistic sensibilities are not keen in this setting as well, nor that the celebration is any less important. For this reason, the representation of skulls in sugar, chocolate, paper cutouts and papier-mâché will be the focus of a later publication on the Day of the Dead. For the present, we hope that this book will transport you to a world full of beauty and serenity. ◆

—Translated by Michelle Suderman

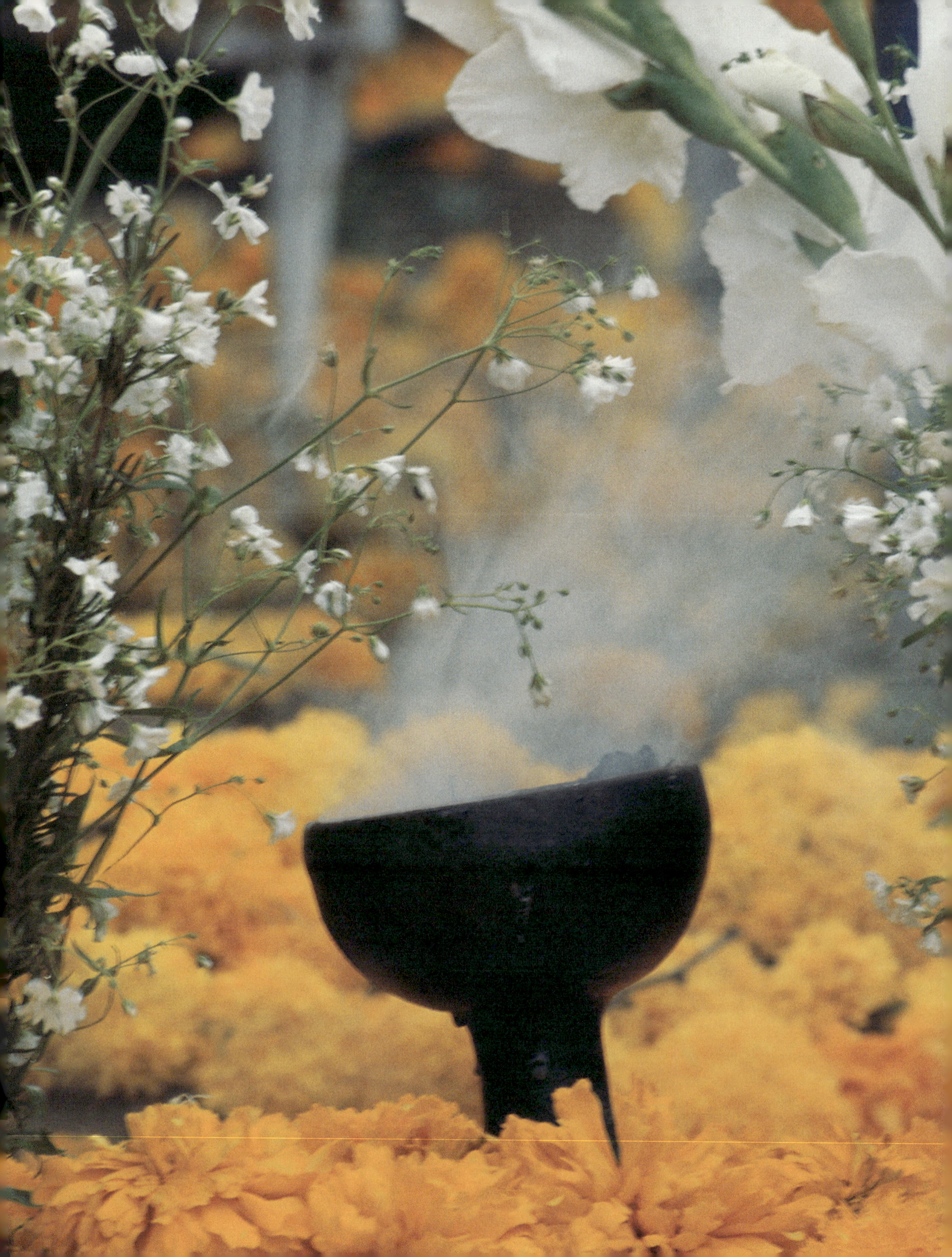

OCCULT ANCESTORS

Dominique Dufétel

◆◆◆◆◆

Who would dispute that the shaggy orange flower known as *cempasúchil* or marigold has a relationship with the Day of the Dead that stretches far back into pre-Hispanic times? To realize just how profoundly ancient the tradition is, suffice it to wander through the great markets of Mexico City—such as the one at Xochimilco—during the days prior to All Souls' Day and see the stalls heaped with these "flowers of the dead;" to visit any Mexican graveyard on November 2 and become dizzy from the pungent scent; to surrender to the environment created by these blooms as they steep altars, tombs and the paths of souls in a unique aesthetic. The flower of countless petals, the flower of infinity (*cempasúchil: cempoalxóchitl*, flower of twenty petals, i.e., an infinite number of them) is piled into golden drifts over anything connected with the deceased during those days. But despite this evidence, a glance at the principal sources of our knowledge regarding the holy days and ceremonies of the ancient Mexicans will indicate that no such association existed, that while the plant is assuredly both antique and native, it was used in a range of festivals as just one among many other species that were considered no less important in the endless game of fiesta, life, and sacrifice.

◆ PRE-HISPANIC FESTIVALS OF DEATH ◆

There were not one but many ways to honor the deceased throughout the eighteen months of the Aztec year, and these occasions tended to be tied to other events, which might lead us to the hasty conclusion that following the

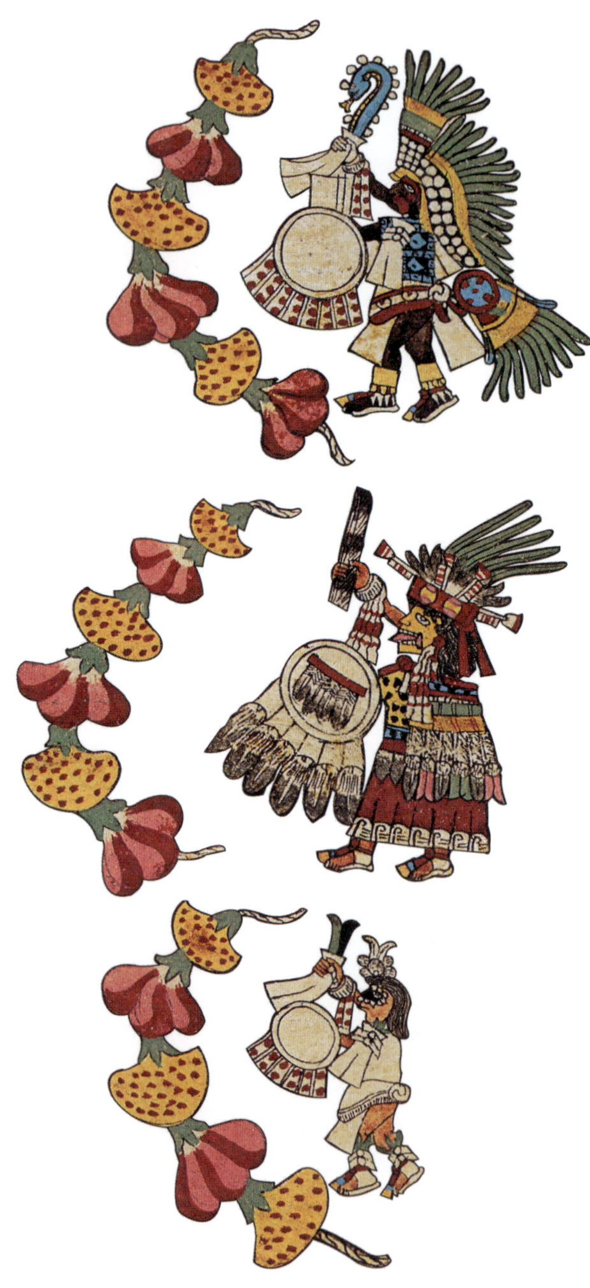

Tlaxochimaco, little festival of the dead. Codex Borbonicus. • **PAGE 20:** Paul Czitrom. Tetelcingo, Puebla, 1999.

conquest, all the forms of celebrating the afterlife became condensed into the days ordained for this purpose by the Christian religion. Nevertheless, closer study reveals that there were two ceremonies valued over and above all other rituals of death: the first fell in the ninth month, Tlaxochimaco, also known as Miccailhuitontli which means "small feast of the dead" or "feast of the small dead;" the second took place during the following month, Xócotl Uetzi, or Hueymiccaihuitl, meaning the great feast of the dead. It is very likely that the proceedings were scheduled for the last of the twenty days that made up each month. This is perhaps the reason why the two days of commemoration of the dead came to be held on the first and second days of November in the Gregorian calendar, first the children's day, then the adults', as in the old tradition.

Aside from these two major celebrations, the cult of the dead was practiced on other occasions, each consecrated to a different category of souls. In the Mesoamerican conception of the World, the individual's conditions of existence after death depended not so much on the manner in which he or she had lived—like it does for the profoundly ethical Christian religion—as on the manner of death, a circumstance which was in any case predestined by the magical calendar from birth. During the feast of Tepeilhuitl, for example, people made "images of mountains out of *tzoalli* paste in honor of the high peaks where the clouds gather, and in memory of those who had perished in water or after being struck by lightning, or those whose bodies were not incinerated but buried"—that is, those destined for the paradise ruled by Tláloc. During the month of Quecholli, the victims of battle were remembered: the warriors who were now escorting the Sun in its climb to the zenith, before descending during the afternoon in the form of butterflies and hummingbirds. Izcalli was the month of the Tamale Feast, in honor of the fire god Xiutecuhtli. The ceremony involved an offering of five tamales to the flames of the hearth; to honor them, one was also placed on every grave, to indicate that this was not the resting place for common remains. "This was done before eating the tamales and afterward they would eat them all, not leaving a single one."

Such ceremonials were part and parcel of other more important ones, for each month was dedicated to a god who was—in Mesoamerican cosmology as in many other religions—originally or most primitively an ancestor. Numerous Amerindian myths feature an ancestor who becomes a hero and eventually, over time, acquires the status of a god. In the highly complex structure of the Mexican religion, dominated by the pantheon of gods, the cult of the dead seems to be confined to the familial sphere and closely concerned with lineage. The custom of cremating the dead (probably inherited from the Toltecs but ideally suited to the physical conditions of the Valley of Mexico, a vast lagoon which did not lend itself to the excavation of large-scale tombs) doubtless had a marked effect on the nature of the mortuary rites and may go some way toward explaining the secondary role of the Day of the Dead. The tomb as such, a physical space that enjoys considerable relevance in today's ritual, was virtually nonexistent then; hence, perhaps, the stress on altars to the dead as stand-ins for the memorial headstone.

• DEATH'S GREAT ANNUAL CYCLE OF THE DEAD •

It is important to explore the possible symbolic relations between pre-Hispanic tributes to the dead and the larger feasts with which they were articulated, since, as Mircea Eliade asserts, "The symbol delivers its message and fulfils its purpose even when its meaning is not consciously apprehended."

One point must be emphasized with regard to the ancient calendar. The Mexicas had a solar year of 365 days (divided into eighteen twenty-day months, plus five spare days of ill omen), but it seems they neglected to adjust for the astronomical error (for instance by adding, as we presently do, one day every four years). Given that their calendar originated sometime during the Toltec era, corresponding to the eighth century AD, it must have been at least six months behind by the time of the conquest. This led to a glaring mismatch between the point in the agricultural cycle which each month purported to mark—especially in its way of worshipping gods who were consistently associated with nature—and the actual season of the fiesta's celebration. We may suppose that, as in any tradition whose origins have been lost, the Mexicas soldiered on with their rites but in some confusion, suggesting a cult which stands closer to religiosity than to mysticism.

The first of the two main feasts of the dead—dedicated to the children as we mentioned earlier—was dubbed Miccailhuitontli by the other peoples of the Mexican Altiplano, but the Mexicas called it Tlaxochimaco, or "birth of flowers." The central act of this ceremony was to offer up "the early and incipient buds," the chroniclers tell us; unfortunately, though, during the sixteenth century the date fell in August, when flowers are in full bloom.

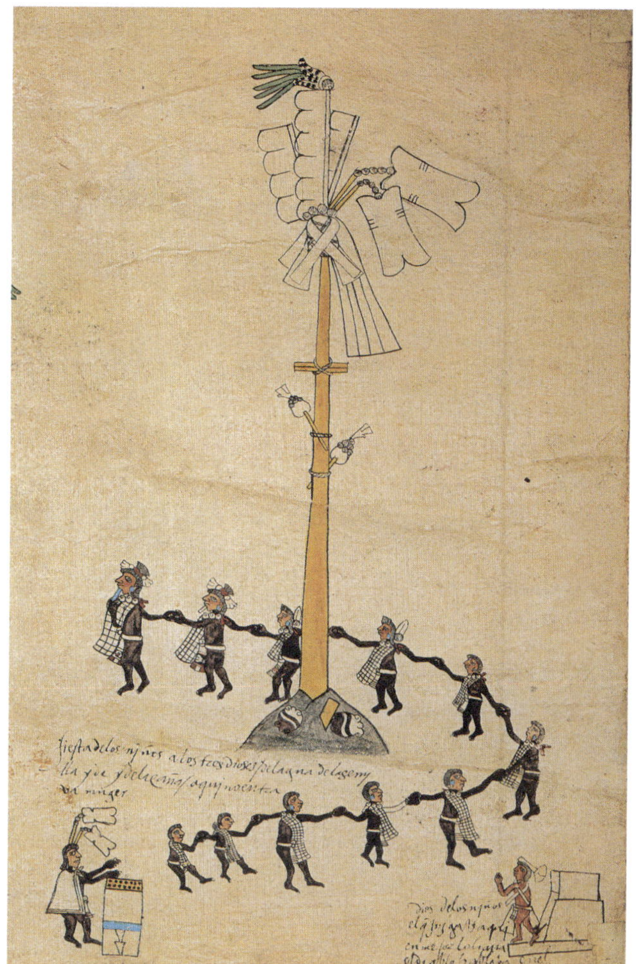

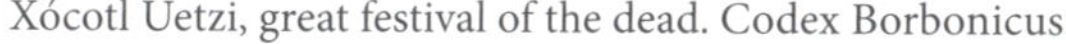

Xócotl Uetzi, great festival of the dead. Codex Borbonicus.

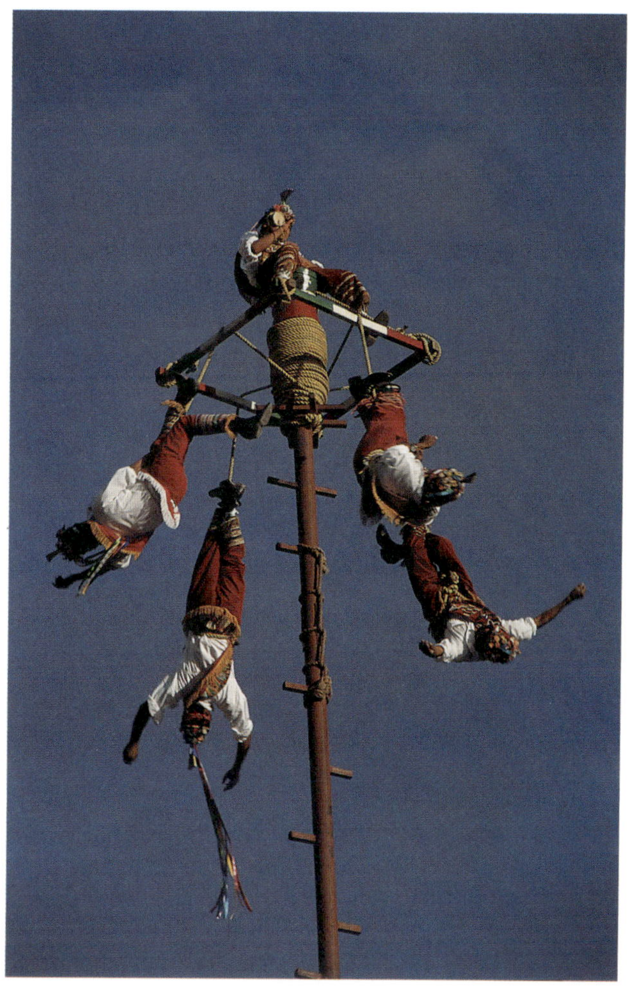

Jorge Pablo Aguinaco. Flying stick ceremony, a rite with echoes of the Xócotl Uetzi.

Back in the eighth century, of course, it came in February, around the time when the first buds begin to emerge across the Altiplano. This enables us to understand the significance of the infant deaths that were offered up on this occasion to the supreme deity, Huitzilopochtli, alongside the first flowerings of the natural cycle: these small dead souls were headed directly for the highest heaven, that is, for the divine place above all others, where they would be reabsorbed into the vital magma that gave birth to every being. Hence their premature death was no misfortune, but a divine sacrifice. "Two days before this feast," relates the anthropologist and friar Sahagún, "the whole populace took to the meadows and cornfields to look for flowers, blossoms of the woods and of the countryside, some of which are called . . ." and he writes out a long list of floral names, all corresponding to the rainy

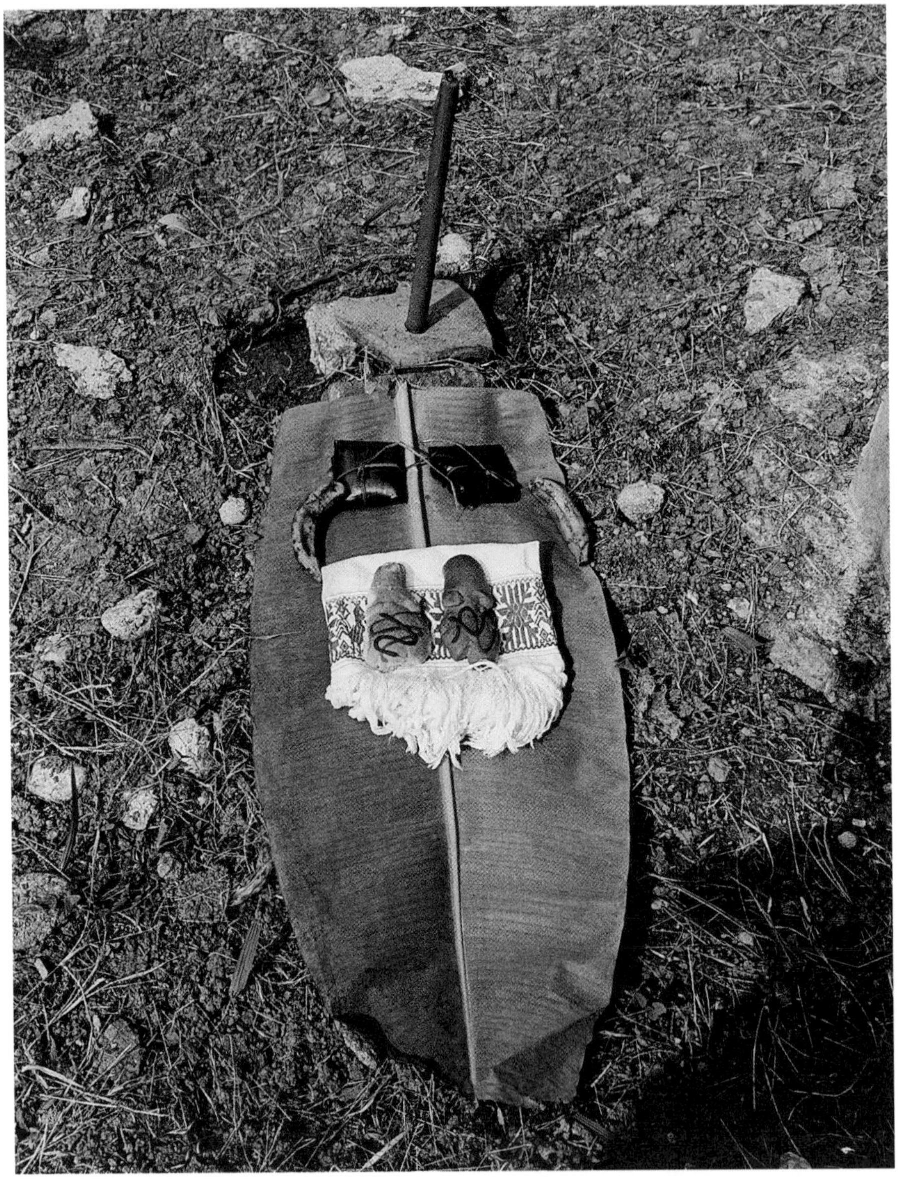

Alicia Ahumada. Offering in Huautla, Hidalgo. 2000.

season, except for the marigold which in those days seems to have flowered earlier than its usual season. The next day at dawn, he continues, "they braided them with cord to make thick ropes from them, long and twisted, which they then hung in their patios, to be presented to the god whose feast they were celebrating."

Within this ritual, the flowers did not constitute an offering to the dead children: rather they were a representation of those same children who were to be offered up to the god. Then "on the last day of the month, the men went into the hills to cut down a whole tree, smoothed it and brought it as far as the entrance to the city. This log was worshipped with offerings, foodstuffs and incense. They called it by the name of *xócotl*" (which evolved into the word *jocote*, the bitter-tasting fruit of the yellow *jocotero* tree).

The following month was the feast of Xócotl Uetzi, dedicated to the "large" or adult dead. At this time, writes Durán "they lifted the tree off the ground and set it upright in the temple forecourt and placed on top a richly decorated bird formed of dough." Alternatively, Sahagún wrote that this crowning figure was a molded image of the god Xiutecuhtli, as it was his feast day. The climactic moment of the proceedings occurred when a band of youthful volunteers shinned up the smooth trunk in a race to reach the bird and wrench off its head and other parts. The first four to make it were the winners, and these had to perform immediate penitence. Later that same day the trunk was pulled down and hacked to pieces by the crowd, who took these chips home with them as though they were relics—adds Durán—"because that is the meaning of the name Xócotl Uetzi, the fall of the *xócotl*."

This fiesta, originally held in February, reminds us of the modern ritual of the "flying trunk," a legacy of the prestigious cultures of the Gulf coast. Though it is most notorious in the Papantla area, among today's Totonac groups, it takes a more integral form among the Otomí peoples who live in the mountains of Puebla and Hidalgo states. Here it occupies a prime place in the Carnival, in keeping with the indigenous cosmovision. According to the anthropologist Jacques Galinier, who has recorded all the variants of this Otomí rite, "Carnival marks the beginning of the annual count (of days)" and is the first of the two markers of the year: "the first inter-equinoxial phase, lasting six months (from March to October) is separated from the second (November to February) by the two hinge dates: Carnival and the Day of the Dead." These twin poles of the calendar display another feature in common: both are moments when, "every year, the dead come and go between their abode and the village." To the extent that it may be legitimate to extrapolate pre-Hispanic thinking from the study of contemporary indigenous peoples, there appears to be ample evidence for the conclusion that the Mexica feast of Xócotl Uetzi (whose possible Otomí origins cannot be dismissed, argues Galinier) combined the nature of today's Carnival with that of the Day of the Dead.

In the Otomí dance of the *volador*, or flying man, four "viejos" or elders climb to the eyrie at the top of the pole and another performer called

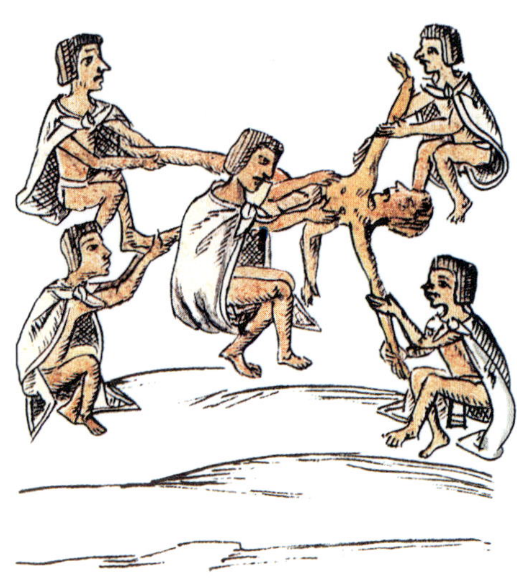

THIS PAGE AND OPPOSITE: Festival of the Tlacaxipehualiztli. Florentine Codex.

the "Malinche" dances there in the character of an eagle or hawk, representing the solar bird. The "viejos" come spinning down again, in reference to the descent into the underworld of the dead, while the flight of the "Malinche" enables it to soar up to heaven. In Galinier's view, "the Huastecs regard the *voladores* as godlike departed souls who escort the Sun until it disappears." Like the ancient *xócotl*, the pole (a cosmic phallus) from which *voladores* launch their descent to the ground can be interpreted as an axis of the world that enables people to circulate between its several levels. "The pole is the numen of fertility, linked to a life-principle symbolized by the eagle and to a death-principle embodied in the presence of the old men," Galinier writes. The ancient ritual of climbing the pole to behead the solar bird of corn paste (surviving in the Otomí "Malinche") is a way of taking hold of the Sun, fount of all life, precisely on a day that celebrates the dead, or more exactly, one of the periodic visits the souls make to humankind. It took place originally, just like the present-day Otomí carnival, during a barren season for the land, around February, when it was necessary to call

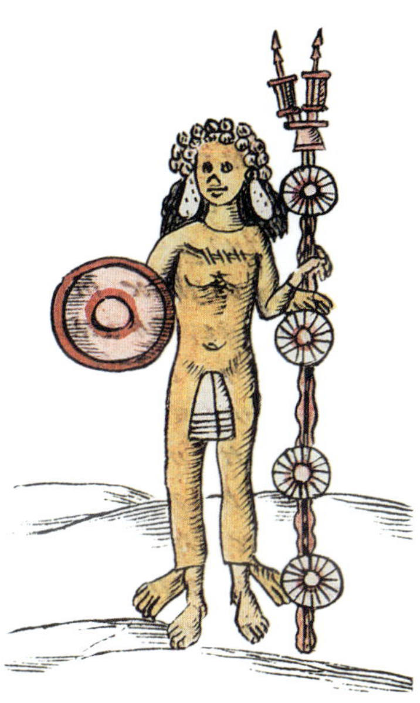

upon the power of the gods—that is, of the people's occult ancestors—in order for the Earth to become fruitful once more.

It so happens that the sacred days we have already mentioned corresponding to the month of Quecholli—those dedicated to men slain in battle—coincided during the sixteenth century with the feast of All Saints in the Gregorian calendar. During those days, also consecrated to Mixóatl, god of hunting and astral fire, the Mexicas got together to make arrows and darts for use in war and the hunt. On the last day of the month, they made smaller arrows which were lashed together in fours, mixed with splinters of ocote pine. These bundles were placed on the graves of the warriors as offerings, next to a pair of tamales. They lay there for the space of a day, until at nightfall, the bunches of wood were burned. Here as on other occasions we note the absence of marigolds, and yet the image of those bundles of arrows flaring orange in the night cannot but remind us of those flowers, with their fiery hues and masses of slender petals, placed on tombs now.

This other feast of the dead took place in early November, when at the exact point where the sun went down it was possible to discern the figure of Mixcóatl, the principal Chichimeca deity, adopting his form as the Cloud Serpent. In this case there seems to have been an adjustment made to match the ritual with the appropriate season—a later adaptation, perhaps. Whatever the reason, the fact that it coincided, at the time of the Conquest, with the Catholic ritual of All Saints' must surely have some bearing on the fervor and pomp with which this Christian holy day—not of first-rank importance in Europe—has been observed in Mexico since then. This syncretic adaptation manages to concentrate into just two days, November 1 and 2—all the expressions of the great annual cycle of death.

However, if we accept—as Galinier's testimonies about present-day Otomí tribes suggest—that in pre-Hispanic times, the ancestors manifested themselves twice a year, at the time of the equinoxes, then what ancient rites associated with this twofold break in the Earth's lifecycle might be related with the cult of the dead?

The month after Xócotl Uetzi was Ochpaniztli, which would have corresponded to March during the eighth century. This was a time to celebrate the divine Toci, mother of the gods and heart of the Earth. On the last of its twenty days, a woman representing the goddess was sacrificed by being skinned alive. The high priest put on her skin to dance all day long, and the skin of her things was used to make the mask of the corn god, Cintéotl.

Six months later, during the month of Tlacaxipehualiztli, it was the god Xipe Tótec's turn to be honored with a similar sacrifice, but this time it was a man whose skin was worn by the priest. And thus, it becomes clear that contrary to the common belief, the Náhuatl scholar Salvador Díaz Cíntora is correct to argue that Xipe Tótec was not the god of spring we once thought, he was a deity of the fall. The man's fresh skin donned by the high priest was subsequently preserved for days "until it tore"—this was now a yellow, stained, decaying scrap of hide, not the firm flesh of

Toci that heralds spring and summer. It is the parchment-textured skin of a "*viejo*"—a dead man indeed—that ushers in the fall and winter. As Díaz Cíntora writes, "Half the year, then, is governed by Xipe Tótec, the god of the Zapotec and Tlapanec coasts; the other half, by the mother goddess of the Huasteca regions, and the coast of the Seno Mexicano. (. . .) During Tlacaxipehualiztli, one man, the priest, dresses in the skin of another, the sacrificial victim: this is undiluted masculinity, necessarily sterile. In Ochpaniztli, the priest covers himself with a woman's skin: (. . .) here the masculine element conjoins with the feminine, getting literally under her skin, as a sacrament of fertility ensuring life on Earth."

Furthermore, during the month consecrated to Xipe Tótec a kind of bread called *cocolli* was prepared from the sacred grains of certain ears of corn known as *ocholli* that were strung from the eaves by their wrappings after the harvest. It was exclusively these grains and no others that had to be sown the following year, because these were the seed of a god who both embodied and heralded death: Cocolli was thus a sacred offering of bread, corn bread, yellow as the leathery skin of Xipe Tótec, a food that augured the death of nature and might well lie at the origins of our contemporary *pan de muerto* (a special bread baked for the Day of the Dead).

When the rains have vanished from the sky and the Earth enters a period of repose—before it becomes cloaked in the parched skin of vegetation burnt by frosts and winter sun, before the ordeal of coming drought—then the land sprouts a fleece of yellow flowers: sunflowers, Santa María flowers and above all the extraordinary heads of marigold, with their warm golden shades, like the reflection of a nocturnal sun, an orange-yellow as beautiful and poignant as the feeling of farewell to summer. Who could deny that this symbol of hidden forefathers has its roots buried deep in pre-Hispanic Mexico? ◆

—Translated by Lorna Scott Fox

Dominique Dufétel. Translator, writer, and University of Paris teacher in Hispanic literature. Dufétel was a researcher and writer of the video series *Ciudades del México* (*Cities of Mexico*). He has coordinated several issues of *Artes de México* and is a FONCA literary translation scholarship recipient.

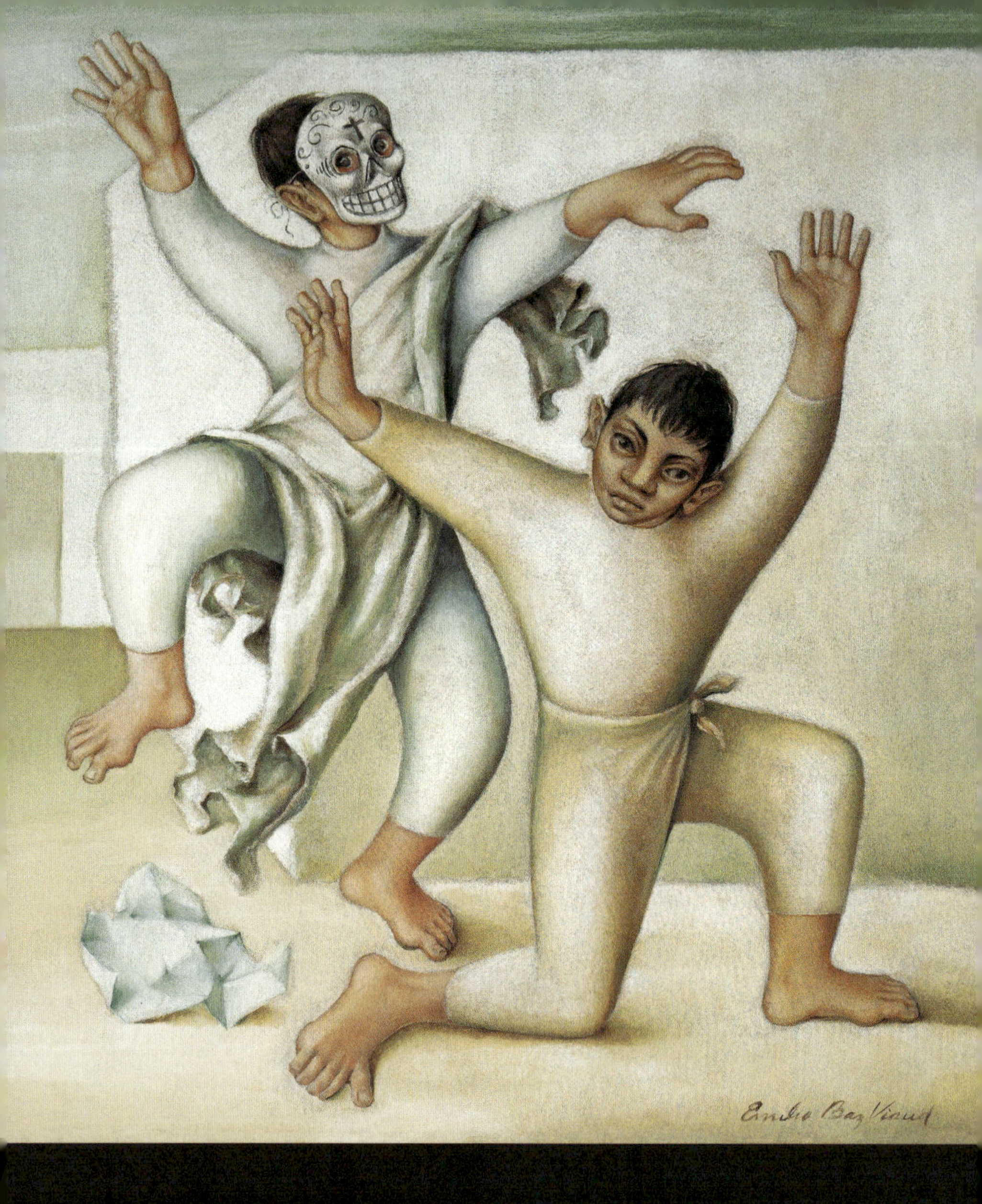

Emilio Baz Viaud, *El coco*, 1995. Oil on canvas, 50 × 40 cm. Courtesy Fundación Andrés Blaisten.

DAY OF THE DEATH RITUALS

Ruth D. Lechuga

◆◆◆◆◆

As Paul Westheim notes, "The only thing Mexico's Day of the Dead has in common with All Souls' Day, as celebrated in Europe, is the fact that on both sides of the ocean it is a day dedicated to the memory of deceased loved ones."

Whereas for Europeans the very mention of death is taboo—as if by rejecting the idea one could avoid the fact—Mexicans accustom themselves with the notion from childhood. This familiarity is evidenced in many ways; for example, in the many expressions to say that a person died: he got peeled, hit the mat, stretched a leg, carpeted the floor, went cold, took off, left us, turned in the equipment, left with the skinny one (Death), became defunct; and, they brought him out sneakers first, the witch gobbled him up, he was carried away legs akimbo, we drank coffee with him (as at a wake), and so forth.

There is a difference in the ritual too: Europeans visit the cemetery on All Souls' Day to remember departed loved ones whereas Mexicans see this as a time when their deceased return to the Earth to spend the day with their relatives. Even the pre-Hipanic custom of dedicating one day to dead children and another to dead adults has been handed down. Currently, the fiesta might last several days longer than the two assigned to dead children and adults respectively.

María Cristina Morales tells us, for example, that in the Huastec Indian region of the state of Hidalgo, St. Michael is believed to open up the gates of Heaven for souls to begin their pilgrimage to visit the living on September 30, then St. Andrew closes them on November 30, by which date all souls should have returned to their dwelling place.

The Totonacs in the sierra wind up their festivities on St. Andrew's Day as well. Researchers at the Totonac language school claim they also

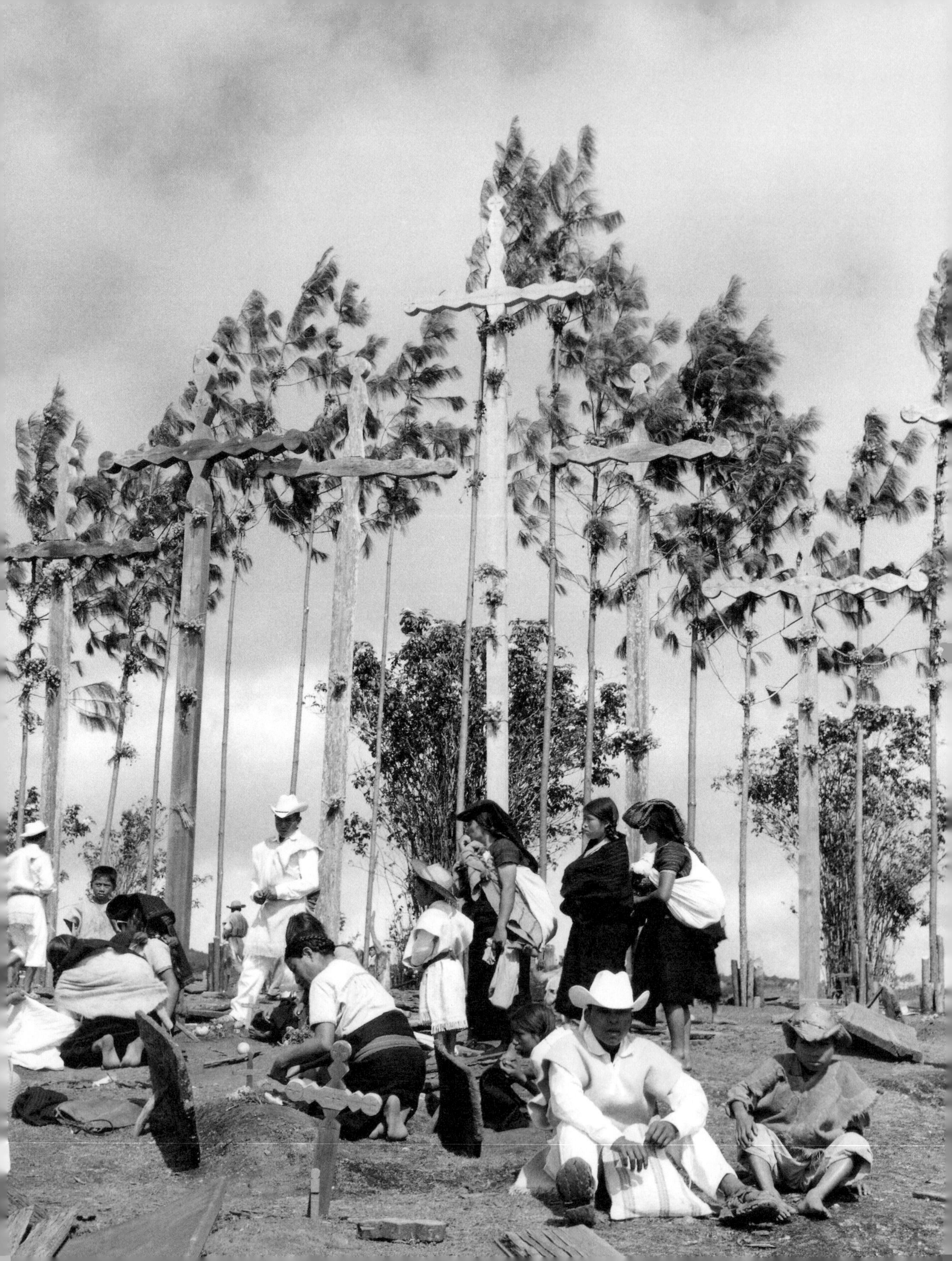

dedicate St. Luke's Day (October 18) to people who have died a violent death: in an accident, murdered, drowned. The Totonacs of Papantla, Veracruz, and the Nahuas of Cuetzalan, Puebla, assign a special day, October 30, to non-baptized children and, according to Simón Gómez Atzin, they call it "the day of people in limbo."

The annual visit from the deceased is no mournful occasion, but an excuse for a party. Perhaps one explanation for that appears in the *Madrilenian Codex*, from Sahagún's Aztec informants: "The elders used to say

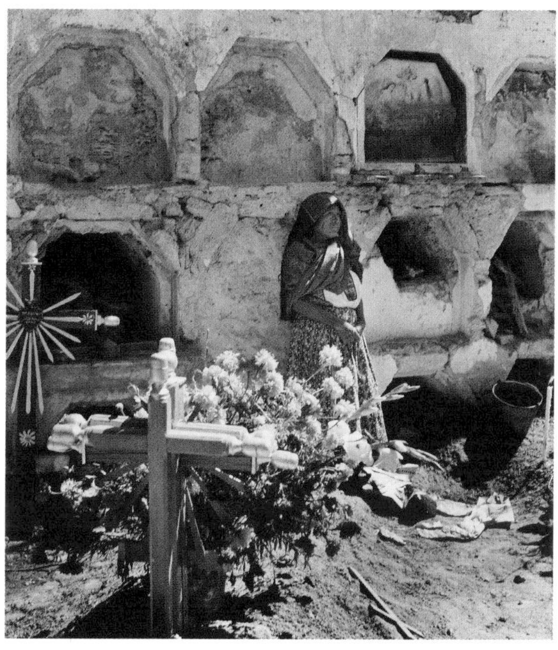

Ruth D. Lechuga. Offering to the lone soul. San Gabriel Chilac, Puebla. 1964. • **OPPOSITE:** Ruth D. Lechuga. Chamula (tzotzil) cemetery. Romerillo, Chiapas. 1968.

he who has died has become a god. Their turn of phrase 'he became god' means 'he died.'" In fact, Robert Childs and Patricia Altman assure us the belief persists that "a dead person's soul becomes a supernatural being with the power to intercede on behalf of family members." They further point out another idiosyncrasy of the Mexican Day of the Dead that differs from the European equivalent: "in the orthodox Catholic faith one prays for the souls of the dead to be saved from purgatory. Indigenous people, on the other hand, do not pray for souls, but to them."

Nacho López. Janitzio, Michoacán. N.d. Reproduction authorized by the INAH.

As they did with the gods of the past, people must pray to their ancestors to look favorably upon the requests of the living: ancestors too expect their offerings. So, descendants must set aside a little of their time and money to fete them accordingly. Every village has its tale about a person who failed to lay out an offering with due respect and was punished by the dead. The penalty imposed may range from a flogging even to the death of the disobliging relative.

For example, in an account discovered by Fernando Horcasitas, a sorcerer in Milpalta relates how a woman asked her son to fetch some wood and buy what was necessary for an offering. Instead, the boy messed around all day playing on the mountain and when he wanted to return, "he noticed a long procession of old people coming up behind him. He saw his father, his grandparents, great-grandparents, great-great-grandparents, all trembling with cold, dying of hunger and thirst, carrying their empty knapsacks and rolled-up sleeping mats under their arms, all anxious to return home where they were awaited, to warm themselves, eat and spend the night. 'What are you doing here?' they complained, 'Why aren't you waiting for us back in the house?' The startled boy was speechless. The dead tied him to a tree and left him there all night. At dawn, as the fragrant smoke from the copal incense lifted and faded, and the offering candles went out one by one, the defunct old people plodded slowly back through the forest again, untied the boy and continued on their way. The boy fled home to his mother crying, 'Now I know that the dead people really do come back; next year we'll buy them their food and wait for all of them.'"

Another story, told by researchers at the Totonac language school, had a more tragic ending. There was a man who did not believe in the dead and disregarded their day. On his way home after a drinking binge, "he suddenly saw a crowd coming towards him, but they were all dead people returning to their world. Among them were his father and mother with empty arms, while others were loaded with offerings. He saw that his deceased family carried only a piece of clay (*tepalcate*) as a censer; it was burning their hands, and they were lamenting their sorry state, full of complaints. Soon after he had returned home, he began to feel dizzy and nauseous, then quickly fell ill and died suddenly. The meal he had asked to be prepared for the offering served only as a meal for his own burial."

After the fiesta, the dead must return to their dwelling place. A few, reluctant to do so, hang around their relatives' house, possibly with the

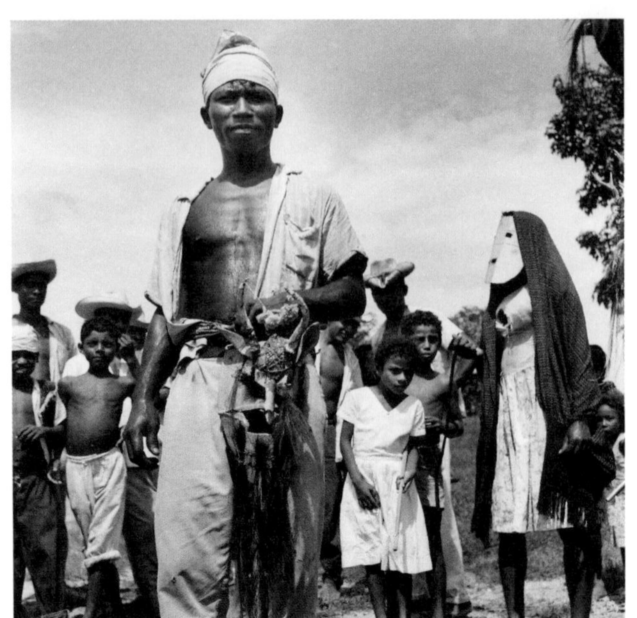

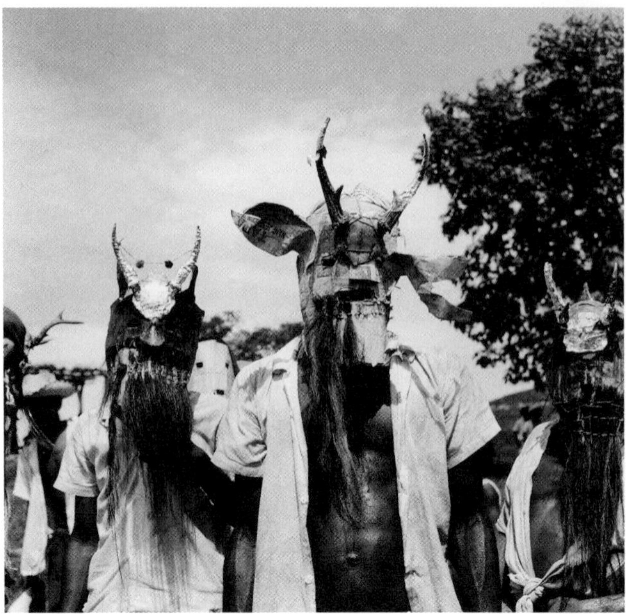

Ruth D. Lechuga. Dance of the devils, staged to entertain the deceased.
La Estancia Grande, Oaxaca. 1963.

idea of becoming prankster spirits. Some communities hold special ceremonies to avoid that. Frances Toor tells us that "in Yalalag, Oaxaca, the priest walks right through the village in the company of musicians chanting prayers for the dead and *Salve Reginas*, with or without music, depending on how much people are prepared to spend. The chanting takes place both inside and outside the houses to ensure that no soul is hiding, because some of them get lost along the way and others are reluctant to go back where they came from. At the sound of the prayers, they must depart and stop upsetting their relatives."

The Totonacs in the sierra make another small offering on St. Andrew's Day. "In the afternoon they go to the graveyard, bearing the cross and part of their offering. As a farewell they recite the rosary and sing praises to dissuade departed souls from returning to bother family members."

The Chatino Indians of Yaitepec, Oaxaca, make a procession to the cemetery to escort adult souls back to their tombs. Masked dancers go from house to house making a lot of noise to expel any souls that have yet to take their due leave.

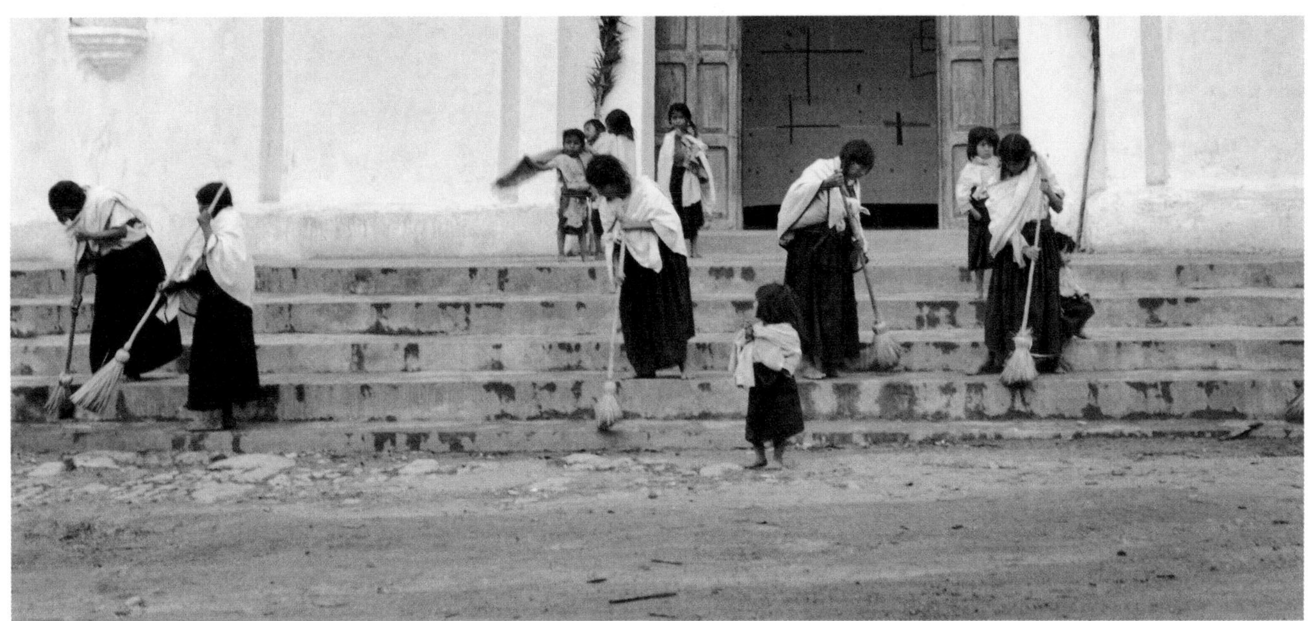

Ceremony reminiscent of the Ochpaniztli, Chiapas. 1968.

• DANCING FOR THE DEAD •

Throughout Mexico it is common to place an offering—inaccurately called an "altar for the dead"—at the house of the deceased, the cemetery, or both. Food, drink, flowers, and lights are the staples. However, local variations abound.

The Totonacs of Papantla, Veracruz, who are meticulous about their appearance and always carry a bag with a change of clothes should they get dirty, place a set of clean clothes for the deceased to put on when they arrive so that they can enjoy the party.

Offerings can be made at the cemetery during the day, such as in San Gabriel Chilac in Puebla. As family members arrive, they will sit down around the graves that are festooned with flowers, candles, baskets, food, and figures of angels. If they can afford it, they will pay a musician with a portable piano or mariachis to cheer up the dead.

As happens elsewhere in Mexico, in the corner of the cemetery locals here will place an offering for those lonely souls without relatives to remember them.

Celebrations take place at night in other parts of the country; the cemetery will be filled with candles creating a festive and magical atmosphere.

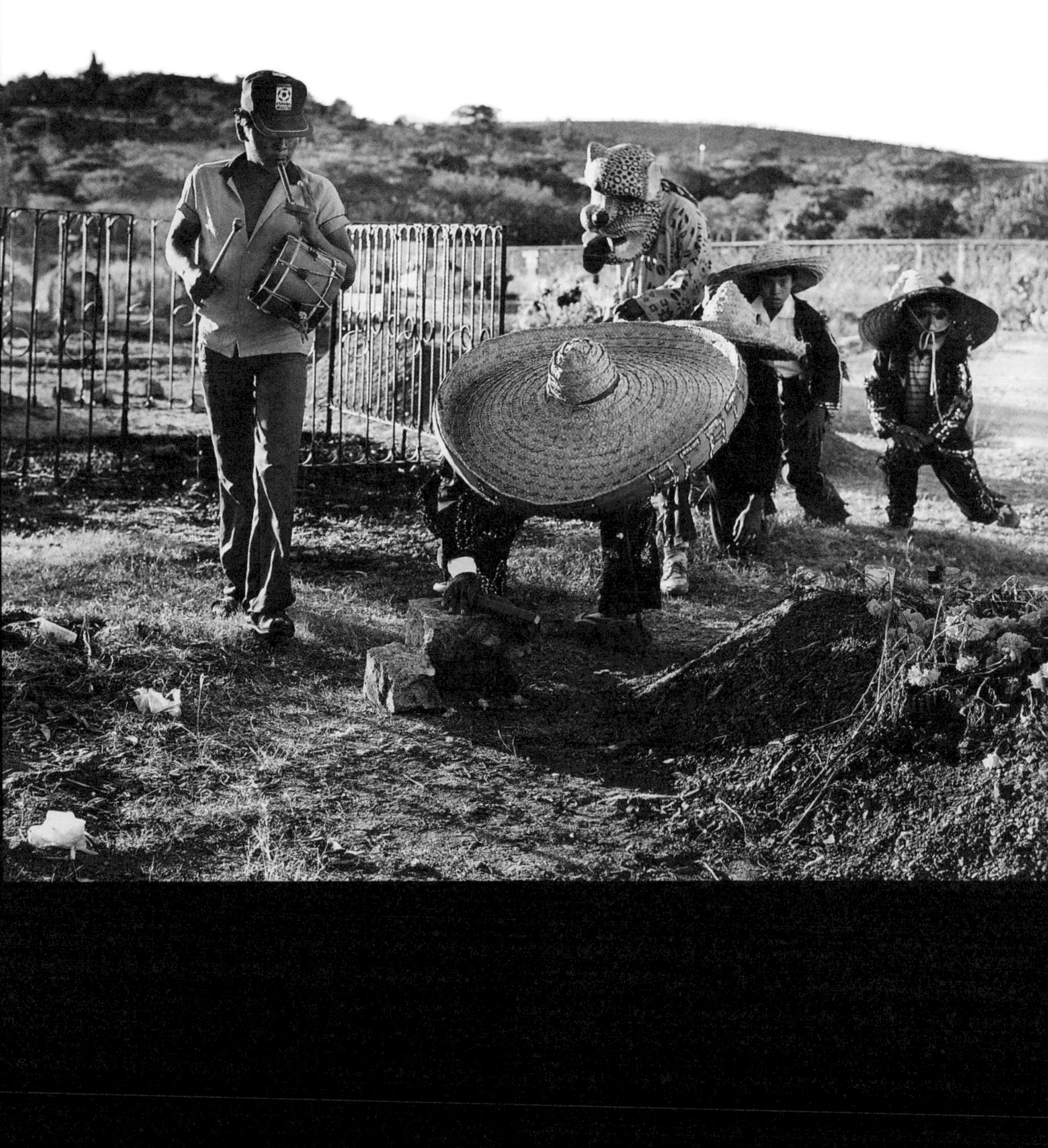

Ruth D. Lechuga. *Danza de tecuanes.* Acatlán, Puebla. 1986.

These ceremonies—aptly called *iluminadas*—also include food, flowers, incense, and, depending on the region, special decorations. In Janitzio and the towns dotted around Lake Pátzcuaro, oranges, bananas and candied figures are hung from large arches clad in marigolds.

In Iguatzio, one of the lakeside communities, a woman with a banana approached me and said: "This is for you—from my dead husband who is glad that you're joining in the party with us."

The most remarkable aspect of the *iluminada* is its pre-Hispanic roots. Sahagún wrote about the fiesta for the month of Quecholli (from October 20 to November 8): "they made small darts in honor of the deceased . . . they would tie four arrows together and four torches with loose cotton threads, and they would place the names on the graves of the deceased. They would also put down a couple of sweet tamales; they left them there for the whole day and at dusk they would light the torches and burn them together with the arrows."

Many villages hold dances during the Days of the Dead. Some dancers perform in the street, some go from house to house and others dance in the cemetery.

In the Huastec region, dancers are called *huehues* ("elders" in the Náhuatl language) and represent the dead. They dance in couples and their jokes often have some sexual innuendo. The Tejorón Indians of Yaitepec, Oaxaca, hide behind the anonymity of a mask when playing practical jokes with ribald humor. In both instances, it is a fertility ritual, which shows that the pre-Hispanic world view of duality and the endless life-death-life cycle continues to live on in the minds of some Mexicans. The Tejorones, however, play another role: they expel souls that drag their feet when the time comes to go home after their day is over.

Other dances are staged to amuse the dead. The black population in the coastal towns of Oaxaca call the dancers "devils." In the street they accompany their vigorous movements with chanted improvised verses in reference to their compatriots and visitors.

In Acatlán, Puebla, the customary dance is called *tecuanes*, in which multiple characters take part, including the tiger. They usually dance in honor of the souls on the afternoon on November 2 in a square outside the cemetery; but when anyone in the troupe has a recently deceased relative, they enter the graveyard and perform around his tomb. The devils of Tanquián, San Luis Potosí, do the exact same thing whenever one of their dancers dies.

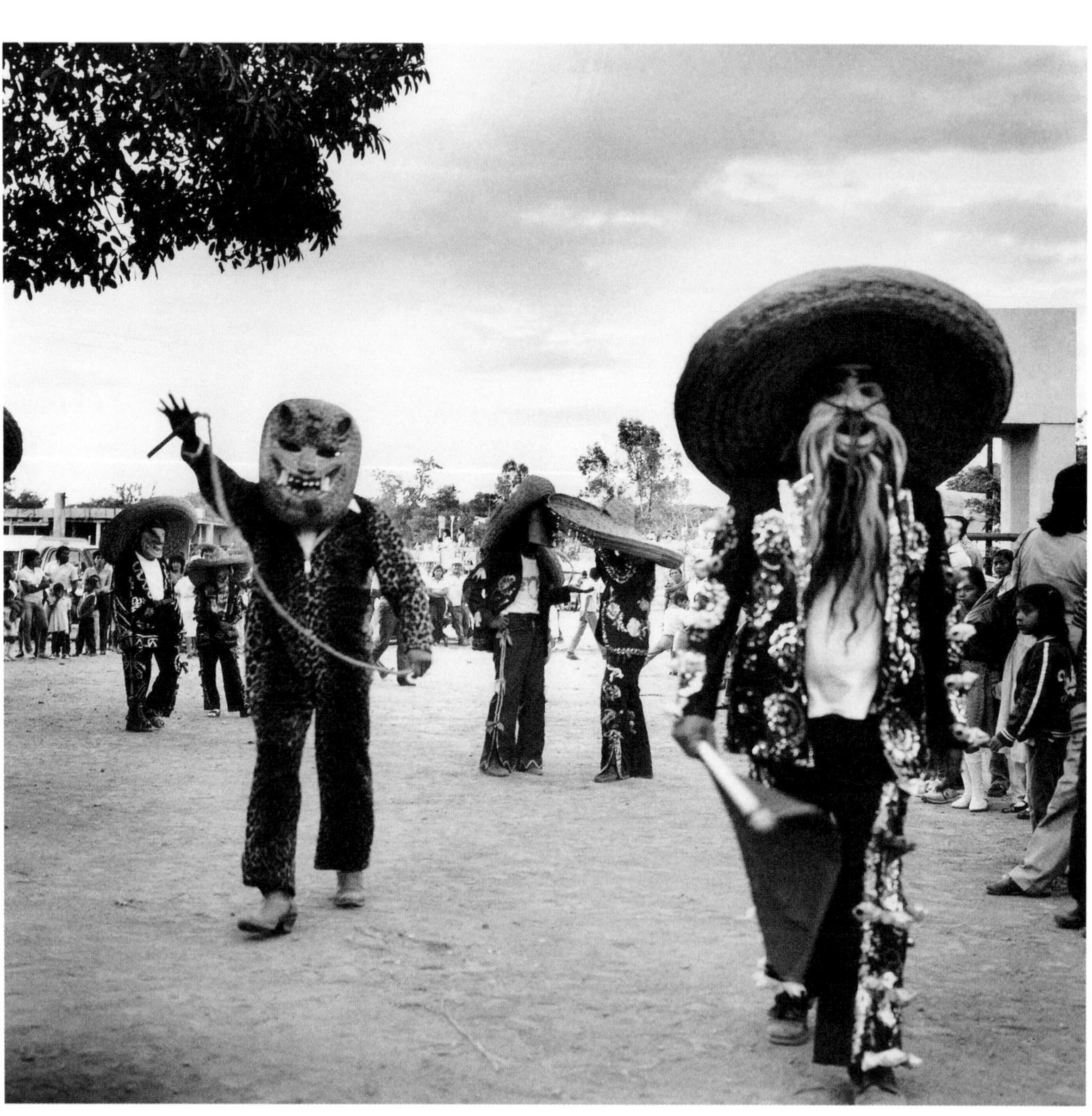

Ruth D. Lechuga. Dance of the tecuanes. Acatlán, Puebla. 1986. • **PAGES 44–45:** Fernando Castro Pacheco. *Hanal Pixan* (Mayan Day of the Dead). Acrylic on canvas. 128 × 180 cm. MACAY.

The old folk of Suchiquiltongo, Oaxaca, and the mimics of Romerillo, Chiapas, always dance inside the cemetery.

Children in Tepoztlán, Morelos, have fun dancing with a skeleton virtually their size, made of reeds and lined with tissue paper.

One unique spectacle is that of the living graves in Iguala, Guerrero. As a tribute to any person who has died since the last Day of the Dead—and who is generally referred to by the population as a "fresh corpse"—the family will vacate the largest bedroom overlooking the street. It then becomes an improvised actors' set for young family members and children, who usually present a tableau of some religious theme, in which they remain motionless long hours through the night. The town's inhabitants do the rounds to admire each family's inventiveness.

Calixta Guiteras relates that in Chenalhó, Chiapas, a special council holds office for one day on behalf of the dead. There is a ceremonial handing over of the cloak and scepter, in the same manner as when a new council is instated each year. The next day, the authoritative symbols are returned to the everyday governors.

Another important ceremony takes place in Huixtán, Chiapas, where women sweep the church and the plaza outdoors. This ritual dates back to pre-Hispanic Mexico. Fray Diego Durán relates, "The eleventh month of the year was called Ochpaniztli, which means day for sweeping. It was the day of solemn of the gods. (. . .) The first ceremony of the day required that everyone dust their belongings and sweep out the house. What is more, they swept every street in the village, an ancient custom that has remained with us throughout the land." Here, like in other related ceremonies, pre-Hispanic rituals and beliefs persist despite almost five centuries of evangelization. ◆

—Translated by Carole Castelli

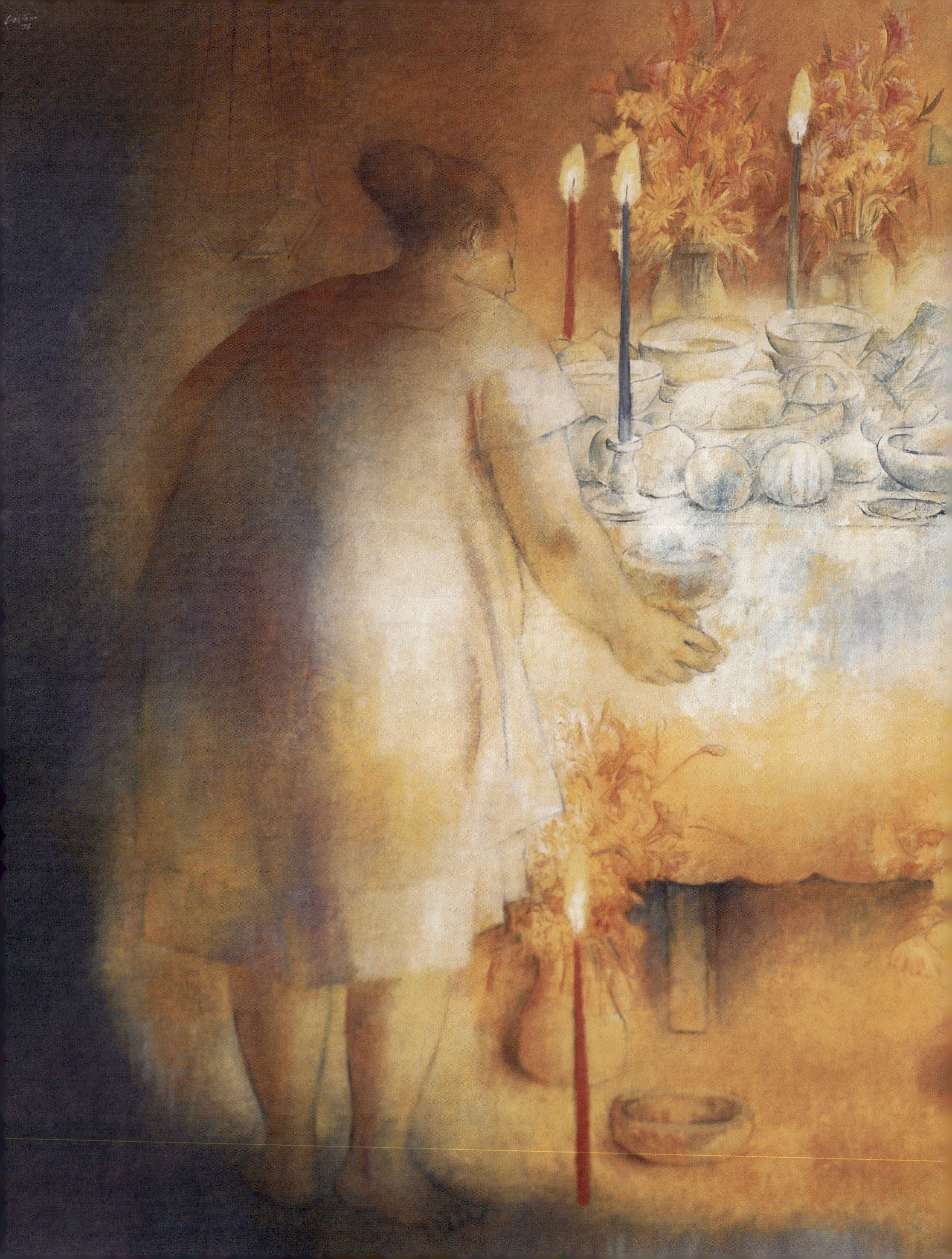

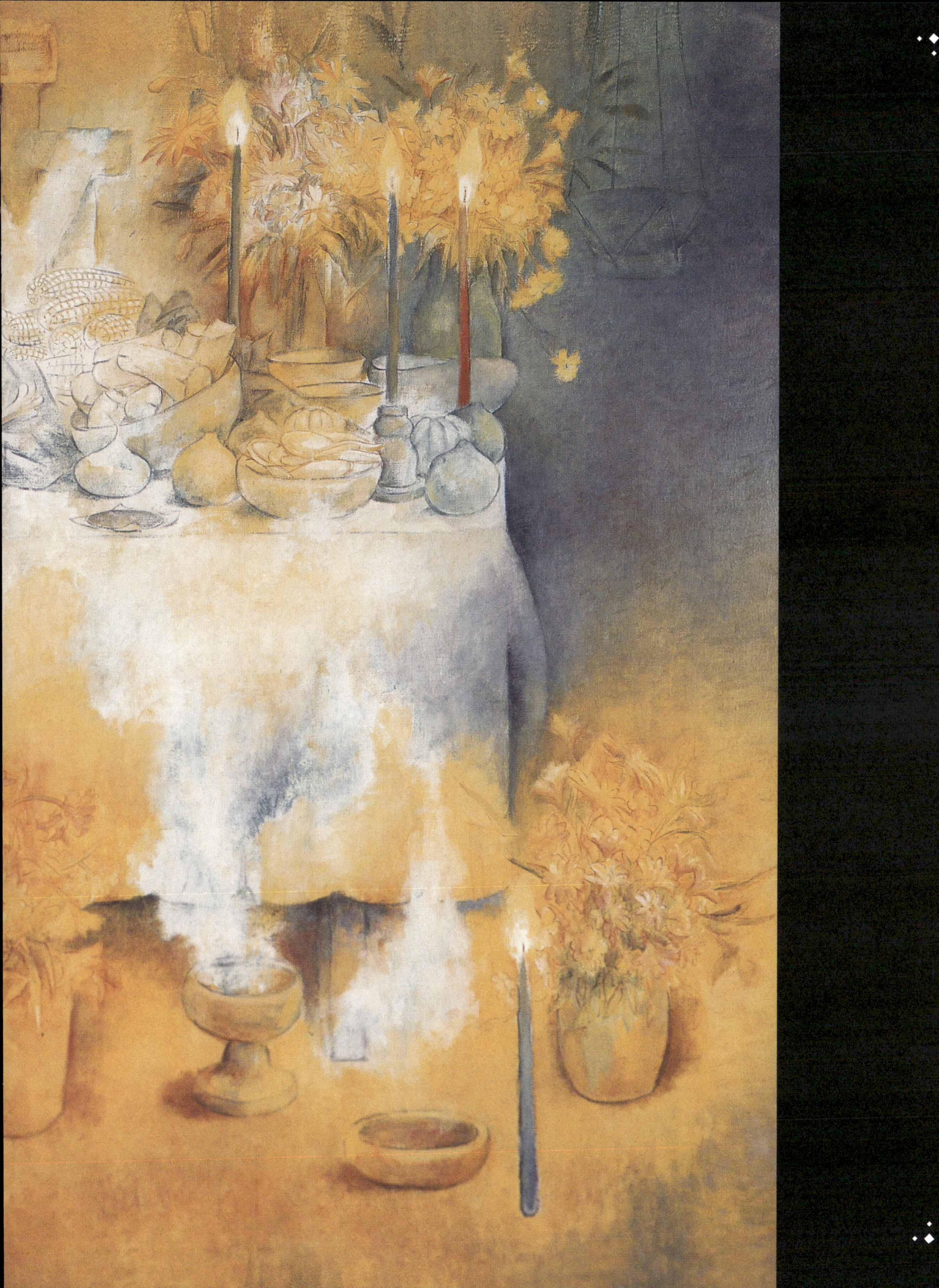

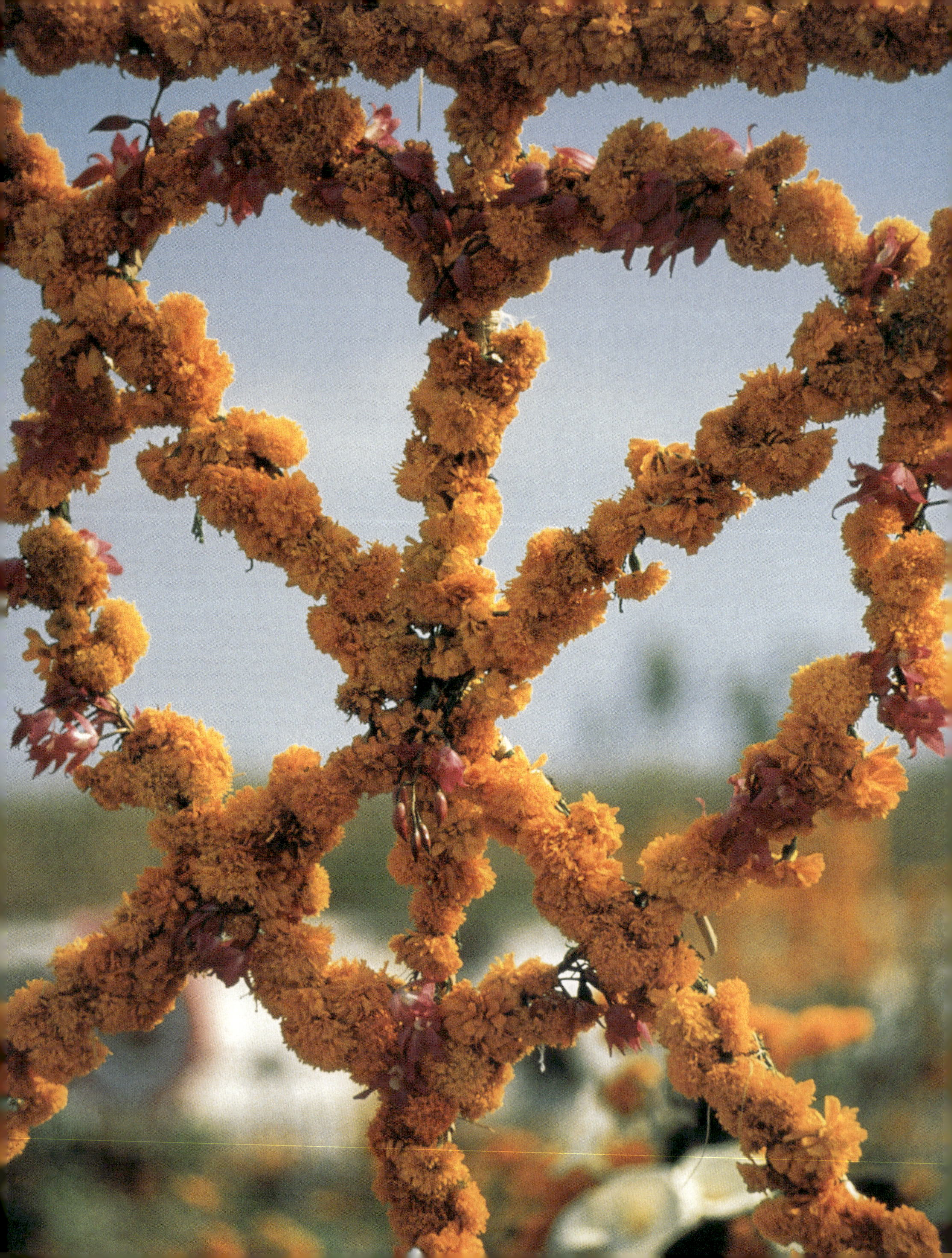

SAN MATEO DEL MAR'S WANDERING SOULS

Laurette Séjourné

◆◆◆◆◆

In San Mateo del Mar, the dead are feared above all as a cause of illness. It even seems that evil is an inherent quality of those who lie buried beneath the earth, since they only appear to manifest themselves by bringing on some kind of calamity. To think about a dead person is a careless deed, which one must swiftly amend by means of offerings and prayers if one wants to avoid becoming ill. To invoke a dead person to do evil is common practice; if one is in trouble, one runs a high risk of getting sick, because if a dead relative realizes one is worried, then he or she will send some affliction one's way—locals say the deceased *dan lástima* which normally means "to be pitiful" but in this case could also be interpreted as "to send woes."

The most pernicious souls are those of men who died in accidents outside town: since they do not find a place of rest, they wander the earth waiting to enter the body of a living being. Thus, it is not uncommon for someone coming back from a long trip to fall gravely ill from having "caught" one of these lost souls. Locals are always concerned about this type of diagnosis, since the treatment carried out by the specialist consists of whippings, repeatedly applied until the patient is cured. However, some people claim that these wandering souls are often very stubborn and will commonly let the patient die from the whipping before agreeing to leave their host.

All this clearly reveals two characteristics of San Mateo del Mar's population's mentality: their humble, submissive worship of supernatural forces and their dependence on the group. They feel the singular need to ask for forgiveness when they fall prey to an illness; moreover, they do not carry out any of the rituals by which *brujos* or witchdoctors usually cure ailments—rituals implying a sense of active resistance—but simply limit themselves to praying and making offerings. This outlook explains the atmosphere of devotion that reigns over the town: indeed, if one must pray to heal oneself, one must also incessantly pray in order to prevent the undifferentiated realm where humans mingle with saints, the departed, and animals from ever losing its harmony—as tragedies mainly occur due to some imbalance in this homogeneous whole.

The community's cohesion is further expressed in the fact that no brujo will agree to make someone sick at a client's request—something so common elsewhere. Only a traveling brujo would be capable of such a thing, and for this reason strict measures have been adopted so that no out-of-town brujo may enter San Mateo. And just in case one of these undesirable characters were to insist on sticking around, the countless chapels erected on every corner in defense against that would surely convince him otherwise.

The All Saints' Day celebrations demonstrate that the San Mateo native's anonymous state of existence as well as his or her unconditional dependency on the group also apply to the dead. Dead people's behavior is closely tied to that of the living, and when a brujo diagnoses a relative as having "dead-person's illness," the invocations he carries out to make the late lamented soul appear are a prime necessity, indispensable to the whole family. In spite of this relationship's intimacy, souls can wander freely about town once a year, and are then received with a solemn welcome—a custom followed by practically all Mexican ethnic groups. However, in San Mateo—unlike other regions of Mexico—the altar each family makes in honor of the celebration is not dedicated to any particular dead person, and this lends the festivities here a totally impersonal character.

Something else distinguishes the people of San Mateo del Mar: their aversion to anything which lies beyond their group identity is so deep-rooted that they even mercilessly "boycott" those townsfolk who died elsewhere, as if their leaving town in the first place makes them as impure as foreigners.

The belief that there are souls who have lost the way to their native land is a prevalent one throughout Mexico; however, this was the first time I witnessed a people turn their backs on these spirits. In the different places where I have spent the Day of the Dead, I have always witnessed a general sense of sympathy for wandering souls: a candle in the doorway or a table of modest offerings inside a house are the alms of human memory that each family presents to the lost souls that might pass through.

Nothing like this takes place in San Mateo del Mar, quite the contrary: stray spirits are closely monitored so they cannot freely mingle with the community of respectable dead individuals. People claim that when one

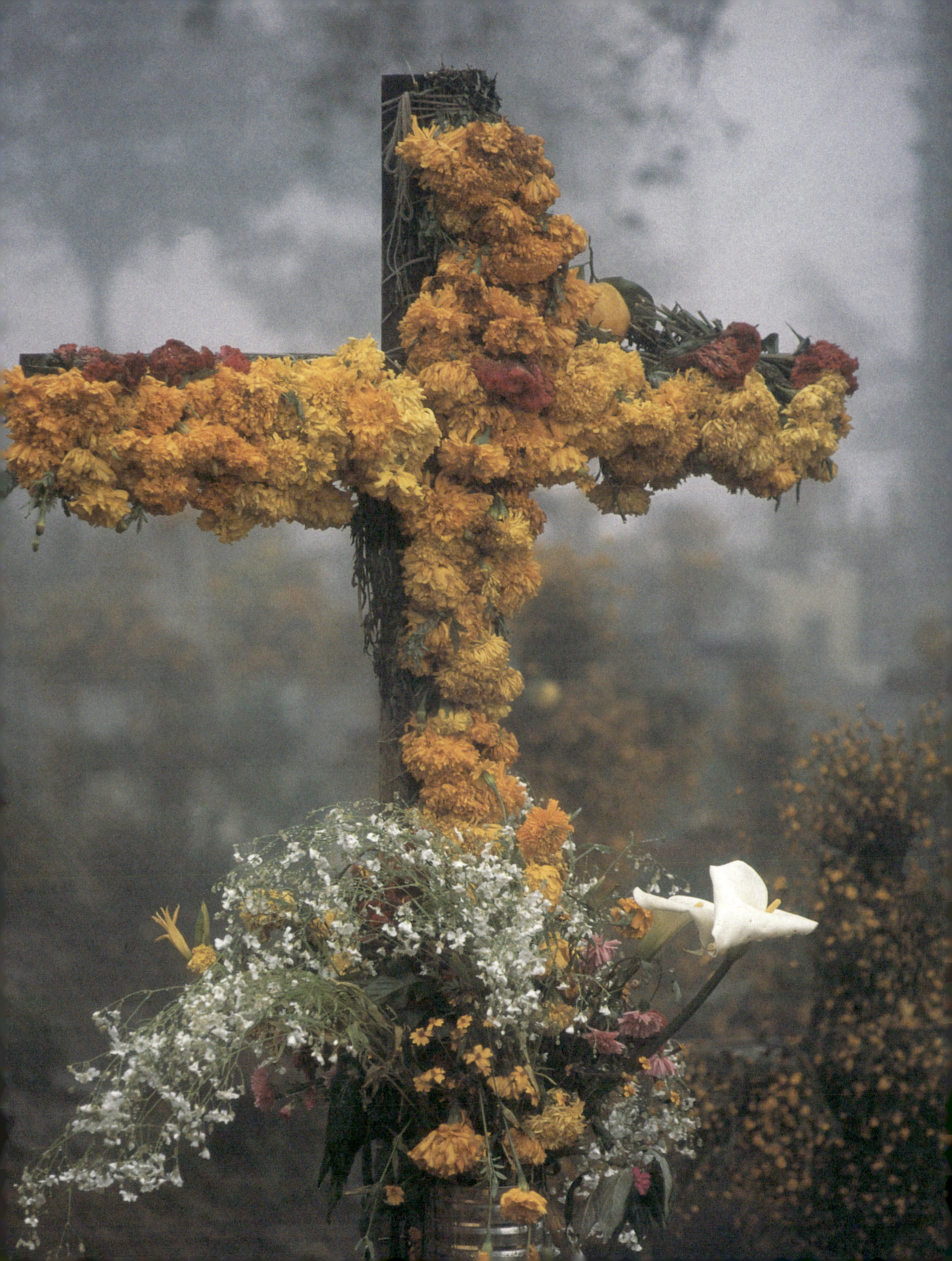

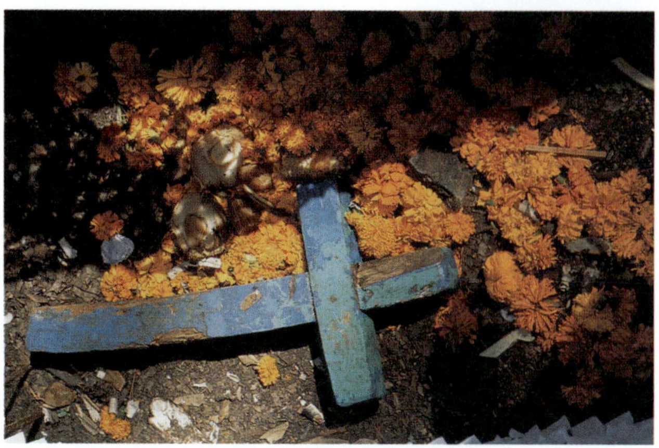

George O. Jackson, Guadalupe Victoria, Chiapas. 2000.
PAGE 46: George O. Jackson, Ihuatzio, Michoacán, 1997. • **PAGE 49**: Jorge Pablo Aguinaco, Ayutla, Oaxaca, 1990.

of these unwanted souls tries to enter the church, hoping to partake in the offerings which would allow it to join the ranks of the pure, the front door to the church, outraged, will stop it from coming in. I have heard it said that the priest often sees the heavy door slam shut of its own accord in the face of one of these renegade spirits.

A few days ahead of time, the whole community prepares to welcome their dead. At home, women work hard to make the kind of food and drink their dead relatives liked; at the market candles are snatched up the minute they are made, and locals eagerly await the arrival of marigold salesman and the Day of the Dead bread made in the shape of angels, rabbits, or deer. (I discovered this kind of bread made for the feast of the Day of the Dead during my trip to San Mateo. When the friendly Zapotec couple's cart in which I was traveling turned over—with all of us inside it, of course—we tried, with the aid of a flashlight that barely dispersed the cold darkness around us, to pick up and clean the objects littered on the ground. I was moved by these oddly shaped breads and did my best so that, in spite of the mishap, they could still grace a table of offerings.)

At midday on November 1, church bells start ringing, and the souls—who are only awaiting this sign—rush to the earth. Come dawn they return to their respective resting places—some even going back to Hell—carrying their offerings from the living. The deceased who leave empty-handed will not forget to shower the worst calamities upon those forgetful enough not to have given them some token of respect.

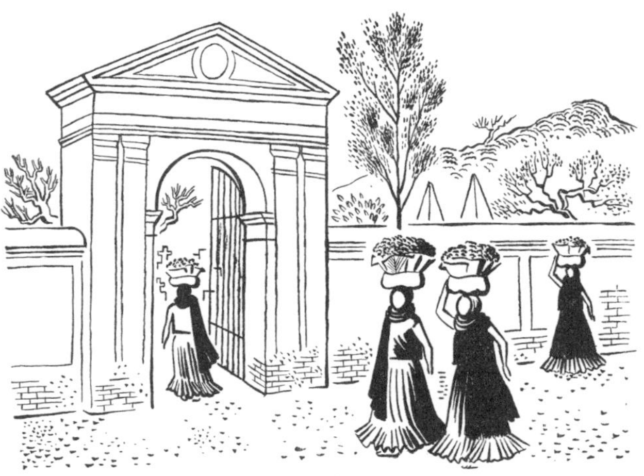

Miguel Covarrubias. Illustration from *Mexico South*, Alfred A. Knopf, New York, 1946.

At the toll of the bell, which does not cease ringing until the next morning, the townsfolk greet their dead. They begin by singing prayers in front of each family altar; in the homes of town leaders, secret ceremonies take place, reserved exclusively for men; women visit each other's homes offering as many candles as people they once knew who have died: there are young girls who stand shyly in the doorway to a house holding out a single candle, and old women carrying great bundles of them.

The narrow streets become impressively beautiful as they bustle with these women carrying their offerings to and fro. Indeed, once the souls have arrived, the town is suddenly revealed in all its authenticity. The women's attire and behavior, for instance, is very much like that of priestesses used to having an intimate relationship with the supernatural: the thick red cloth tied around their waists and dropping to the ground; the wide, square black or yellow blouse over their bare chests; the piece of white cotton, as large as a bed sheet, tied around their heads and draping severely over their shoulders and backs. Silent, standing proud and focused, carrying candles decorated with marigold flowers in their hands, they progress without any apparent movement, and disappear . . .

Homes are simply multiple churches, all forming part of a single sacred place, and the altar that each one houses is the site that is most alive within them. Numerous candles fill the rooms with golden light, dispelling the usual darkness, since these shacks have no other opening than a very narrow door and the space inside is so confined that hardly any light enters. Fruits, flowers, and basil—which plays a very important role in witchcraft—as well as burning wax and copal enshroud everything with an intensely religious perfume. People stand before the tables of offerings to sing prayers with a fervor that will not decline until the next morning.

The night, under the full moon's benevolent glow, further underscores the profound meaning of things, and the whole town appears to be under the influence of a spell; the shacks' dark shapes loom over the narrow streets and alleys, oblivious to any sort of rectilinear order; the ground, warm and shifting, refuses to stay still beneath our feet; groups of men, floating among the alcoholic vapors of ritual drinking, glide by like sleepwalkers; prayers rise above every room like thick columns of smoke . . .

The shack I am staying in can evidently not escape the fate of the others, and I will be unable to sleep by the light of the candles, among the perfumes that get caught in my throat, the noise of the prayers and the constant comings and goings. The moon is still high when the women get ready to go to the cemetery wearing their prettiest dresses. It is my duty as a researcher to follow them, but it seems like a sacrilegious indiscretion for me to witness their farewells to the dead, and I am truly relieved when they tell me I cannot accompany them. In the doorway, the man of the house chats with some friends of his—all of them completely drunk. Not daring to join them, I stand in a corner for a long while unsure of what to do, listening to their chatter sprinkled with Spanish words. And then, in the most unexpected manner, I hear a song rise above the din, more disturbing and stranger than everything else: a few notes of *L'Internationale.*

Suddenly, the plaza, deserted for the past two days—the street vendors have abandoned it knowing they will not sell anything during the festivities—vibrates with color and movement. Women returning from the cemetery pass groups of staggering men without noticing them, apparently, as the latter leave the church where, taking turns since the previous evening, they stood guard over the table of offerings.

A little later, the plaza will look like the aftermath of a battle: bodies are strewn everywhere, men hobble under the hot sun, stoop to regain their balance and take another few faltering steps before collapsing. Once in a while a woman's hieratic silhouette appears: she reverentially bends over one of these prostrate bodies and takes it away like a precious burden. Absolutely all the men are totally inebriated: they had no choice but to

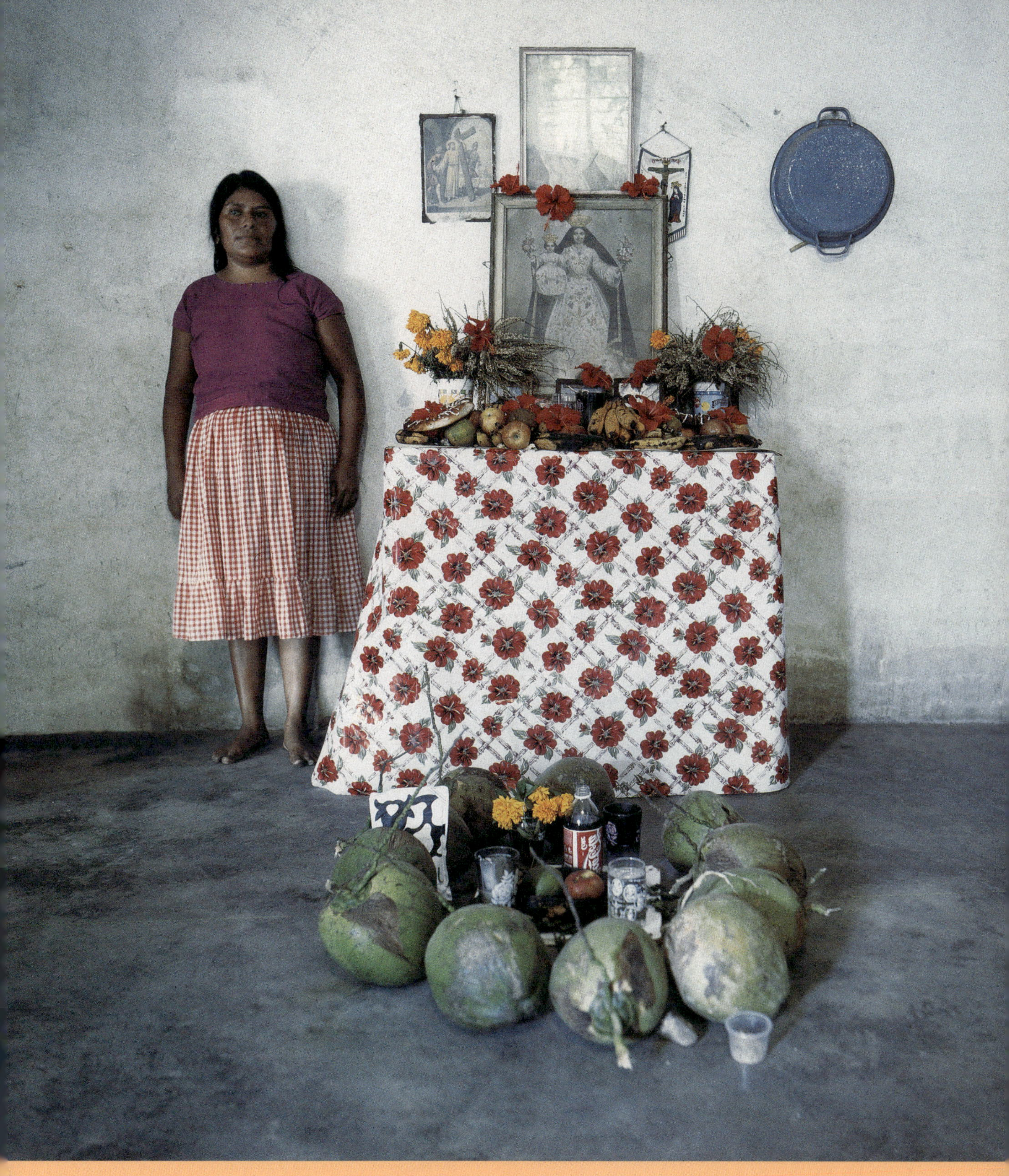

Lourdes Almeida. Offering in Juchitán, Oaxaca. 1995.

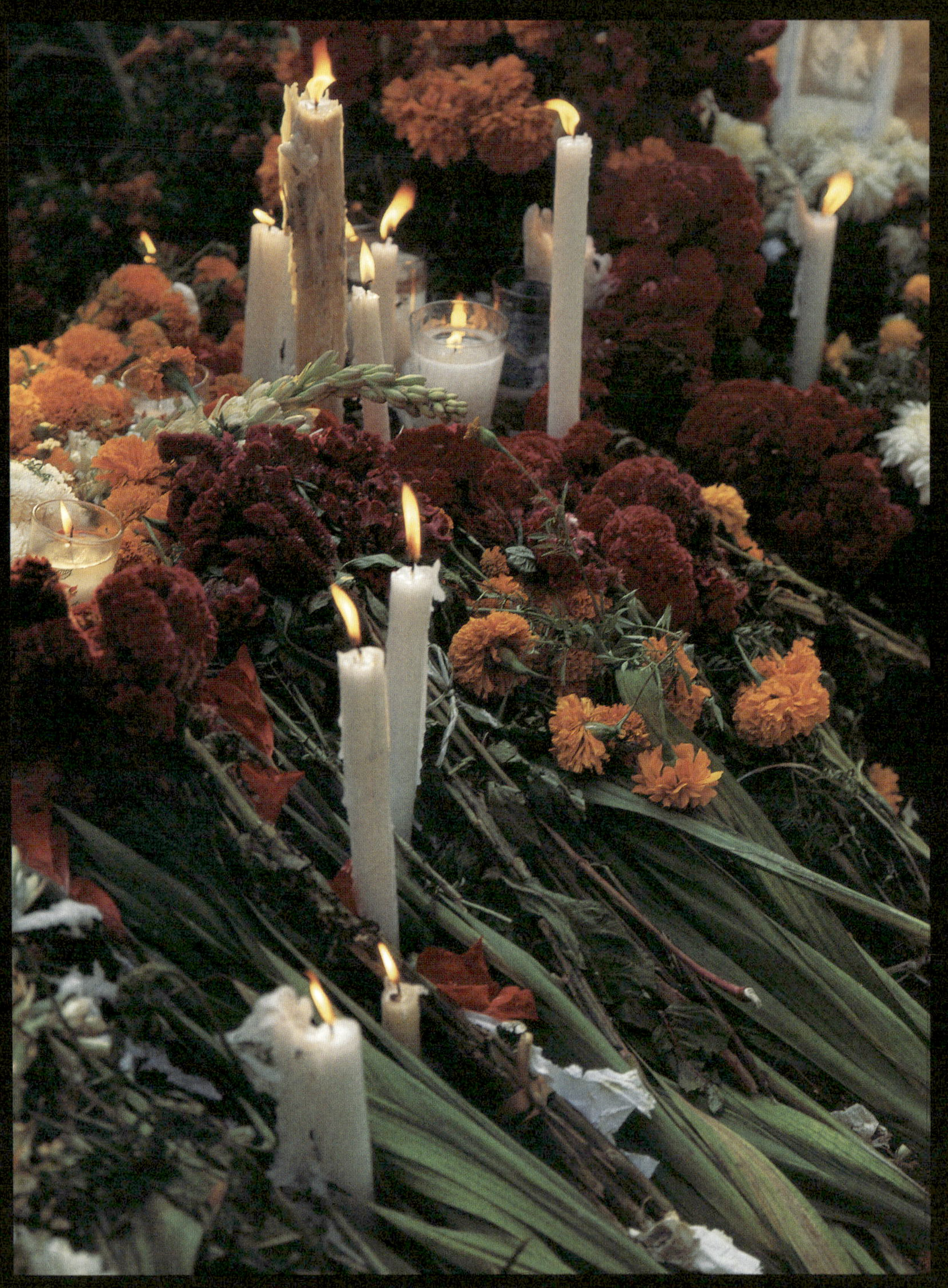

Jorge Pablo Aguinaco, cemetery in Ocotepec, Morelos, 1999.

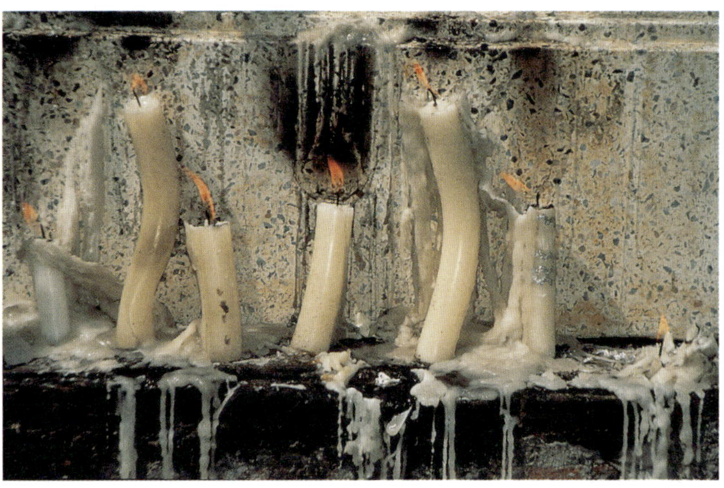

George O. Jackson. Grave in Xalmimilulco, Puebla. 1998.

drink with the visiting souls—indeed, refusing to do so would have been a grievous sin.

I overheard a revealing dialogue in this regard: as the young schoolmaster, himself suffering from a dreadful hangover, was asking a venerable old man why he had not done this or that, the latter, surprised by such a question, answered: “But how? . . . I couldn’t, I was drinking.” I must add that this sacred collective binge is ever so peaceful: during the twenty-four hours the men drank, not a single violent incident occurred. The only novelty to report, besides the plaza’s and streets’ surprising appearance, was that these people, usually so introverted and sullen, had become talkative, even expressing a certain degree of warmth. ◆

—Translated by Richard Moszka

Laurette Séjourné. French archaeologist who participated in the explorations of Monte Albán and Palenque. In 1955, in Teotihuacán, she discovered three complete architectural structures. She is the author of, among other books, *Palenque, una ciudad maya* (*Palenque, a Mayan City*), *Un palacio en la ciudad de los dioses* (*A Palace in the City of the Gods*), *La cerámica de Teotihuacán* (*The Ceramics of Teotihuacán*), *El pensamiento náhuatl cifrado* (*Encrypted Nahuatl Thought*), and *Supervivencias de un mundo mágico* (*Survivals of a Magical World*) (Fondo de Cultura Económica, 1996), from which this fragment was extracted.

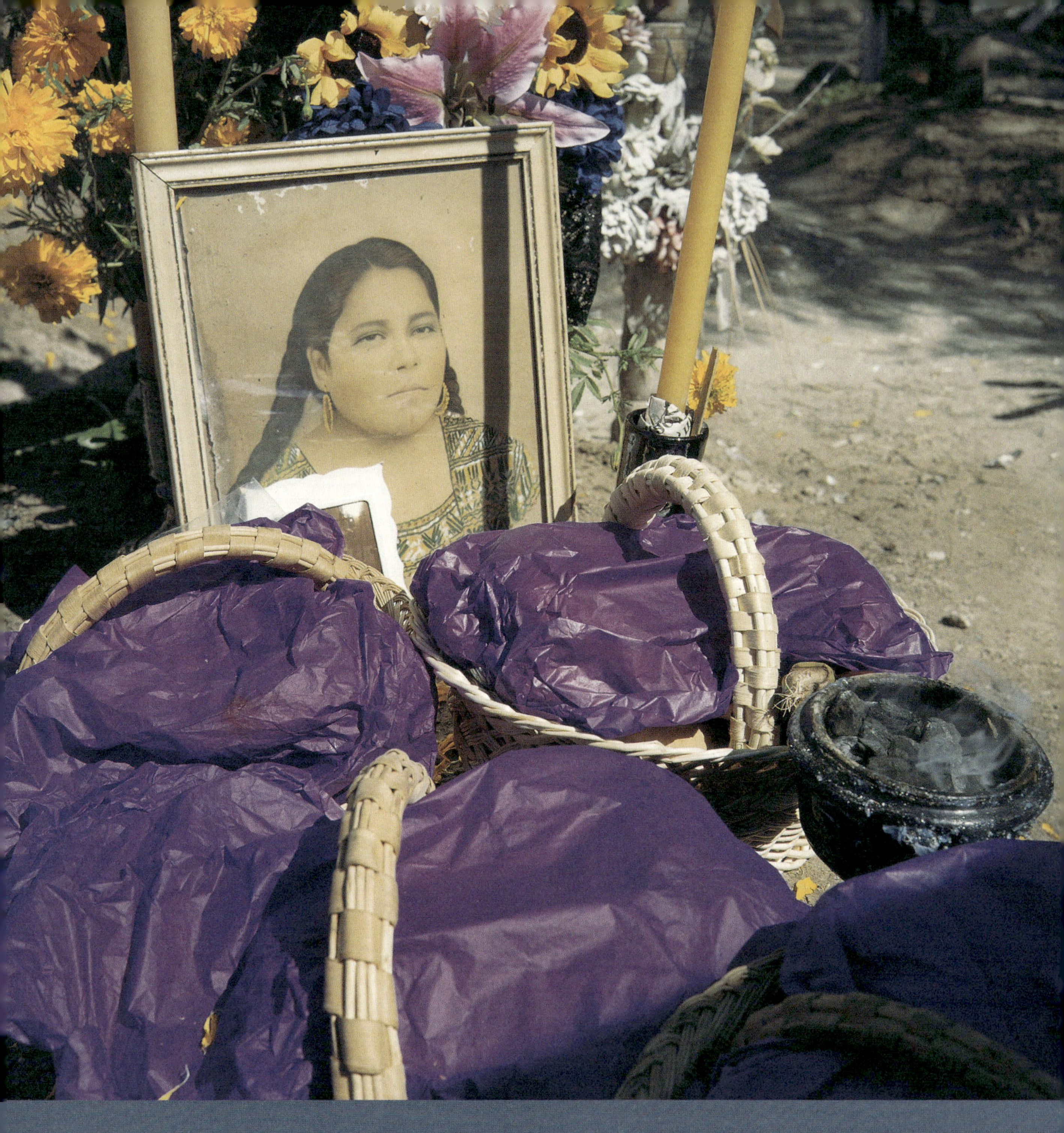

Agustín Estrada. San Gabriel Chilac, Puebla. 1999.

SAN GABRIEL CHILAC

Gutierre Tibón

◆◆◆◆◆

On the second of November, throughout Mexico the air is filled with our grateful and affectionate thoughts about those loved ones who have come before us in this eternal dream; we all wish to show them that we have not forgotten them, that they live on in our memory. In thousands and thousands of cemeteries across the country the faithful departed receive visits from their relatives; countless graves are decorated with the emblematic flower of the dead, the marigold. Though in some places the Day of the Dead is celebrated with more devotion, more solemnity. I was in a cemetery that I consider unique in Mexico, and perhaps in the world. An almost unreal vision of color, beauty, and human tenderness is still etched on my retina. I spent the second of November in Chilac, a town about twenty kilometers from Tehuacán, near the border with the state of Oaxaca. The inhabitants are successful garlic farmers. They are all bilingual, speaking Náhuatl and Spanish with equal ease. They are all literate, and most can even read music.

What is unique about the Chilac cemetery? Small shelters—made out of emerald-green banana leaves, small green *carrizo* reeds, or black or purple cloth—are erected above each grave. Offerings are placed in the shade: *tenate* palm-weave baskets filled with bread baked specially for the occasion, *mole* casseroles, bananas, oranges, and an abundance of the very freshest flowers in elegant arrangements. Marigolds flutter, with their yellowy-orange color contrasting with the blood-red, velvety flower the locals call *moco de pavo* (amaranth); and the pure white lilies, the purple gladioli, the carpets of the blue morning glory known as the "virgin's veil" all add to this impressive display. The latter seemed to have waited to flower especially until this morning. Candles—one for each soul being remembered—flicker softly among the offerings and flowers. Family members, from the grandparents to the grandchildren,

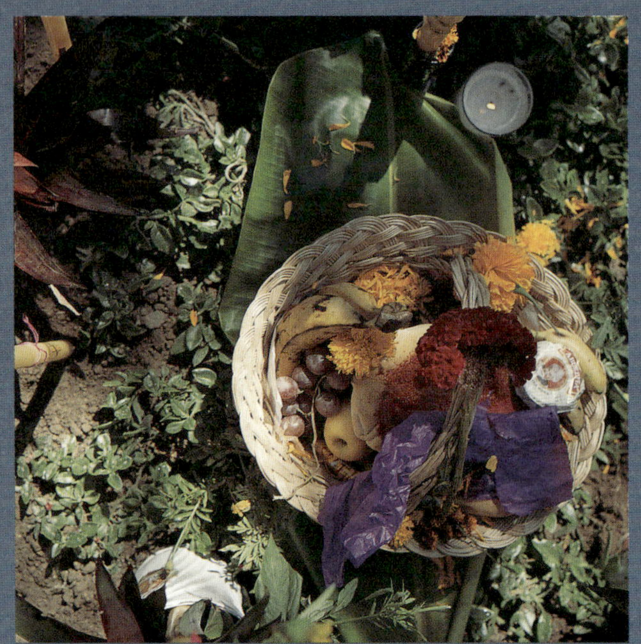

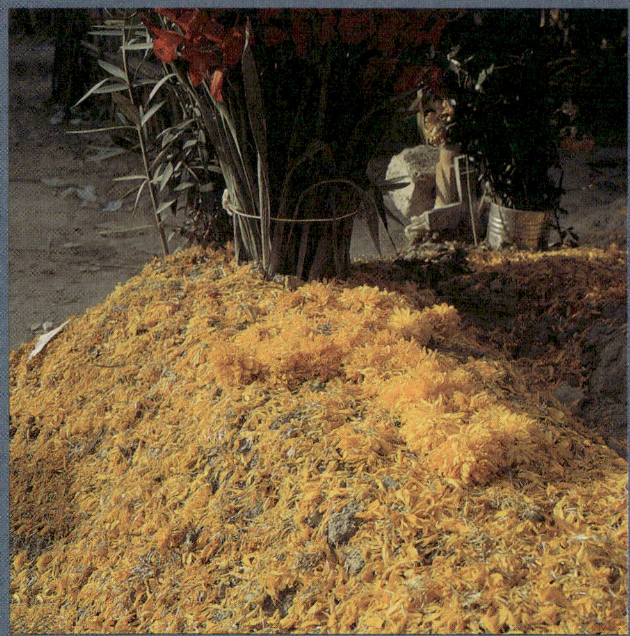

Agustín Estrada. Grave and offering in San Gabriel Chilac, Puebla. 1999

all sit or kneel in prayer in front of the shelters. Numerous harmoniums (I counted sixteen) are distributed among the graves. The campesinos play the instruments themselves, reading the music like expert organists, and operating the pedals in their huaraches or barefoot. The whole family sing to accompany the harmonium, their treble and bass voices all perfectly in tune. They sing and pray in perfect Spanish or well-pronounced Latin, though among themselves they speak the mellifluous tongue of the Mexico of old, Náhuatl. Women would occasionally pass by carrying huge bunches of flowers to add even more decoration to the graves.

The sky is an intense blue; the perfume of marigolds intermingles with the copal incense burning gently in the censers. Melodious, angelic voices rise from amid the sea of green, black, and purple shelters. And flowers everywhere, an apotheosis of flowers. The atmosphere in the cemetery in Chilac is not joyful or sad, but peaceful and serene. I returned to Mexico City with a sense of calm, as though I'd had a foretaste of eternal bliss. ◆

Excerpt from *Aventuras en México 1937–1983*, Diana, 1983

—Translated by Quentin Pope

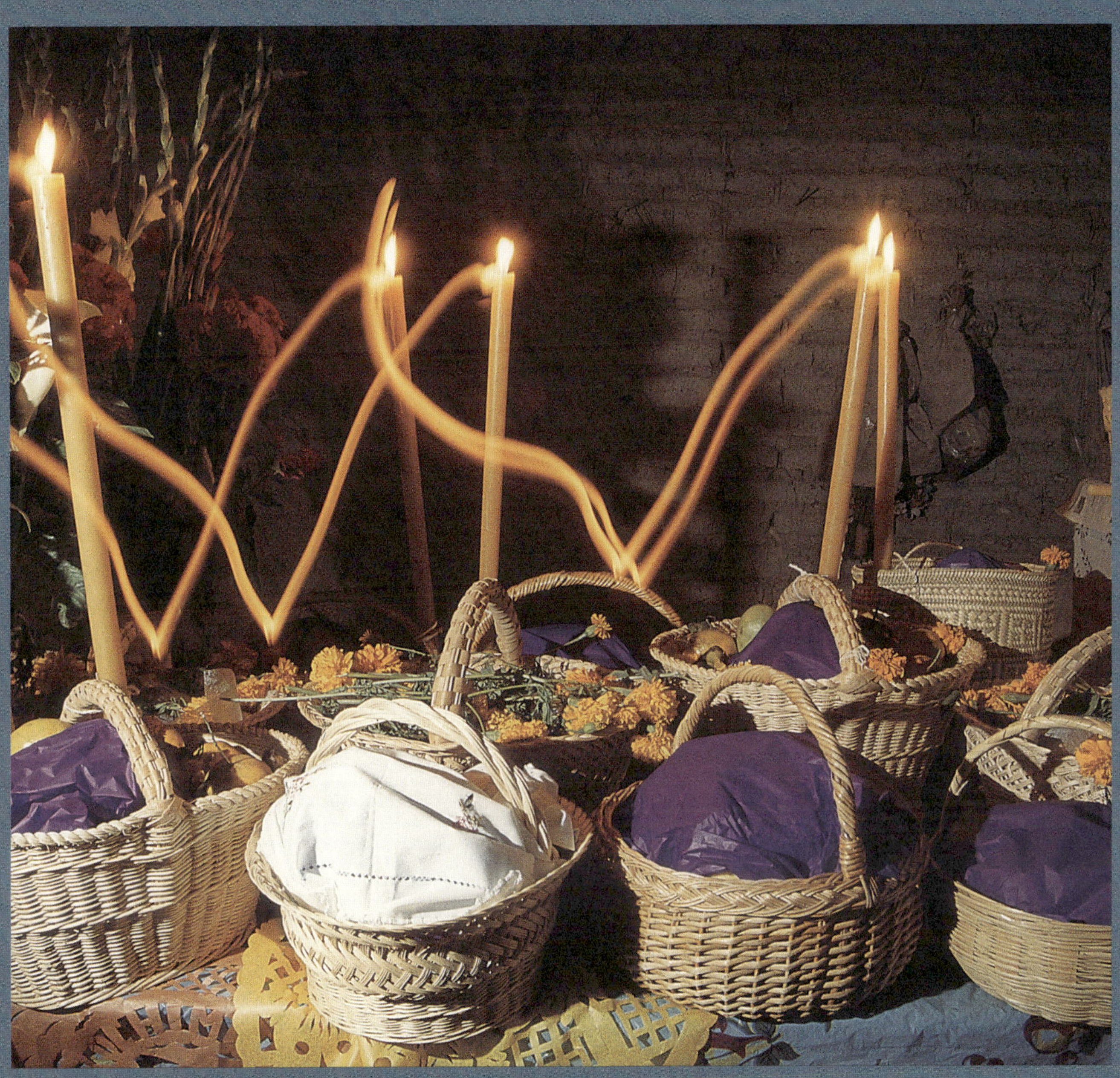

Jorge Vértiz. San Gabriel Chilac, Puebla. 2001.

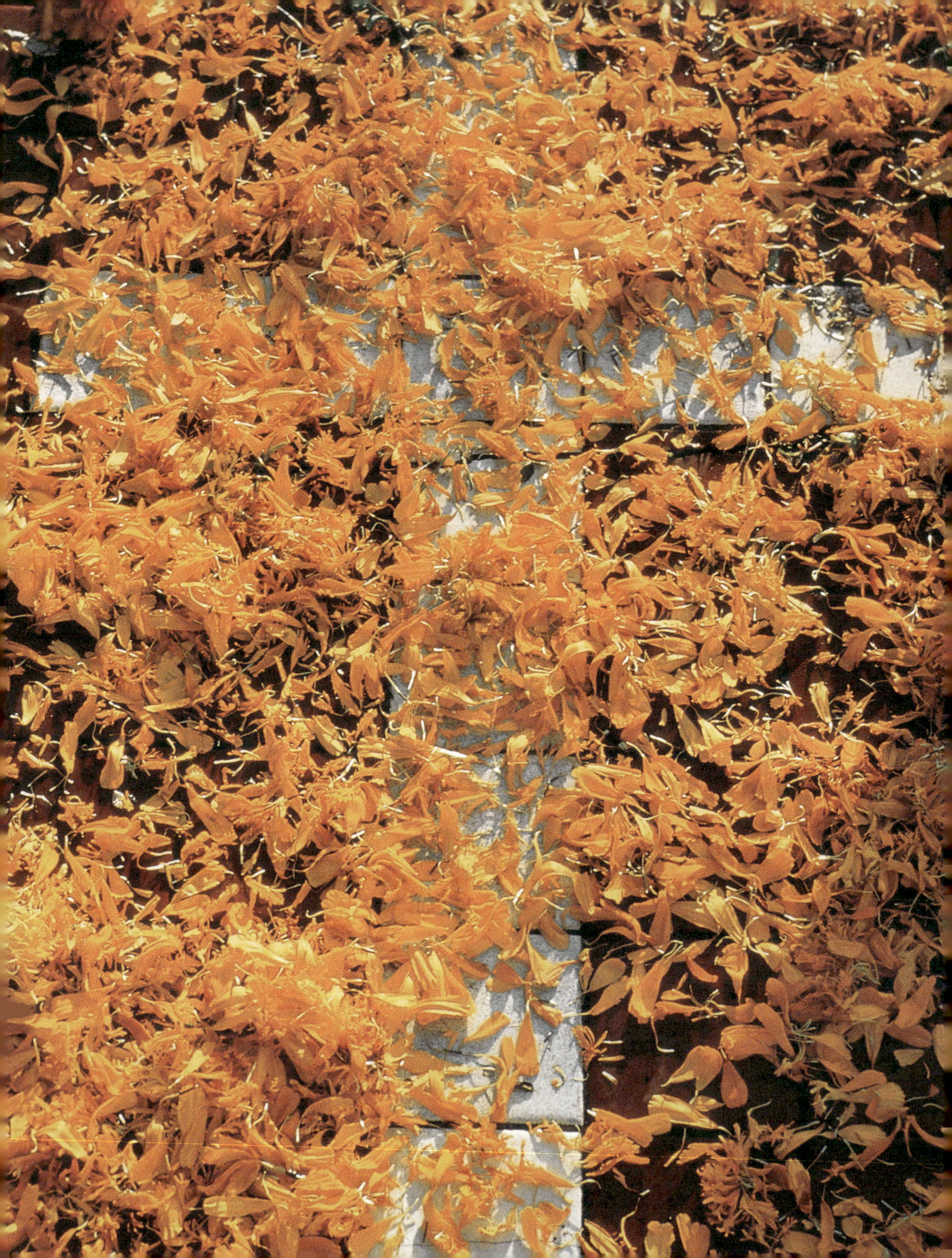

A SPLENDID RECEPTION IN TEOTITLÁN DEL VALLE

Mary Jane Gagnier de Mendoza

◆◆◆◆◆

The people of Teotitlán del Valle, Oaxaca, thirty kilometers from the state capital, are widely recognized as exemplary hosts, and the souls who visit on Day of the Dead receive a truly royal reception. Preparations for their welcome are in the making for days, and beginning October 31, the villagers are already attending spirits. The first to arrive are the *angelitos*—the souls of dead children—on November 1, All Saints' Day, given that angels and saints have much in common, even residing in the same heavenly abode. They depart just after the first adults begin arriving from the "other world" at 3 p.m. the same day. Officially the souls take leave at 3 p.m. on November 2, but should that day fall on a Sunday—the day liturgically reserved for the Lord—the spirits must simply wait and return on November 3. The normally industrious town of Teotitlán comes to a grinding halt during these fiestas. Tradition warns that, "No one should work while the spirits are still visiting!"

◆ CONSTANT COMPANY AND KIND WORDS ◆

It is midday, November 1, and many years have passed since Antonia Ruiz lost her last child. This spirited, compact woman speaks from first-hand experience as she has buried five of her eleven children. She leads me past the newly renovated room where the altar has been set up, across the porch and into her daughter's bedroom. I am initially perplexed to be moving away from the living room, but as we enter the cool darkness a small altar emerges. Antonia explains that this was the original living room in the home built by her husband's parents forty years ago. This room had housed

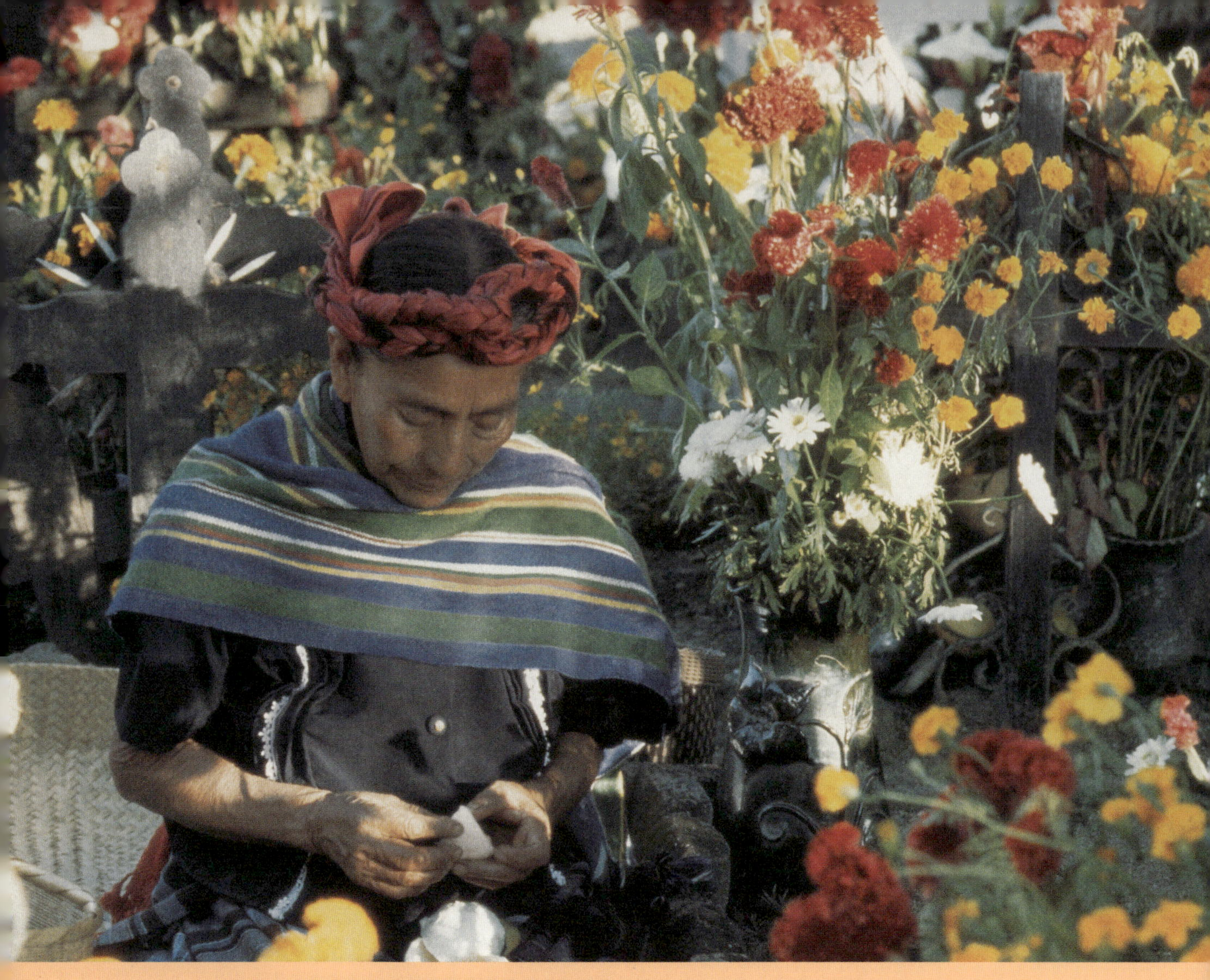

PAGE 60: George O. Jackson. San Gabriel Chilac, Puebla. • **PAGE 62–71:** Ariel Mendoza. Teotitlán del Valle, Oaxaca. 2000.

the altar until 1980 when Antonia and her husband, Félix, built a new living room. She says she still maintains this small altar because it was here, in this room, that the wake was held when her own children died. This is the place they know. This is the place they come back to. "We receive the spirits here," explains Antonia while her daughter Reina takes down the offerings left on the altar for the children's spirits: peanuts and pecans, tiny egg loaves, miniature clay cups filled with hot chocolate, and the tiny bars of chocolate used for making this essential beverage.

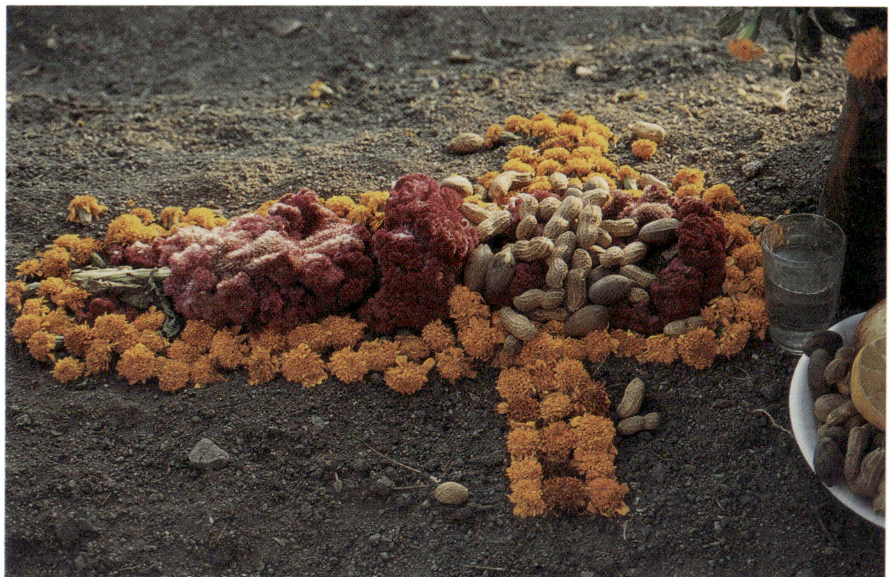

"While the *angelitos* are here we often hear the clinking of ceramics coming from this room," Reina tells me, "the same sound made when you take a drink and place the cup back in the saucer."

The same afternoon in another household in Teotitlán del Valle, Doña Clara Ruiz is already busy attending to four visitors in her living room when another couple arrives. On a day like today, with so many people coming and going, she has left the front door open. Her sister-in-law Leonora, and her husband Renaldo, enter the room quietly while the other guests fall into a respectful silence. The couple goes directly to the altar, unpacking from a large basket their offering of bread, fruit, nuts, and a single taper about a meter tall.

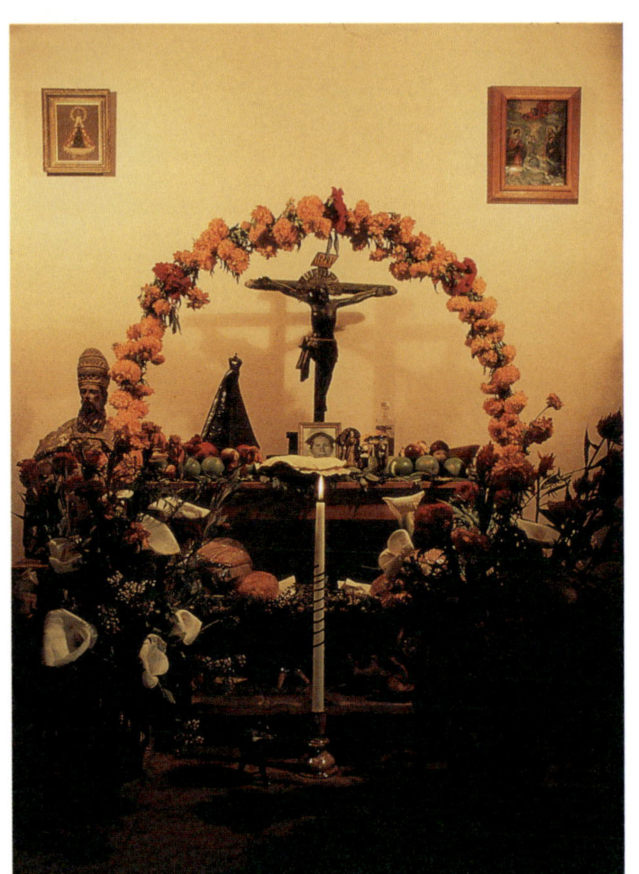

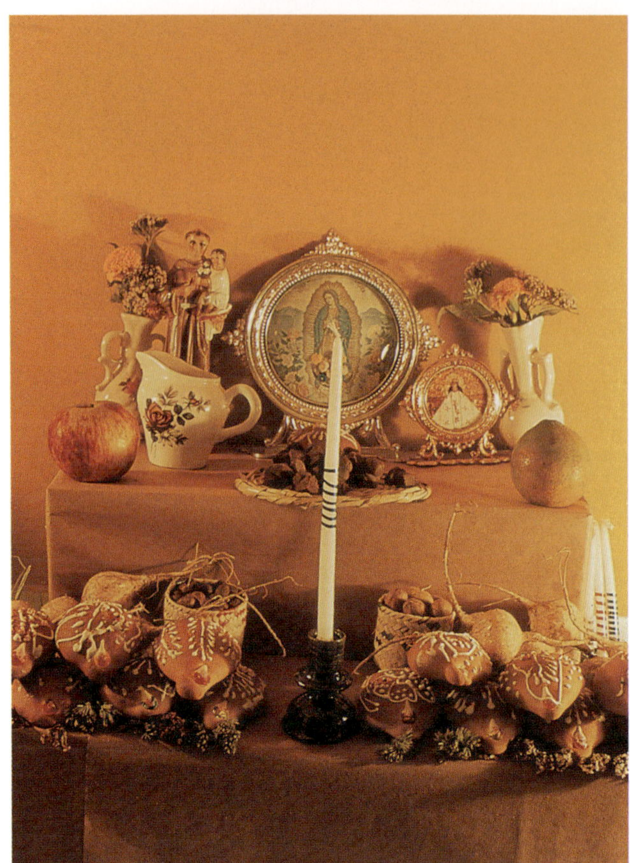

Leonora's lit candle joins six others on the floor at the base of the altar illuminating a framed photograph of Emiliano Mendoza, Clara's deceased husband. According to custom the couple kneels respectfully before the altar. Only after the dead have been properly greeted do the guests direct their attentions to the living, first Clara, then her adult sons and the other guests. They take their places at the large table and comfortable conversation resumes.

The spirits want constant company during their brief twenty-four-hour visit. And while virtually every home has its own spirits to attend to, in a tight-knit community like Teotitlán, most folks spend a good part of the fiesta paying their respects to deceased relatives at other homes.

Hours later, Clara instructs her grown daughter to keep watch over the altar and attend to any visitors while she goes off to visit the homes of several relatives. In the sturdy reed basket tucked under her *rebozo* she carries a bottle of mescal, half a dozen egg loaves, and several blocks of chocolate. She will return home more than once to replenish the basket in the course of her obligatory rounds.

Her first stop is at the home of her deceased mother-in-law. The door is open, and she slips silently into the living room; ignoring the others seated at the long table she moves directly to the altar. She kisses the edge of the altar then kneels to pray.

I asked Doña Clara what she prays for at this moment. "For the spirit of the deceased to be at peace," she replies.

Rising, she greets her brother-in-law, Andrés Mendoza, who as the youngest son, and concurrent with Zapotec custom, still occupies his mother's home. Emerging from the kitchen, Andrés's wife Rosa joins her husband and receives the loaded basket from Doña Clara. This same scene has been played out countless times. Everyone has taken part in it at some point, out of the deep sense of commitment that exists within this community to perform the duties allotted to each person.

Antonia and her husband Félix Mendoza offer their vision of the spirit's comings and goings during the fiesta: "Sometimes the spirits come to visit with friends or maybe a *compadre*. They also visit homes other than those where they lived and died—they go to the homes of their children, godparents and favorite relatives."

So, while the living make their rounds, paying their respects to the spirits of loved ones, likewise the spirits have an open invitation to enjoy the aromas rising from other altars. Even young couples living in new homes where no one they know has died prepare offerings partly for unknown spirits that could return to their ancestral site, and partly for the souls of family members or godparents that might come to visit. Should the need arise to leave their house unoccupied during the fiesta, such an offense may be remedied by leaving the door to the altar room open, which is symbolic of inviting the souls in to visit.

Even worse than offering a half-hearted welcome to the spirits is to not receive them at all. The people of Teotitlán have much to say on this matter. Antonia remembers that as a young girl her family moved to a large property in the heart of the village. "Many people had lived and died on this land long before we came to it but for years it had been abandoned. When our first Day of the Dead came upon us, in the early hours of November 2, my mother heard moans out in the large courtyard."

So, at four in the morning, Victoria González Martínez went out in the dark to reassure the sad souls. She spoke to them and told them that they were welcome. "Don't cry anymore. Even though I don't have much to give you, please join us," she said. Almost half a century has gone by now, and the unknown souls have been content, and never a mysterious moan has been heard since.

• THE OFFERING •

Each element of the family altar assures spirits that they have come to the right home. For that reason, whenever possible, photographs are made central to the arrangement. A simple glass of water is perhaps the most indispensable offering on any Day of the Dead altar. As with the soul's first journey to the "other world," this too has been an arduous one, and the dead need to quench their thirst.

Candles play an important symbolic role. Alejandrina Ríos, the daughter-in-law of Tía Antonia, believes that they illuminate the spirits' path on their return. "If you offer no candles then they light their little fingers to better see the rocks and thorns that line the dark road back," she says. Could this be why lit candles are also placed on the grave immediately following the burial and again on the Day of the Dead, times of travel in the spirit world?

At three in the afternoon on November 1, as the church bells signal the spirits' arrival, the living put the finishing touches on their altars. No hands remain idle at this time of year. Antonia's three daughters are busy in the kitchen. Reina pours a cup of hot chocolate whipped to a thick froth and nestles it among three large *panes de muerto*—sweet loaves of bread marked with a cross baked especially for this fiesta. Elia deftly mounds steaming tamales on a platter while Altagracia ladles the ubiquitous black mole over a cooked turkey leg. All this takes place under the watchful eye of Antonia, who has strategically placed the hot chocolate, tamales, and mole on her altar, anticipating by minutes the arrival of *los muertitos*.

"But things were not always like this," Félix Mendoza emphasizes, comfortably presiding over the long wooden table he has made himself, with his back to the wall and his gaze upon the doorway. This trim, handsome man in his late fifties, dashing with a well-groomed mustache and a thick head of hair, has, like others of his generation, seen more changes in half a century

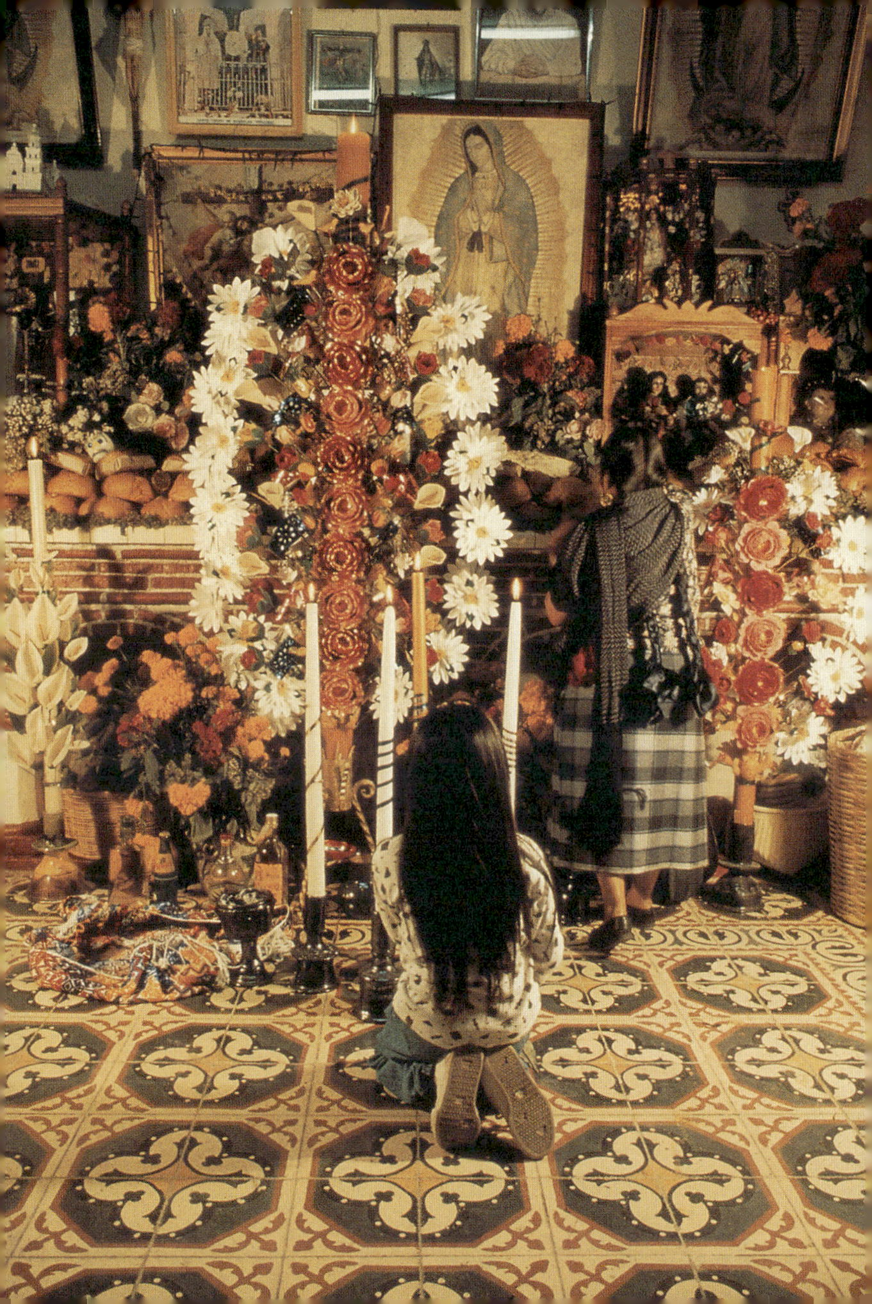

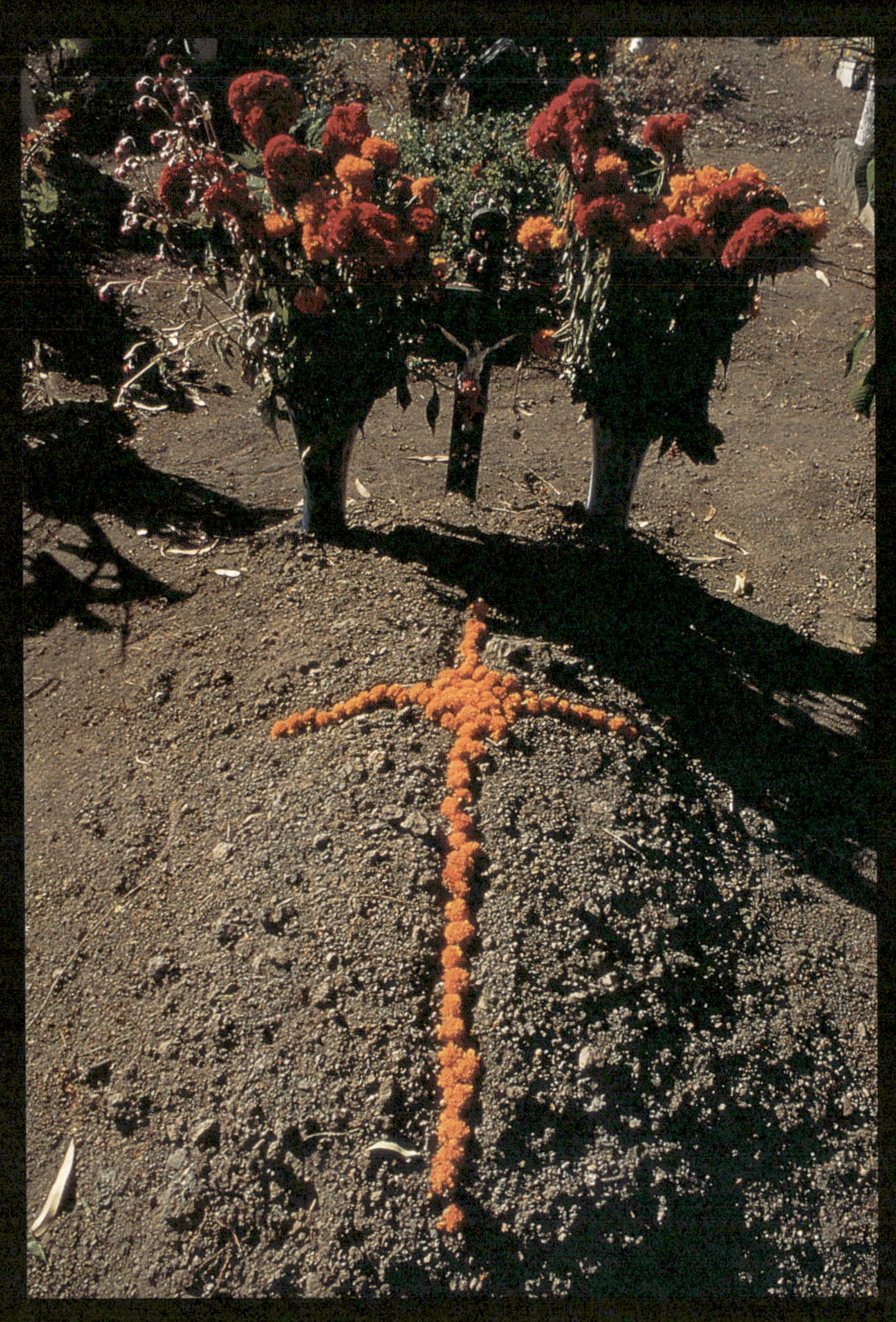

than any Zapotec ancestor since the arrival of the Spaniards. Félix recalls, "I would work day and night to finish weaving a *serape* before the Day of the Dead. I'd take it to sell in the Tlacolula market and there were times when I returned home with the unsold piece after an entire day sitting in the sun. We would be really desperate then! If I didn't sell the serape we would have nothing to offer our dead—not mole, not turkey, not even chocolate! My only option would be to sell it to one of the wholesalers in the village who would pay us whatever they wanted in those days, sometimes only half the value of the weaving because they knew we had no other choice."

Arnulfo Mendoza Ruiz, my husband and son of the deceased Emiliano, says that, in the early nineteen-fifties, before the first day of the dead that they celebrated as a married couple, Emiliano couldn't sell his only rug to cover the costs of the fiesta. But it was so important to place an offering for the departed that they went up into the hills with a mule to gather that deliciously perfumed flower that can only be found in the sierra near to Teotitlán. After loading up the animal, the couple went from town to town exchanging the freshly cut flowers for bread, corn, and beans—acceptable offerings in those times of scarcity.

The grand altar at Clara Ruiz's home now takes first place for its sheer abundance. It entails a true balancing act using plates of apples, oranges, and tamales. Around the edge of the altar a wall over half-a-meter high has been constructed of *panes de muerto* reminiscent of fieldstone walls. This arrangement stands so high that the photographs making up Mendoza Ruiz's family's saintly entourage—concealed within wooden niches and embraced by crepe paper flowers—are barely visible over the oven-browned bread.

Despite being in her sixties, Clara glides gracefully from altar room to patio to kitchen, intent on properly looking after her guests. She miraculously appears serving bowls of scalding *atole*, hot chocolate, and steaming tamales. After 1 p.m. they dispense with the breakfast foods and switch to *mole de castilla*, her deceased husband's favorite dish.

Aroma is to spirits what taste is to the living, so the heady incense of copal resin and tiny scented wildflowers are essential elements on any Teotitlán altar. The intense smells satiate the dead while the living indulge in bowls of rich turkey mole and yellow tamales. The villagers often comment that when they place the bread on the altar it weighs more than when they take it away, or how the food removed from the offering has no flavor.

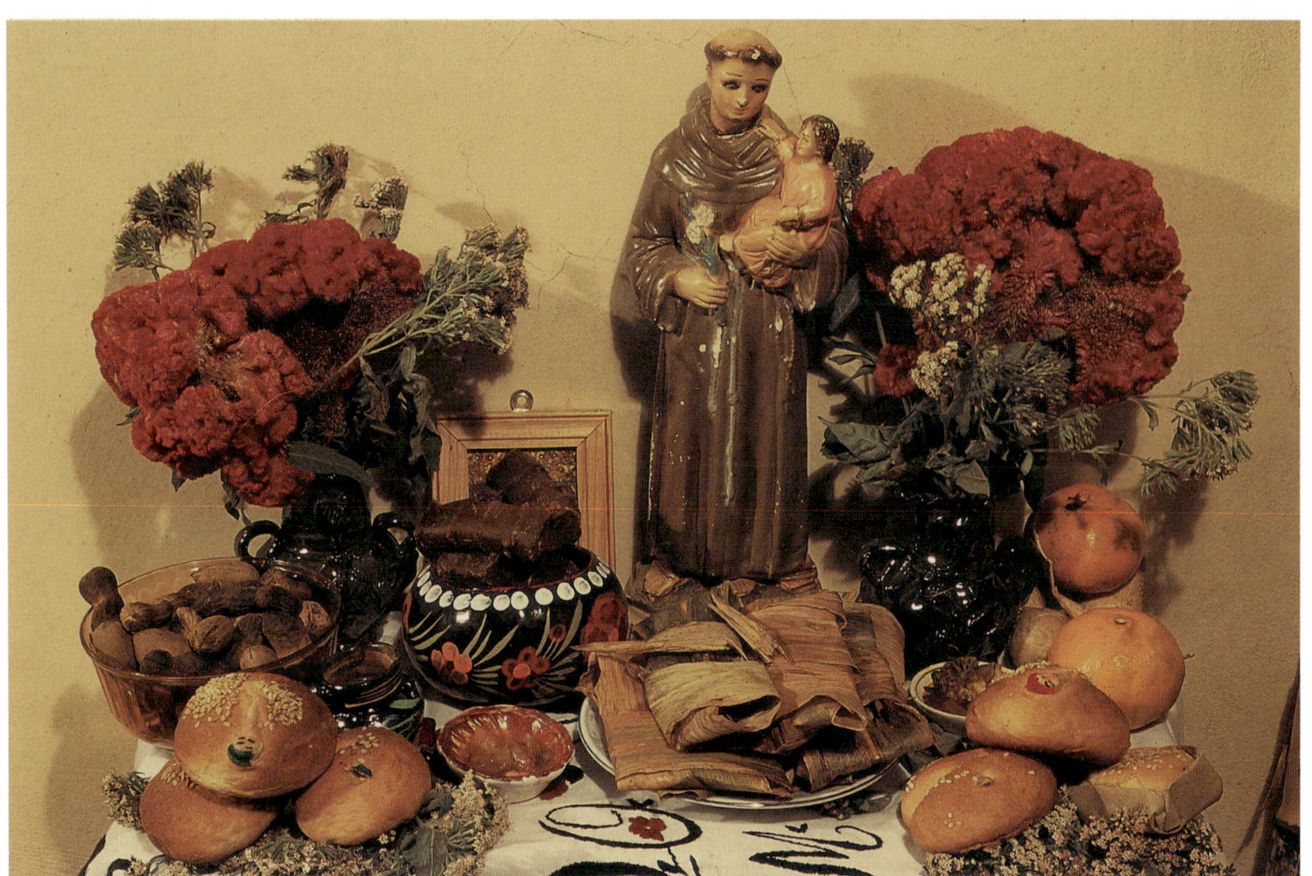

Don Marino Vázquez, a respected village elder, explains: "That happens because the dead feast on the spirit of the food, they take away its essence; that's why we don't eat it afterwards."

"It isn't just food we offer the dead children—we buy them presents too!" Antonia elaborates.

Tiny sheep, turkeys and angels of sugar decorated with colored frosting are made especially for the altars of *angelitos*. Some families will add miniature objects to the altars such as *metates* (grindstones) and tortilla presses for their daughters, and toy hammers and hoes for their sons.

"Every year we buy a brand new *tenate* (woven basket), *molcajete* (mortar and pestle), and *jarrito* (clay jug). Sure, we use them afterwards, but they do take the gifts away—symbolically. We know that," Antonia explains, "because women who have gone to wash clothes in the river before the fiesta is over testify, in spite of their fright, to seeing the dead leading away their pack burros or carrying baskets under their arms and sacks over their shoulders loaded with the offered gifts."

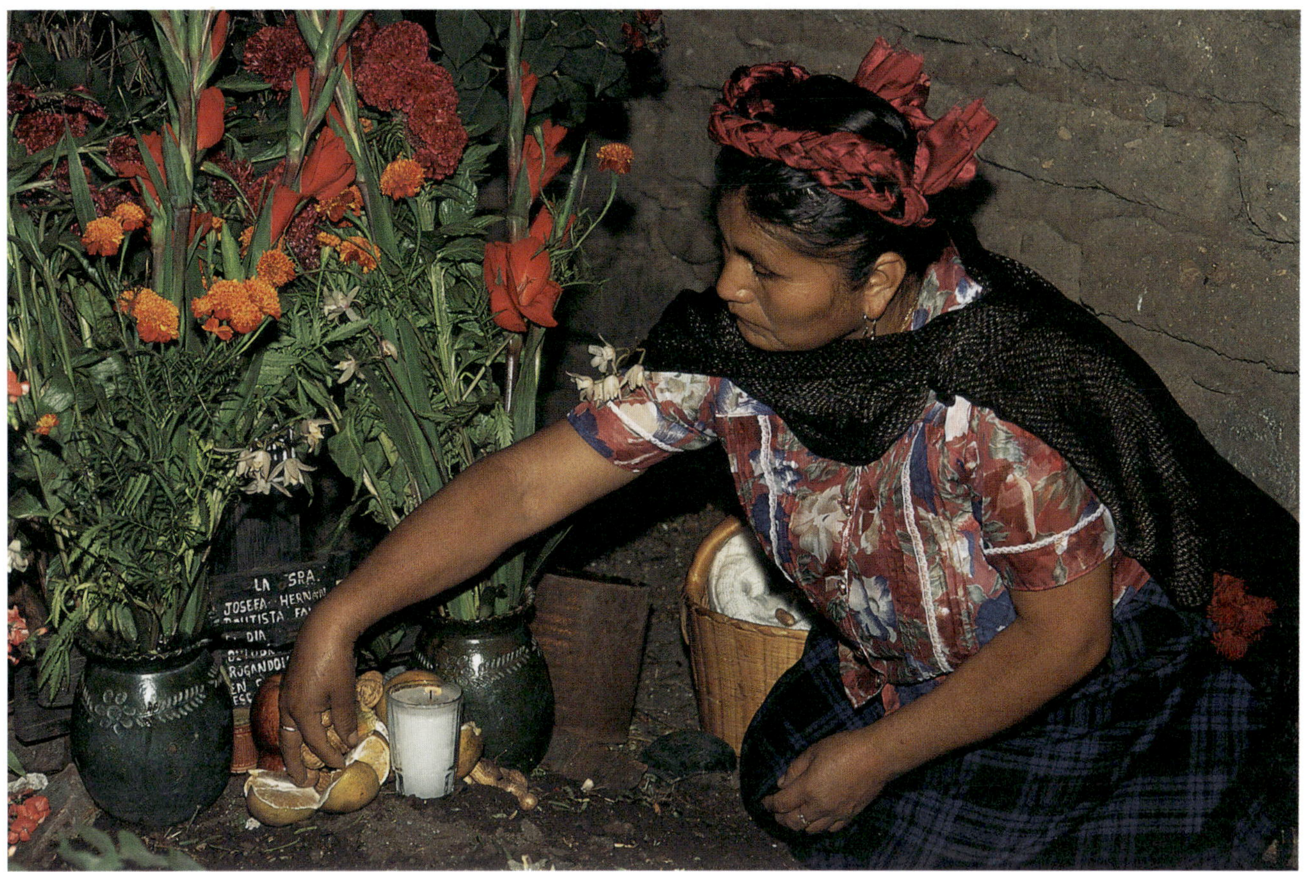

Don Marino explains that if the spirits like to drink mescal, then a toast is made. The *juez* (judge or official mezcal sever) will first pour a shot and drizzle it in the form of the cross on the offering at the foot of the altar. Having offered a drink to the deceased, he will then pass out shots of mezcal to all the visitors at the table, in order of importance.

• THE RETURN TRIP •

Many villagers insist on “seeing off” their loved ones at the cemetery. Others, like Félix Mendoza and Antonia Ruiz never go to the cemetery on November 2. Félix explains “this would be like kicking someone out of the house. Some spirits leave slowly and others get drunk and so the fiesta spills over to the third.”

At 3 p.m. on November 2, deafening explosions from firecrackers in the churchyard and homes signal to the entire populace, living or dead, that it is time for the souls to think about their journey back.

A visit to the cemetery on this same afternoon is a sight to behold: the graves dance with enormous bunches of oxblood, cock's comb, and brilliant marigolds, dotted with delicate calla lilies. Many families go to the cemetery bearing fruits, peanuts, bottles of mezcal and cases of beer. This is a time to clean the tombstones, some are even diligently scrubbed with soap and water. Candles are lit and long-winded toasts are made to the departing loved ones.

At this time of year, the warm glowing rays of the late afternoon sun heighten the intense tones of the flowers, and as one draws near the cemetery's tiny chapel the woeful chants of the *alabanceros* (members of Teotitlan's highly respected lay clergy) invite those present to indulge in the moment's sweet sorrow.

The band plays emotive dirges and slow marches, the same sad songs played for the funeral processions that every villager has accompanied on countless occasions, escorting close and extended family on their last and ultimate rite of passage—the journey we will all, one day, make to the "other side."

Just as Sunday is dedicated to the Lord, every Monday in November belongs to the dead. For five weeks, Padre Rómulo—who attends to the spiritual needs of Teotitlán as well as four other nearby villages—will visit each community in turn, celebrating *los responsos* in the town cemetery. On the Monday designated for Teotitlán, even those who stayed at home with the languishing souls on November 2 will likely visit the cemetery making a small donation to the priest for which he will recite individual prayers at the graves of their departed ones. The exuberance of fresh flowers and the chanted prayers heighten the senses to take in every detail of this moment suspended in time and space, somewhere between Heaven and Earth. ◆

Mary Jane Gagnier de Mendoza was born in Canada and studied music and visual arts at Vancouver Community College. She curated the exhibition *Myth and Magic: Oaxaca Past and Present*, which was presented at the Palo Alto Arts Center, the Santa Cruz Museum of Art, and the Mexican Fine Arts Museum in Chicago. Featured in the *Artes de México* collection titled *Libros de la Espira*l, her work *Rituales de Armonía* treats the festivities of Teotitlán del Valle, where the most important celebrations of this Oaxacan community take place.

POSTHUMOUS REVENGE

Recorded by Fernando Benítez
As told by Manuel Zugaide

◆◆◆◆◆

All Saint's Day is the most important day of the year for us Indians. This is the day when the dead come back. Dead children come at midday on October 31 and they leave at noon on November 1. The dead adults arrive at that time, and they leave at midnight on November 2.

They are summoned by bells. The bells ring twenty-four hours without stopping, from noon on the last day of October until noon on the first day of November, and the bell ringers take turns throughout the day they are rung in a minor key for the dead children, and a major key for dead adults.

The dead arrive and they smell the bread, tamales, and fruit making up the offerings, and they take away their essence. And we are always there eating with them. They don't need anything else. The essence is enough for them to last a whole year.

People go from door to door praying. They are paid fifty *centavos* or a peso to mention the name of dead family members, and they and their helpers share in the food from the offering.

In Cihualtepec they are also summoned with bells, but it isn't the same thing here. Take an example: I buried my mom in La Joya but, unfortunately, we have to celebrate All Saint's here. We don't know if the dead can come here, if they know how to get to some unknown place even though we're calling them with prayers and bells. Some still go to Old Ixcatlán or Old Soyaltepec. We also have the dead who were buried previously on this land. Besides, they're poor people who don't know how to get around outside their customary places.

It's the old people and not the young ones who still talk to their dead in the cemeteries. They say, "Pray to God so you will reach Glory soon." Others say,

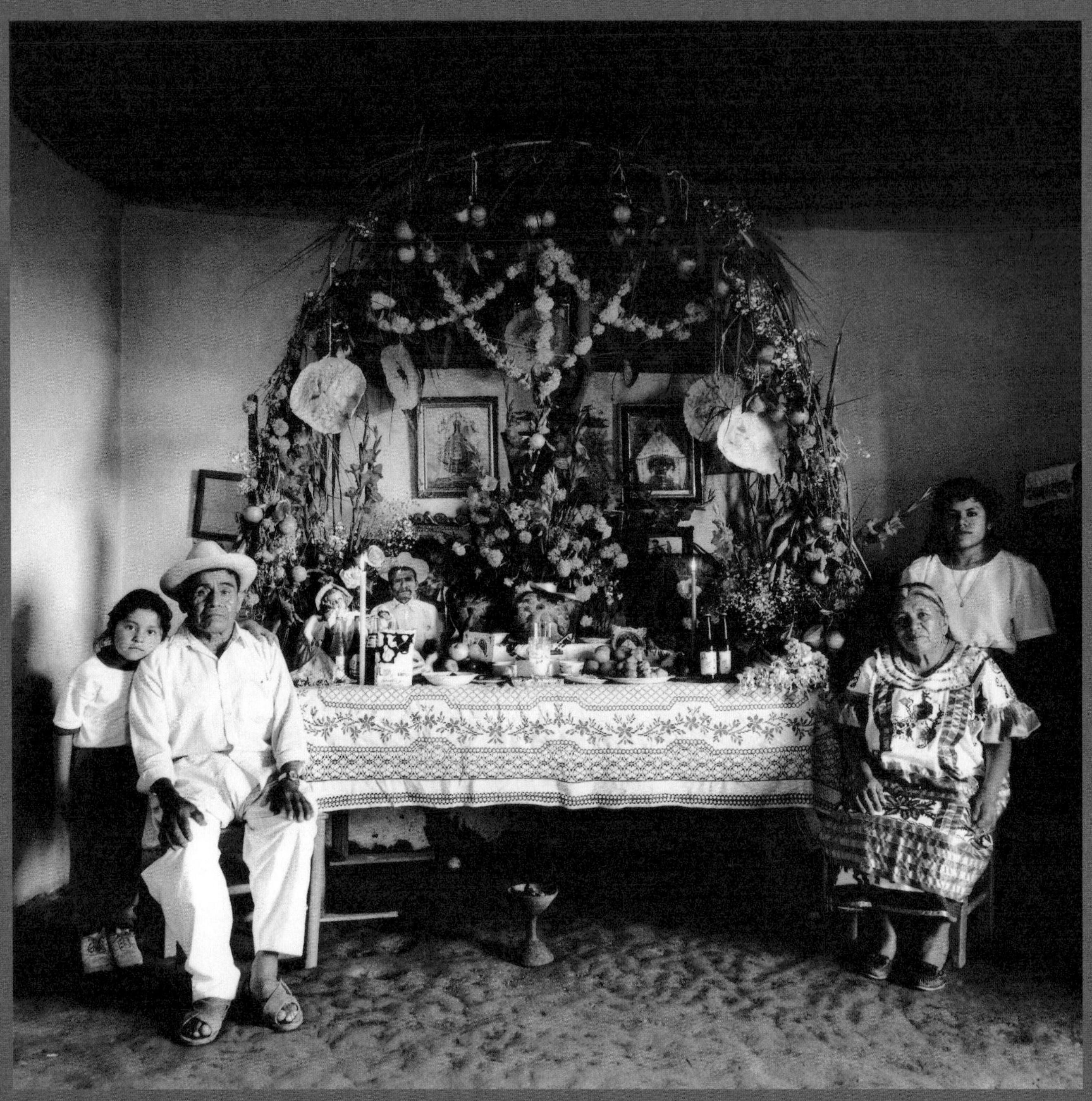

Lourdes Almeida. Mazatec family next to their altar in Huautla, Oaxaca. 1995.

"Here I am suffering in the knowledge that I'm bound to die before long. We all travel the same road eventually." They just talk to them from above and say the dead hear them.

Sorcerers visit the cemeteries so the dead can call whoever they're thinking of harming. Say that person has a bad dream: he gets stabbed, or falls off a cliff, or his house burns down, and if he has sex with a woman after that dream, well he's done for: he's sure to get sick or even die if he doesn't go to a good medicine man. The medicine man is supposed to protect him against the sorcerer and talks to God, to ask for his health to be restored: "Lord Jesus Christ, you can't let some bad person cut the life of another human being short just like that."

Since we're talking about All Saint's Day I'm going to tell you a story. There was a man whose wife died so he remarried. He was broke and had to go away to work, so a few days before the Day of the Dead, he told his bride, "Look, do me a favor, everything you're going to put on the altar for your dead relatives, just put the same there for my dead wife. Will you do as I ask?"

"Yes," answered the woman. "Don't worry. I'll do as you ask."

"When the dishes and fruit are taken to the altar, it's customary to say, 'This fruit is for you, Juana (assuming this was the name of the dead wife) or this chicken, or this coffee.' Do you understand?"

"Yes, Pafnucio, I think I understand."

So, the new wife heated up a stone and when it was so red-hot it was giving off sparks, she took it to the altar saying, "Juana, I'll put this stone here for you to eat."

The husband returned that same night and, on the way home, found the dead woman crying and moaning. "Ay, ay," the poor dead woman cried. "I've burned my mouth!"

When the man entered the house, he asked his wife, "What did you put on the altar for my dead wife?" "Food and fruit, like you ordered." He went closer and then he saw the burnt altar. He understood that his wife had tricked him. As he was a peaceful man, he just gave her a good thrashing. ◆

—Translated by Michelle Suderman

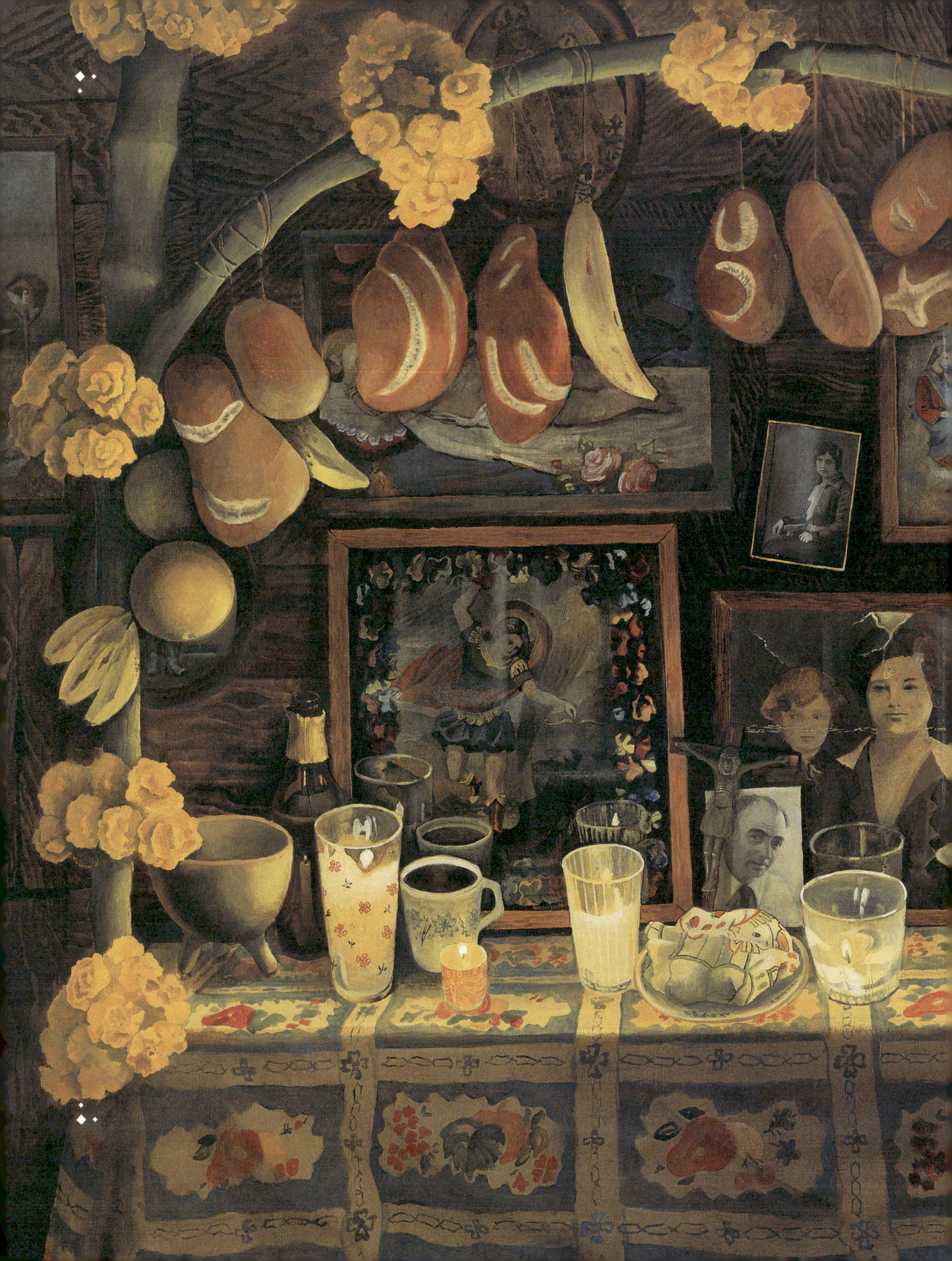

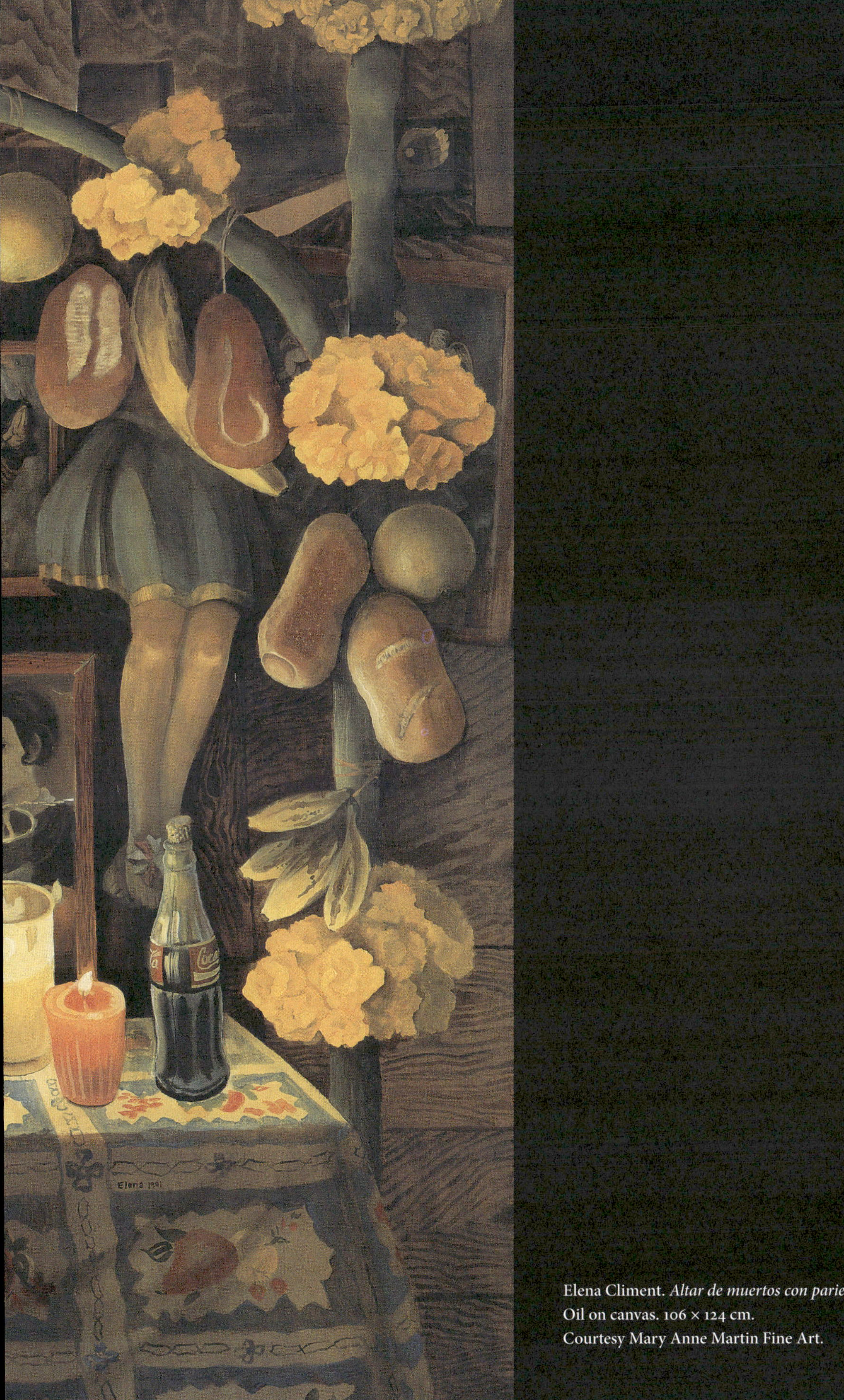

Elena Climent. *Altar de muertos con parientes*
Oil on canvas. 106 × 124 cm.
Courtesy Mary Anne Martin Fine Art.

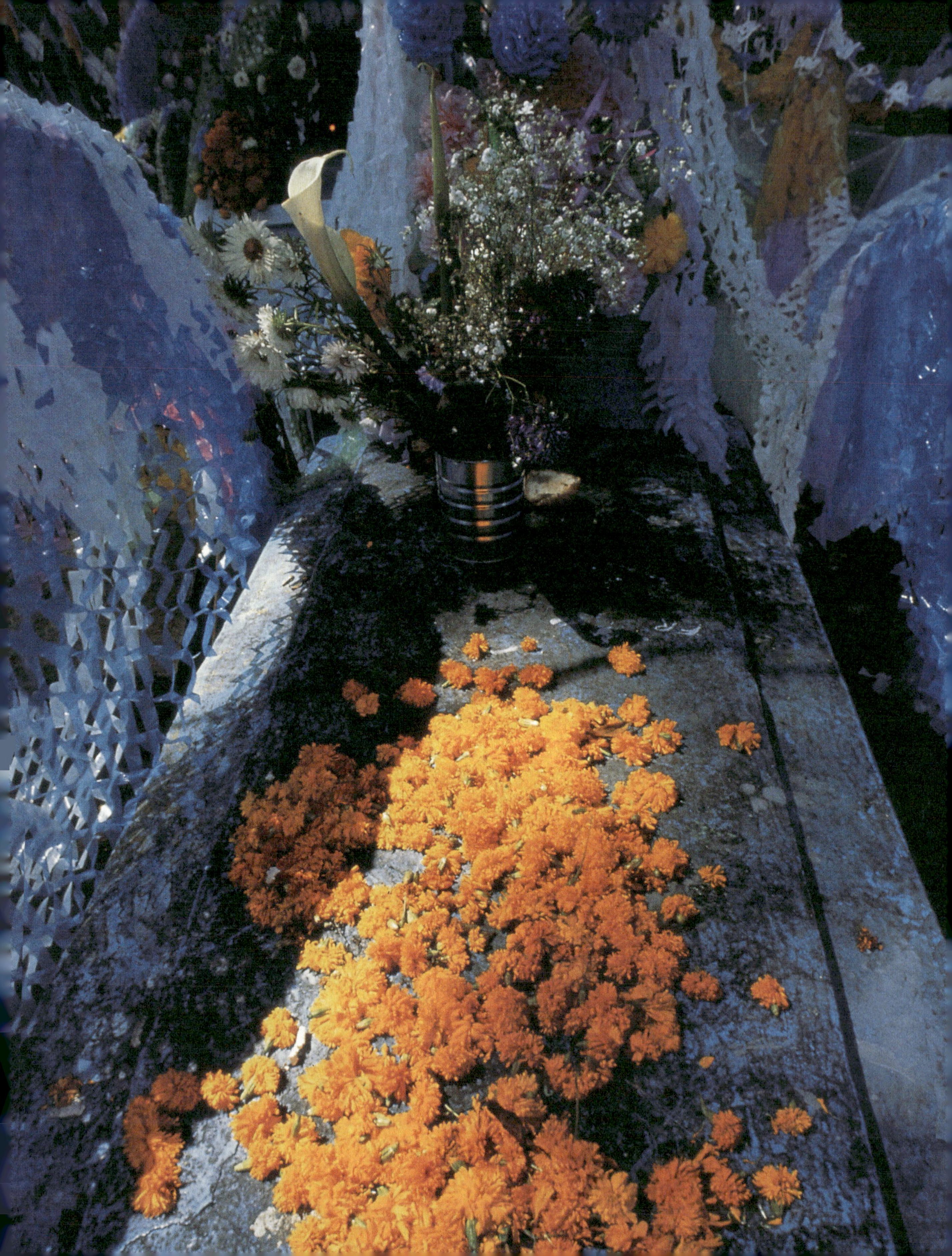

THE ALTAR: A CREATIVE HORN OF PLENTY

Marta Turok

◆◆◆◆◆

The penetrating smell and bright color are unmistakable. It is October, the harvest is almost done, and the marigold has arrived in the street markets, seeming to signal the approach of that time of year when we remember those who have passed away. Stands begin to pop up, selling objects for the Day of the Dead. Here we find strips of *otate* (cane), copal, censers, clay candelabras, little chocolate or sugar skulls, and crepe paper decorations . . .

From the (mainly urban) collective consciousness, the prototype of the Mexican who plays with death has emerged and, over the course of time, become fashionable. It is a figure that mocks death and treats it with irreverence. This image is juxtaposed against that of the indigenous communities, guardians of ritual, who carry out the ceremony with discretion and reverence.

In these communities, the Day of the Dead celebrations are held by the family. They are private, but possess a collective, communal dimension. Like any ritual, they consist of several acts: the welcome and farewell of the spirits, the preparation and setting up of the offering in the family altar, the decoration of the graves, the vigil in the cemetery, and religious services from the Catholic liturgy. In this ceremony, the family's dead relatives as spirits. As they come from a world that is similar to that of the living, they are received for a brief get-together and are sent off with music, food and gifts. There is no smell of death, nor any fear.

In many places, the spirits of the dead are guided by the aroma of flower petals—preferably of marigolds—which lay a fragrant trail from the street to the shrine.

The arrival of the dead is announced by a peal of bells, prayers, the burning of copal, and the lighting of candles, just as setting off fireworks

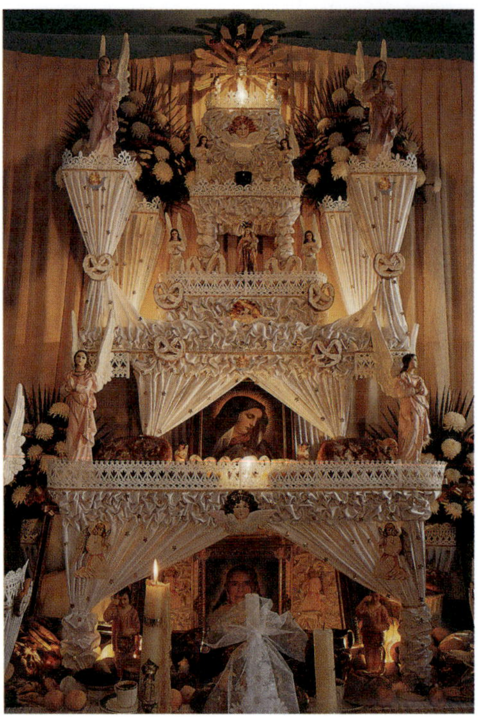

Jorge Vértiz. Huaquechula, Puebla. 1999.

or another peal of bells bids them farewell. However, in places such as the Huasteca area of Hidalgo, the celebrations continue until Carnival, when those spirits still at large are captured with ropes called *micahuitl* to return them to the underworld.

The ceremony is prepared in advance. First, the cemetery is cleaned, the tasks and chores generally being done on a communal basis. Next, families take charge of the decoration of their particular graves, although the adornment of graves belonging to the anonymous dead or those who have lost their families are never forgotten. These people are remembered because they will still be missed in some part of the world.

The grave decoration is followed by the vigil. This is the act of accompanying the dead all day or night, sometimes sharing food with them, and often serenading them with their favorite songs or ritual masked dances. In this way, the devotion at the family shrine is replicated in the cemetery.

Altars are located next to the traditional shrine to the saints or in the main reception room of the house. While they display great differences between regions, they share certain formal elements. A table or shelf covered

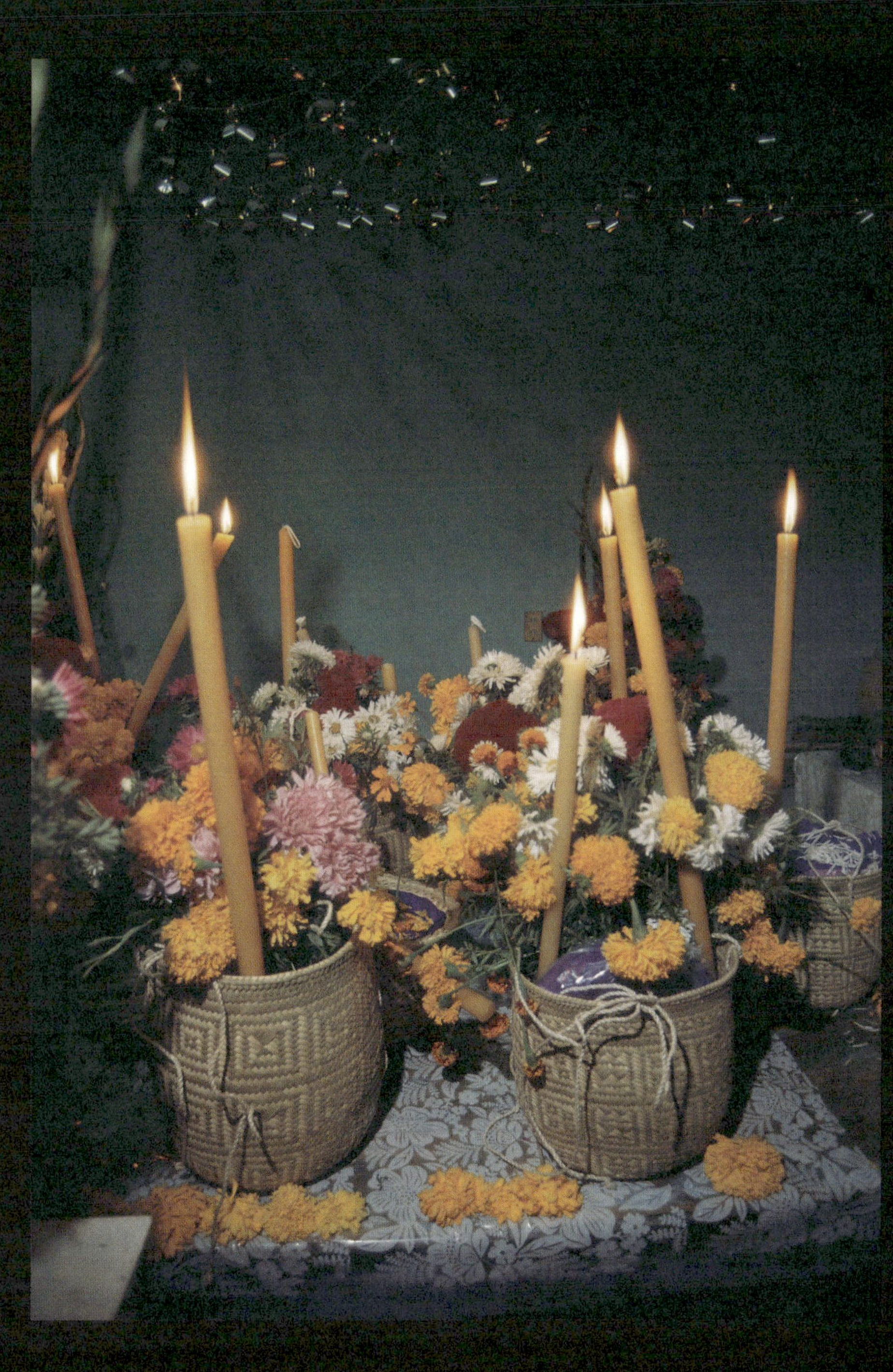

Jorge Vértiz. San Gabriel Chilac, Puebla. 2001. • **PAGE 78:** George O. Jackson. Grave in Guadalupe Victoria, Chiapas, 2000.

with a tablecloth forms the basis of any shrine in Mexico. The tablecloth is preferably white and embroidered, although these have tended recently to be replaced by patterned plastic ones. In order to mark out the sacred space for the offering, one or more sugarcane, *otate*, or *carrizo* (reed) arches are tied to the feet of the table. These are adorned with marigolds, palm leaves, *cucharilla* (lemongrass), banana leaves, fresh fruit, dried chilies, and bread. The most spectacular shrines are constructed in the form of a *catafalque*, using covered boxes or shelves to make them taller. The most outstanding works of this nature are those of the Nahua community in Mexico City and the Huasteca region, the Purépecha of Michoacán and the Zapotecs in the Oaxaca valley.

Paper flowers and crepe paper decorations are occasionally hung in front or behind the table. These accompany photographs of those family members who have passed away, which are generally placed between several vases. One or more censers may be placed on a new *petate* (palm mat) in front of the table. Garments or objects associated with the deceased may also be placed on the altar; these may include a machete, a hat, a sash, children's toys, and so forth.

Traditional dishes to be offered to the dead are cooked between October 30 and November 1. It is common that all the clay dishes in which food is offered be new; these then become part of the everyday crockery.

• RITUAL OBJECTS •

Although produced and used expressly for the celebration, the objects associated with the cult of the dead can be considered examples of ritual craftsmanship. Many of them form part of the offering, whose ephemeral nature demonstrates the abundance of creativity that the annual transformation demands. The syncretic nature of this celebration is palpable above all in the pieces that form part of an offering, although traditions that were part of the European rites of the sixteenth century can also be appreciated. These found an echo in pre-Hispanic customs, such as the act of offering gifts to the dead, visiting the cemeteries to share in the ephemeral return of the dead, and the special treatment of deceased children.

As regards the objects, it is interesting to note, for example, that there is a page in the *Magliabecchiano Codex* showing strings of paper with designs probably painted in *ulli* (gum oil). These are direct ancestors of the strings of perforated crepe paper decorations used to this day, which have pre-Hispanic, Chinese, and French influences. Nowadays, the manufacture of perforated crepe paper decorations is traditionally carried out in San Salvador Huixcolotla, Puebla, as well as Uruapan, Michoacán, and Tláhuac in the Federal District, although they are produced in many other areas in a less commercial way.

In Metepec, state of Mexico and Santa Fe de la Laguna, Michoacán, candelabras and censers are made of black clay or with a black glaze. In Ocotlán, Oaxaca, these are made of baked clay, the figures adorning them being painted white and cobalt blue with earth and pigments. The censers are crowned with anthropomorphic figures whose upraised arms are linked, and candelabras have paste skulls affixed to the tube and base. These hark back to a pre-Hispanic piece found in Zaachila, Oaxaca: a three-legged ceremonial vessel in the Mixtec style. Leaning against this orange clay work, we find a skeletal figure attributed to the god Mictlantecuhtli, whose head swivels on its neck and whose expression fluctuates between macabre and playful. In the neighboring town of Atzompa, Oaxaca, the censers and candelabra are decorated with a green glaze and small cherubic faces. The censers from Huaquechula and Izúcar de Matamoros, Puebla, whose colors are achieved through the use of anilines, are made of baked clay with a white glaze. These have a cherub and two molded flowers on the rim, as do the candelabras, which also have a figure of St. Michael the Archangel. The candles bear a scaly design and elaborate figures of flowers and leaves, or simple diagonally snaking colored ribbons.

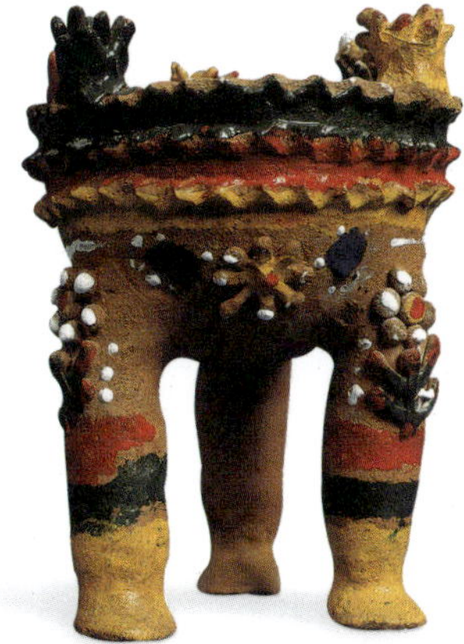

Chatino censer. 1985. Clay with pastillaje, painted. Panixtlahuaca, Oaxaca. Franz Mayer Museum / Ruth D. Lechuga Collection of Popular Art.

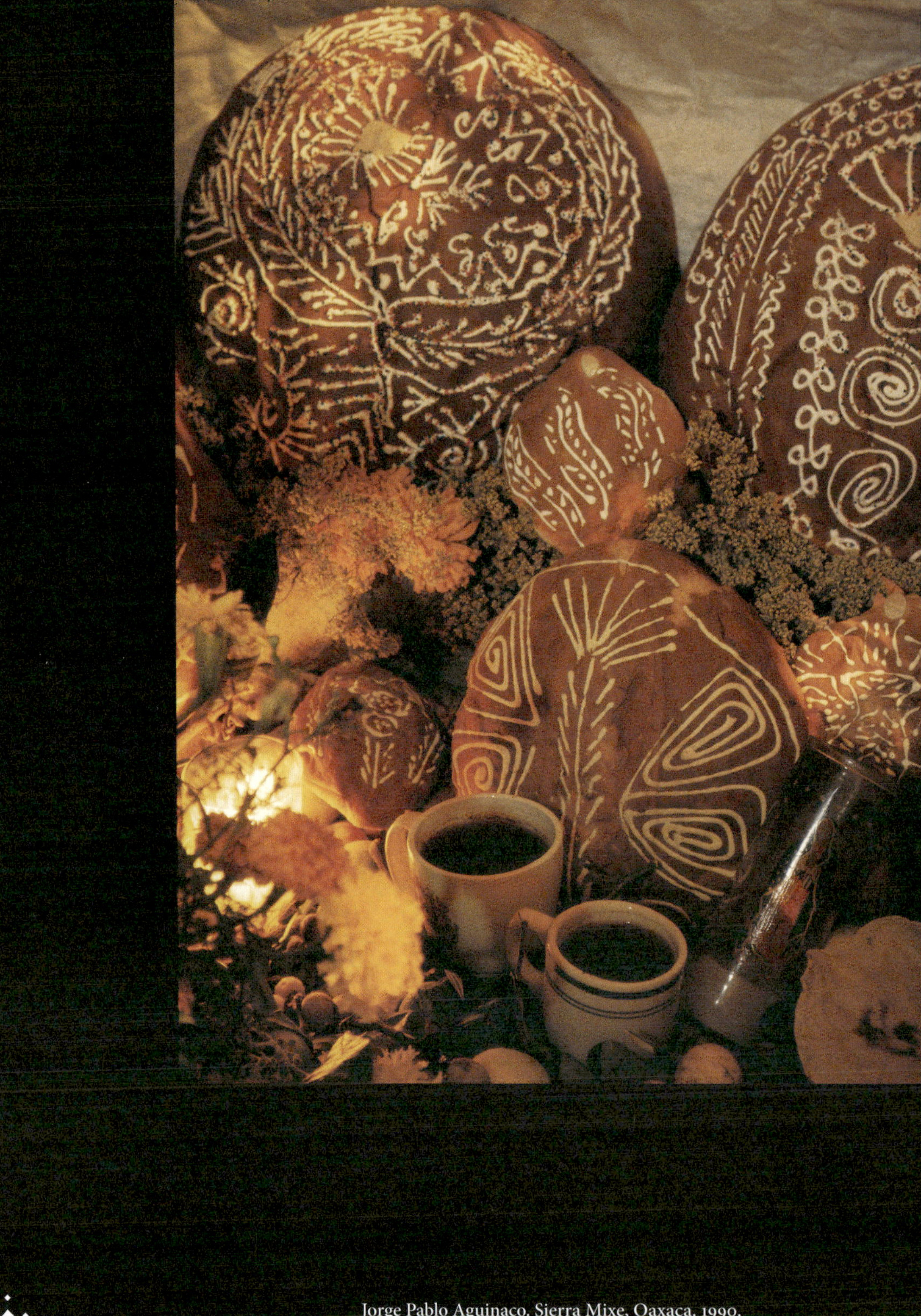

Jorge Pablo Aguinaco. Sierra Mixe, Oaxaca. 1990.

Amaranth mixed with tamale dough forms a paste called *tzoalli*, with which the Aztecs molded the figures of certain deities used in celebrations and ceremonies, some of which were linked with death. In colonial times, this dough could possibly have been replaced by anthropomorphic figures made of wheat bread, or molded sugar faces, which have since become quite ubiquitous in Day of the Dead offerings.

• FROM RITE TO MYTH, POPULAR RE-CREATION TO ARTISTIC INSTALLATION •

On comparing Mexico City practices with rural indigenous traditions and even those of urban mestizo in the rest of the country, we realize that a new vision of the Day of the Dead has developed in the capital, and has extended to other cities within and beyond the borders of Mexico. José Guadalupe Posada obviously played an important role in this movement. In close association with the work of this engraver, we encounter the *calavera*, a macabre cartoon combined with witty literary satire, criticizing politicians and public figures.

The ritual of living with the dead, in this context, tends to remove the element of the sacred. Another development worthy of consideration is that experienced by those communities—such as Mixquic in the Federal District, or the island of Janitizio in Pátzcuaro, Michoacán—whose fervor is mixed with mass tourism. The inhabitants of such places have learned, little by little, that preserving tradition is also good business.

In the ambit of popular craft expression and the staging of offerings, we also find an explosive reinterpretation of semantics that turns the cult of death into the cult of spectacle. We should acknowledge that, for the last few years, the urbanized image of death (that of skeletons, skulls, and certain offerings) has tended to lose its ritual meaning in order to re-create itself. Ritual craft has become decorative folk art, to be collected and exhibited. Numerous craftsmen, such as the brothers Alfonso and Tiburcio Soteno of Metepec, state of México, the Linares family of Mexico City, Alfonso Castillo of Izúcar de Matamoros and Roberto Ruiz of Oaxaca and Ciudad Nezahualcóyotl, have testified that they started to make figures of skulls due to the interest of buyers and agents in the 1950s and 1960s. At no time, however, did this compromise the creativity and enjoyment with which they create their works.

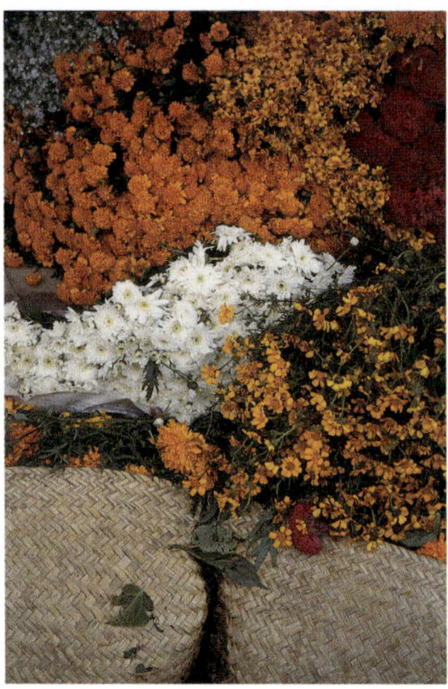

Jorge Pablo Aguinaco. Oaxaca, Oaxaca. 1990. • **NEXT PAGE:** Jorge Pablo Aguinaco. San Miguel de Allende, Guanajuato. 2000.

The offering has also taken on new values: it has become a symbol *par excellence* for artists and the educational system. On the one hand, it occurs in artistic installations and performances, which are taken to museums and cultural centers in Mexico and other countries. On the other, it becomes a medium for reaffirming Mexican cultural values in schools, countering the Anglo-Saxon tradition of Halloween. The celebration of the Day of the Dead is unequivocal evidence that we live in times of change. We are poised between the rite and the conversion into myth of something that seeks to be defined as a national archetype. ◆

—Translated by David Bevis

Marta Turok is an anthropologist from Tufts University who studied at Harvard and UNAM. She has chaired the Mexican Association of Popular Art and Culture (AMACUP) since 1989. She has published, among other titles, *¿Cómo acercarse a la artesanía?* (*How to Approach Crafts?*), *El caracol púrpura, una tradición milenaria* (*The Purple Snail, an Ancient Tradition*), *Fiestas mexicanas* (*Mexican Festivals*), and *Living Traditions: Mexican Popular Arts*. She was co-curator, along with Mark Winter, of the exhibition *El sarape de Saltillo: Enigma y Trace*, presented at the Franz Mayer Museum.

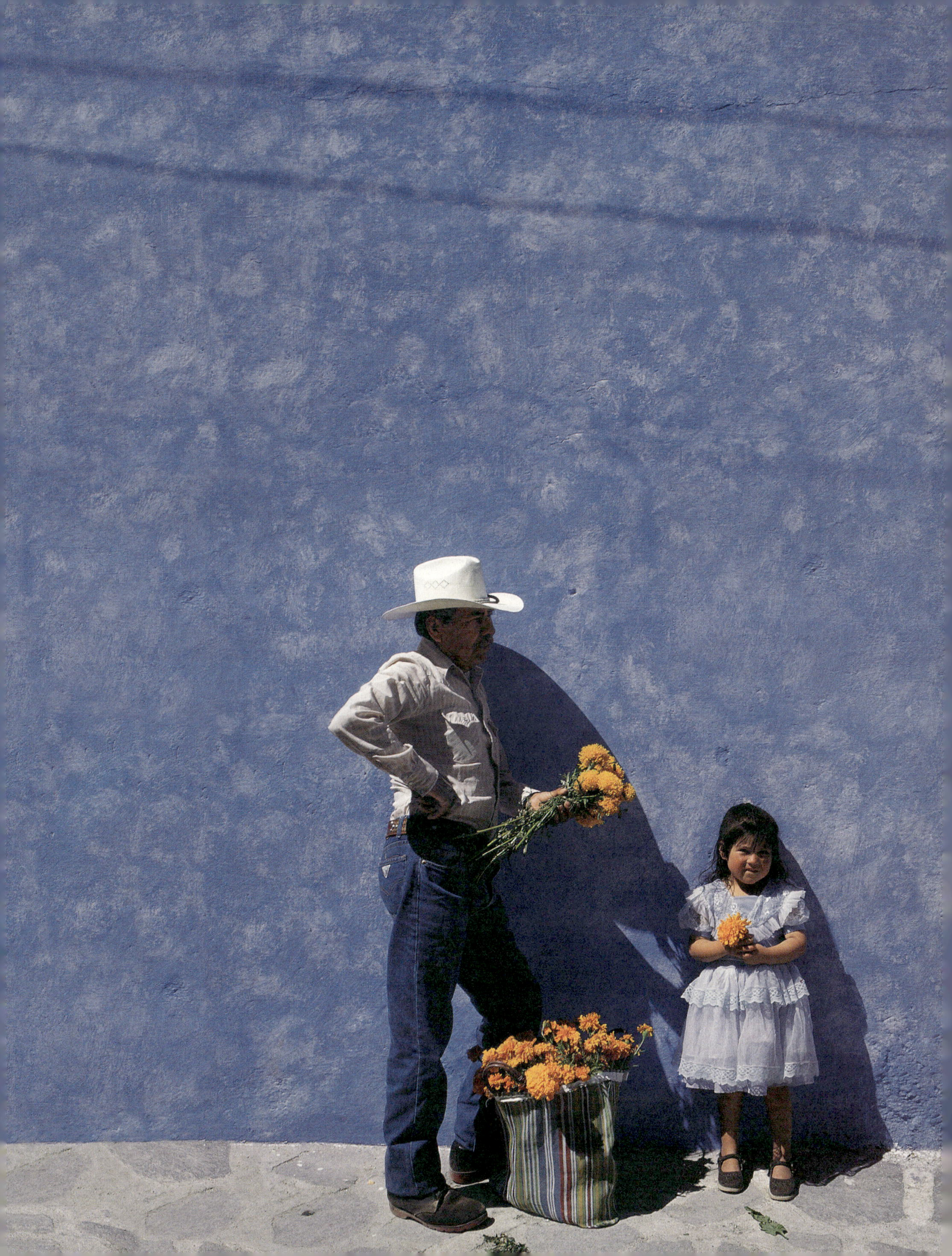

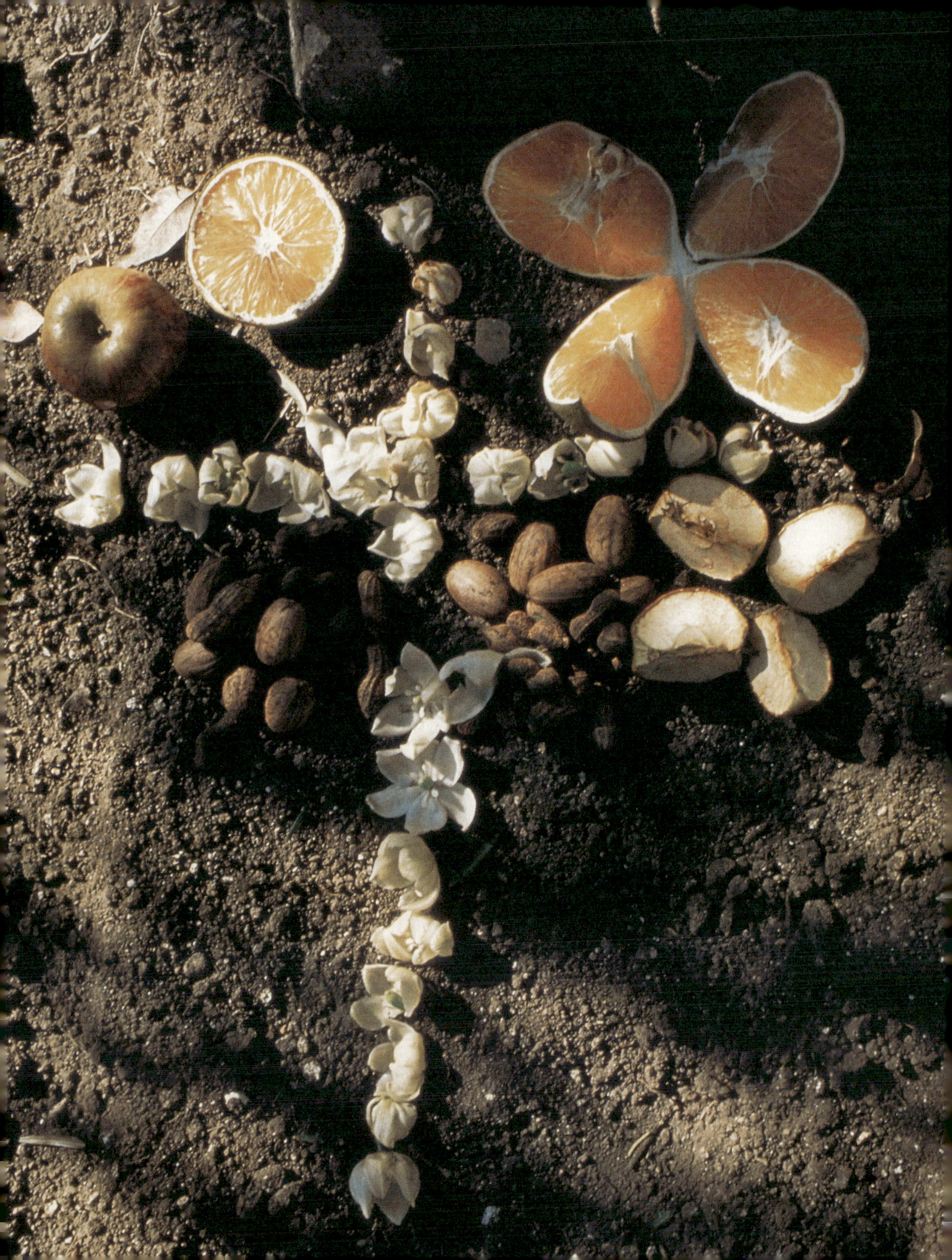

ON SEEDS AND DEATH

Gabriela Olmos

◆◆◆◆◆

Ever since humanity's discovery of agriculture, there have been peoples whose religions associated death rituals with the fertility of the Earth. Mircea Eliade, in his *Tratado de historia de las religiones*, cites India's commemoration of the dead that coincides with the harvest festival, as well as an ancient Nordic cult that associated death with the ceremony of vegetation.

Mexico's Day of the Dead festivities can structurally be counted amongst these traditional rites that recognize the relationship between seeds and the dead, as they too take place on the eve of the harvest, just before the onset of winter, between September and October. Among other things, both share a similar physical location—by planting the seed, do we not desecrate the Earth, the dead's natural resting place? Furthermore, both are in a larval state, having proceeded from a living state, and they share an intermediate existence in which life lies latent. Thus, in Mexican rural communities, the celebrations of November 1 and 2 contain vestiges that predate the arrival of the Judeo-Christian tradition, hinting at the splendor of the pre-Columbian civilizations. Deep within the Day of the Dead substrata lies evidence of a ceremony that springs from a time when agricultural rites linking death and the possibility of renewal were being born.

What does the arrival of the dead during these dates mean to Mexican cultures? According to Eliade, it is a sacred time, a time of ritual and prayer—our means of establishing a dialogue with the gods—in which the slate of human history is wiped clean to begin anew. However, re-creating the world can only be accomplished by repetition of the divine creation, which in the beginning separates order from chaos, followed by the establishment of a cosmic balance. This is what takes place during the festival.

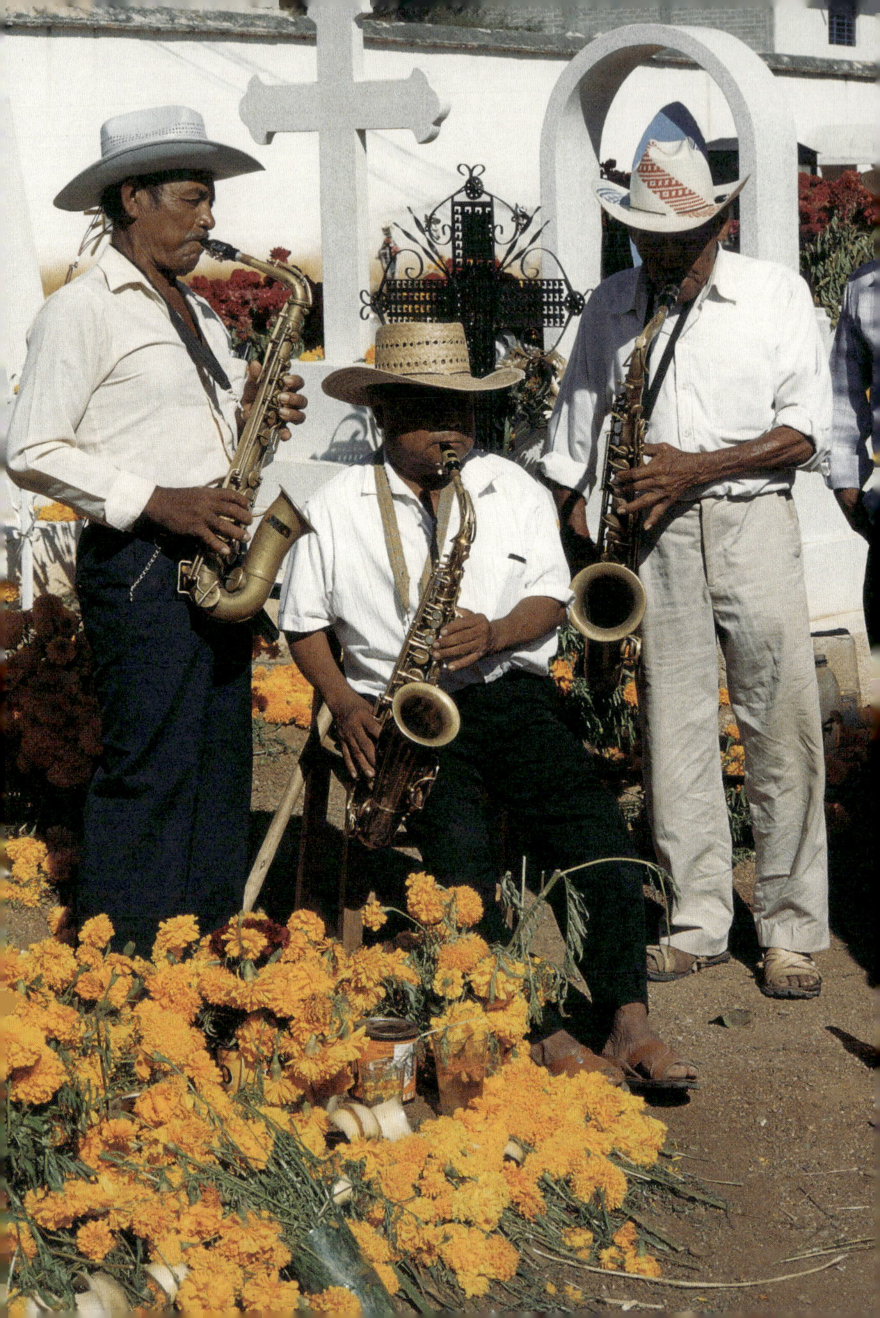

How does one enter sacred time without offending the gods? A ritual preparation is necessary, and Mexican communities begin a few days before the arrival of the dead by sprucing up and decorating the cemeteries, and preparing the offerings (what better way to compensate for the offense of having penetrated into the space of the dead to plant seeds than by making them offerings of the fruits of those seeds?), while some communities include a ritual purification.

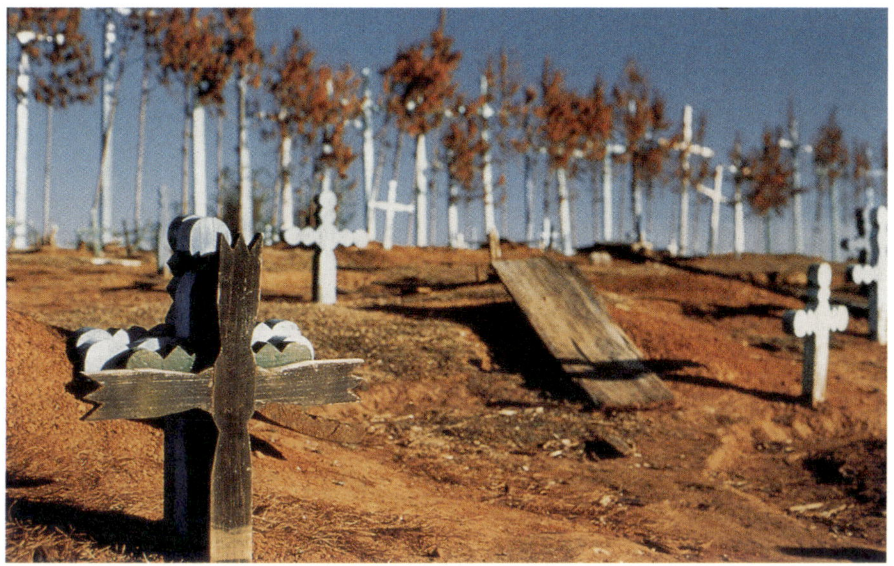

Diana Molina. Sierra de Chihuahua. N.d.

In their study of the Chatino Indians of Oaxaca, anthropologists Miguel Bartolomé and Alicia Barabas describe how in Yolotepec, the All Souls' Day celebration begins with a *novena* starting a week before November 1, during which time the offering is prepared, altars dedicated to the Sun and the Moon are adorned so they will watch over the dead's safe return to Earth, people bathe in the river (perhaps as an act of purification), and a welcoming altar for the visitors is set up. These acts, along with some trips to the cemetery and other civic preparations, are called "caring for the days," and what better reason to care for the days than to avoid annihilation? Especially if you take into account that the farmers are faced with the onset of winter, the death of the Earth. This is the ceremony that transcends the encounter of the living with the dead. The Sun and the Moon, perhaps overseeing this cosmic balance, are called into action by their altars.

The ritual preparation is followed by a reenactment of the age-old battle. According to Eliade, the arrival of the dead represents the cosmic night. In the dark, things lose their shape, outlines are blurred, chaos reigns. The souls of the dead that visit the living are an indicator that boundaries have

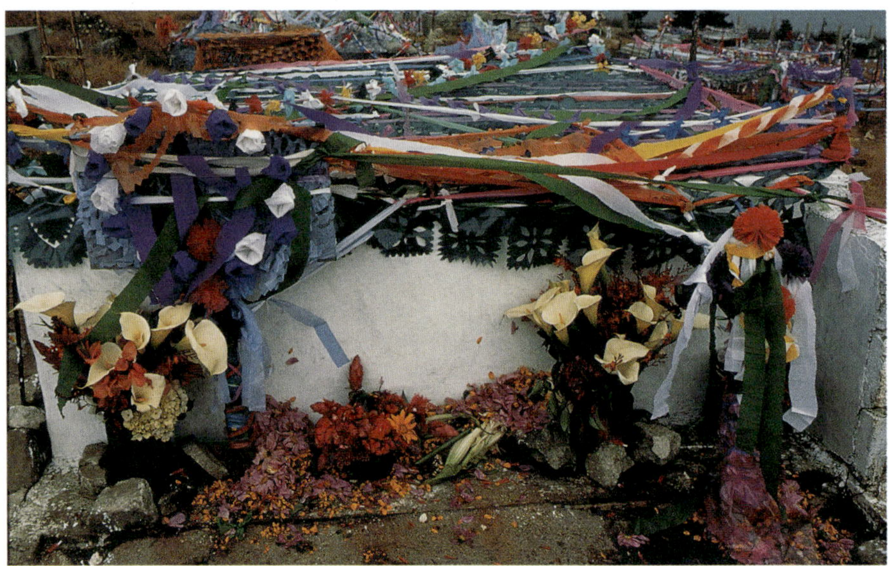

George O. Jackson. Grave in El Malé, Chiapas. 2000.

been annulled and are replaced with confusion. In many parts of Mexico—one of them the Huasteca region—masked dances are performed in which, within a universalized context, the dancers might represent the soul of the ancestors. This is why they are referred to as *viejos* (the elders) or, as Ruth Lechuga prefers, *huehues*, given that Náhuatl contains more specific reference to the ancestors. Communication between the living and the dead denotes unbalance, opening the door to licentiousness and drunkenness, the inversion of order. Fernando Benítez, in his study of the Huichol Indians, quotes a source who affirms the world of the dead is a "reverse world."

Another link to agricultural festivities can be traced here. The re-creation of primal chaos by archaic civilizations is experienced as time out of time, orgiastic, tied into fertility, like classical bacchanalias celebrating the grape harvest. Nietzsche characterized them as "signifying the redemption of the world and days of transfiguration." Eliade spoke of them as moments in which the unstoppable power of nature takes shape and humans become symbolically transformed into seeds; the recovery of a larval state that is ready to sprout. Perhaps the sexual allusions of the Huasteca's *huehue* dances or the Tejorones dance in Yaitepec, Oaxaca, as related by Ruth D. Lechuga, are remnants of the orgiastic sense of the Day of the Dead festivities.

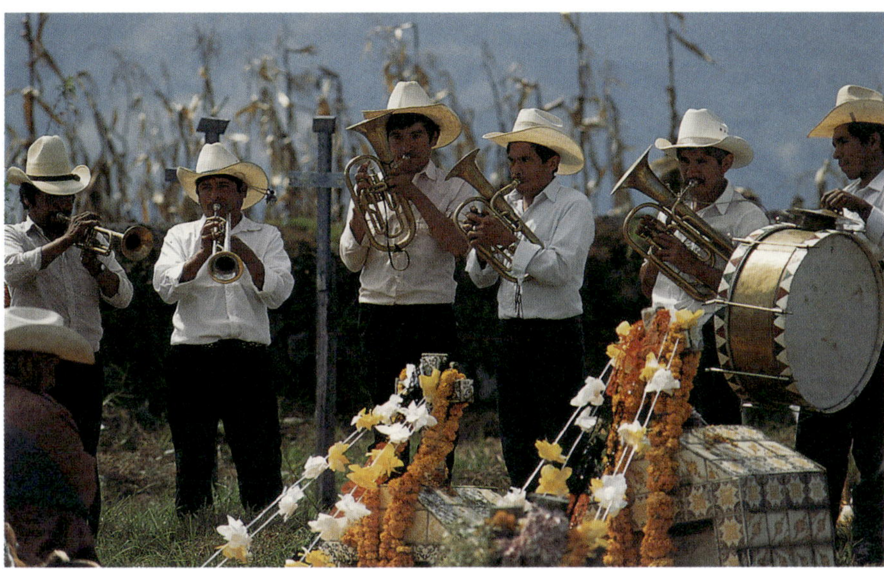

Jorge Pablo Aguinaco. Tutotepec, Hidalgo. 1995.

The ritual terminates in the restoration of cosmic order with the divine action of separating light and darkness. The dead—for the most part—take their leave, thankful for the offerings. Some are offended for having been forgotten, and they vow to deny their blessings for the regeneration of the Earth to those who have offended them. An affront to the dead, in effect, dooms the community to an ultimate death. Linked as they are to a consciousness of collective fate, in ancient times this implied a total annihilation of life.

Then comes the repetition of the specific action for creation. In the Day of the Dead festivities in Acatlán, Puebla, this occurs in the final episode of the dance of the Tecuanes, when the tiger is killed. This is no generic tiger. It happens to be Tezcatlipoca, who stood for the nocturnal forces in the pre-Hispanic pantheon.

In *Los indios de México*, Benítez states that among the Chamula and Cora Indians, the change of *mayordomo* (steward of religious matters) in the respective communities is followed by the Day of the Dead ceremonies. This occurs among the Chatinos as well, as documented by Miguel Bartolomé and Alicia Barabas.

Eliade asserts that "any enthroning has the value of a re-creation or regeneration of the world," citing two examples that confirm the idea. Fiji Islanders refer to the installation of a new chief as "the re-creation of the world," and the emperors of China created a new calendar upon acceding to power, thereby abolishing the old order so as to establish a new one.

Cosmic equilibrium having been reestablished, the world is now ready for life to be reborn. Once winter has passed, the seeds will be planted to live alongside the dead, who will procure that they germinate and bear fruit.

Seen from this perspective, the Day of the Dead ceremony among native Mexican people is not—as is frequently and ignorantly claimed—a tribute to death, but rather a tribute to death's link to life, to the possibility for renewal. This continues to be palpable in the traditions of those places where the inhabitants fear individual death to a lesser degree than the annihilation of the community. According to Philippe Ariès, since the late Middle Ages, city dwellers have undergone an individualization of death. More and more, dying is a personal tragedy. "I die" has substituted yesteryear's "we will all die," which can still be perceived in Mexico's rural communities.

Perhaps this explains why the nervous laughter the Day of the Dead provokes among city-dwellers is replaced in the countryside by a sense of making community, of pardoning faults and sharing food—acts that usually follow the restoration of the new order. The collective guarantees perpetuation, for after we die, our descendants remain. ◆

—Translated by Harry Porter

Gabriela Olmos is a writer and editor. She is deputy director of *Artes de México*, where she has published *El zopilote y la chirimía* (*The Buzzard and the Shawm*), *Pintores mexicanos de la A a la Z* (*Mexican Painters from A to Z*), and *Con los ojos cerrados, sueños de los niños indígenas* (*With Eyes Closed: Dreams of the Indigenous Children*), among other titles. In 2009 she was named the Mexican candidate for the Astrid Lindgren Memorial Award, one of the most important children's literature awards in the world.

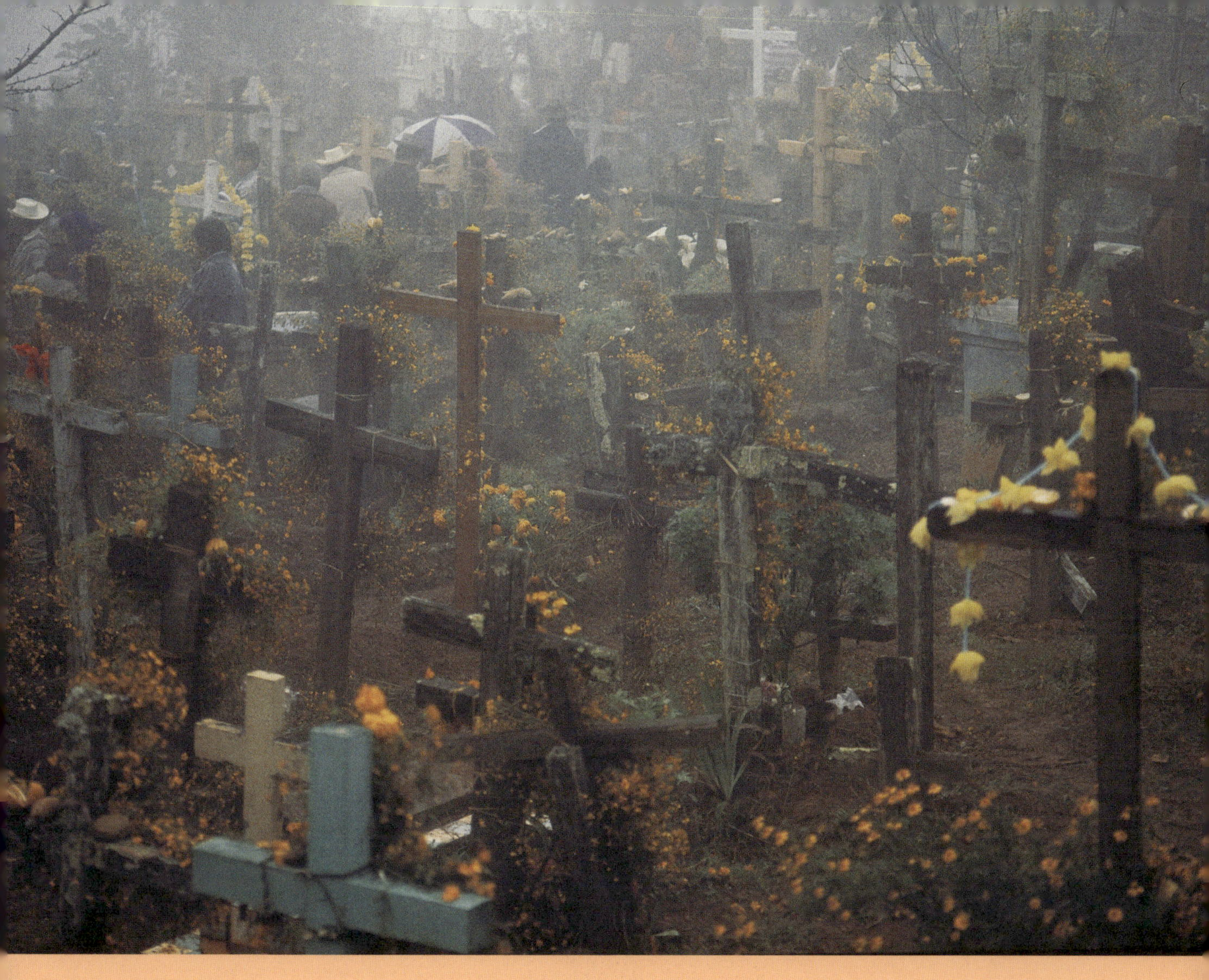

Jorge Pablo Aguinaco. Ayutla, Oaxaca. 1990.

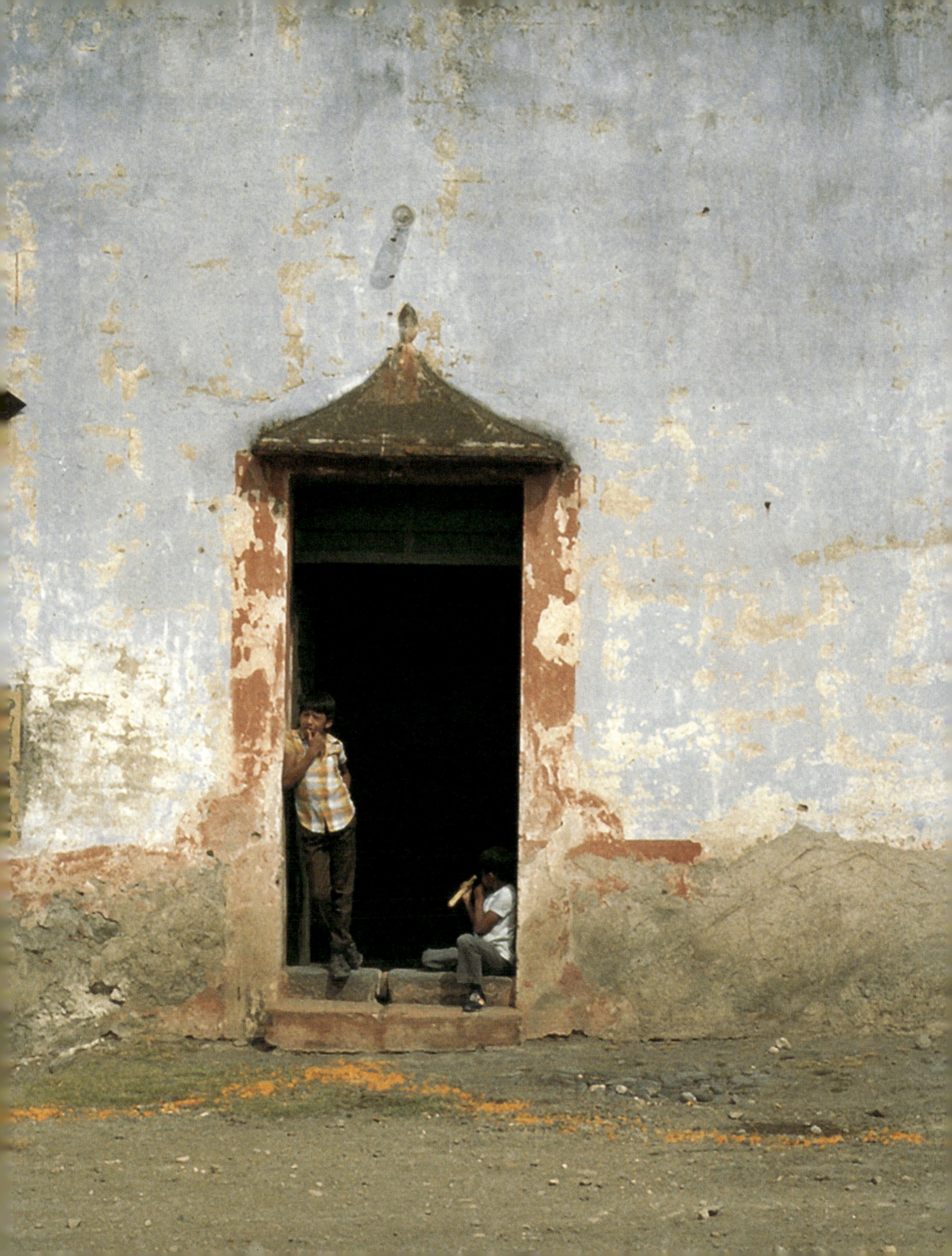

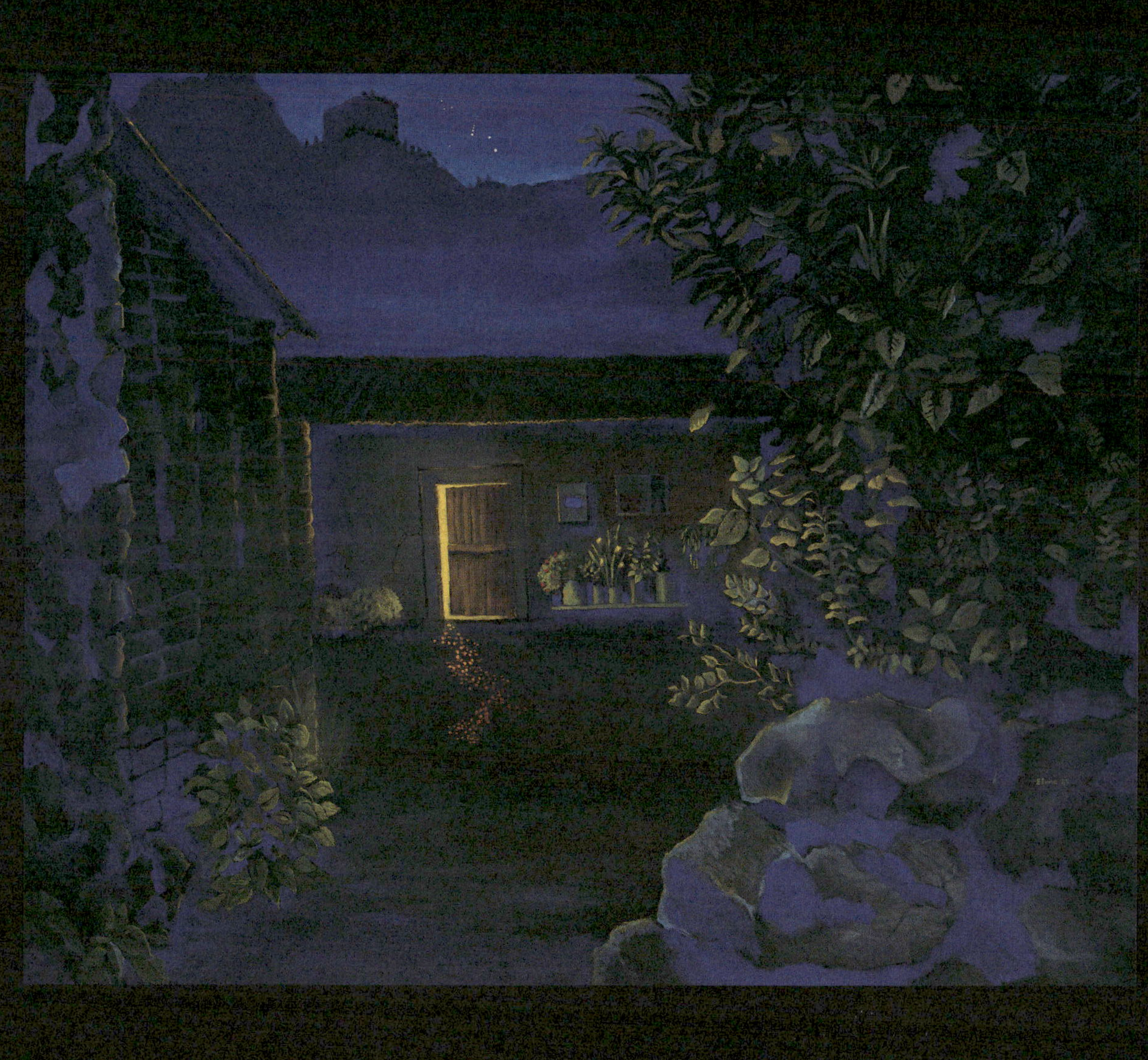

Elena Climent. Day of the Dead in Tepoztlán (detail). Oil on canvas. 100 × 150 cm. Private collection.
OPPOSITE: Lilia Martínez. Huaquechula, Puebla. N.d.

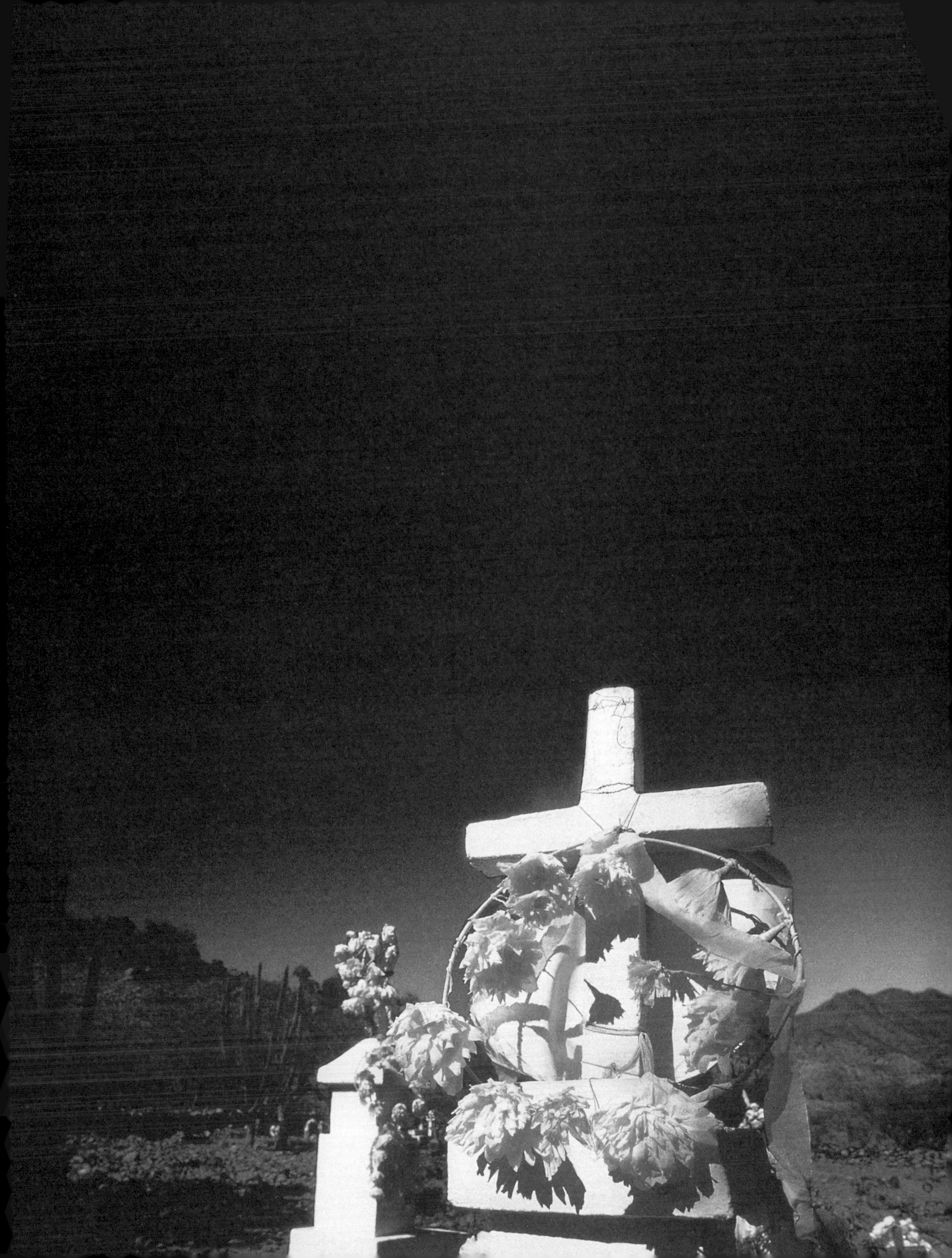

PARTE I

◆

SERENIDAD RITUAL

◆◆◆◆◆

En la noche del primero al dos de noviembre,
el cementerio es muy impresionante. Las flores sobre las
tumbas son muchísimas. Pero las velas encendidas
sobre ellas son más. [. . .] Todo el cementerio, esa noche,
es un gran jardín de fuego. El rumor de las oraciones da calor
al viento frío. A media noche hay que comer y que beber.
Y se bebe fuerte porque los recuerdos así lo necesitan.
Caminando encontré una tumba fresca. Rezaban terminando
el rosario. Me uní al grupo y respondí a la letanía.
Cuando escuché "Consoladora de los afligidos" miré al cielo,
me dolió la vida, y di gracias por estar viviendo.

Carlos Pellicer

◆◆◆◆◆

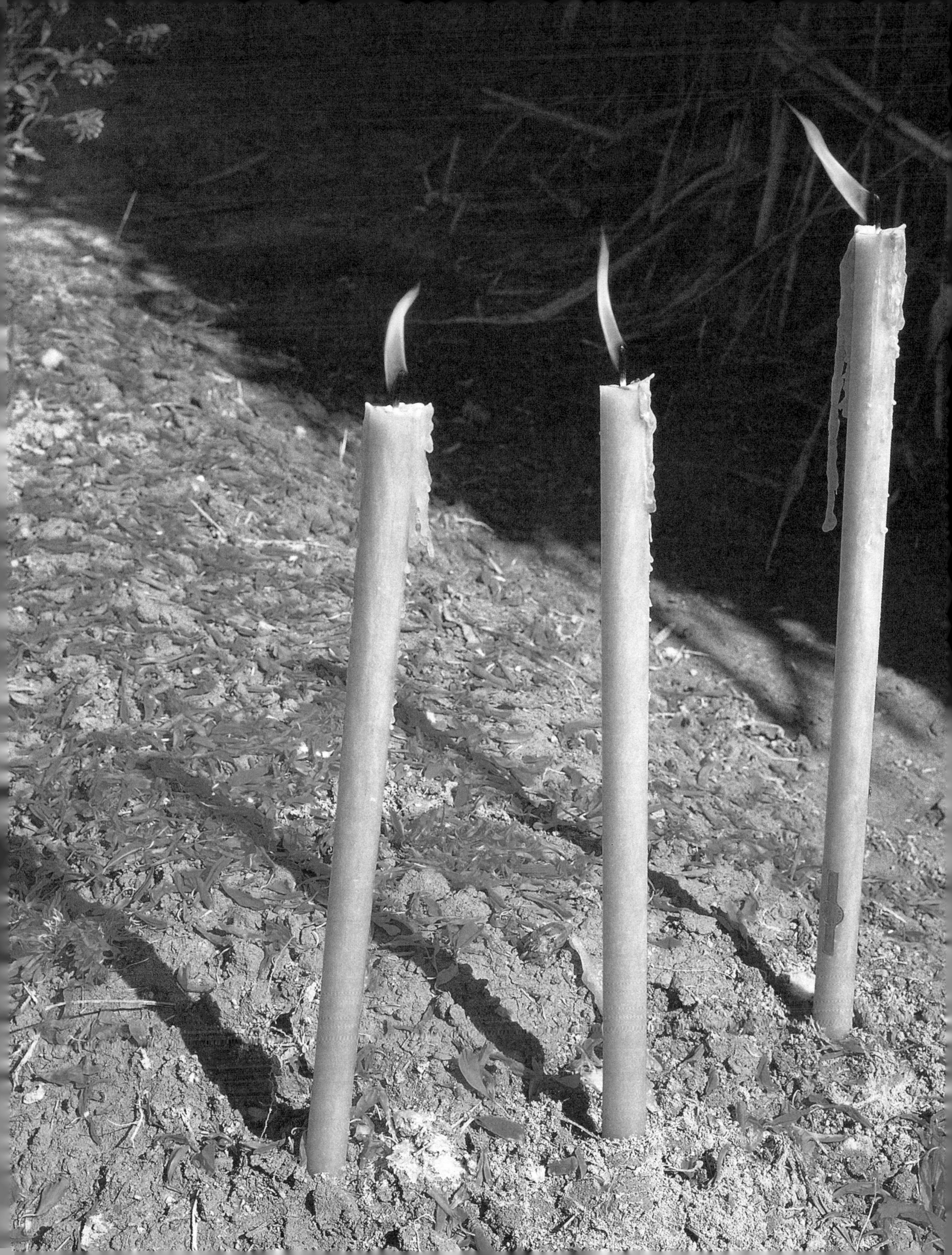

PREGUNTAS AL DÍA DE MUERTOS Y LA MUERTE SONRIENTE

Margarita de Orellana

◆

"Los mexicanos de la ciudad encuentran a la muerte con juegos y diversiones y los indios de los pueblos con toda tranquilidad".

—Frances Toor

◆

La curiosidad, el asombro y la fascinación son las emociones que impregnan este número de *Artes de México*. Al contrario de quienes piensan que la cultura sobre la muerte en México ya ha sido completamente explorada, nosotros creemos que comprende un universo más rico de lo que comúnmente se piensa, y del cual falta mucho por ser estudiado. Cada una de nuestras ediciones busca alejarse de los estereotipos y de los lugares comunes, al plantearse diversas interrogantes desde ángulos con frecuencia inesperados. Nuestra primera exploración sobre este tema (*El arte ritual de la muerte niña*, número 15 de nuestro catálogo) nos llevó a difundir un género artístico, hasta entonces poco conocido, que forma parte de los rituales de la muerte en México, e incluso dimos a la representación plástica de infantes difuntos un nombre que ha sido usado a partir de entonces, como si siempre se hubiera llamado así. Abrimos caminos y creamos conceptos, maneras de comprender: labor fundamental del proyecto cultural que es *Artes de México*.

En esta ocasión hemos querido abordar el fenómeno del Día de Muertos en su variada celebración en muchas de las comunidades rurales del país, la mayoría de ellas indígenas. En el lapso de esta fiesta se suspenden casi todas las actividades cotidianas. Los espacios dentro de los hogares y en los cementerios toman formas distintas y significados muy variados. Los muertos cobran vida en los recuerdos de los vivos, quienes evocan sus formas de ser, sus gustos, sus virtudes y defectos. Entre las almas que son esperadas y los de este mundo se establece un diálogo intenso. No hay lugar para el rechazo; pero quizá sí para un reproche o dos.

Cada pueblo ha establecido sus formas para este diálogo: sus estrictas normas de hospitalidad, sus códigos de conducta centenarios, que cada integrante conoce perfectamente, porque las leyes de esa convivencia son pautas de vida. En las comunidades que celebran el Día de Muertos no hay sorpresa. Para quienes las observamos desde afuera, sí la hay. En ese diálogo entre vivos y muertos, encarnados en los altares u ofrendas, notamos un rasgo común asombroso: un sentido estético avasallador. En composiciones efímeras hechas con tierra, flores, velas, canastas, papeles de colores, cruces de madera o de fierro, y hasta adornos

PÁGINA 98: Diana Molina. Sierra de Chihuahua. s.f. • **PÁGINA IZQUIERDA:** Agustín Estrada. San Gabriel Chilac, Puebla. 1999.

de plástico, reconocemos una de las más fértiles dimensiones del arte popular. En cada una de las majestuosas ofrendas descubrimos un arte de trascendencia vital, además de una descarga del alma que resulta en una explosión de formas y colores.

Hay ofrendas que, con unos cuantos pétalos de cempasúchil y dos o tres velas, forman, bajo un profundo color ocre, una composición de gran sencillez y armonía. Hay otras, muy barrocas, que revelan una dimensión estética que nos hace sentir más plenos, al mostrarnos esa natural capacidad de crear belleza. Más que celebrar a los muertos, los artífices de estas obras ¿no estarán celebrando la vida? ¿No serán estos rituales una intensa prolongación de la vida en las inmediaciones de la muerte?

Es imposible dar cuenta de los miles de rituales del Día de Muertos que se llevan a cabo en México. La pequeña muestra que aparece en estas páginas es bastante elocuente. Varios de nuestros autores han señalado los ecos prehispánicos en algunos de ellos, pero también las influencias directas de nuestro pasado hispánico.

Dominique Dufétel nos muestra algunas similitudes en creencias y costumbres de ambas vertientes culturales, y sugiere que, al haber coincidido al momento de la Conquista una celebración mexica de la muerte con el día de Todos Santos europeo, estas fiestas se fundieron para dar pie a toda la grandilocuencia y el fervor con la que se celebra hasta hoy el Día de Muertos.

A grandes rasgos, Ruth D. Lechuga nos describe algunas características específicas de esta ceremonia entre los Huastecos, totonacos, nahuas, chatinos, y encuentra reminiscencias prehispánicas en algunas de ellas. Además, nos aclara que mientras "los cristianos rezan por las almas de los muertos, los indígenas les rezan a ellas". Cinco siglos después de la evangelización, este tipo de religiosidad se mantiene vigente.

Laurette Séjourné, en su estancia entre los huaves de San Mateo del Mar durante la década de 1950, se percató de que en este poblado del istmo de Tehuantepec los altares de muertos no estaban dedicados a algún difunto en particular. Esos días se recibe a todas las almas, que tienen la libertad de circular por donde les plazca. Sin embargo, son rechazadas aquellas que murieron fuera del pueblo, porque las consideran extranjeras indeseables.

Teotitlán del Valle, en Oaxaca, es un pueblo de tejedores extraordinarios, que guarda sus tradiciones con celo extremo. Mary Jane Gagnier es parte de esa comunidad desde hace más de quince años. Conoce profundamente los detalles imperceptibles y los significados del ritual del Día de Muertos, y generosamente los comparte con nosotros. Su historia nos revela los lazos profundos que existen en esa comunidad, y la manera en que se estrechan a través de estos rituales. Su testimonio nos enriquece y nos asombra.

El relato que recoge Fernando Benítez de un indígena mazateco de la sierra de Oaxaca nos advierte del castigo que ameritan los anfitriones que no reciben a sus difuntos como se debe.

Más adelante, Marta Turok nos señala cómo el mercado ha generado, en algunos lugares del centro del país y en las mismas ciudades, una demanda por los objetos antiguamente utilizados para ofrendas, hasta convertirlos en artesanía decorativa desprovista de su uso original. Es obvio que muchos talladores, ceramistas y otros creadores encontraron el lado espectacular de este ritual y sus beneficios económicos.

La lectura simbólica que realiza Gabriela Olmos del Día de Muertos, basada en las ideas del reconocido historiador de las religiones Mircea Eliade, nos remite a las muy antiguas ceremonias agrícolas "en las que la muerte está vinculada con la posibilidad de renovación".

Las calaveras, que forman parte del paisaje urbano del Día de Muertos, no aparecen en el ámbito rural. La calaca participa en la tendencia a pensar que la relación específica que tiene la muerte con los mexicanos nos da una identidad. Además, representa otra forma de relación vinculada con el desafío y la risa. La fiesta urbana se ha despojado de religiosidad, pero eso no significa que la sensibilidad artística no se agudice en este escenario. Por eso, las calacas de azúcar, chocolate, papel picado y papel maché serán protagonistas de un número posterior dedicado al mismo tema. Por lo pronto esperamos que este los transporte a un mundo lleno de belleza y serenidad.

◆

Al investigar en *Artes de México* el Día de Muertos, la primera evidencia que se nos impuso iba en contra de lo que comúnmente se piensa: esta celebración no se vive de la misma manera en el mundo rural y en el mundo urbano. En el primero, el Día de Muertos está aún muy ligado a las creencias ancestrales. Su forma ritual de expresar su creatividad está impregnada de una solemnidad inflexible y de un rígido código protocolario acompañado de un derroche de colores, composiciones y texturas. En el Día de Muertos urbano también existe un estallido de colores y formas, pero estas se hallan desprovistas de religiosidad y poseen un sentido festivo más desenfadado y lúdico. En este ejemplar de *Artes de México*—así como en el número 62, dedicado al Día de Muertos en el ámbito rural—hemos intentado representar estas dos formas de celebrar el Día de Muertos.

También hemos querido explorar ciertas interrogantes que nos hemos planteado desde que concebimos las dos ediciones. ¿Cómo y cuándo esta celebración se diferenció en el mundo rural y en el mundo urbano? ¿Por qué en la ciudad se abandonó el carácter ritual para convertir a esta fiesta en una experiencia exaltada y desafiante? ¿Por qué muchos de nosotros pensamos que se trata de una fiesta que se celebra igual en todo el país?

Se ha pensado que el Día de Muertos de la ciudad es una fiesta secular, debido a la Revolución mexicana. La obsesión de muchos intelectuales posrevolucionarios por impulsar nuestras raíces culturales desproveyéndolas de su catolicismo y su herencia española, para privilegiar el pasado prehispánico, hizo que la reflexión en torno al Día de Muertos optara por este camino. Sin embargo, encontramos que ese distanciamiento entre el ámbito rural y el urbano ya se daba desde las últimas décadas del siglo XIX. En una sociedad que deseaba ser moderna y formar parte de la serie de naciones que ya lo eran, estas celebraciones parecían un atavismo, un obstáculo para el progreso. Hay quienes expresaban (sobre todo en las clases medias ilustradas) su repudio ante estas muestras de "atraso". Otros más tradicionalistas se lamentaban de que un día que había estado por siglos dedicado al dolor y la nostalgia adquiriera tintes de frivolidad. Según su peculiar punto de vista, los muertos ya no venían a compartir sus alimentos, sino a contemplar "grandes comilonas con glotones que ingerían sin cesar golosinas y bebidas alcohólicas". En los panteones, en vez de plegarias se escuchan voces altisonantes y hasta carcajadas.

En la ciudad y en lugares como Toluca, con su Mercado del Alfeñique, había una inundación de colores y sabores encarnados en sus panes y sus dulces, sobre todo las calaveras de azúcar. En el ámbito rural no se ve esta proliferación de azúcar, sino la preparación de alimentos tradicionales ligados a los gustos de los difuntos. Y de ninguna manera encontramos las calaveras de dulce en las ofrendas.

Las calacas en la ciudad nos son muy familiares. Son estas figuras las que expresan la actitud de desafío ante la muerte que supuestamente es parte de nuestra idiosincrasia. Es curioso cómo en el México del siglo XX se le dio tanto realce a esta representación, cuyos orígenes se encuentran en la Europa medieval, como si se tratara de un rasgo nacional. La calavera en todas sus representaciones se convierte, sobre todo en ese día, en parte de la comunidad, y las calaveras de dulce que nos comemos, en una especie de comunión con la muerte. Dos autores clásicos, Luis Cardoza y Aragón y Paul Westheim, intrigados, desde su llegada a México, por este fenómeno, examinan y reflexionan sobre diversos aspectos de la plástica derivada de los esqueletos. El primero lo hace a través de las calaveras de José Guadalupe Posada. Para Westheim, estas representaciones descarnadas nos hablan más de la angustia de la vida que de la convivencia con la muerte.

Ruth Lechuga destaca que la calavera no solo baila y participa jocosamente de nuestros Días de Muertos. La calaca tilica y flaca se inventa y reinventa sin cesar en el México cotidiano. No podíamos dejar fuera la exportación de esta tradición hacia la frontera norte. ¿Qué papel jugó y juega entre los chicanos? Tomás Ybarra Frausto define esta tradición exportada como una lucha contra el olvido que permite afrontar—y quizá transformar—esa nueva realidad del emigrante. Después, la escritora Ana García Bergua nos ofrece un altar de muertos literario insospechado.

El brillante ensayo de Alfonso Alfaro nos responde muchas de las interrogantes que nos hicimos al iniciar este número. ¿Cómo el Día de Muertos y sus calaveras urbanas han servido como instrumento simbólico dentro de la estrategia posrevolucionaria para crear una identidad nacional? ¿Cómo, poco a poco, se ha interiorizado en nuestra sociedad la idea de que los mexicanos tenemos una relación privilegiada con la muerte? Este autor, además, analiza la actitud que las clases superiores urbanas toman frente a la muerte, similar a la de sus homólogas europeas y estadounidenses. Y finalmente invoca a esa muerte que, día a día, aparece en el país al escuchar los tiros de un cuerno de chivo. Y plantea una certeza con respecto a esa muerte: "nuestro país no tiene la menor idea de qué hacer con ella".

El tema de la muerte es inagotable. Habrá que seguir explorándolo en nuevas publicaciones, intentando provocar entre nuestros lectores más interrogantes e inquietudes que las aquí planteadas. ◆

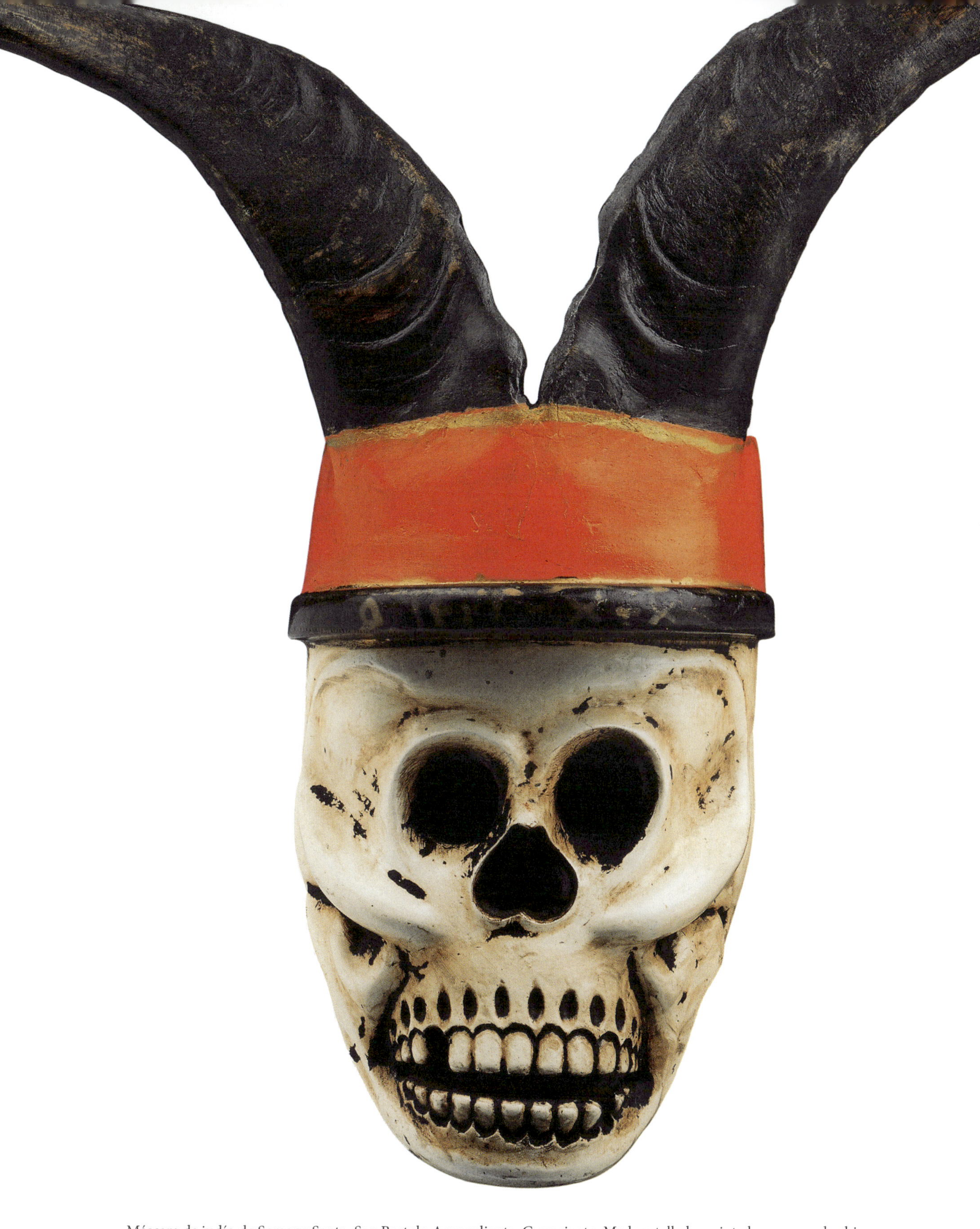

Máscara de judío de Semana Santa. San Bartolo Aguacaliente, Guanajuato. Madera tallada y pintada, cuernos de chivo.
Colección Ruth D. Lechuga de Arte Popular/ Museo Franz Mayer.

FIESTA CÍCLICA

LOS ANTEPASADOS OCULTOS

Dominique Dufétel

◆

En el México prehispánico se celebraban varias fiestas que tenían relación con la muerte, y que estaban repartidas en el calendario agrícola. En estas páginas, el autor enumera las ceremonias que integraban el gran ciclo de la muerte en las tradiciones del Altiplano, y que, durante la Colonia, se fundieron con la ceremonia cristiana de Todos Santos.

◆

¿Quién podría negar que la flor de cempasúchil y el Día de Muertos mantienen una relación cuyas raíces se hunden en la época precortesiana? Para persuadirse de lo profundamente antiguo de esta tradición, basta con rondar por los grandes mercados de la Ciudad de México, como el de Xochimilco, los días precedentes a Todos Santos y ver los amontonamientos de la flor de muertos; pasear por cualquier panteón mexicano el dos de noviembre y embriagarse con su olor penetrante; dejarse envolver por el ambiente que es creado por esta flor, que presta su estética a los altares, las tumbas, los caminos de las ánimas. Esta flor de innumerables pétalos, pues es la flor infinita (cempasúchil, *cempoalxóchitl*, la flor de veinte, es decir de infinitos pétalos), cubre en estas fechas cualquier cosa relacionada con los difuntos con su cálida nieve amarilla. Y, sin embargo, el estudio de las principales fuentes que nos hablan de las fiestas y ceremonias de los antiguos mexicanos nos revela que no existía tal asociación; que, si bien la flor es eminentemente autóctona y antigua, se usaba en numerosas festividades junto con muchas otras flores, tan importantes en aquel juego sin fin de la fiesta, la vida y el sacrificio.

LAS FIESTAS MEXICAS DE LA MUERTE

La manera de celebrar a los difuntos en el México prehispánico no era una, sino varias, a lo largo de los 18 meses del año azteca, casi siempre colaterales de otras festividades; de ahí que podamos concluir fácilmente que, a partir de la Conquista, las múltiples formas de celebración se concentraron en los días impuestos por la religión cristiana. No obstante, al indagar más a fondo encontramos que entre todas las ceremonias dedicadas a los muertos destacaban particularmente dos: la primera, celebrada en el noveno, llamada *Tlaxochimaco* o *Miccailhuitontli*, es decir, fiesta pequeña de los muertos o fiesta de los muertos pequeños, y la otra, *Xócotl Uetzi*, también nombrada *Hueymiccaihuitl*, la fiesta grande de los muertos, festejada en el décimo mes. Es muy probable que el rito se celebrara en el último día de la veintena que englobaba cada mes. Quizá por ello los días de celebración de los difuntos se establecieron en México el primero y el dos de noviembre,

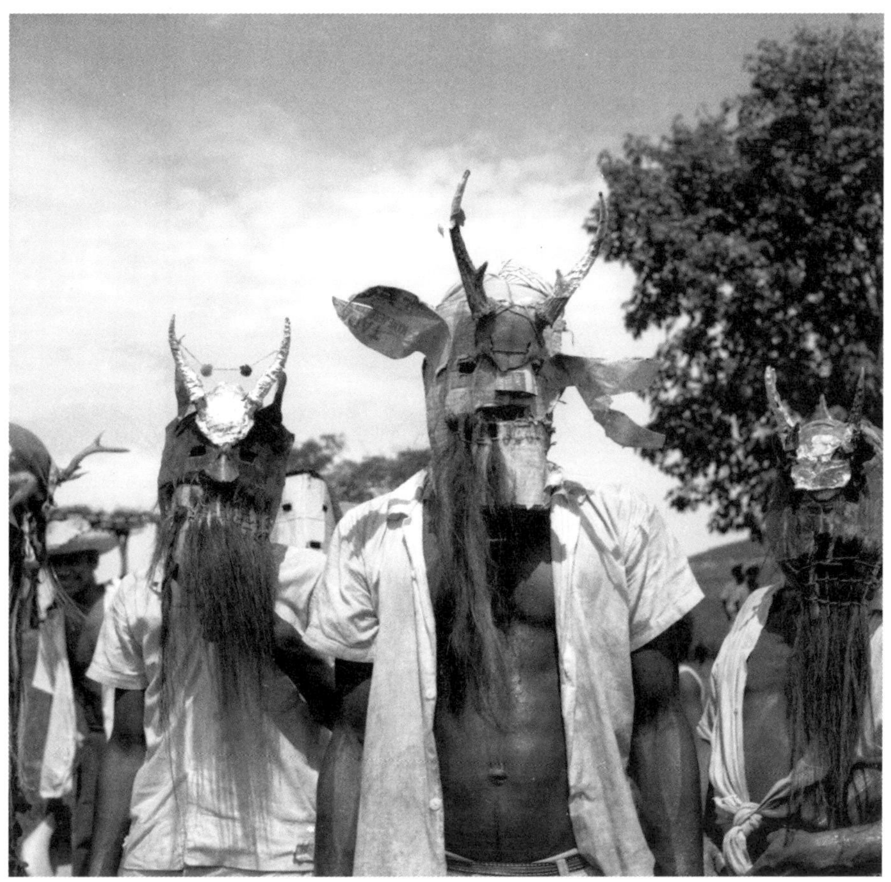

Ruth D. Lechuga. Devils' Dance. La Estancia Grande, Oaxaca. 1963.

primero la fiesta de los niños, y luego la de los adultos muertos, como en la tradición antigua.

Fuera de estas dos grandes celebraciones se rendía culto a los difuntos en otras ocasiones, aunque en cada una se celebraba a diferentes clases de ánimas. En la concepción mesoamericana del mundo, la existencia del ser después de la muerte no dependía de la manera en que se había vivido—como en la religión cristiana, profundamente ética—sino de la circunstancia en que se había muerto, y esta estaba predestinada en el calendario mágico desde su nacimiento. Durante la fiesta de Tepeilhuitl, por ejemplo, se "hacían imágenes de montes de pasta de tzoalli a honra de los montes altos donde se juntan las nubes, y en memoria de los que habían muerto en agua o heridos de rayo, o de los que no se quemaban sus cuerpos sino que los enterraban", es decir a los que iban al paraíso de Tláloc. En el mes de Quecholli, se celebraba a los muertos en la guerra, los que iban a acompañar al sol en su carrera hasta el cenit y bajaban por la tarde transformados en mariposas y colibríes. Durante el mes de Izcalli se celebraba la fiesta de los tamales en honor al dios del fuego Xiutecuhtli. En esta ceremonia se ofrecían cinco tamales a las llamas del hogar; para honrarlos, se disponía uno sobre cada sepultura, por lo que se entiende que no eran difuntos comunes. "Esto se hacía antes de comer los tamales y después se los comían todos, no dejaban ni uno".

Estas fiestas se sumaban a otras mucho más importantes, pues cada mes estaba dedicado a una divinidad. Y los dioses, al igual que en cualquier religión, para los mesoamericanos eran, en su manifestación más primitiva, los mismos antepasados. En muchos mitos amerindios, estos se transformaban en héroes y, con el tiempo, estos mismos héroes en dioses. En la estructura tan compleja de la religión mexica, en la que los dioses ocupan un lugar preponderante, el culto a los muertos parece limitarse al ámbito familiar, ligado desde luego al linaje. El hecho de incinerar a sus muertos—costumbre al parecer heredada de los toltecas, pero que se adaptaba perfectamente a la situación física del Valle de México, espacio lacustre que dificultaba la excavación de tumbas a gran escala—seguramente influiría mucho en los ritos mortuorios y puede explicar parcialmente el papel secundario del culto del Día de Muertos. La tumba, espacio físico tan importante en la celebración actual, estaba casi ausente; quizá por ello tenga tanta relevancia el altar de muertos como un doble de la lápida sepulcral.

EL GRAN CICLO ANUAL DE LA MUERTE

Es importante explorar las relaciones simbólicas posibles entre las celebraciones prehispánicas de los difuntos y las fiestas a las que se sumaban, ya que, como afirma Mircea Eliade, "el símbolo entrega su mensaje y cumple su función aun cuando su significado escape a la conciencia".

Es necesario hacer una aclaración con respecto al calendario antiguo. Los mexicas consideraban el año solar de 365 días (18 veintenas más 5 días aciagos), pero es muy probable que no hayan corregido el error astronómico (agregando, por ejemplo, como hacemos en la actualidad, un día cada cuatro años). Considerando que el origen de su calendario se remontaba a la época tolteca, hacia el siglo VIII de nuestra era, en el momento de la Conquista este se había retrasado cuando menos seis meses. Esto provocaba un desfase significativo entre el momento del ciclo agrícola al que pretendía estar relacionado cada mes—sobre todo en su manera de festejar a los dioses siempre asociados con la naturaleza—y el momento real en que se celebraba cada fiesta. Podemos pensar que, como en cualquier tradición cuyos orígenes se han perdido, los mexicas seguían realizando los ritos pero con cierta confusión, lo que nos hace pensar en un culto que se ubicaba más cerca de la religiosidad que del misticismo.

La primera fiesta de los muertos, la que—decíamos—estaba dedicada a los muertos pequeños, llamada *Miccailhuitontli* entre otros pueblos del Altiplano, era conocida por los mexicas como *Tlaxochimaco*, es decir "nacimiento de flores". En esta ceremonia "se ofrecían las primicias de las flores", según nos dicen los cronistas, con el inconveniente de que en el siglo XVI ocurría en agosto, momento en que la flora está en su apogeo. En cambio, en el siglo VIII esta fiesta se celebraba en febrero, momento

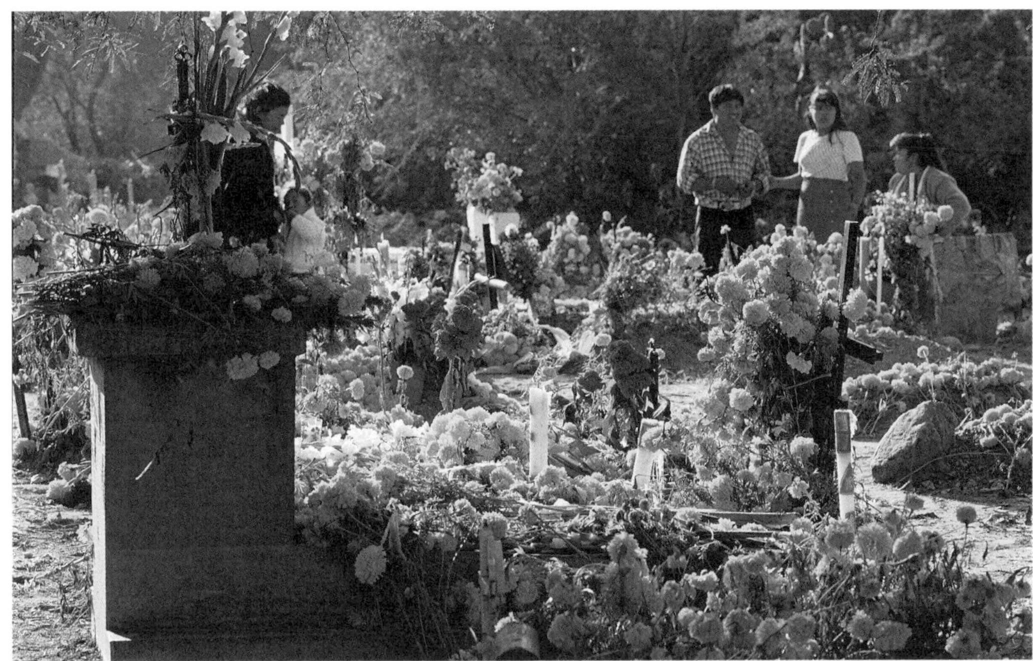

Paul Czitrom. Tetelcingo, Puebla. 1999.

en que en el Altiplano brotan los primeros retoños. Así se entiende el significado de las muertes niñas ofrecidas en la fiesta al dios supremo, Huitzilopochtli, al igual que las primeras flores del ciclo natural: estos muertos chicos iban directamente al cielo más alto, es decir al lugar divino por excelencia, donde se reintegraban al magma vital, de donde nacía todo ser. Su muerte prematura no era una desgracia sino un sacrificio divino. “Dos días antes que llegase esta fiesta—nos cuenta el padre Sahagún—toda la gente se derramaba por los campos y maizales a buscar flores, así silvestres como campesinas de las cuales unas se llamaban . . .” y cita una larga lista de nombres de flores, todas de la temporada de lluvias excepto el cempasúchil que parecía entonces adelantarse a su estación y que, al día siguiente, “en amaneciendo ensartaban en sus hilos [para hacer] sogas gruesas de ellas, torcidas y largas, y las tendían en el patio de aquel *cu*, presentándolas a aquel dios cuya fiesta hacían”.

En esta fiesta, las flores no se ofrecían a los pequeños muertos, sino que representaban a los niños mismos que se ofrecían al dios. Además, “el último día del mes, los hombres iban al monte a cortar un árbol entero, lo alisaban y lo traían a la entrada de la ciudad. A este palo le rendían culto con ofrendas, comidas e inciensos. Le ponían el nombre de *xócotl*” (que derivaría en la palabra jocote, fruto ácido del jocotero, un árbol amarillo).

En el mes siguiente, durante el *Xócotl Uetzi*, dedicado a los muertos grandes, “levantaban el madero—dice Durán—del suelo y lo enhestaban en el patio del templo y ponían en la cumbre un pájaro de masa todo adornado”. Sahagún

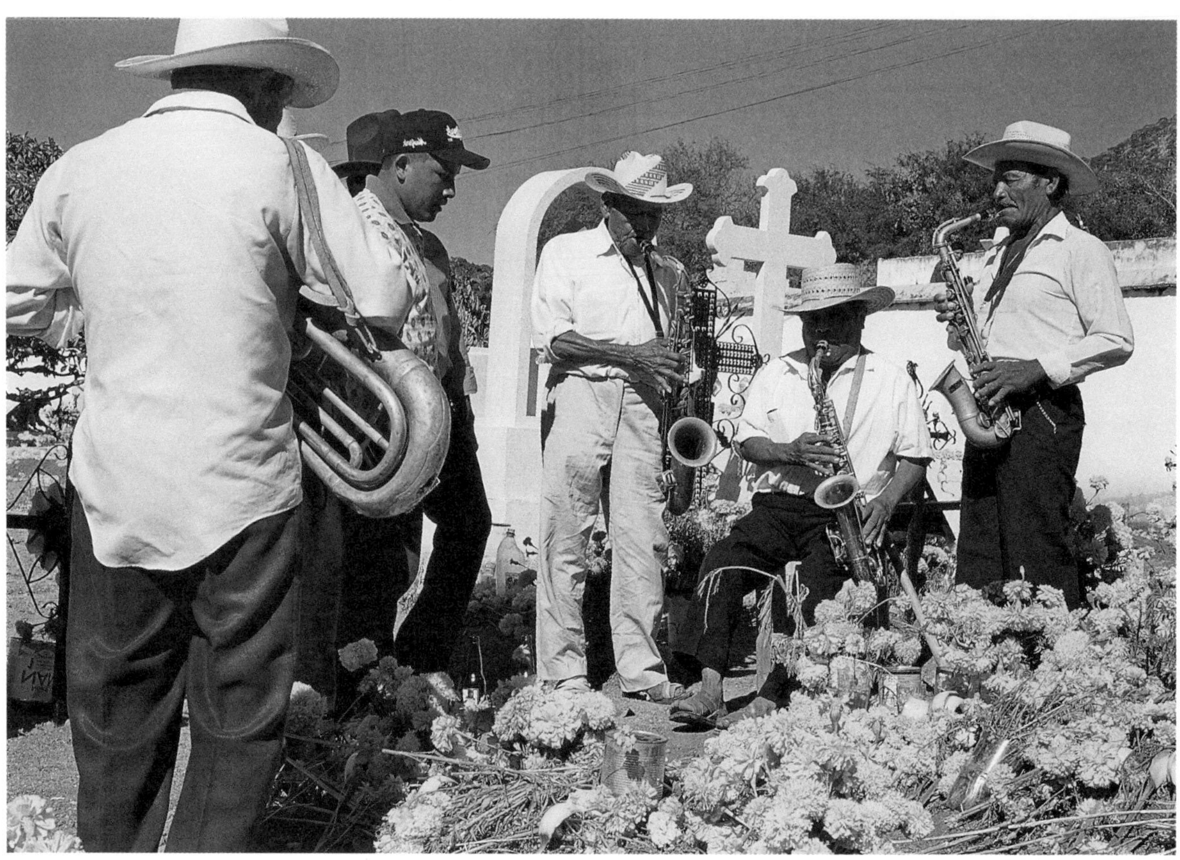

Paul Czitrom. Tetelcingo, Puebla. 1999.

dice que arriba se colocaba la figura de pasta del dios que se celebraba, es decir, Xiutecuhtli. El momento culminante de la fiesta sucedía cuando todos los voluntarios jóvenes acudían a subir como podían al palo liso para arrancar la cabeza y otras partes del pájaro. Los cuatro primeros eran los ganadores y enseguida hacían penitencia. El mismo día se derribaba el palo y la multitud lo deshacía hasta volverlo astillas que se llevaban como si fueran reliquias—agrega Durán—"porque esto era el significado del nombre Xócotl Uetzi, la caída de xócotl".

Esta fiesta, que ocurría originalmente en febrero, nos recuerda al actual rito del palo volador, herencia de las prestigiadas culturas de la costa del Golfo, famoso en la región de Papantla entre los actuales totonacos, pero mucho más completo entre los otomíes de la sierra poblanohidalguense, donde ocupa un lugar preponderante en la fiesta del carnaval, acorde con la cosmovisión indígena. Según el antropólogo Jacques Galinier, quien ha registrado las variantes de este rito otomí, "el carnaval inaugura el inicio del cómputo anual", y se sitúa en uno de los dos límites del año: "la primera fase interequinoccial que dura seis meses (de marzo a octubre), está separada de la segunda (de noviembre a febrero) por dos fechas límite: la del carnaval y la del Día de Muertos". Estos dos polos calendáricos comparten otra coincidencia: son los momentos en que "los muertos efectúan cada año dos idas y venidas de su morada al pueblo". Toda vez que es válido interpretar lo prehispánico por la etnología de los indígenas actuales, podríamos concluir que pareciera que la fiesta mexica de *Xócotl Uetzi* (cuyo origen otomí no se debe descartar, afirma Galinier), reunía a la vez el carácter del carnaval actual y el del Día de Muertos.

En la danza otomí del volador, cuatro son los "viejos" que se suben al palo y uno el "Malinche", que baila arriba del palo y que es el águila o gavilán, que representa al ave solar. Los "viejos", al bajar, descienden al mundo de los muertos, mientras el "Malinche", con su vuelo, alcanza el cielo. Diría Galinier que "los Huastecos consideran a los voladores como muertos divinizados que escoltan al sol hasta donde se oculta". Tanto el palo (que es un falo cósmico) de los voladores como el *xócotl* antiguo pueden considerarse ejes del mundo que permiten la circulación entre sus diversos estados. "El palo es el numen de la fertilidad, ligado a un principio de vida, simbolizado por el águila, y a un principio de muerte, marcado por la presencia de los viejos", concluye Galinier. El rito antiguo de subir al palo para decapitar al ave solar de pasta de maíz (que se encarnará en el "Malinche" otomí), es decir al apropiarse del sol que es la vida en una celebración a los muertos, ocurría originalmente, al igual que el carnaval otomí actual, en un momento de esterilidad de la tierra (hacia febrero), cuando era necesario invocar las fuerzas de los dioses—de los antepasados ocultos—, que volverían a fecundar la tierra.

Casualmente, las fiestas del mes de *Quecholli* ya mencionadas, en que se celebraba a los muertos en la guerra, coincidían, en el siglo XVI, con las de Todos Santos del calendario gregoriano. En estos días, en que se festejaba a Mixcóatl, deidad de la caza y del fuego astral, los mexicas se reunían para confeccionar saetas y dardos para la guerra y la cacería. El último día del mes hacían flechas chicas y las ataban de cuatro en cuatro junto con astillas de ocote. Depositaban los manojos sobre los sepulcros de los guerreros como ofrendas. Junto colocaban dos tamales, los dejaban un día entero sobre la sepultura y en la noche quemaban los ramilletes de flechas. Como en otras ocasiones notamos la ausencia del cempasúchil, pero aquellos ramilletes que arden en la noche no pueden sino hacernos pensar en estas flores, con su color ígneo y su proliferación de pétalos, depositadas sobre las tumbas actuales.

Esta otra fiesta de muertos ocurría a principios de noviembre, cuando en el punto exacto donde se ocultaba el sol podía verse la figura de Mixcóatl, principal dios de los chichimecas, que tenía la forma de la Serpiente de Nubes. Parecería que aquí hubo una adecuación del ritual con el momento del año, quizá una adaptación tardía. De cualquier forma, el que coincidiera en el momento de la Conquista con el ritual católico de Todos Santos puede haber influido para dar a esta fiesta cristiana—secundaria en Europa—todo el fervor y el fasto con que la celebramos desde entonces. Con esta adaptación se cristalizaron en dos fechas todas las manifestaciones del gran ciclo anual de la muerte.

Sin embargo, si admitimos—como lo atestigua Galinier para los otomíes actuales—que los antepasados prehispánicos se manifestaban dos veces al año, en cada equinoccio, ¿qué ritos antiguos asociados con esta doble ruptura en el ciclo vital de la tierra podrían relacionarse con el culto a los muertos?

El mes que seguía a *Xócotl Uetzi*, *Ochpaniztli*, que hubiera correspondido a marzo en el siglo VIII, se celebraba a la diosa Toci, madre de los dioses y corazón de la tierra. El último día de esta veintena se realizaba el sacrificio de una mujer, doble de la diosa, por desollamiento. El gran sacerdote revestía aquella piel para bailar durante todo el día y con la piel de sus muslos se hacía la máscara del dios del maíz, Cintéotl.

Medio año después, en el mes de *Tlacaxipehualiztli*, se celebraba a Xipe Tótec, con otro desollamiento, pero esta vez el sacerdote revestía la piel de un hombre que representaba al dios. Así que, como lo demuestra el nahuatlato Salvador Díaz Cíntora y contrariamente a la idea difundida, Xipe Tótec no era el dios de la primavera que se pretende, sino una deidad del otoño. La piel desollada que reviste el sacerdote en esta ocasión la conserva durante días "hasta que los cueros se rompían"; es una piel amarilla, apergaminada, manchada, descompuesta, no es la piel joven de Toci que anuncia la primavera y el verano, es la piel del "viejo", la piel del muerto que anuncia el otoño y el invierno. "La mitad del año, pues—escribe Díaz Cíntora—está regida por el dios de la costa zapoteca y tlapaneca, Xipe Tótec; la otra mitad, por la diosa madre de la Huasteca, de la costa del seno mexicano. [. . .] En *Tlacaxipehualiztli* un hombre, el sacerdote, viste la piel de otro hombre, el sacrificado; es la pura masculinidad, necesariamente estéril. En *Ochpaniztli*, el sacerdote se reviste de la piel de una mujer; (. . .) es el elemento masculino en unión al femenino, metido literalmente en su piel, sacramento de la fertilidad y de la vida en la tierra".

También durante el mes dedicado a Xipe Tótec, se fabricaba un pan, *cocolli*, con los granos sagrados de unas mazorcas, llamadas *ocholli*, las cuales se colgaban de los techos por sus envolturas después de la cosecha. De esta semilla, y no de otra, se tenía que sembrar al año siguiente, pues era semilla de un dios que exhibía y anunciaba la muerte. El *cocolli* era, pues, un pan de ofrenda sagrada, pan de maíz, amarillo como la piel apergaminada de Xipe Tótec, pan que auguraba la muerte de la naturaleza y que podría ser el origen del actual pan de muerto.

Cuando las lluvias se han retirado del cielo, y la tierra entra en un periodo de calma, antes de cubrirse con la piel seca de la vegetación quemada por las heladas, antes de las torturas de la sequía futura, la tierra se viste con una piel de flores amarillas: entonces brotan el girasol, la flor de Santa María y, entre todas ellas, el tan peculiar cempasúchil, de un color amarillo íntimo, como el reflejo de un sol nocturno, un amarillo anaranjado, bello y triste como ese sentimiento de pérdida del verano. ¿Quién negaría que este símbolo de los antepasados ocultos hunde sus raíces en el México prehispánico? ◆

Dominique Dufétel. Traductor, escritor y maestro en letras hispánicas por la Universidad de París. Fue investigador y escritor de la serie de videos *Ciudades del México* antiguo. En Artes de México coordinó varios números. Fue becario de traducción literaria del FONCA.

FIESTA OBLIGADA

RITUALES DEL DÍA DE MUERTOS

Ruth D. Lechuga

◆

Esta autora, en sus múltiples viajes por los pueblos mexicanos, testificó algunas de las distintas maneras de recibir a los muertos en su día. En este artículo, relata las similitudes, las diferencias, y encuentra algunos ecos de los ritos prehispánicos que, a pesar de los siglos, siguen vivos en la conciencia de ciertas comunidades indígenas.

◆

Como hizo notar Paul Westheim: "Lo único que tiene en común el día de los muertos mexicano con la fiesta de los fieles difuntos, tal como se celebra en Europa, es el hecho de tratarse aquí y allá de un día consagrado a la memoria de los muertos queridos".

Mientras que para el europeo la simple mención de la muerte es tabú, como si al rechazar el pensamiento se pudiera evitar el hecho, el mexicano se familiariza con la idea desde la niñez. Esta cercanía se manifiesta de muchas maneras; por ejemplo, las múltiples expresiones para decir que una persona murió: se peló, se petateó, estiró la pata, lo sacaron con los tenis por delante, felpó, se difunteó, se enfrió, se ausentó, se nos fue, se lo chupó la bruja, se lo cargó patas de catre, entregó el equipo, acompañó a la flaca, dobló el pico, lo cafeteamos, etcétera.

La diferencia también se deja ver en el ritual: el europeo visita el cementerio el día de los fieles difuntos para recordar a sus seres queridos ya fallecidos, mientras que el mexicano piensa que en estos días los difuntos regresan a la tierra para pasar el día con sus parientes. Incluso se ha heredado de la tradición prehispánica la costumbre de dedicar un día a los niños y otro a los adultos muertos. Actualmente, la fiesta puede durar muchos días, además de los dedicados a los muertos pequeños y adultos, respectivamente.

Cuenta María Cristina Morales, por ejemplo, que en la Huasteca hidalguense se considera que san Miguel abre las puertas del cielo, para que las ánimas inicien su peregrinar y visiten a los vivos el 30 de septiembre y san Andrés las cierra el 30 de noviembre, fecha en la que todas las almas deben haber regresado a su morada.

También los totonacos de la sierra concluyen las festividades hasta el día de san Andrés. A decir de los investigadores de El Colegio del Idioma Totonaco, ellos dedican, además, el día de san Lucas—18 de octubre—a aquellos que han muerto con violencia: accidentados, asesinados, ahogados. Los totonacos de Papantla, Veracruz, y los nahuas de Cuetzalan, Puebla, asignan un día, el 30 de octubre, a los niños que no han sido bautizados y, a decir de Simón Gómez Atzin lo llaman "el día de los limbos".

La visita anual de los muertos no es ocasión de luto, sino motivo para celebrar una gran fiesta. Quizá una explicación para ello se encuentre en el *Códice matritense*: "Decían los viejos: quien ha muerto, se ha vuelto dios. Decían: Se hizo dios, quiere decir que murió". De hecho, Robert Childs y Patricia Altman aseguran que todavía se cree que "el alma del difunto se vuelve un ser sobrenatural con el poder de interceder por los familiares vivos". Más adelante, agregan otro elemento distintivo del Día de Muertos mexicano con respecto al europeo: "en la práctica católica ortodoxa, uno reza por las almas de los muertos para salvarlas del purgatorio. Los indígenas, por el contrario, no rezan por las almas, sino que les rezan a ellas".

Al igual que los dioses del pasado, hay que agradar a los antepasados para que miren favorablemente las peticiones de los vivos: ellos también esperan sus ofrendas. Los descendientes deben destinar algo de su tiempo y de su dinero para agasajarlos convenientemente. En todos los pueblos se relata cómo una persona que no puso su ofrenda con el debido respeto fue castigada por los difuntos. La pena impuesta puede ir desde los azotes, hasta la muerte del pariente desobligado.

Por ejemplo, en un relato recogido por Fernando Horcasitas, un hechicero de Milpalta cuenta que una señora encargó a su hijo ir por leña y comprar lo necesario para la ofrenda. El muchacho se distrajo todo el día, jugando en el monte y, cuando quiso regresar, "advirtió que detrás de él venía la larga procesión de los viejitos. Vio a su padre, sus abuelitos, bisabuelitos, tatarabuelitos, todos temblando de frío, muertos de hambre y sed, cargando sus morrales vacíos y sus petatitos enrollados bajo el brazo, todos deseosos de volver a su casa, donde eran esperados para calentarse, comer y dormir por una noche. '¿Qué haces aquí?', le riñeron, '¿por qué no nos estás esperando allá en tu casa?'. El muchacho, azorado, no pudo contestar. Los difuntos lo amarraron a un árbol y lo dejaron allí toda la noche. Al amanecer, cuando ya se desvanecía el humo perfumado del copal, cuando se iban apagando las ceras de cada ofrenda, los viejitos difuntitos volvieron a pasar lentamente por el bosque, desataron al muchacho y siguieron su camino. El muchacho regresó a su casa llorando. '¡Ahora sí, mamacita, ya sé que vuelven los muertitos; el año que entra les compraremos su comida y los esperaremos a todos!'".

Otra historia, referida por los investigadores de El Colegio del Idioma Totonaco, acabó más trágicamente: un señor que no creía en los muertos y no hizo caso de su día, cuando iba rumbo a su casa después de una parranda: "de pronto vio que venía mucha gente a su paso, pero que todos eran difuntos que ya retornaban a su mundo; entre ellos iban su papá y su mamá sin ofrenda, en cambio los otros iban bien cargados de sus ofrendas. Vio que sus difuntos solo cargaban un pedazo de tepalcate como incensario, y que les quemaban las manos; iban lamentándose muy tristes. Entonces aquel hombre no dudó más, de carrerita y muy apresurado fue a poner la ofrenda. No tenía mucho rato de haber llegado a su casa, cuando empezó a sentir mareos y ascos, luego enfermó y repentinamente murió. La comida que había mandado a preparar para la ofrenda, solo sirvió de comida para su entierro".

Pasada la fiesta, los muertos deben regresar a su morada. Hay algunos que, renuentes a hacerlo, rondan en las cercanías de la casa de los parientes, quizá con el objetivo de volverse espíritus chocarreros. En algunos pueblos se hacen

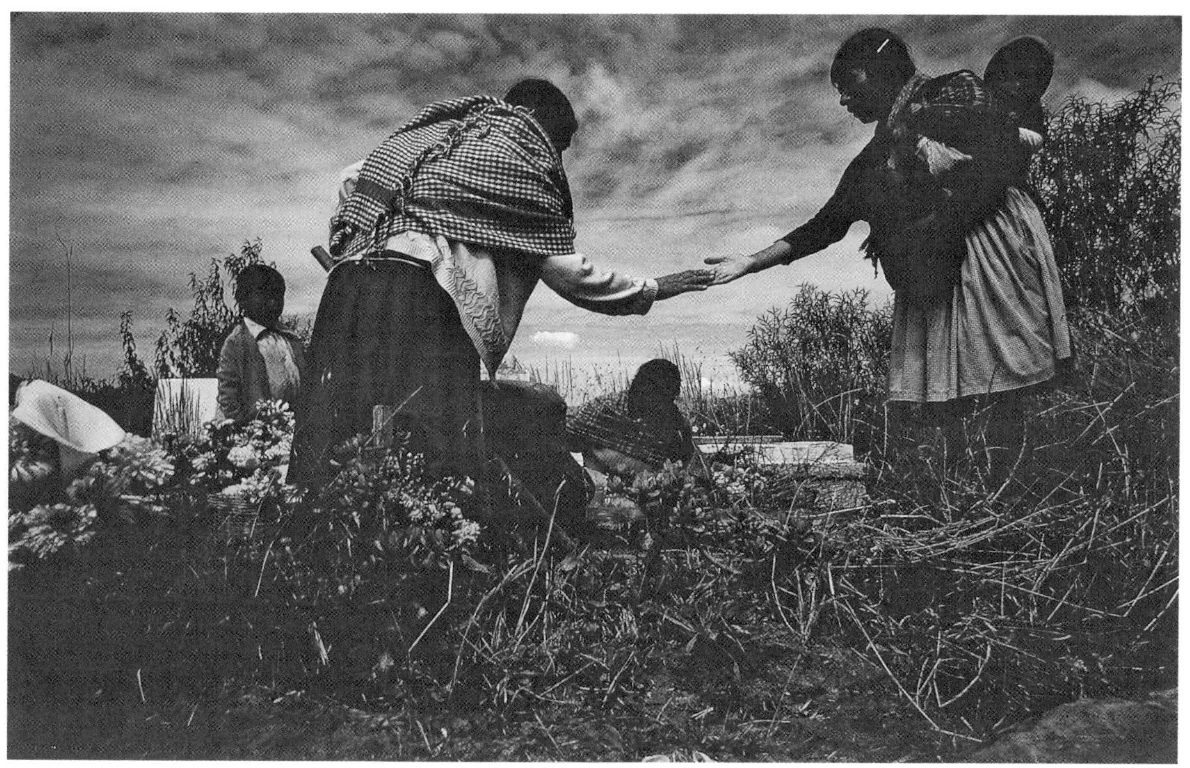

Julio Galindo. Mazahua cemetery. 1985.

ceremonias especiales para evitarlo. Frances Toor relata que "en Yalalag, Oaxaca, el sacerdote, acompañado de músicos, camina a lo largo del pueblo, recitando responsos y Salve Reginas, con o sin música, según lo que la gente esté dispuesta a gastar. Se dicen dentro y fuera de las casas para asegurar que ningún alma se está escondiendo, porque algunas se pierden en el camino y otras están renuentes a regresar; con los rezos tienen que partir y dejar de perturbar a sus parientes".

Los totonacos de la sierra hacen otra ofrenda pequeña el día de san Andrés. "Por la tarde se van al camposanto, llevando la cruz y parte de la ofrenda. En forma de despedida, rezan un rosario y unas alabanzas para que no vuelva el difunto a molestar a los familiares".

Los chatinos de Yaitepec, Oaxaca hacen una procesión al cementerio, para retornar a las almas adultas a las tumbas. Danzantes enmascarados van de casa en casa, haciendo mucho ruido, para expulsar a las ánimas que no hayan regresado oportunamente.

La ofrenda, llamada impropiamente "altar de muertos", es costumbre general en todo México. Puede hacerse en la casa del difunto, en el cementerio, o en ambos lugares. Consiste fundamentalmente en comida, bebidas, flores y luces. Sin embargo, hay muchas variantes locales.

Los totonacos de la región de Papantla, Veracruz, que son extremadamente pulcros e invariablemente llevan en un morral una muda

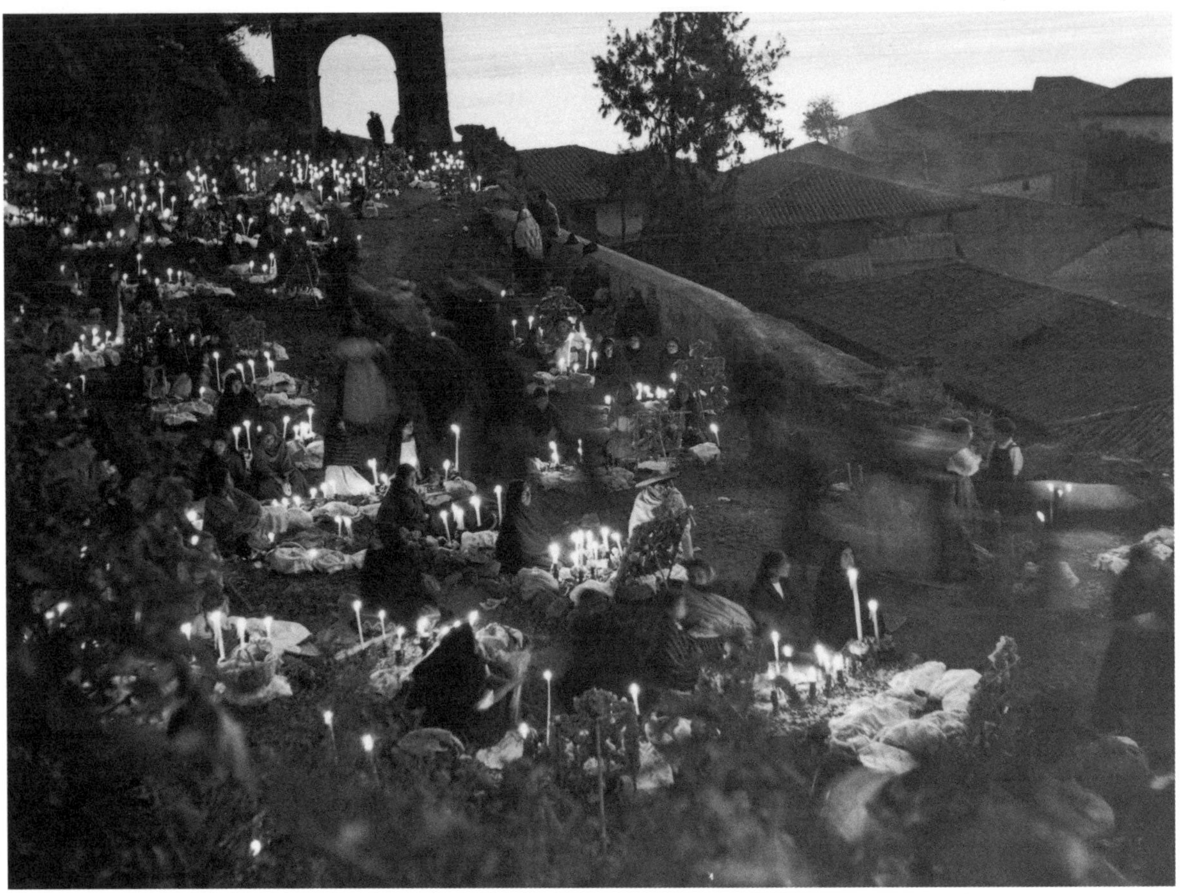

Julio Galindo. Mazahua cemetery. 1985.

de ropa, por si se llegaran a ensuciar en el camino, ponen junto a la ofrenda un vestuario limpio, para que el muerto pueda cambiarse al llegar y, entonces, pueda disfrutar de la fiesta.

Las ofrendas en el cementerio pueden hacerse durante el día, como en San Gabriel Chilac, Puebla. Conforme llegan las familias, se sientan alrededor de las tumbas adornadas con flores, velas, canastas, comida, figuras de ángeles y otros elementos. De acuerdo con sus posibilidades económicas, contratan un músico con un piano portátil o un grupo de mariachis para alegrar a los difuntos. Aquí, como en muchos otros sitios, la comunidad pone en un rincón del camposanto, una ofrenda para el ánima sola, dedicada a todos aquellos difuntos que ya no tienen familiares que los recuerden.

En otros lugares, la celebración tiene lugar en la noche. Entonces, el cementerio se llena con velas encendidas que propician un ambiente festivo y mágico. En estas ceremonias, llamadas atinadamente "iluminadas", hay también comida, flores, incienso y, según la región, adornos distintivos. En Janitzio y en pueblos alrededor de la laguna de Pátzcuaro, se colocan grandes arcos forrados de flores de cempasúchil, de los que cuelgan naranjas, plátanos y figuras de azúcar.

En Iguatzio, una de las poblaciones a la orilla del lago, se me acercó una señora con un plátano y me dijo: "Es para ti, te lo manda mi difunto marido por el gusto de que compartas con nosotros esta fiesta".

Lo más notable de "la iluminada" es que tiene un antecedente prehispánico. Relata Sahagún sobre la fiesta del mes de *Quecholli* (del 20 de octubre al 8 de noviembre): "hacían unas saeticas pequeñas a honra de los difuntos... amarraban de cuatro en cuatro saeticas y cuatro teas con hilo de algodón flojo, y ponían los nombres sobre las sepulturas de los difuntos. También ponían juntamente un par de tamales dulces; todo el día estaba esto en las sepulturas y, a la puesta del sol, encendían las teas y allí se quemaban las teas y las saetas".

En muchos pueblos hay danzas durante los días de muertos. Algunas se llevan a cabo en la calle, otros grupos van de casa en casa y otros más actúan en el cementerio.

En las Huastecas los danzantes se llaman *huehues* ("viejos" en idioma náhuatl) y representan a los difuntos. Danzan en parejas y sus bromas a menudo hacen referencia a un contenido sexual. También los tejorones de Yaitepec, Oaxaca, hacen bromas pesadas con chistes sexuales, amparándose en el anonimato de la máscara. En ambos casos se trata de un rito de fertilidad, lo que demuestra que la cosmovisión prehispánica respecto a la dualidad y al devenir constante del ciclo vida-muerte-vida sigue viva en el pensamiento de algunos mexicanos. Sin embargo, los tejorones juegan otro papel: expulsar a las ánimas que se retrasaron en salir después de que acabó su día.

Otras danzas se escenifican para divertir a los difuntos. Los negros de los pueblos costeros de Oaxaca llaman a sus danzantes diablos, actúan en la calle, sus pasos son vigorosos y dicen versos improvisados, aludiendo a sus compatriotas y a los visitantes.

En Acatlán, Puebla, la danza habitual se llama tecuanes e intervienen muchos personajes, entre otros el tigre. Suelen danzar la tarde del 2 de noviembre en honor a las ánimas en una plaza afuera del cementerio; sin embargo, cuando en el grupo hay un pariente recientemente fallecido entran al camposanto y ejecutan un número alrededor de su tumba. Lo mismo hacen los diablos de Tanquián, San Luis Potosí, cuando se muere un compañero danzante.

Los viejos de Suchiquiltongo, Oaxaca, y los monos de Romerillo, Chiapas, danzan siempre dentro del cementerio.

Los niños de Tepoztlán, Morelos, se divierten bailando con un esqueleto de carrizo, forrado de papel de china que es casi de su tamaño.

Un espectáculo único son las tumbas vivientes en Iguala, Guerrero. Cuando hay una persona fallecida después del Día de Muertos anterior, o como lo llama la población "un muerto fresco", la familia desocupa el cuarto más grande con vista a la calle y allí se improvisa toda una escenografía, con los familiares jóvenes y niños como actores. Generalmente se representa algún cuadro de tema religioso, con la particularidad de que los participantes tienen que permanecer inmóviles en la noche durante largas horas; los habitantes de la ciudad van en romería para admirar la inventiva de cada familia.

Calixta Guiteras relata que en Chenalhó, Chiapas, hay un ayuntamiento especial que gobierna en nombre de los muertos por un día. Se hace una entrega ceremonial del gabán y del bastón de mando, como se acostumbra cuando se instala el nuevo ayuntamiento anual. Al día siguiente, las insignias del mando se regresan a los regidores ordinarios.

Otra ceremonia importante tiene lugar en Huixtán, Chiapas, donde las mujeres barren la iglesia y la plaza de enfrente. Es una acción ceremonial que tiene sus raíces en el México prehispánico. Fray Diego Durán relata: "El undécimo mes del año llamábase *Ochpaniztli* que quiere decir día de barrer en el cual día celebraban la fiesta de Toci que era la madre de los dioses. [. . .] La ceremonia primera de aquel día era que todos habían de barrer todas sus pertenencias y todas sus casas. De más de esto se barrían todas las calles del pueblo, la cual costumbre ha quedado en toda la tierra, porque era rito antiguo". Aquí, al igual que en algunas otras ceremonias relatadas, se observa la persistencia de ritos y creencias prehispánicas, a pesar de casi cinco siglos de evangelización. ◆

Ruth D. Lechuga fue investigadora de arte popular y fotógrafa. Creó un museo de arte popular con su colección de cerca de 10 000 piezas, al que está dedicado el número 42 de Artes de México. Publicó *Traje indígena de México*, *Las técnicas textiles en el México antiguo*, *La indumentaria en el México indígena* y *Mask Arts of Mexico*, entre otros. En la colección Uso y Estilo, el título *Ruth D. Lechuga, una memoria mexicana* rescata la obra fotográfica de esta autora. Legó su archivo fotográfico, con más de 20 000 negativos, a *Artes de México*.

FIESTA ENSIMISMADA

ALMAS *NON GRATAS* EN SAN MATEO DEL MAR

Laurette Séjourné

◆

Entre los huaves, como entre casi todos los indígenas mexicanos, el tiempo profano, el del sudor y el trabajo, se interrumpe con el Día de Muertos, para dar paso a los instantes sagrados en los que los ancestros vuelven a la tierra. En este relato, escrito en la década de 1950, la autora nos señala un elemento distintivo de esta celebración: el rechazar las almas de los que han muerto fuera del pueblo, quizá para que el sentido de comunidad que reina entre los vivos se extienda hasta el mundo de los difuntos.

◆

En San Mateo del Mar, a los muertos se les teme por encima de todo como causa de las enfermedades. Hasta parece que el mal es parte inherente de los que están bajo tierra, porque estos no se manifiestan de otro modo que infligiendo desgracias. Pensar en un muerto es una imprudencia que se debe reparar apresuradamente por medio de ofrendas y de rezos, si no se desea caer enfermo. Servirse de un muerto para malear es cosa corriente; encontrarse en una situación difícil representa gran peligro de enfermedad, porque si un pariente desaparecido se da cuenta de la inquietud que uno siente, entonces—"de lástima", así dicen ellos—no dejará de enviarle alguna infección.

Las almas más perniciosas son las de los hombres muertos por accidentes fuera del pueblo, porque, no encontrando lugar de reposo, recorren los caminos con esperanza de introducirse en el cuerpo de un ser viviente. Así, no es raro que, al regreso de un viaje, se caiga gravemente enfermo por haber atrapado una de esas almas perdidas. La posibilidad de que se diagnostique esta enfermedad no deja de inquietar, porque el tratamiento que aplicará el especialista en tal caso consistirá en la administración de latigazos hasta que la cura sea completa. Sin embargo, hay quien se queja de que estas almas errantes suelen ser muy testarudas y muchas veces dejan que el paciente se muera bajo los golpes antes que consentir en abandonar su refugio.

Todo esto deja entrever claramente dos actitudes mentales que caracterizan al habitante de San Mateo del Mar: su veneración humilde y sumisa a la fuerza siempre sobrenatural y su dependencia respecto del grupo. No solo sienten singular necesidad de pedir perdón por una enfermedad recibida, sino que además se limitan a rezar y hacer ofrendas sin llevar a cabo ninguna de las operaciones por las cuales los brujos extirpan generalmente las infecciones, y que suponen un sentido activo de rebeldía. Esta mentalidad explica la atmósfera de devoción que reina en este pueblo, porque, si se necesita rezar para curarse, es necesario también hacerlo incesantemente como medida de higiene a fin de que este conjunto indiferenciado en que los hombres, los santos, los muertos y los animales se confunden no pierda jamás su armonía: la razón principal de la desgracia es el desequilibrio de este todo homogéneo.

La cohesión de la comunidad se manifiesta también en el hecho de que no hay brujo que consienta provocar una enfermedad a petición de un cliente, cosa tan usual en otras partes. Solo un brujo forastero sería capaz de tales operaciones, motivo por el cual se han tomado serias medidas para prohibir la entrada en el pueblo de todo brujo extranjero. En el caso en que uno de estos personajes indeseables persistiera en querer entrar, los innumerables oratorios situados en cada esquina a manera de defensa no tardarían en hacerlo sucumbir.

En ocasión de las fiestas de Todos Santos se hace manifiesto que el anonimato en el cual está sumergido el individuo en San Mateo del Mar, así como su dependencia incondicionada respecto al grupo, se extienden hasta los mismos muertos. La actuación de los seres desaparecidos está estrechamente mezclada a la de los vivos y las invocaciones para hacerlos aparecer cuando el brujo diagnostica un "mal de muerto" son un artículo de primera necesidad, indispensable para toda la familia. A pesar de la intimidad de esas relaciones, no es más que una vez al año cuando las almas pueden circular libremente en el pueblo, oportunidad en que se les reserva una solemne recepción, tal como sucede con casi todos los grupos étnicos de México. Pero, contrariamente a lo que pasa en otras partes, el altar que cada familia levanta en su honor no está aquí dedicado a algún difunto en particular, lo que imprime a las fiestas un carácter completamente impersonal

Hay algo más que destaca la singularidad de la gente de San Mateo del Mar: su hostilidad hacia todo lo ajeno al grupo es tan consecuente, que llegan incluso a boicotear sin piedad a aquellos de los suyos que han muerto fuera del pueblo, como si el hecho de haber salido de él los arrojara en la impura condición de extranjeros.

El concepto de que existen almas que han olvidado el camino de su tierra natal se halla muy difundido; era, en cambio, la primera vez que veía yo rechazar esas almas. En los diferentes lugares en que he asistido al Día de Muertos, observé siempre la existencia de un pensamiento caritativo hacia las almas errantes: un cirio en el umbral de una puerta o una modesta mesa de ofrendas en el interior de la casa son las limosnas de recuerdo humano que cada familia da a las almas perdidas que pudieran pasar por ahí.

Nada parecido se da en San Mateo del Mar, sino que, al contrario, se vigilan las almas de cerca, a fin de que no puedan mezclarse impunemente con la comunidad de los muertos respetables. La gente asegura que cuando una de esas almas extrañas intenta colarse en la iglesia con la esperanza de compartir las ofrendas que le permitirían incorporarse a las filas de los puros, el portal, indignado, le impide entrar. He oído decir que el sacristán ve a menudo la pesada puerta del templo cerrarse sola en la nariz de una de estas almas fuera de la ley.

Con algunos días de adelanto, la población entera se prepara para recibir a sus muertos. En las casas, las mujeres trabajan duramente para elaborar las bebidas y los alimentos gratos a las almas; en el mercado, se arrebatan las velas a medida que son confeccionadas y se espera con impaciencia la llegada de los vendedores de cempasúchil, y los panes de muerto en forma de ángeles, de conejos o de ciervos. (Conocí estos panes para la comida de los muertos durante mi viaje de ida a San Mateo. Habiéndose volcado la carreta de la simpática pareja zapoteca—con nosotros dentro, se entiende—, nos esforzábamos, con la ayuda de una lámpara que penetraba con dificultad las frías tinieblas que nos rodeaban, en recoger y limpiar los objetos esparcidos en el barro. Estos panecillos de graciosas formas me conmovieron y les dediqué todos mis cuidados a fin de que pudieran todavía, a pesar de su desgracia, figurar dignamente en una mesa de ofrendas.)

Al mediodía del primero de noviembre, las campanas comienzan a tocar, y las almas, que no esperan más que esta señal, se precipitan sobre la tierra. Regresarán al alba a sus residencias respectivas—las hay que vienen hasta del infierno—, cargadas con las ofrendas de los vivos. Las que vuelven con los brazos vacíos no dejarán de enviar las peores calamidades a los olvidadizos que no las han ayudado con un recuerdo.

Al son de la campana que se hará escuchar sin descanso hasta la mañana siguiente, los aldeanos dan la bienvenida a sus muertos. Se comienzan a cantar las oraciones delante de cada altar familiar; en casa de las autoridades se llevan a cabo ceremonias secretas, reservadas exclusivamente a los hombres; las mujeres van las unas a casa de las otras ofreciendo tantas velas como difuntos recuerdan: hay niñas que se detienen tímidamente en el umbral de una puerta y tienden una vela solitaria, y viejas cargadas con haces de cirios.

Animadas por el paso incesante de estas portadoras de ofrendas, las callejuelas adquieren una belleza impresionante. Es que, con la presencia de las almas, el pueblo aparece de pronto en toda su autenticidad. El atavío y el comportamiento de las mujeres, por ejemplo, son precisamente los de sacerdotisas acostumbradas a la intimidad con lo sobrenatural: la gruesa tela roja que ciñe la cintura y que cae hasta el suelo; la amplia blusa cuadrada, negra o amarilla, bajo la cual el busto está desnudo; la pieza de algodón blanco, grande como una sábana que, de la cabeza, cae severamente sobre los hombros y las espaldas. Silenciosas, erguidas y concentradas, llevando en la mano cirios ornados de cempasúchil, avanzan sin moverse y desaparecen . . . Las casas no son más que los templos múltiples de una misma área sagrada, y el altar que cada una posee en su interior es el punto más vivo en ellas. Numerosos cirios expanden su luz dorada en la pieza, generalmente oscura, pues las chozas no tienen otra abertura que la muy estrecha de la puerta, y el techo y las paredes son tan estrechos que no dejan filtrar la menor luz. Las flores, las frutas, la albahaca—planta que desempeña papel predominante en la hechicería—, la cera y el copal que arden llenan todo de un intenso perfume religioso. La gente se va relevando ante la mesa de las ofrendas para cantar las oraciones con un fervor que no decaerá hasta la mañana siguiente.

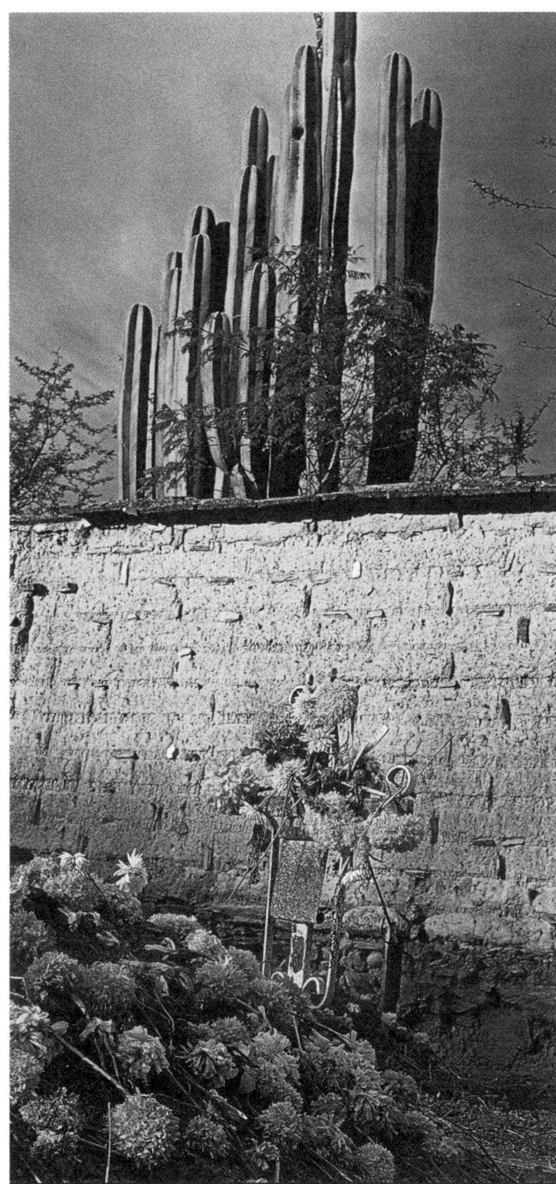

Paul Czitrom. Tetelcingo, Puebla. 1999.

La noche, ayudada por la luna llena, pondrá más en relieve todavía el sentido profundo de las cosas, y el pueblo entero aparecerá como encerrado en un sortilegio: las masas sombrías de las chozas que avanzan sobre las callejuelas como mejor les parece, según un orden totalmente extraño a la línea recta; el suelo, caliente y movedizo, que se desplaza obstinadamente bajo los pies; los grupos de hombres, que flotando entre los vapores del alcohol ritual pasan como sonámbulos; las plegarias que se elevan por encima de cada habitación como espesas columnas de humo . . .

La choza que me abriga no escapa evidentemente a la suerte de las otras, y me será imposible dormir a la luz de los cirios, entre los perfumes que atacan la garganta, el clamor de los rezos y las continuas idas y venidas. La luna está todavía alta cuando las mujeres se aprestan a ir al cementerio vestidas con sus más bellos atavíos. Mi deber de investigadora me obliga a seguirlas, pero me parece que cometería una indiscreción sacrílega asistiendo a sus adioses con los muertos y siento verdadero alivio cuando me prohíben hacerlo. En la puerta, el dueño de la casa conversa con varios amigos, todos en completa ebriedad. No atreviéndome a enfrentarlos, me quedo largo rato bloqueada en un rincón de la pieza escuchando sus parloteos, en que mezclan a veces palabras en español. Y es entonces cuando, de la manera más imprevista, se eleva un canto cuya perturbadora extrañeza sobrepasa todo lo demás: son algunas notas de La internacional.

De repente, la plaza, vacía desde hace dos días—los vendedores ambulantes la han abandonado sabiendo que durante estas fiestas no se pesca—, vibra de color y movimiento. Las mujeres que vuelven del cementerio se cruzan, sin parecer verlos, con los grupos de hombres titubeantes que salen de la iglesia, donde, desde la víspera, montan la guardia turnándose alrededor de la mesa de las ofrendas.

Un poco más tarde, la plaza tomará el aspecto de un campo después de la batalla: cuerpos tendidos por todas partes; hombres que avanzan penosamente bajo el duro sol se detienen para recobrar el equilibrio, dan algunos pasos inciertos antes de derrumbarse. De vez en cuando aparece la silueta hierática de una mujer: se inclina con veneración sobre uno de estos cuerpos tendidos y lo lleva como un precioso botín. Toda la población masculina, sin excepción, está completamente ebria, porque ningún hombre podría, sin pecar gravemente, dejar de brindar con las almas de visita.

Asistí a un diálogo revelador a este respecto: cuando el joven maestro de escuela, sufriendo él mismo los efectos de una borrachera atroz, preguntaba a un venerable anciano por qué no había hecho no sé qué cosa, este último, sorprendido de que le pudiera hacer tal pregunta, contestó: "Pero, cómo . . . no podía . . . estaba bebiendo". Es necesario agregar que esta borrachera colectiva y sagrada es de lo más pacífica: durante las 24 horas que los hombres bebieron, no se registró incidente alguno. La única novedad, aparte del aspecto chusco de la plaza y de las calles, fue que esta gente, de ordinario tan taciturna y cerrada, se volviera locuaz y llegara hasta a manifestar cierta ternura. ◆

Laurette Séjourné. Arqueóloga francesa que participó en las exploraciones de Monte Albán y Palenque. En 1955, en Teotihuacán, descubrió tres estructuras arquitectónicas completas. Es autora, entre otros libros, de *Palenque, una ciudad maya*, *Un palacio en la ciudad de los dioses*, *La cerámica de Teotihuacán*, *El pensamiento náhuatl cifrado* y *Supervivencias de un mundo mágico* (Fondo de Cultura Económica, 1996), de donde fue extraído este fragmento.

SAN GABRIEL CHILAC

Gutierre Tibón

El día dos de noviembre el aire de todo México está impregnado de pensamientos de afecto y gratitud hacia los seres queridos que nos han precedido en el sueño eterno; el anhelo de todos es probarles que no los olvidamos y que siguen viviendo en nuestro recuerdo. En mil y mil panteones del país los fieles difuntos reciben la visita de sus familiares; la flor emblemática de los muertos, el cempasúchil, decora innumerables tumbas. Hay, sin embargo, lugares donde se celebra el Día de Muertos con más devoción, con más solemnidad. Yo estuve en un panteón que considero único en México, y tal vez en el mundo. Tengo todavía grabada en la retina una visión casi irreal de color, belleza y ternura humana. He pasado el dos de noviembre en Chilac, un pueblo que está a unos veinte kilómetros de Tehuacán, casi en los linderos con Oaxaca. Su población se dedica con éxito al cultivo del ajo. Todos son bilingües: hablan con igual soltura el náhuatl y el español. Todos saben leer y escribir, y la mayoría hasta lee música.

¿En qué consiste el carácter único del cementerio de Chilac? Cada tumba tiene, construida encima, una cabaña de hojas de plátano color esmeralda, o de pequeños carrizos verdes o de tela negra o morada; en la sombra están las ofrendas: tenates con pan de muerto, ollas con mole, plátanos, naranjas, flores, todas fresquísimas, en increíble abundancia y arregladas con garbo. Campean los cempasúchiles, que contrastan, por su amarillo anaranjado, con el rojo sangre de una flor aterciopelada que llaman moco de pavo; también se destaca el blanco virginal de las azucenas, el morado de las gladiolas y las cubiertas de los convólvulos azules que llamamos manto de la Virgen. Pareciera que estas últimas hubieran esperado esa mañana para florecer. Entre las ofrendas y las flores se agitan suavemente las llamas de las ceras, tantas como los difuntos que se conmemoran. Delante de las cabañas están sentadas o arrodilladas las familias, desde el abuelo hasta los niños, y todos rezan. Distribuidos entre las tumbas están los armonios, muchos armonios (he contado dieciséis). Los tocan los propios campesinos; leen la música como expertos organistas, en tanto que mueven los pedales del instrumento con sus pies calzados de huaraches, o descalzos. Toda la familia canta, acompañada por el armonio; voces blancas, voces bajas, siempre afinadas. Cantan y rezan en un perfecto español o en latín bien pronunciado, aunque entre sí hablan el melodioso idioma del México antiguo, el náhuatl. De vez en cuando pasa una mujer con inmensos ramos de flores, para adornar aún más las tumbas.

El cielo es de un azul intenso; flota en el aire el perfume entremezclado de los cempasúchiles y del copal que humea en los pebeteros. Del mar de cabañas verdes, negras y moradas, llega la armonía del canto y de la música, como si se tratara de voces angelicales. En todas partes, flores: una apoteosis de flores. La atmósfera, en el panteón de Chilac, no es de alegría, ni de tristeza, sino de paz, de sosiego. Regresé a México con el corazón sereno, como si hubiera saboreado un anticipo de la bienaventuranza eterna. ◆

Tomado de *Aventuras en México 1937–1983*, Diana, 1983.

FIESTA SERENA

ESPLÉNDIDA RECEPCIÓN EN TEOTITLÁN DEL VALLE

Mary Jane Gagnier de Mendoza

◆

En el pueblo oaxaqueño de Teotitlán del Valle, durante la celebración del Día de Muertos los habitantes recorren las casas para saludar a quienes conforman la comunidad. Pero estas rondas son también obligación de los muertos, quienes se llevan de cada altar la esencia de sus ofrendas.

◆

A los habitantes de Teotitlán del Valle, Oaxaca, se los reconoce por ser anfitriones excepcionales, por lo que las almas que los visitan el Día de Muertos reciben un trato verdaderamente generoso. La preparación para darles la bienvenida dura días; pero a partir del 31 de octubre, la gente del pueblo ya se afana en atender a los espíritus. Los primeros que regresan son los angelitos, que son las almas de los niños muertos. Ellos llegan en las primeras horas del primero de noviembre, día de Todos Santos, porque ángeles y santos tienen mucho en común, entre otras cosas, que habitan en el mismo lugar celestial. Los espíritus de los niños se retiran justo cuando los adultos que residen en el más allá comienzan a llegar, a las tres de la tarde del mismo día. Oficialmente, los muertos se retiran a las tres de la tarde del dos, pero si esta fecha cae en domingo, día de descanso, reservado por la liturgia al Señor, los espíritus simplemente esperan y regresan a su morada el tercer día del mes. En Teotitlán, un pueblo de hábiles tejedores, ubicado a 30 kilómetros de la capital del estado, las actividades artesanales se detienen durante estas fiestas, pues como advierte la tradición: "¡nadie debe trabajar mientras los espíritus estén de visita!".

COMPAÑÍA CONSTANTE Y PALABRAS CARIÑOSAS

Es el mediodía de un primero de noviembre. Ya han pasado varios años desde que la tía Antonia Ruiz perdiera un hijo. Esta mujer, vigorosa y compacta, habla por experiencia propia: ha enterrado a cinco de sus once hijos. Pasamos junto al cuarto, recién renovado, en donde se encuentra la ofrenda, cruzamos el pasillo y llegamos al dormitorio de sus hijas. Al principio me sorprende que nos alejemos de la sala; pero, al entrar en la fresca penumbra, se dibuja la forma de un pequeño altar. Ella me explica que esta era la sala original, que formaba parte del hogar construido por los padres de su marido hace 40 años. Este lugar albergó el altar de la casa hasta que ella y su esposo, Félix, construyeron otra sala, en 1980. Nos cuenta que mantiene este pequeño altar porque fue aquí donde velaron a sus hijos cuando murieron. Este es el lugar que ellos conocen. Aquí es adonde regresan.

—Aquí atendemos a los espíritus—explica Antonia, mientras su hija Reina baja del altar la ofrenda que se deja a los espíritus de los niños: cacahuates y nueces, panecillos de huevo, tacitas de barro llenas de chocolate y pequeñas tabletas de cacao, las mismas que se usan para preparar esta bebida.

—Mientras los angelitos están aquí, oímos ruidos, escuchamos cómo tintinea la cerámica—cuenta Reina—, el mismo ruido que se hace cuando uno bebe un trago de chocolate y luego pone de nuevo la taza en el plato.

Esa misma tarde, en otro hogar de Teotitlán del Valle, mi suegra, doña Clara Ruiz, atiende a cuatro visitantes en su sala, cuando llega otra pareja. En un día como este, con tantos ires y venires, doña Clara ha dejado abierta la puerta de la casa. Su cuñada Leonora y su esposo, Renaldo, entran discretamente, mientras los otros visitantes guardan un respetuoso silencio. La pareja se dirige directamente al altar. Saca de una canasta su ofrenda de pan, fruta, semillas y un cirio de casi un metro de altura.

La vela de Leonora, ahora encendida, se suma a otras seis puestas sobre el suelo cerca del altar, que iluminan una fotografía de Emiliano Mendoza, el fallecido esposo de Clara. De acuerdo con la costumbre, la pareja se arrodilla respetuosamente. Solo después de haber saludado de manera adecuada a los difuntos, los huéspedes dirigen su atención a los vivos, primero a Clara, luego a sus hijos adultos y por último a los otros invitados. Finalmente, los visitantes toman asiento en un extremo de la mesa, y la fluida conversación continúa. La plática se centra en los difuntos. A veces la memoria arranca risas o lágrimas.

Los espíritus desean tener compañía durante toda su visita de un día. Y aunque cada morada tiene espíritus propios que atender, en una comunidad de lazos tan estrechos, la mayoría de la gente pasa gran parte de la fiesta presentando sus respetos a los espíritus familiares de otros hogares.

Horas después Clara Mendoza pide a su hija adulta que vigile el altar y que atienda a quienes lleguen, mientras ella visita las casas de varios parientes. En la resistente canasta que lleva bajo el rebozo trae una botella con mezcal, media docena de panes de huevo y varias tablillas de chocolate. Regresará a su casa más de una vez durante las obligadas rondas, para volver a llenar la canasta.

Su primera parada es en casa de su fallecida suegra. La puerta está abierta, así que entra y se desliza silenciosamente dentro de la sala. Sin prestar atención a quienes ocupan la mesa, se dirige hacia el altar. Besa las orillas de este y se hinca a rezar.

Le pregunté a Clara qué es lo que rezaba en ese momento.

—Que los espíritus de los fallecidos estén en paz—me contestó.

Al levantarse, saluda a su cuñado Andrés Mendoza, quien, de acuerdo con la costumbre zapoteca, por ser el hijo menor, todavía vive en casa de su madre. Rosa, la esposa de Andrés, sale de la cocina y, junto con su marido, recibe la canasta de las manos de doña Clara, y se dirige automáticamente hacia el altar para distribuir la ofrenda. Todos han sido partícipes, en incontables ocasiones, de esta misma escena, porque hay en esta comunidad un profundo compromiso por llevar a buen fin las obligaciones de cada quien.

Tía Antonia y su esposo, Félix Mendoza, a quienes habíamos visitado al iniciar el día, nos ofrecen su versión de los quehaceres de los espíritus durante la fiesta:

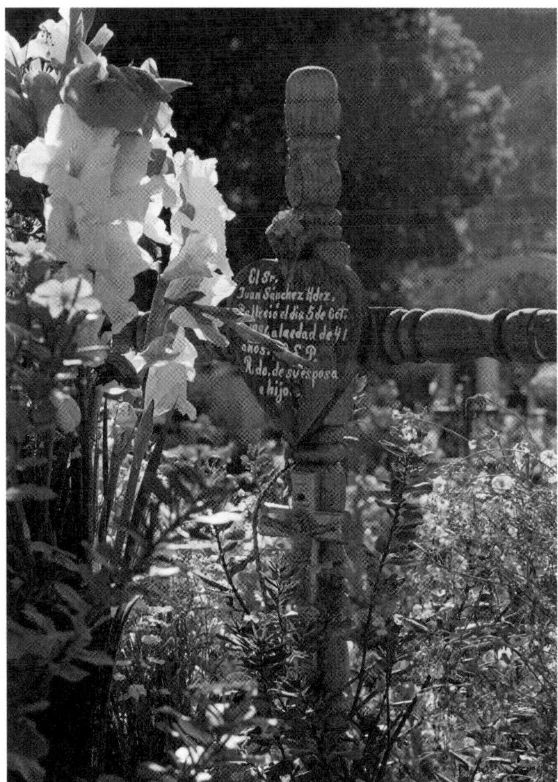

Paul Czitrom. Tetelcingo, Puebla. 1999.

—A veces vienen a ver a sus amigos o a un compadre. Además, visitan otras casas, no solamente aquellas en las que vivieron y murieron, también van a las de sus hijos, a las de sus padrinos y a las de sus parientes favoritos.

Así, mientras los vivos hacen sus rondas, ofreciendo sus respetos a los espíritus de las personas que amaron, los muertos también recorren el pueblo, pues tienen una invitación abierta para disfrutar los aromas que se elevan desde otros altares.

Incluso las parejas jóvenes que viven en casas nuevas, en las que nadie ha muerto todavía, preparan ofrendas, en parte para los espíritus desconocidos que regresan a su lugar, o por si acaso el alma de algún miembro de la familia o padrino quiere visitarlos. Si por alguna razón se vieran obligados a salir de sus casas en esta fiesta, una situación por demás indeseable, podrían remediar su afrenta dejando abierta la puerta de la habitación donde se ha puesto el altar. Con este gesto invitan simbólicamente a los espíritus a visitarlos.

Si hay algo peor que atender mal a los espíritus, es no atenderlos. Los teotitecos tienen mucho que contar acerca de este asunto. Antonia recuerda que, cuando era apenas una muchachita, su familia se mudó a un solar en medio del pueblo.

—Mucha gente había vivido y muerto en este pedazo de tierra mucho antes de que viniéramos, pero luego fue abandonada por años. Cuando llegó nuestro primer Día de Muertos, en la madrugada del dos de noviembre, mi madre escuchó los gemidos que venían del patio grande.

A las cuatro de la mañana, Victoria Gónzalez Martínez salió al patio en medio de la oscuridad para tranquilizar a esas almas tristes. Les habló y les aseguró que serían bienvenidas.

—No lloren más, las vamos a atender. Aunque no tenemos mucho que ofrecerles, por favor vengan—les dijo.

Casi medio siglo ha transcurrido, y las almas desconocidas están satisfechas; ni un solo gemido misterioso se ha vuelto a escuchar.

LA OFRENDA

Todos los elementos del altar familiar aseguran al espíritu que ha llegado al hogar que le corresponde. Por eso, cuando hay posibilidad de usar fotografías, estas son elementos centrales en los arreglos. Un simple vaso de agua es, quizá, la ofrenda indispensable en cualquiera de ellos. Así como el viaje del espíritu al otro mundo ha sido arduo, su regreso al hogar también lo es: necesitan agua para apagar su sed.

Las velas tienen un importante papel simbólico. Alejandrina Ríos, la nuera de la tía Antonia, cree que estas iluminan el camino de regreso de los espíritus:

—Si no las colocas en la ofrenda, los muertos se verán obligados a encender sus deditos para ver mejor las rocas y las espinas que bordean el camino de regreso.

¿Será por esto que se encienden algunas sobre la tumba, justo después del entierro, y otras más el Día de Muertos, en los momentos del viaje hacia y desde el otro mundo?

A las tres de la tarde del primero de noviembre, mientras suenan las campanas de la iglesia que anuncian la llegada de los espíritus, los vivos dan los toques finales a los altares. Estos días hay muchas cosas que hacer. Las tres hijas de Antonia están ocupadas en la cocina. Reina sirve chocolate caliente, batido hasta formar una espesa espuma, en una taza que acomoda en medio de tres panes de muerto. Elia coloca, hábilmente, montones de tamales humeantes sobre un platón, mientras Altagracia pone cucharones del omnipresente mole negro sobre una pierna de guajolote. Todo esto se lleva a cabo con la dirección de Antonia, quien ha acomodado estratégicamente, minutos antes de la llegada de los muertitos, el chocolate, los tamales y el mole sobre el altar.

—No es que las cosas hayan sido siempre así—enfatiza Félix Mendoza, que preside la situación, con la mirada fija en la puerta, de espaldas a la pared y sentado cómodamente en la cabecera de la mesa que él mismo fabricó y, de acuerdo con la costumbre, ocupando el lugar más cercano al altar. Delgado, guapo, de bigote cuidado y pelo abundante, este hombre, de 76 años, ha vivido más cambios en los últimos 50 años que la mayoría de sus ancestros zapotecos, después de la llegada de los españoles. Félix recuerda—: Antes yo podía trabajar noche y día para terminar de tejer un sarape antes del Día de Muertos. Me lo llevaba a vender al mercado de Tlacolula, pero hubo ocasiones en que, después de estar todo el día bajo el rayo del sol, me regresaba a la casa sin haberlo vendido. ¡Ahí sí que nos desesperábamos! Si no lo colocaba, pues no teníamos nada que ofrecer a los difuntos: ¡ni mole, ni guajolote, ni siquiera chocolate! Ya lo único que me quedaba por hacer era venderlo a los mayoristas del pueblo, que en aquellos días me pagaban lo que ellos querían, a veces menos de la mitad de lo que valía el tejido, porque sabían que yo no tenía otra opción.

Arnulfo Mendoza Ruiz, mi esposo e hijo del difunto Emiliano, cuenta que, a principios de la década de 1950, antes del primer Día de Muertos que celebraron sus padres como matrimonio, Emiliano no pudo vender su único tapete para cubrir los gastos de la fiesta. Pero como era importante poner una ofrenda para los difuntos, subió al monte con su burro a recortar esa florecita tan aromática que solo se encuentra en la sierra aledaña a Teotitlán. Con la bestia cargada, la pareja recorrió los pueblos vecinos cambiando la recién cortada mercancía por pan, maíz y frijoles, regalos aceptables en aquellos tiempos difíciles.

Actualmente, el gran altar de Clara Ruiz, con su desbordante abundancia, es una verdadera hazaña de equilibrio casi circense, en la que se colocan platos de tamales, naranjas y manzanas. Sobre la orilla ha sido levantada una especie de pared, de aproximadamente 80 centímetros de alto, construida con panes de muerto y que parece un muro hecho de piedra sin argamasa. Es tan alta, que casi no puede verse la colección de santitos que cotidianamente presiden el altar de la familia Mendoza. Ocultas en sus nichos de madera, adornadas con flores de papel crepé, estas figuras son apenas visibles tras las montañas de pan dorado.

Clara tiene más de 60 años, pero su edad no es obstáculo para que se deslice hábilmente desde el cuarto del altar al patio y del patio a la cocina, concentrada en la atención a sus huéspedes. Llega como una aparición, cargando tazones de atole hirviente, chocolate y tamales en su punto. Después de la una de la tarde se dejan de servir tanto el atole como el chocolate, bebidas que se asocian con el desayuno, para ofrecer, en su lugar, mole de castilla, el guiso favorito de su difunto marido.

El aroma es a los espíritus lo que el gusto es para los vivos, de ahí que el embriagante perfume del copal y de las pequeñas flores silvestres sea un elemento esencial en cualquier altar de Teotitlán. Los intensos olores sacian a los muertos, mientras los vivos se complacen comiendo platos de rico mole con guajolote y tamales calientes de amarillo. Los habitantes del pueblo comentan a menudo, que, cuando pusieron el pan en la ofrenda, este era mucho más pesado que cuando lo retiraron, o que al llevarse la comida de ahí descubrieron que ya no poseía ningún sabor. Don Marino Vázquez, uno de los señores más respetados del pueblo, explica:

—Esto sucede porque los difuntos se alimentan con el espíritu de la comida, y se llevan su esencia; por eso, no la consumimos después.

—¡No solo ofrecemos comida a los angelitos; les compramos regalos también!—agrega Antonia.

Hay juguetes hechos especialmente para colocar en su ofrenda: borreguitos, guajolotes y ángeles de azúcar, decorados con betún de colores. Algunas familias ponen en sus altares, además, objetos miniatura: metates y prensas para hacer tortillas para las hijas, y martillos y azadones para los hijos.

—Cada año compramos tenates, molcajetes y jarritos nuevos. Claro que los usamos después, pero ellos se llevan los regalos, simbólicamente. Lo sabemos—explica—porque hay mujeres que han ido al río a lavar la ropa antes de que termine la fiesta, y ellas pueden atestiguar, a pesar del susto, que han visto a los muertitos irse del pueblo con sus burros, o llevando canastas bajo el brazo y costales al hombro cargados de ofrendas.

Dice don Marino que, si a los espíritus les gusta el mezcalito, entonces hay que hacer un brindis. El juez, el escanciador oficial del mezcal, primero sirve uno y lo salpica, en forma de cruz, sobre la ofrenda hecha en la base del altar. Una vez servido el mezcalito a los muertos, reparte varias copas, según la jerarquía, entre los visitantes que están sentados alrededor de la mesa.

EL REGRESO

Muchos habitantes del pueblo insisten en acompañar a sus difuntos hasta las puertas del camposanto. Otros, como Félix Mendoza y Antonia Ruiz, nunca van al cementerio el dos de noviembre. Félix tiene una justificación:

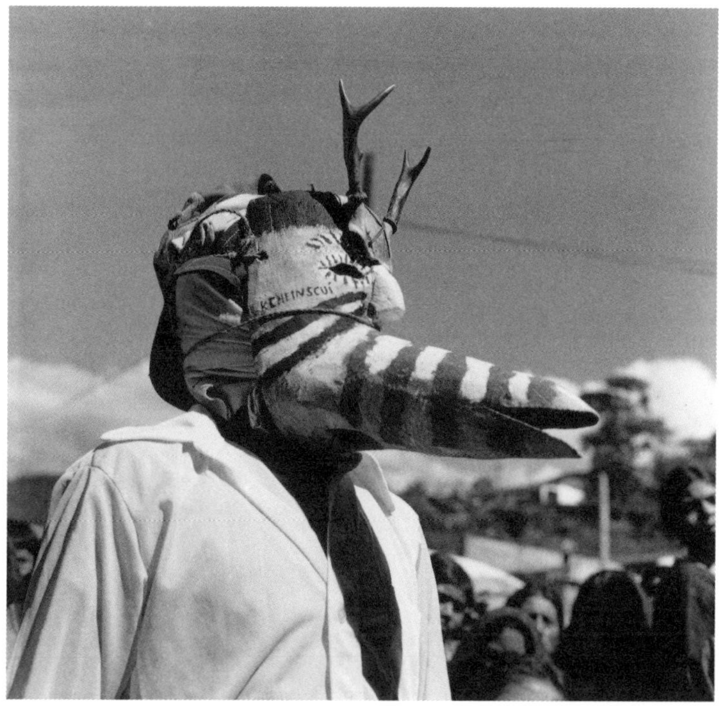

Ruth D. Lechuga. Tejorones Dance. Panixtlahuaca, Oaxaca. 1980.

—Sería como correr a alguien de la casa. Algunos espíritus se van despacio y otros se emborrachan, así que la fiesta sigue hasta el tres de noviembre.

El ruido ensordecedor de los cohetes que truenan desde el atrio de la iglesia y en las casas a las tres de la tarde es una señal para que los asistentes a la fiesta, vivos y muertos, sepan que ya es hora de que los difuntos comiencen los preparativos para el viaje de regreso.

Una visita al cementerio en la tarde del dos de noviembre ofrece un espectáculo inolvidable: pareciera que las tumbas danzan bajo el aluvión de flores, entre las que destacan enormes manojos de cresta de gallo color escarlata, brillantes flores de cempasúchil punteadas por delicados alcatraces. Muchas familias acuden al cementerio cargadas con frutas, botellas de mezcal y cartones de cerveza. Este es el momento de limpiar las tumbas, algunas de ellas incluso con agua y jabón. Se encienden las velas, y se hacen largos brindis en honor de aquellos que se ama y que se vuelven a marchar.

En estas fechas, los rayos luminosos de la tarde tibia hacen aún más intensos los colores de las flores. Mientras uno se acerca a la pequeña capilla del cementerio, los melancólicos cantos de los alabanceros, miembros de la muy respetada clerecía secular de Teotitlán, invitan a todos los presentes a disfrutar la dulce tristeza del momento.

La banda toca trenos emotivos y lentas marchas, las mismas tristes tonadas que acompañan a las procesiones funerarias, a las que todos los habitantes del pueblo han asistido en innumerables ocasiones, escoltando a los padres, a los hijos, a los padrinos o a los compadres en su último rito, el más importante, el viaje hacia el otro lado, que todos haremos algún día.

Así como los domingos se dedican generalmente al Señor, los lunes del mes de noviembre corresponden a los muertos. Durante este mes, el padre Rómulo, encargado de las necesidades espirituales de la gente de Teotitlán y de los pueblos vecinos, celebra los responsos, cada semana en el cementerio de un pueblo diferente.

En el lunes que corresponde a Teotitlán, incluso aquellos que se quedaron en sus casas con las almas que aún languidecen, van de visita al cementerio y entregan al padre una pequeña dádiva para que rece plegarias individuales en las tumbas de sus familiares desaparecidos. La exuberancia de las flores frescas y las plegarias, llenas de emoción, cantadas por los alabanceros, elevarán entonces nuestros sentidos hasta un estado de conciencia más profundo, en el que pareciera que se vive, por un instante, suspendido en algún lugar entre la tierra y el cielo. ◆

—Traducción de Verónica Murguía

Mary Jane Gagnier de Mendoza nació en Canadá, estudió música y artes visuales en el Vancouver Community College. Dirigió la curaduría de la exposición *Myth and Magic: Oaxaca Past and Present*, que se presentó en el Palo Alto Arts Center, en el Santa Cruz Museum of Art y en el Mexican Fine Arts Museum en Chicago. En *Artes de México* publicó, en la colección Libros de la Espiral, *Rituales de Armonía. Fiestas de Teotitlán del Valle*, en donde se da cuenta de las más importantes celebraciones de esta comunidad oaxaqueña.

VENGANZA PÓSTUMA

Fernando Benítez
Informante: Manuel Zugaide

Todos Santos es el más grande día para nosotros los indios. Los muertos chicos vienen al medio día del 31 y se van a las doce del día primero. A esa misma hora entran los muertos grandes y se retiran a la media noche del dos de noviembre.

Los llaman con campanas. Las campanas doblan veinticuatro horas sin parar, desde las doce del día último a las doce del día primero, y los campaneros se cambian por turnos constantemente. Para los muertos chicos se dobla en tono menor, y en tono mayor para los grandes.

Llegan los muertos y huelen el pan, los tamales, la fruta de las ofrendas, y se llevan la sustancia. Allí estaremos nosotros comiendo con ellos. No necesitan más. La sustancia les basta para vivir un año entero.

Los rezadores van de casa en casa rezando. Se les paga cincuenta centavos o un peso por mencionar el nombre de los diferentes familiares, y ellos y sus ayudantes participan en la comida de la ofrenda.

En Cihualtepec también se los llama con campanas, pero ya no es lo mismo. Digamos un ejemplo: yo dejé enterrada a mi jefa en La Joya y con gusto hacemos aquí el Todos Santos. No sabemos si los muertos pueden venir, si saben llegar hasta un lugar desconocido a pesar de que los llamen con rezos y campanas. Unos van todavía al viejo Ixcatlán o al viejo Soyaltepec. Nosotros tenemos a los difuntos pasados enterrados en el ejido, y además la gente está muy pobre y no sabe andar fuera de sus lugares.

Son los viejos y no los jóvenes los que todavía hablan con sus muertos en los cementerios. Les dicen: "Ruégale a Dios para que llegues pronto a la gloria". Otros dicen: "Yo aquí sufro sabiendo que me voy a morir en cualquier chico rato. Todos seguiremos el mismo camino". Solo hablan con ellos. No es que los vean; les hablan desde arriba y dicen que los muertos los oyen.

Los brujos visitan los cementerios con el fin de que los difuntos le llamen al fulano a quien piensan dañar. Entonces el fulano sueña un sueño pesado: que le tiran una puñalada, o que se cae en un barranco, o que se le incendia su casa, y si después de tener ese sueño monta a una mujer, ya estuvo que se enferma o puede morir cuando no lo asiste un buen curandero. El curandero debe defenderlo contra el brujo y le habla a Dios, para pedirle su curación: "Señor Jesucristo, no puede ser que un malo le corte así nomás la vida a un ser humano".

Y ya que hablamos de Todos Santos te voy a contar un cuento. Dice que a un señor se le murió su esposa y se volvió a casar. Pocos días antes de la fiesta, como estaba jodido y debía salir a trabajar fuera, le dijo a su nueva mujer:

—Mira, por favor, todo lo que le pongas a tus muertos en el altar se lo pones también a mi finada esposa. ¿Harás lo que te pido?

—Sí—contestó la mujer—, vete tranquilo. Yo haré lo que me pides.

—Cuando se llevan los platos y las frutas al altar es costumbre decir: "Esas naranjas son para ti, Juana", suponiendo que se llamara Juana la señora muerta, o "esta gallina" o "este café". ¿Has entendido?

—Sí, Pafnucio, creo que he entendido.

Bueno, pues la mujer calentó chica piedrota y cuando estaba roja la llevó al altar diciendo:

—Juana, aquí te pongo esta piedra para que te la comas.

El marido regresó esa misma noche y en el camino encontró a la difunta llorando y quejándose mucho.

—Ay, ay—gritaba la pobrecita—, me he quemado la boca.

Cuando el hombre entró a su casa, le preguntó a su mujer:

—¿Qué le pusiste en el altar a la finada mi esposa?

—Comida y fruta, como tú lo ordenaste.

Él entonces se acercó y vio el altar quemado. Comprendió que su mujer lo había engañado. Como era un hombre pacífico, nada más le dio sus buenos cuarterazos. ◆

Tomado de *Los indios de México*, Era, 1977.

FIESTA CONTRASTADA

LA OFRENDA, UN DERROCHE CREATIVO

Marta Turok

◆

La tradición ritual del Día de Muertos casi no se ha modificado en las comunidades indígenas, pero en las grandes urbes ha sufrido una metamorfosis, en la que los objetos sagrados se transforman en motivos de ornato o en banderas de la nacionalidad. ¿Qué piezas forman aún parte del diálogo que los hombres establecen con los dioses, y cuáles integran el universo decorativo?

◆

El olor y el color son inconfundibles, fuertes y penetrantes; llegan por ahí de octubre cuando la cosecha está a punto. Arriba a los mercados y tianguis la flor de cempasúchil como señal de que se acerca esa particular fecha en que recordaremos a los que han partido. Empiezan a montarse los puestos en los que se venden objetos destinados a la celebración del Día de Muertos: las rajitas de ocote con el copal, los incensarios y candelabros de barro, el papel picado . . .

En la conciencia colectiva—sobre todo urbana—aparece la figura, que con el tiempo ha logrado imponerse, de un mexicano que juega con la muerte, se burla de ella, la trata con irreverencia. Y esta imagen se yuxtapone con la de las comunidades indígenas, guardianas de la ritualidad, que viven esta ceremonia con sigilo y reverencia.

Las festividades que estos grupos consagran al Día de Muertos se celebran en familia; son íntimas, aunque poseen una dimensión colectiva, comunitaria. Como en todo ritual, se componen de varios actos: la recepción y despedida de las ánimas, la preparación y colocación de las ofrendas en el altar familiar, el arreglo de las tumbas, la velación en el camposanto y la celebración de oficios religiosos dentro de la liturgia católica. En esta ceremonia los parientes muertos regresan, en su estado de ánimas. Como vienen de un mundo parecido al de los vivos, se los recibe con una breve convivencia y se los despedirá con música, comida y recuerdos. No hay olor a muerto ni hay temor.

En muchos lugares, las ánimas de los muertos serán guiadas por el aroma de pétalos de flores—preferentemente de cempasúchil—que trazan una vereda desde la calle hasta el altar.

El repique de campanas, los rezos, la quema de copal y el encendido de velas anuncian su llegada, en tanto que el tronar de los cohetes o un nuevo repiquetear de campanas los despide. Aunque hay lugares, como la Huasteca hidalguense, en que las festividades del Día de Muertos tienen repercusiones hasta el Carnaval, cuando algunas ánimas que quedaron sueltas son capturadas con mecates (el *micahuitl*) para que regresen al más allá.

La ceremonia se prepara con antelación: se limpia el panteón, generalmente con tequio

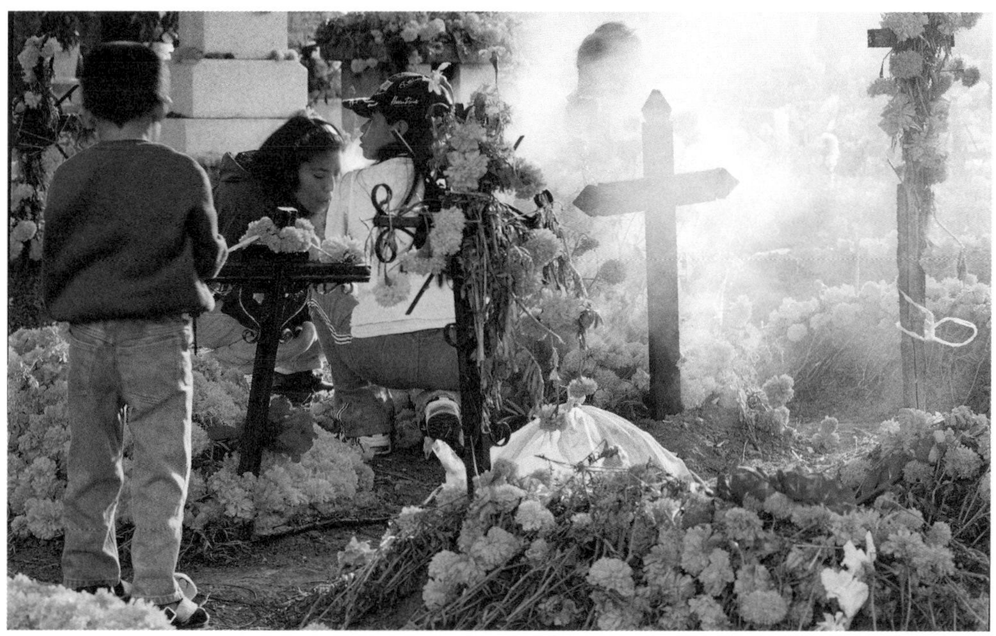

Paul Czitrom. Tetelcingo, Puebla. 1999.

y faenas comunales. Las familias se encargan del arreglo de los sepulcros particulares, aunque nunca falta el atavío de la tumba de algún muerto anónimo, o de algún otro que ha perdido a sus familiares, quienes son recordados porque en algún lado del mundo se los echa de menos.

Después del arreglo de la tumba viene la velación, el acompañar todo el día o toda la noche a los muertos, a veces compartiendo los alimentos, y con frecuencia llevándoles serenatas, o ejecutando danzas rituales con máscaras, de modo que la devoción ante el altar familiar se replica en el camposanto.

Ubicada junto al altar tradicional a los santos o en la estancia principal de la casa, la ofrenda muestra variaciones regionales, y a la vez comparte ciertos elementos formales. Una mesa o una repisa cubierta por un mantel, preferentemente blanco con bordados—que en la actualidad ha sido sustituido en ocasiones por uno de plástico estampado—, son la base de cualquier altar en la República mexicana. Para delimitar el espacio sagrado que será destinado a la ofrenda, se amarran a las patas de la mesa uno o varios arcos de caña, otate o carrizo, que son adornados con palmas, cucharilla, flores de cempasúchil, hojas de plátano e incluso frutas frescas, chiles secos y panes. Los altares más espectaculares se construyen a modo de catafalco con cajas o repisas cubiertas para ganar altura. En este tipo de trabajos destacan los pueblos nahuas de la Ciudad de México y la Huasteca, los purépechas de Michoacán y los zapotecos del valle de Oaxaca.

Delante o detrás de la mesa en ocasiones se cuelgan flores de papel, papeles picados o recortados, que acompañan a las fotografías de los parientes que han partido, generalmente

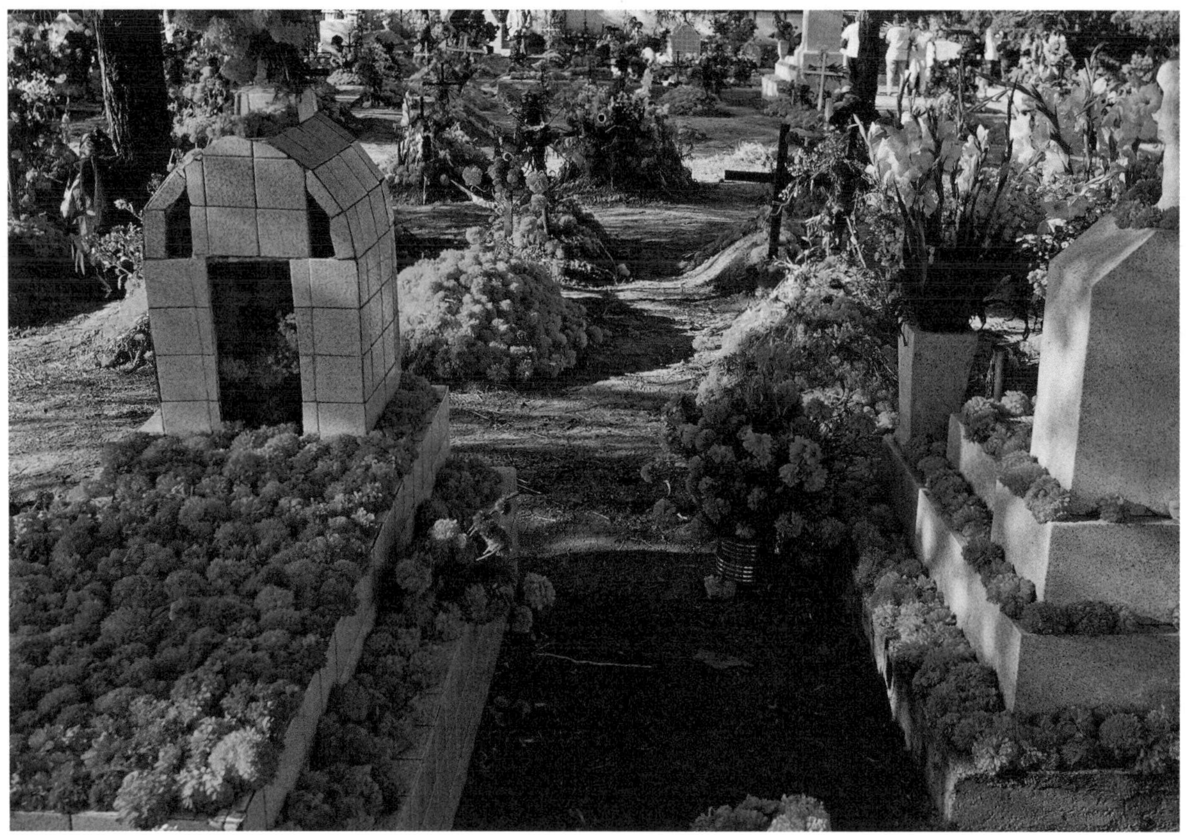

Paul Czitrom. Tetelcingo, Puebla. 1999.

colocadas entre varios floreros. Delante de la mesa, sobre un petate nuevo, pueden ponerse uno o más incensarios. También la ofrenda puede integrar alguna vestimenta u objeto emblemático del difunto, como un machete, un sombrero, una faja, juguetes para los niños, etcétera.

Entre el 30 de octubre y el primero de noviembre se habrán cocinado ya los platillos tradicionales que serán ofrendados a los muertos. Se acostumbra que todos los trastes de barro en los que sean ofrendados los alimentos sean nuevos, y que después pasen a conformar la vajilla cotidiana.

LOS OBJETOS RITUALES

En tanto sean producidos y utilizados exprofeso para la festividad, los objetos asociados con el culto a los muertos son considerados artesanía ritual. Muchos de ellos integran la ofrenda, cuya naturaleza efímera testifica el derroche creativo al que obliga la transformación anual. El sincretismo de esta fiesta es palpable sobre todo en las piezas que integran una ofrenda, aunque también puede apreciarse en tradiciones que fueron parte de los ritos europeos del siglo XVI, y que encontraron eco en las costumbres prehispánicas, como el ofrendar regalos a los muertos, el visitar los panteones para

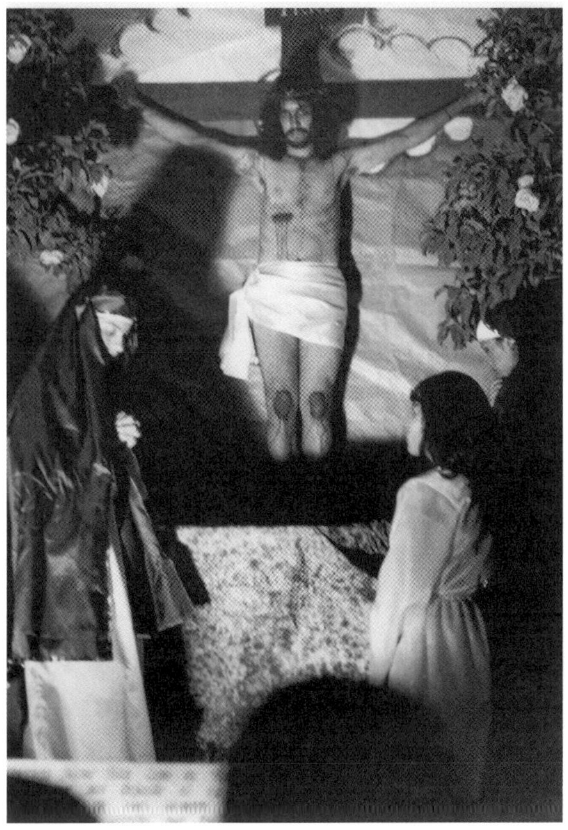

Ruth D. Lechuga. *Living Tombs, Fresh Dead.* Iguala, Guerrero. 1986.

compartir con los difuntos su efímero regreso y el trato especial a los niños fallecidos.

En cuanto a los objetos, resulta interesante, por ejemplo, que en el *Códice magliabecchiano* aparezca una página que muestra enramadas de papel con diseños probablemente pintados con *ulli* o hule, antecedente directo de las enramadas de papel picado que se utilizan actualmente y cuya influencia es una combinación de elementos prehispánicos, chinos y franceses. En la actualidad, la manufactura de papel picado se ha desarrollado como tradición en San Salvador Huixcolotla, Puebla, así como en Uruapan, Michoacán y Tláhuac, en el Distrito Federal, aunque en muchas otras localidades se produce de manera menos comercial.

En Metepec, Estado de México, y Santa Fe de la Laguna, Michoacán, los candelabros e incensarios son elaborados con un barniz o greda color negro. En Ocotlán, Oaxaca, se realizan de barro cocido y las figuras que los adornan son pintadas con tierras y pigmentos color blanco y azul cobalto. Los incensarios llevan una corona de figuras antropomorfas con los brazos en alto y enlazados, y a los candelabros se les aplica, en pastillaje, una calavera adosada al tubo y base, lo que nos recuerda una pieza prehispánica: la vasija trípode, de uso ceremonial, estilo mixteco, encontrada en Zaachila, Oaxaca. Esta, hecha de barro anaranjado, tiene adosada a un costado una figura atribuida al dios Mictlantecuhtli en forma de esqueleto, cuya cabeza puede girar sobre el cuello, y cuya expresión oscila entre lo macabro y lo juguetón. En el vecino pueblo de Atzompa, Oaxaca, los incensarios y candelabros son de barniz verde, y se decoran con pequeños rostros de querubines. En Huaquechula e Izúcar de Matamoros, Puebla, los incensarios son de barro cocido con engobe blanco, y son decorados con anilinas de diversos colores; lucen un querubín y dos flores de molde sobre el borde, en tanto que los candelabros llevan adicionalmente una figura de san Miguel Arcángel. Las velas son decoradas con escamas y elaboradas figuras de flores y hojas, o con simples listones de colores que serpentean diagonalmente.

El amaranto mezclado con tamal formaba una pasta llamada *tzoalli*, con la cual los aztecas moldeaban figuras de algunas deidades que se utilizaban en las fiestas y ceremonias, algunas vinculadas con la muerte. En la época colonial esta masa fue posiblemente remplazada por panes de harina de trigo con figuras antropomorfas, o con rostros de azúcar hechos con molde, que desde entonces se distribuían en las ofrendas del Día de Muertos.

DEL RITO AL MITO: DE LA RECREACIÓN POPULAR A LA INSTALACIÓN ARTÍSTICA

Al comparar las tradiciones rurales indígenas e incluso las mestizas urbanas del interior de la República con las de la Ciudad de México, nos percatamos de que en esta urbe se ha desarrollado una nueva visión del Día de Muertos que se extiende hacia otros centros dentro y fuera del país. Evidentemente, en este giro jugó un papel importante José Guadalupe Posada. En cercana asociación con la obra de este grabador, encontramos "la calavera" como sátira literaria, llena de ingenio, utilizada como recurso de censura hacia los políticos y las figuras públicas.

El ritual de convivir con los muertos, en este contexto, tiende a desacralizarse. Otra evolución digna de tomarse en cuenta es la que se vive en aquellos pueblos, como Mixquic en la Ciudad de México, o la isla de Janitzio en Pátzcuaro, Michoacán, donde el fervor se mezcla con el turismo masivo. Los habitantes de estos lugares han aprendido, paulatinamente, que también es negocio conservar la tradición.

En el ámbito de la expresión artesanal popular y del montaje de ofrendas se produce una explosiva resemantización que convierte el culto a la muerte en un culto al espectáculo. Debemos reconocer que desde hace unos años la imagen urbanizada de la muerte—la de las calacas, las calaveras y ciertas ofrendas—ha perdido sentidos rituales para recrearse a sí misma. La artesanía ritual se convierte en arte popular decorativo, para ser coleccionado y exhibido. Numerosos artesanos—como los hermanos Alfonso y Tiburcio Soteno, de Metepec, Estado de México; la familia Linares, de la Ciudad de México; Alfonso Castillo, de Izúcar de Matamoros; Roberto Ruiz, de Oaxaca y Ciudad Nezahualcóyotl—comenzaron a hacer figuras de calaveras a partir del interés de los compradores y promotores en las décadas de 1950 y 1960, lo que en ningún modo demerita la creatividad y el gusto con el que realizan sus obras.

La ofrenda también ha cobrado nuevos valores: se ha convertido en un símbolo por excelencia para artistas y para el sistema educativo. Por una parte, deviene en instalación artística y en *performance*, y es llevada a museos y centros culturales de México y otros países; por la otra, se convierte en las escuelas en un medio de reafirmación de los valores culturales de México, para contrarrestar al anglosajón *Halloween*.

Indudablemente, la fiesta del Día de Muertos es un testimonio de que vivimos una época de transformaciones entre el rito y la mitificación de algo que quiere ser definido como arquetipo nacional. ◆

Marta Turok es antropóloga por la Universidad de Tufts, con estudios en Harvard y en la UNAM. Preside la Asociación Mexicana de Arte y Cultura Popular (AMACUP) desde 1989. Ha publicado, entre otros títulos, *¿Cómo acercarse a la artesanía?*, *El caracol púrpura, una tradición milenaria*, *Fiestas mexicanas* y *Living Traditions: Mexican Popular Arts*. Fue cocuradora, junto con Mark Winter, de la exposición *El sarape de Saltillo: Enigma y huella*, presentada en el Museo Franz Mayer.

Las flores en la ofrenda

Cada especie de flor, además de agradar al olfato y a la vista de las almas, cumple una función: el cempasúchil es como el fuego, grato para quienes en vida no pecaron e insufrible para quienes pecaron en demasía, porque les quema, les molesta, y de esta manera no olvidan sus culpas ni sus castigos; las gladiolas, por el contrario, atenúan el fuego, lo templan; las flores de terciopelo, que son de color morado, representan la pasión y el sufrimiento de Jesucristo; las xochicalaveras, orquídeas moradas que exhiben en el pistilo la forma de una calavera diminuta, son como un espejo en el que las ánimas ven reflejada su condición; las nubes, blancas, múltiples y diminutas, sirven para que las ánimas descansen y reposen en su blancura. El incienso, por su olor penetrante, llega hasta las ánimas para notificarles que son esperadas para que gocen su fiesta. Las velas y veladoras tienen el fuego que las ilumina y da calor. El mantel es necesario para que puedan alimentarse, compartir y gustar de la ofrenda con limpieza. El petate es para que los vivos y las ánimas se hinquen a rezar frente a la ofrenda. Los vasos de agua son para que beban y se refresquen al llegar a sus casas, porque los difuntos vienen de un camino lleno de polvo.

Tomado de *31 de octubre Yotacico Miccailhuitl: ya llegamos a la fiesta de los muertos.*

FIESTA AGRÍCOLA

DE SEMILLAS Y MUERTOS

Gabriela Olmos

◆

En esta lectura simbólica de la tradición del Día de Muertos, la autora propone una osada hipótesis: en este culto late uno anterior, que liga la muerte con la fertilidad de la tierra; de ahí que la ceremonia actual conserve algunos rasgos de los ritos agrícolas que se celebraban en ocasión de la cosecha.

◆

Desde que el ser humano descubrió la agricultura, han existido pueblos cuyos cultos ligan los ritos de la muerte con los de la fertilidad de la tierra. En su *Tratado de historia de las religiones*, Mircea Eliade cuenta entre ellos la conmemoración india de los muertos, que coincide con la fiesta de la cosecha, y un culto antiguo, cuyo escenario eran los países nórdicos, que asociaba a la muerte con la ceremonia de la vegetación.

Por su estructura, podríamos inscribir la fiesta mexicana del Día de Muertos, que también ocurre tras la cosecha—entre septiembre y octubre—, y antes del invierno, en esta tradición de ritos que hermanan a los muertos con las semillas, entre otras cosas porque ambos comparten la misma ubicación física—al sembrar una semilla, ¿no profanamos los hombres esa tierra simbólica que es el espacio natural de los muertos?—y porque, además, comparten el estado larvario: ambos vienen de la vida y participan de esa condición intermedia en que la vida sigue latiendo. De esta manera, en la celebración del primero y dos de noviembre en las regiones campesinas de nuestro país, podemos encontrar reminiscencias más antiguas a la llegada de la tradición judeocristiana e incluso al esplendor de las civilizaciones precolombinas. En los sustratos más profundos de la fiesta del Día de Muertos puede leerse una ceremonia proveniente de aquellos tiempos en que nacieron los cultos agrícolas, en los que la muerte está vinculada con la posibilidad de renovación.

¿Cuál es el sentido de la llegada de los muertos en estas fechas a los pueblos mexicanos? A decir de Eliade, es en el tiempo sagrado—el tiempo del ritual y de la plegaria, que es nuestra forma de dialogar con los dioses—, donde la historia humana puede abolirse para empezar nuevamente. Pero la recreación del mundo sólo podrá efectuarse repitiendo el gesto divino de la creación, que comienza con la separación del orden del caos y es seguida por la instauración de un equilibrio cósmico. Y esto es lo que sucede en la fiesta.

¿Cómo penetrar en el tiempo sagrado sin ofender a los dioses? Es necesaria una preparación ritual que en los pueblos mexicanos comienza unos días antes de la llegada de los muertos, con la restauración y adorno de los cementerios, la preparación de la ofrenda—ofrendar los frutos de las semillas a los muertos, ¿no será ésta una manera de resarcir la ofensa hecha el año anterior al haber penetrado en su espacio para sembrar?—e, incluso, en algunos casos con la purificación ritual.

En su estudio sobre los chatinos de Oaxaca, los antropólogos Miguel Bartolomé y Alicia Barabas cuentan que, en Yolotepec, la celebración de Todos Santos comienza con un novenario que inicia una semana antes del primero de noviembre y que implica un ritual en el que se prepara la ofrenda, se adornan altares dedicados al sol y a la luna, para que estos vigilen el sano retorno de los muertos a la tierra, la gente se baña en el río—quizá un acto de purificación—y se prepara el altar que recibirá a los visitantes. Estas acciones—junto con algunos viajes al cementerio y ciertos preparativos municipales—son denominados "cuidado de los días". ¿Y para qué cuidar los días, sino para evitar la aniquilación, pues—recordemos—el escenario al que se enfrentan los campesinos en los días próximos al invierno guarda alguna relación con la muerte de la tierra? Estamos ante una ceremonia que trasciende el encuentro de los vivos y los muertos. El sol y la luna, quizá los responsables del equilibrio cósmico, han sido convocados por medio de sus altares.

A la preparación ritual sucede la repetición de la lucha primigenia. A decir de Eliade, la llegada de los muertos representa la noche cósmica. En las tinieblas, las formas se pierden, los contornos se desvanecen, reina el caos. Las almas de los muertos que visitan a los vivos son indicios de que las fronteras han sido anuladas y sustituidas por la confusión. En varios sitios de México, como en la Huasteca, hay danzas de enmascarados que en el contexto universal pueden representar el alma de los antepasados,

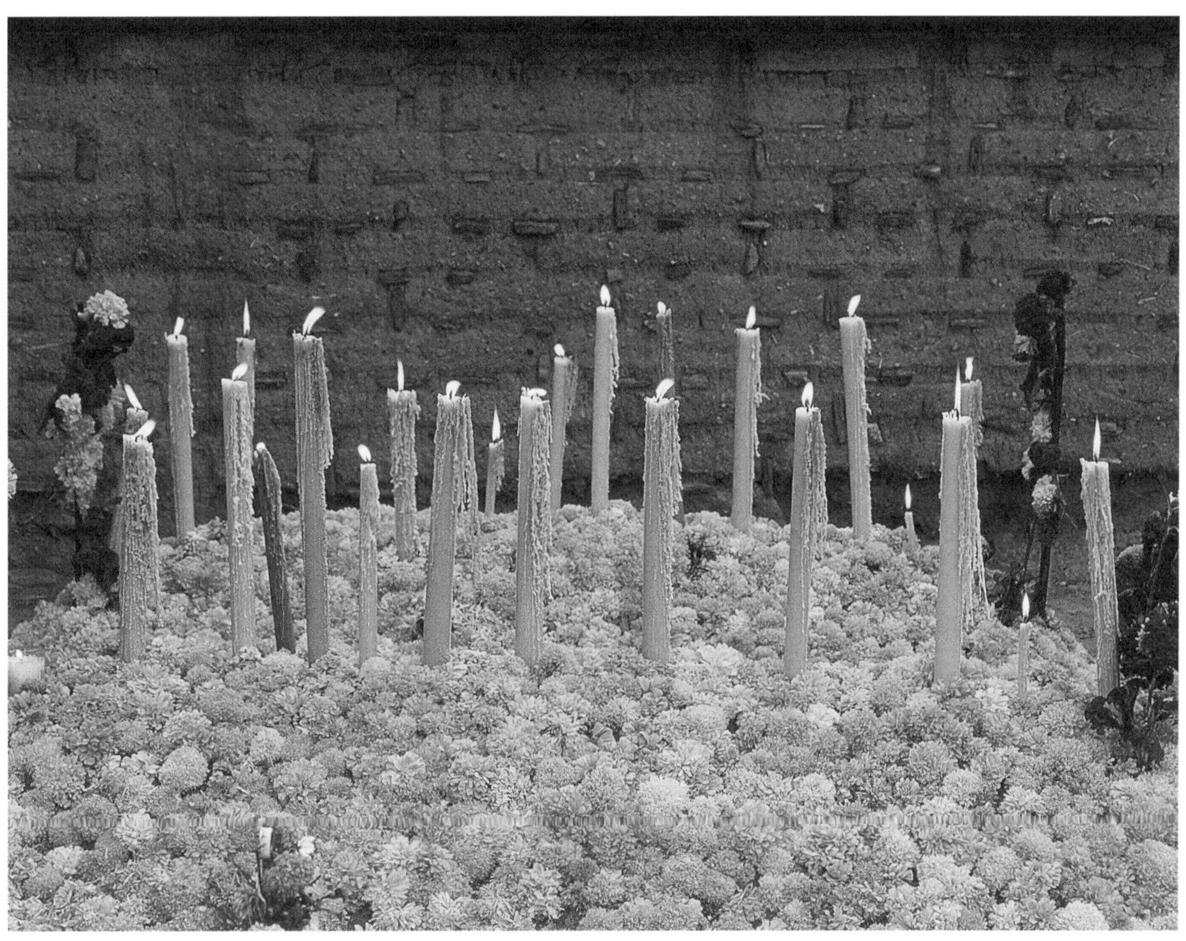

Paul Czitrom. Tetelcingo, Puebla. 1999

y por eso se los suele llamar "viejos", o "*huehues*", porque en náhuatl este término alude a los ancianos. La comunicación entre el mundo de los vivos y el de los muertos denota que el equilibrio ha sido roto; estamos en el espacio del desenfreno, de la embriaguez, de la inversión del orden. En su estudio sobre los huicholes, Fernando Benítez reproduce las palabras de un informante, quien asegura que el mundo de los muertos es el "mundo de al revés".

Aquí se puede trazar otro vínculo con las fiestas agrícolas: la recreación del caos primigenio es vivida por las civilizaciones arcaicas como un espacio de excepción, de orgía, que tiene una liga con la fertilidad, como las bacanales de la época clásica, celebradas tras la cosecha de la vid, fiestas que, en palabras de Friedrich Nietzsche, también "tienen el significado de redención del mundo y de días de transfiguración". En estos momentos toma forma el poder irrefrenable de la naturaleza, y los seres humanos—diría Eliade—se transforman simbólicamente en semillas, es decir, recobran ese estado larvario en el que se hallan prestos a engendrar. Quizá las alusiones sexuales de las danzas de *huehues* de la Huasteca o de tejorones en Yaitepec, Oaxaca, que relata Ruth D. Lechuga, sean remanentes del sentido orgiástico de esta festividad.

El ritual termina con la reinstauración del orden cósmico, con la repetición de aquel gesto divino de separar la luz de las tinieblas. Se despide a los muertos que parten agradecidos por sus ofrendas, la mayoría, salvo los ofendidos a los que se ha olvidado, que juran negar los favores de la regeneración de la tierra a los autores de la afrenta. Y es que ofender a los muertos es garantizar la muerte definitiva de la comunidad que, para las sociedades arcaicas, vinculadas a la conciencia del destino colectivo, implica la aniquilación de la vida.

Entonces tiene lugar la repetición del gesto definitivo de creación. En la fiesta de muertos en Acatlán, Puebla, esto ocurre en la danza de tecuanes, en cuyo episodio final se mata al tigre. No es un tigre cualquiera quien ha muerto: es Tezcatlipoca, quien en el universo prehispánico representa a las fuerzas nocturnas.

Cuenta Benítez, en *Los indios de México*, que, entre los chamulas como entre los coras, la ceremonia del Día de Muertos es seguida por el cambio de mayordomía. Esto también sucede entre los chatinos, y está documentado por Miguel Bartolomé y Alicia Barabas. Presenciamos el inicio de una nueva era. Eliade asegura que "toda entronización tiene el valor de una re-creación o regeneración del mundo", y cita dos ejemplos que confirman esta idea: entre los fidjanos se llama "creación del mundo" a la instalación de un nuevo jefe, y los emperadores chinos, al subir al poder, creaban un nuevo calendario y abolían el orden viejo para instaurar uno nuevo.

Con el equilibrio cósmico restablecido, está preparado el mundo para el renacer a la vida. Pasado el invierno se sembrarán las semillas, y los muertos, que vivirán junto a ellas, procurarán que germinen y den frutos.

Desde esta perspectiva, la ceremonia del Día de Muertos de los pueblos indios de México no es, como se dice superficialmente, un tributo a la muerte, sino a la muerte y a su vínculo con la vida, a la posibilidad de renovación, que aún es palpable en las tradiciones de estos lugares porque sus habitantes viven menos la muerte individual como el aniquilamiento absoluto. A decir de Philippe Ariès, los hombres de las ciudades asistimos, desde finales de la Edad Media, a la individualización de la muerte. Morir es, cada vez más, una tragedia personal. El "yo muero" ha sustituido al "todos moriremos" anterior, cuyos latidos todavía se alcanzan a percibir en el mundo campesino.

Quizá por eso la risa nerviosa del Día de Muertos de las ciudades es sustituida en los pueblos por el sentido de hacer comunidad, de perdonar las faltas y de compartir el alimento, actos que generalmente suceden a la reinstauración del nuevo orden. Es la colectividad lo que garantiza la perpetuación: cuando uno muere, queda la descendencia. ◆

Gabriela Olmos es escritora y editora. Es subdirectora de *Artes de México*, donde ha publicado *El zopilote y la chirimía*, *Pintores mexicanos de la A a la Z* y *Con los ojos cerrados, sueños de los niños indígenas*, entre otros títulos. En 2009 fue nombrada la candidata de México al Astrid Lindgren Memorial Award, uno de los más importantes premios de literatura infantil del mundo.

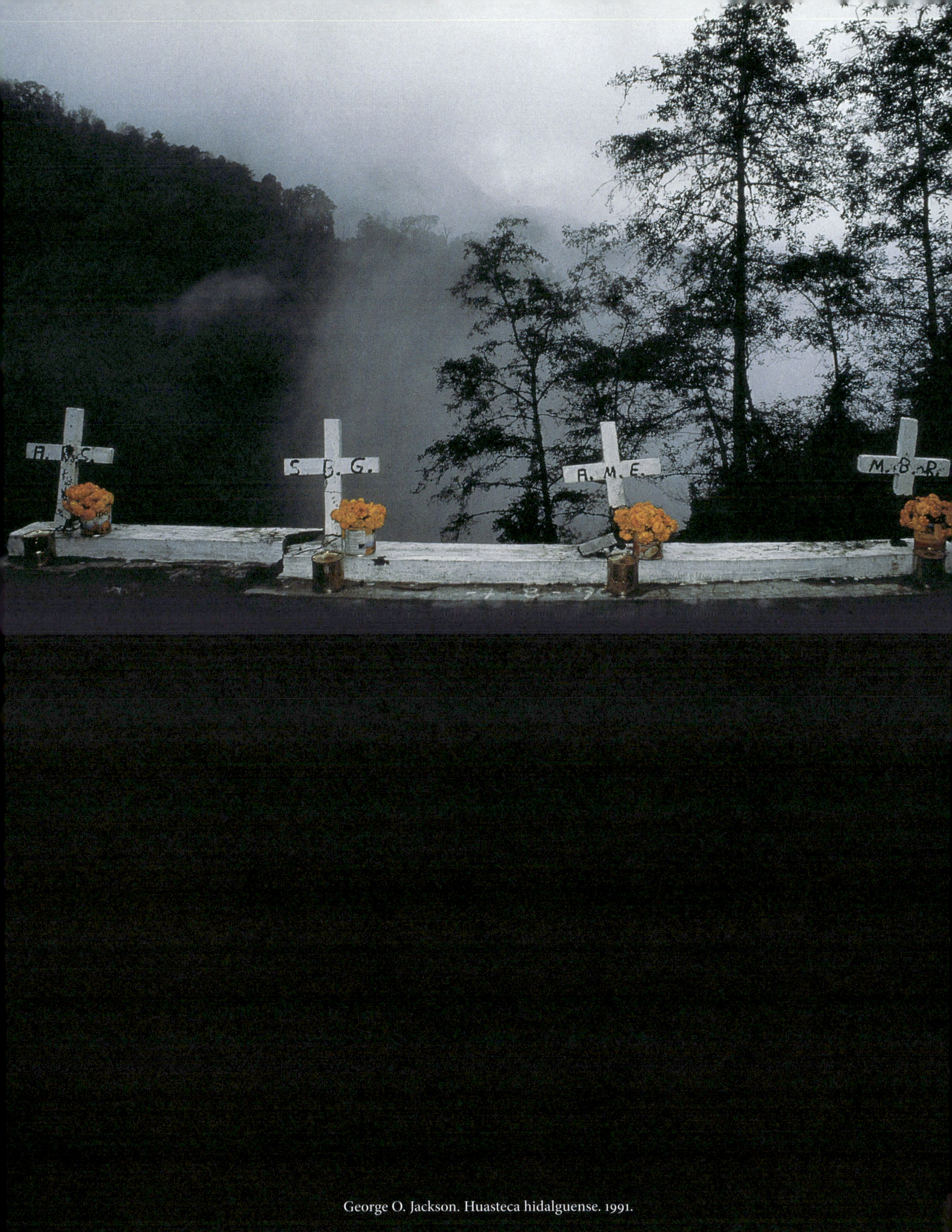

George O. Jackson. Huasteca hidalguense. 1991.

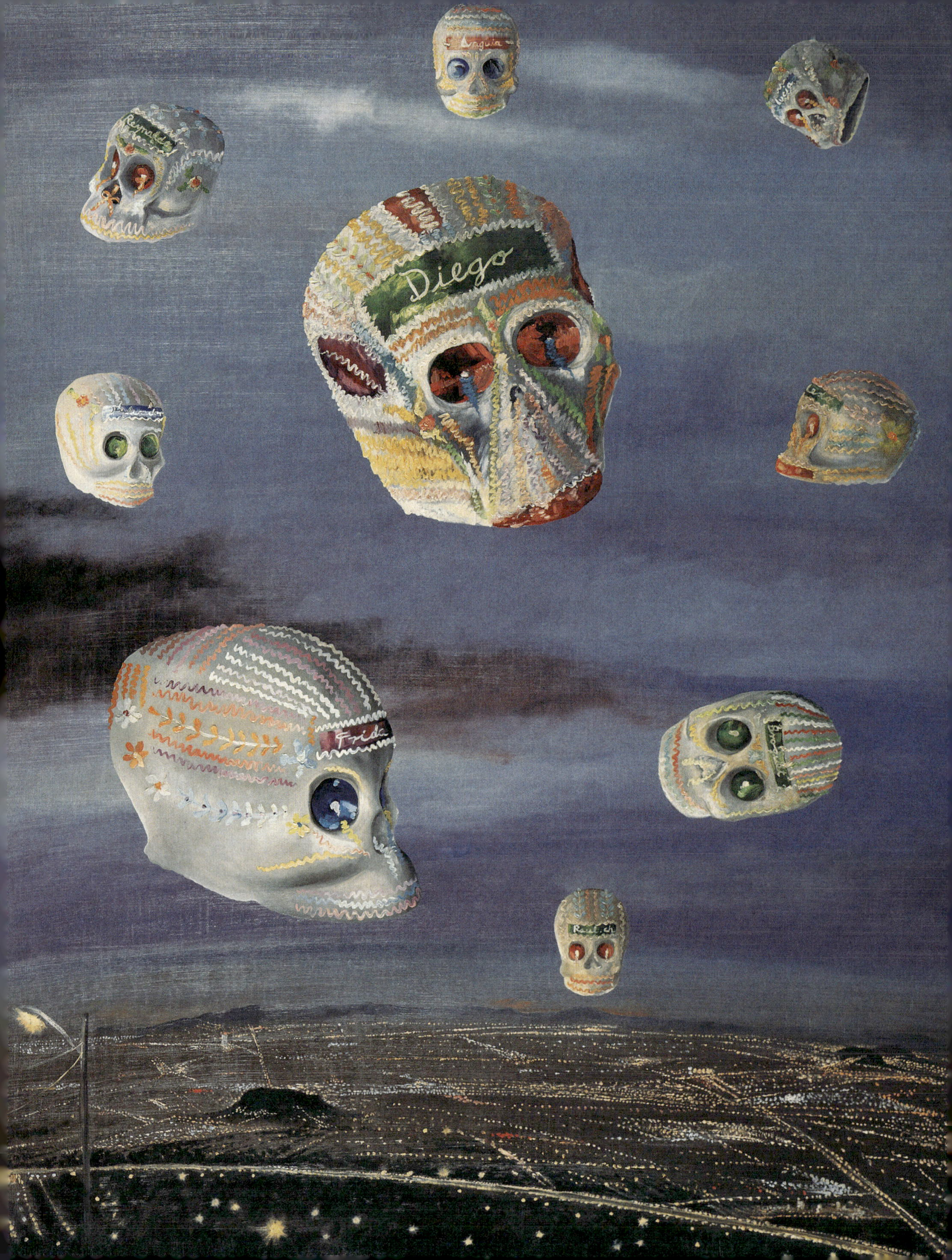
Diego
Frida

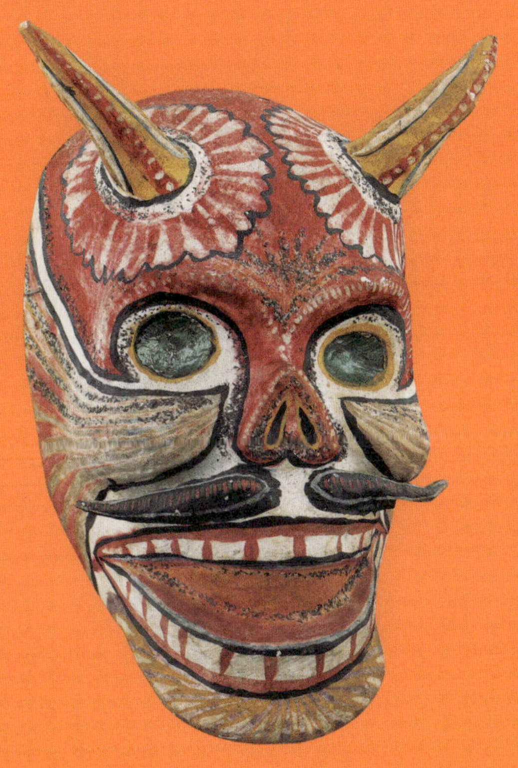

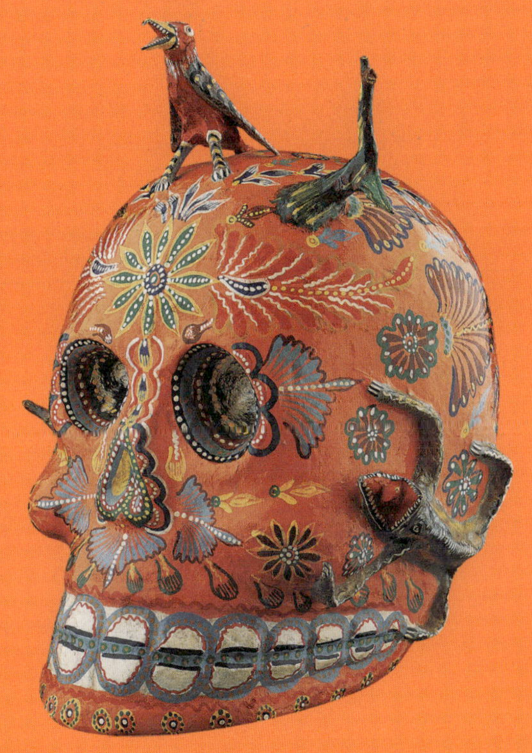

PART II

SKULLS AND LAUGHTER

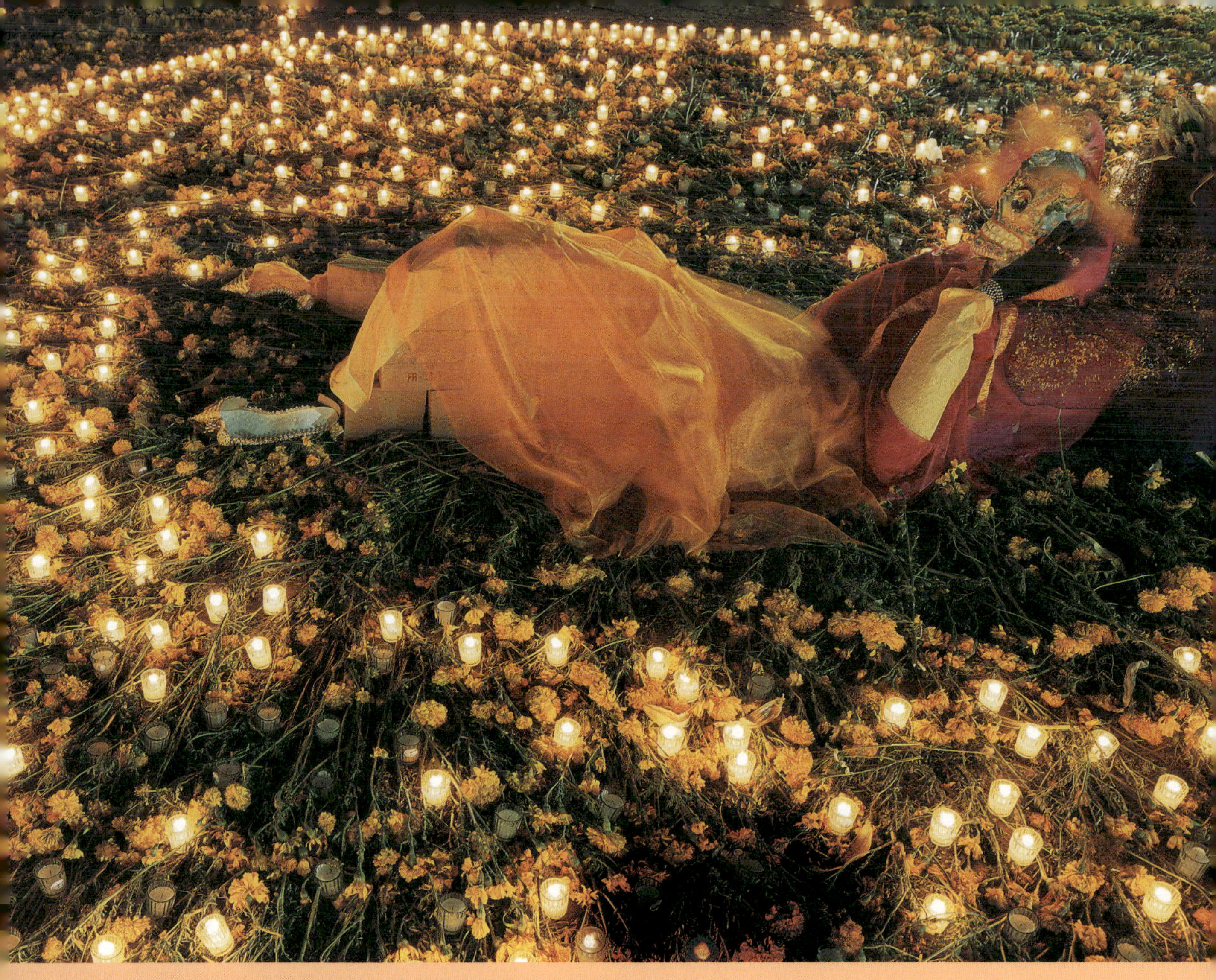

Day of the Dead offering in the Plaza de Santo Domingo. Mexico City, 2002. • **PREVIOUS PAGE:** Linares family. Decorative skulls. Mexico City, 1980 and 1985. Bound and painted paper. Ruth D. Lechuga Collection of Popular Art / Franz Mayer Museum.

FROM RITUAL TO FESTIVAL

◆◆◆◆◆

THE DAY OF THE DEAD IN THE NINETEENTH CENTURY

1763–1764
ALFEÑIQUE FOR ALL SOULS' DAY

Francisco de Ajofrín

◆◆◆◆◆

Before All Souls' Day, they sell countless sugar-paste figures of sheep, rams, and so forth. Called offerings, they are a compulsory gift for neighborhood children. Other items sold are coffins, tombs, and numerous figurines from every religion, bishops, and knights. These are ostentatiously displayed along the roofed walkways around markets, and draw a surprisingly long stream of members of the Mexico City élite the day before All Souls' Day [. . .]. With exquisite workmanship, common people make all these figures and knickknacks, as well as other more substantial items, in a very short time and for a small price. But if they receive a special order, they ask for money in advance (common for all official dealings in America), and then either do not do the work—meaning the buyer loses what he has given them—or they do it poorly, late, and at a high price. So, people lose their patience. ◆

Diario del viaje a la Nueva España

—Translated by Carole Castelli

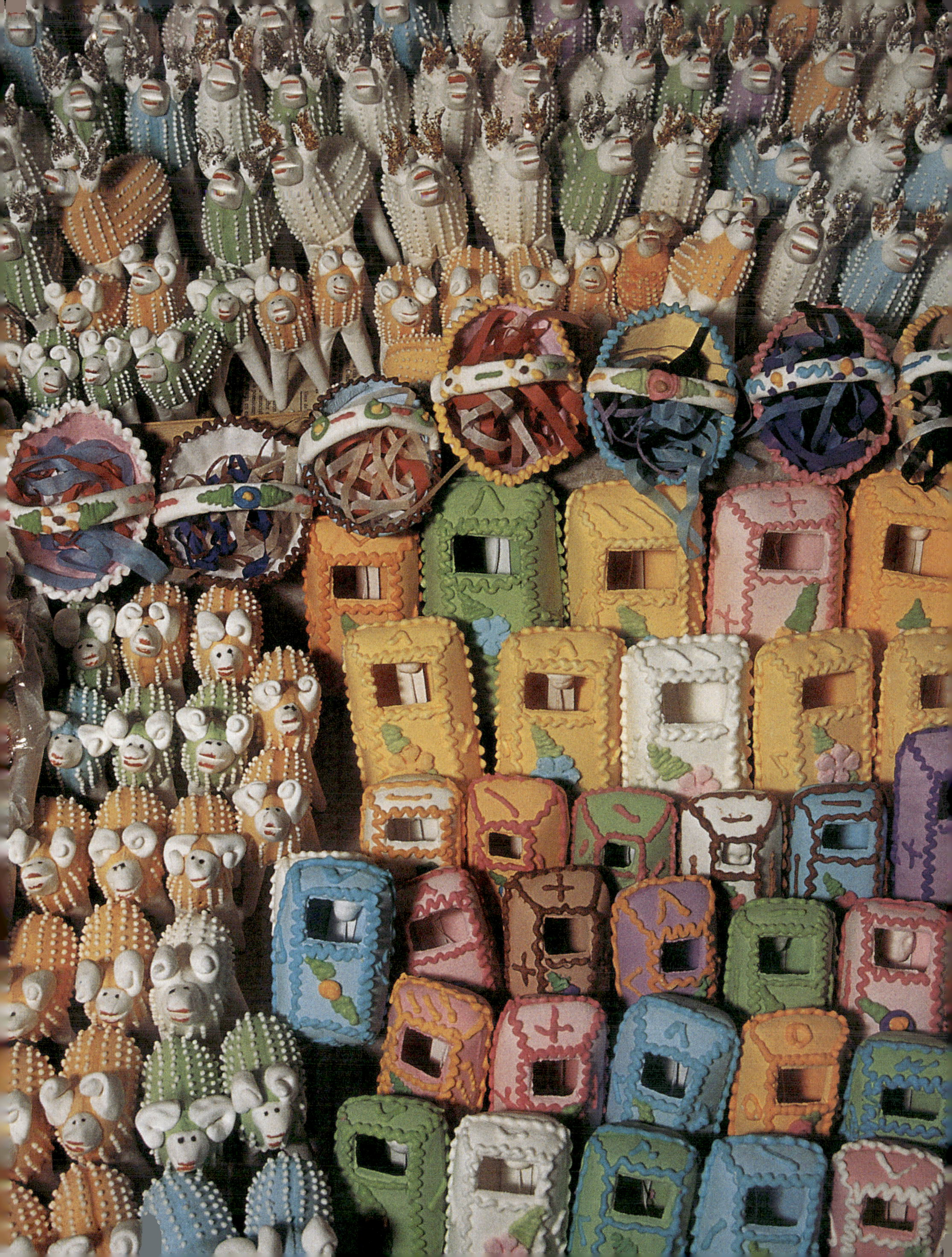

1878
CITY GRAVEYARDS ON DAY OF THE DEAD

Guillermo Prieto

◆◆◆◆◆

I remember the gloomy tolling of the death knell that from the first pale light of dawn heralded the day devoted to the memory of death, to those mortal remains which have no special name and which lived with us.

In many houses, lamps and wax candles were lit as if to rekindle with greater intensity memories of loved ones within the intimacy of the home.

Wailing and weeping emanated from every corner; people made tombstone decorations with tenderness, diligence, and loving care: hand-carved candles, crêpe flowers, wreaths, ornaments, anything suggestive of endearment or adulation when honoring the tombs.

It was for the populace a true day of sorrow and pleasure.

Weeping for the deceased, burying bones, buying fruit, laying out the offering, promenading in the plaza; these were the multiple pleasures and attractions of a day of tears.

Pastry shops and bakeries sold—still do—enormous quantities of Day of the Dead buns with their symmetrical pattern and powdered sugar sprinkled on top. De rigueur were such traditional items as hot fruit punch, a delectable jelly made of hawthorn berries, and *alfeñiques*, sugar-paste figures which appealed to every social class.

The jelly and the *alfeñiques* came in all kinds of special presentations, and there were also the famous hawthorn berries themselves. The success of the jelly lay in its transparency, shown off by placing the dedicatory card on the platter under it, so it could be read through the jelly.

Alfeñiques, particularly those of the San Lorenzo Convent, were justifiably famous. They came in the shape of pyramids, obelisks, rocks, pretty scenes such as riverscapes, and other quirky shapes, and generated a sizeable trade among poor people. Moreover, in private homes *alfeñiques* and sugar skulls supplied an excuse and the raw materials for family parties.

From the middle class on down, strapping young girls, fresh-skinned and ruddy, in loose tunics with the sleeves rolled up, would pour syrup on

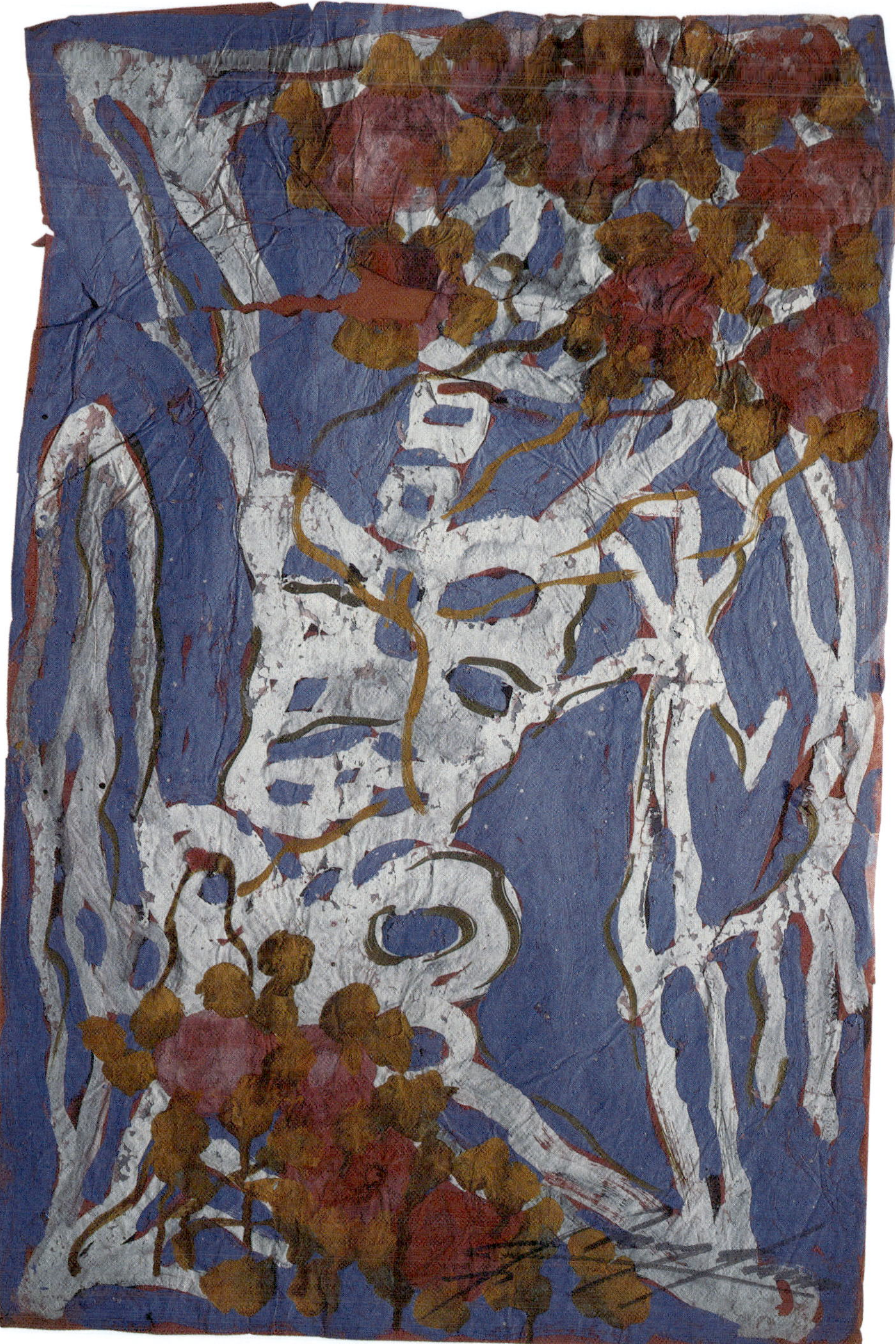

cold plates to harden it, then tear off chunks to knead and mold them like skillful sculptors into hens and sheep, mules and toys. All this amid the hustle and bustle, to and fro, and the little filching hands of bouncing children who were the life and soul of the fiesta.

Children, servants, acquaintances, and endless believers in the obligatory loan thought it their right to ask everyone for spare change. This extraordinary contingent would descend upon the market to convert their earnings into funeral processions of tiny figures with chickpeas for heads, or figures of dead people, scribes, tombs, funeral pyres, and other assorted offerings.

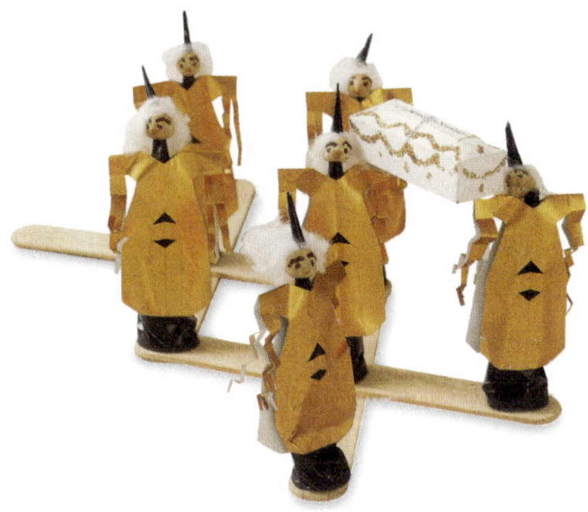

Six-figure procession of the dead. Paper bodies, decorated chickpea heads.

On the gastronomical side, some foods were compulsory. Primarily for the working classes there were the very popular pastry "heads" straight from the oven. The best bakeries were Necatitlán, La Retama, Nana Rosa, Don Toribio, outside the pulque bars La Garrapata and Tío Juan Aguirre, and around the Santiago Tlatelolco cemetery which reestablished its repute as a burial ground during the first cholera outbreak in 1833.

The upper classes who had servants to assist in their preparations chose turkey in mole sauce, and death figurines made of bread or of chacualole (pumpkin cooked in raw sugar syrup). These were the dishes they placed on the tombs, among the candles, abundant fruits and candies that made up the offering.

An offering, particularly among indigenous people, was, and is, considered a lucrative benefit for the Church, curates, and sacristans.

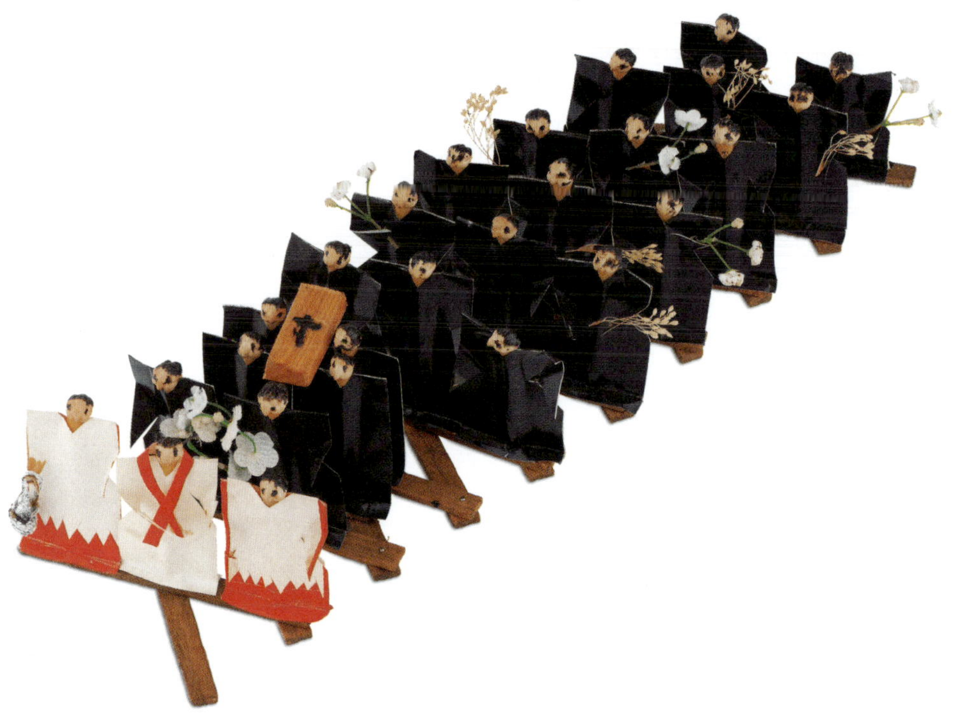

Twenty-six-character funeral procession arranged in a scissored configuration. Luster paper bodies, decorated chickpea heads. Guanajuanto, 1993. Ruth D. Lechuga Collection of Popular Art / Franz Mayer Museum.

When the weeping subsided and the shadows lengthened, the owls around the church pounced upon the offerings to the dead, and the plentiful booty gave pleasure to those whose soul was still in their body in this valley of tears. [. . .]

The Church could not remain indifferent to the manifestations of mourning. At the entrance of each church, scattered around the sanctuary and inside the cemeteries, tables stood covered with dirty black cloths dribbled with wax. On each sat a yellow skull, a holy water basin, the aspergillum, and behind it, the priest's heavy chair and the characteristic *tololoche*, or Mexican bass guitar, its thin scraggy neck rising above the mercantile-mortuary apparatus.

The charge in these abundant collections was simple enough: half a real for a recited response, double that for a response sung to the accompaniment of the decrepit tololoche.

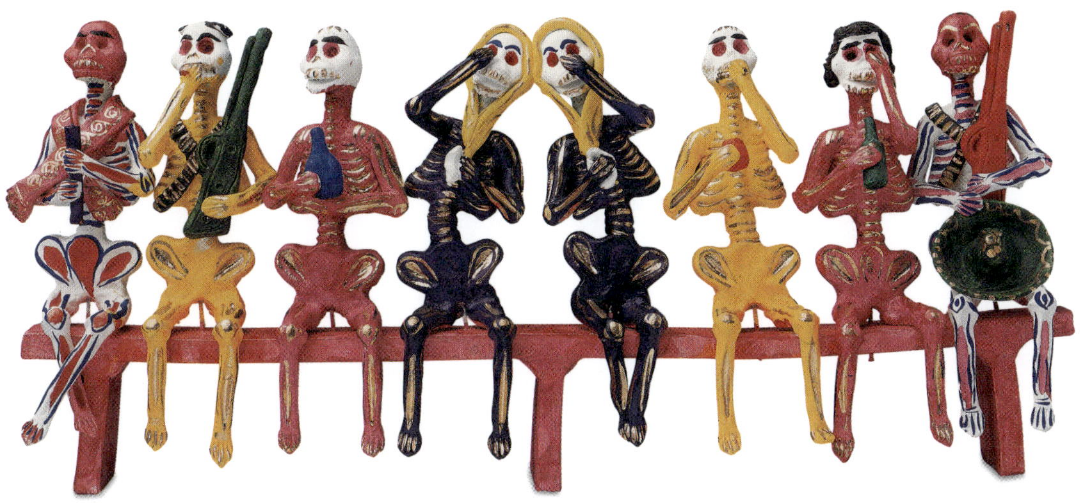

PAGES 150–51: Pedro Soteno. Waltz. Modeled, molded, fired, and painted clay. Metepec, State of Mexico, 1986. Ruth D. Lechuga Collection of Popular Art / Franz Mayer Museum.

All alms were deposited in the holy water basin. Under the table were one or two pitchers of water to replace the raw material for the prayers and singing, while the holy water basin was there to be filled and emptied many times. In a working-class cemetery, as much as six or eight thousand pesos were collected in responses alone.

In these vast non-aristocratic graveyards, the afternoon and evening would bring orgies, disorder, dreadful fights and crying; the flirting, blaspheming, and bloodletting presented scenes to which we fortunately do not sink now, even though we are said to have reached the absolute depths of corruption. [. . .]

The night was devoted to recitations of rosaries for the souls, or ecclesiastical patrols led by their singers and a *tololoche*, praying and dispensing responses right and left in the streets.

The many voices were the attraction of the procession, a kind of funereal serenade. The amount of care and vanity invested in it were measured by proclaiming the names of the departed beneficiaries, letting it be understood in the neighborhood that those poor dead people would not spend the night without their own kind of fandango.

Scorned lovers or quarrelsome married couples frequently paid lay brothers and singers to mention the name of the fickle dandy or unfaithful woman in their responses. Whereupon if the alluded person or one of his or her kin was in overly high spirits and given to anger, he or she would then deal out blows all around. Those cries, that commotion, and those hot, genuine tears were, as they say, the glorious complement to the day. [. . .]

On the other hand, artistically beautiful and exquisitely tasteful monuments have proliferated. The cult of flowers persists, and it is nice to see families take their children to pay tribute to their beloved relatives with floral offerings, the symbol of prayer and love. [. . .]

The French Cemetery is truly lovely, worthy of its purpose and of a civilized people. Majesty, beauty, good sanitation, spiritual grandiosity, perfection, respect for religious practices may be found there.

The rosaries and nocturnal parties have disappeared, doubtless because participants recalled the verses that vulgar people would chant at that time: "My dear bald friend, I'm pleased to see you." "Don't poke fun, for I am Lady Death."

Or this other verse, equally "boorocratic": "As I wandered the Earth, I happened upon a skeleton, and I mumbled to it: it's all the same to me, unless you're from the afterworld." ◆

—Translated by Carole Castelli

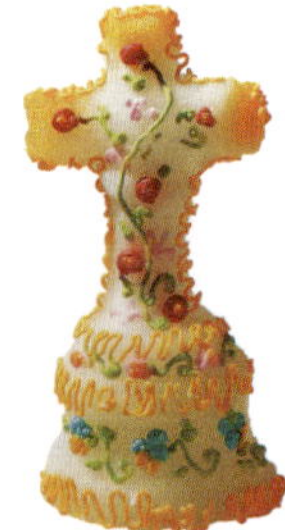

Guillermo Prieto. Born and deceased in Mexico City (1818–1897). Prieto studied at the Colegio de San Juan de Letrán. He was the private secretary of Valentín Gómez Farías and Anastasio Bustamante and a professor of economics at the military college. He fought against the United States in the War of 1847, collaborated in the drafting of the reform laws, and was a deputy eighteen times and secretary of the treasury seven times. He began his journalistic career as editor of *El Cosmopolita* and the *Diario Oficial.* In 1890, the newspaper *La República* named him the most popular poet in the country. He belonged to the Letrán Academy and the Mexican Ateneo.

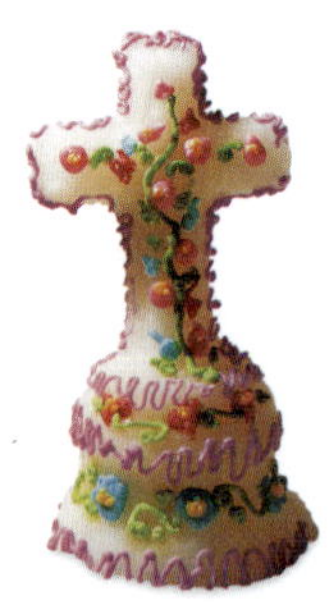

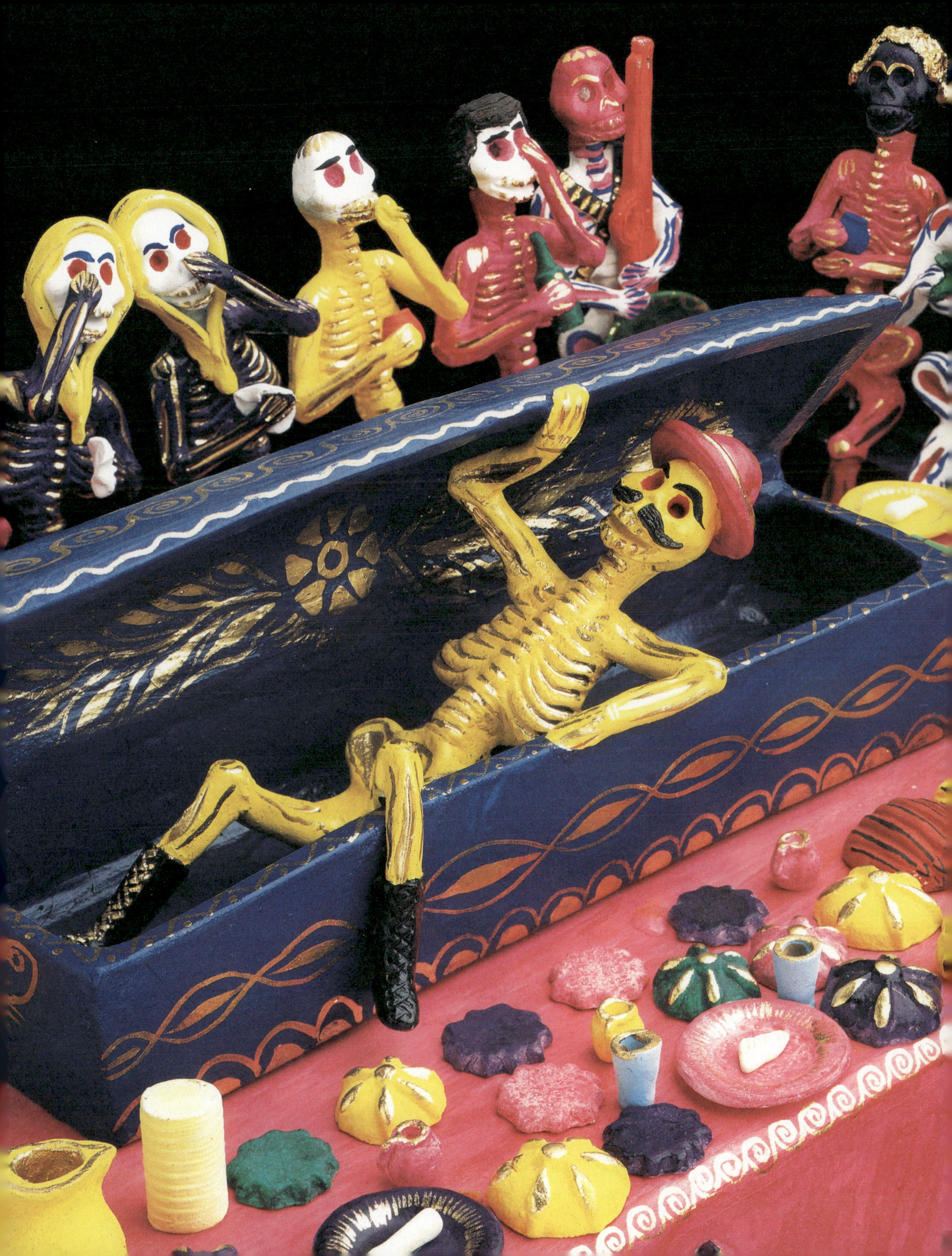

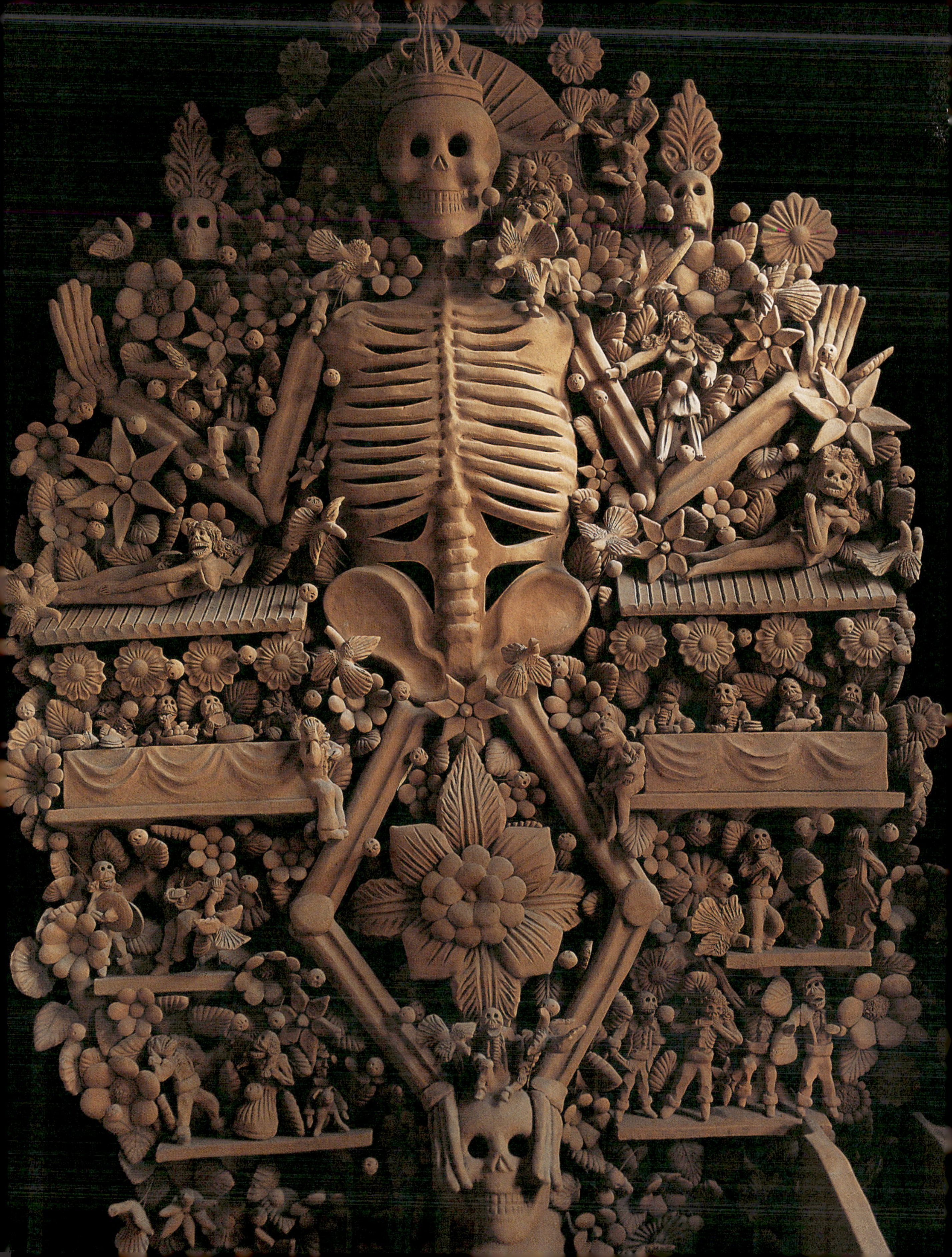

1880
DAY OF THE DEAD

Ignacio Manuel Altamirano

◆◆◆◆◆

In the old days, that is before the Reform, Mexico would awaken on November 2 to the funereal clamor of the bells ringing in all the churches, reminding people that this was the day when the faithful departed were commemorated.

Ah! What sadness and tedium inflicted the continuous funereal clamor that began in the Cathedral and was echoed in the hundred belfries of the convents, and in all the churches, chapels and hermitages that surrounded the city from east to west, from north to south! It was an incessant rhythmic vibration, hoarse, dismal, that gave rise to many feelings, all of them bitter. Sorrow, regret, despair overpowered the heart, like the dreadful procession of the day's memories. For, who had not lost some loved one whose memory was evoked by the chiming of the bells?

And so moved, the faithful obey the sacred mandate, just as they did in the old days. For while the bells have been silenced in the past and muted in the present, the pious custom of commemorating the departed has remained firm, maintained by tradition and family sentiment.

Although I was already familiar with present-day Mexican customs, and though I had to overcome the repulsion I feel at big-city cemeteries—since, when I want to meditate on the profound issue of death, and envelop myself in the shadows of tombs to dream of them, I, like the English poet Gray, prefer to seek out a village cemetery—I set out for the graveyard.

Have Mexican religious customs on the Day of the Dead changed at all, I wondered? Were they different before the Reform?

I climbed aboard a rental carriage that, like all the abominable vehicles of its kind, was charging one or two pesos per hour that day. The one I found by chance was pulled by two unmatched sallow nags, but more spirited than even the brightest person would ever guess.

It is well known that in the city there are new graveyards, arranged differently than in the old days. The French Cemetery and the neighboring La Piedad, Dolores in the hills of Tacubaya, the two named Guadalupe, San

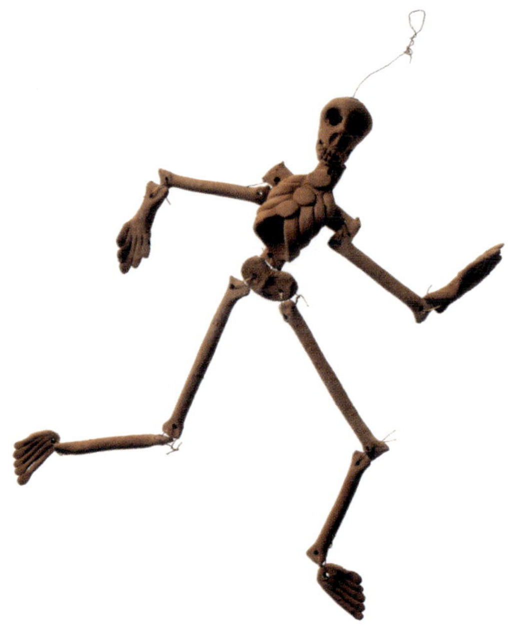

PAGE 154: Tree of death. Modeled, molded, and fired clay. Metepec, State of Mexico, 1995.

Fernando (no longer accepting new occupants), the Flowery Field in the south end of the city and Los Ángeles in the northeast. Buried there are the bones of the dead that the Mexicans mourn.

But La Piedad and the French Cemetery are the most notable and the most widely frequented.

I am saddened as I make my way there, moved as anyone who makes a pilgrimage to the dwelling of the dead ought to be. Ah! I said, forgetting for a moment that I was familiar with the customs of this noble city. How the air must be filled with sighs all along this road! What gloomy faces people must wear! How their eyes must be clouded over with tears!

It is the *via sacra*, the way of pain and tenderness. This is where silent grief passes, with its slow gait . . .

My melancholy phrase was interrupted by a concert of happy guffaws, and shrieks of joy. I stuck my head out the carriage door to see better.

The nags had already passed the Belén watchtower and were trotting down Calzada de la Piedad. On both sides of the highway and the railroad, under the shade of the poplars bordering the avenue, there was an uninterrupted procession of noisy, happy people divided into groups of varying size. It was the Mexican hoi polloi on foot, presenting such a vivid, picturesque scene.

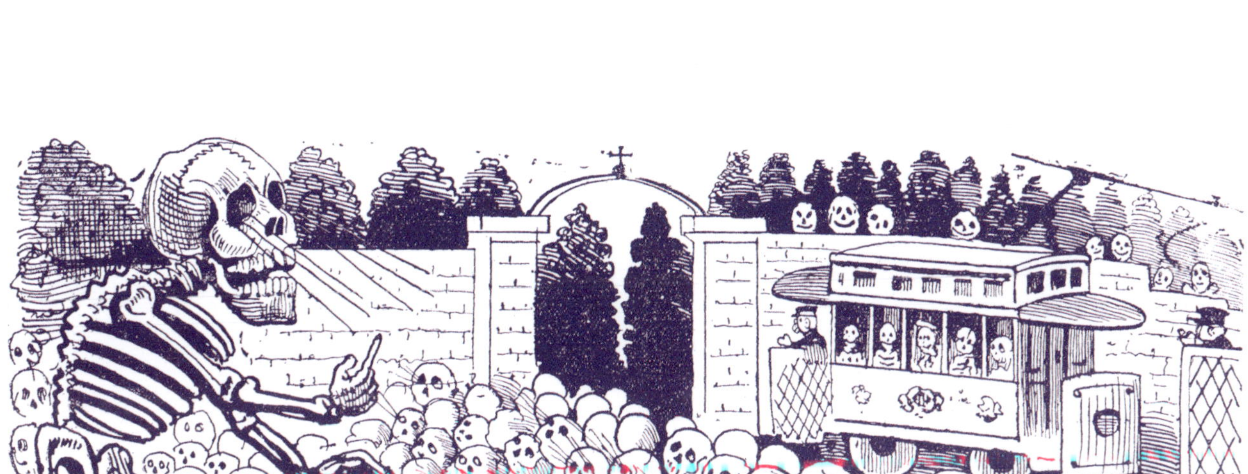

José Guadalupe Posada. Great pantheon of skulls.

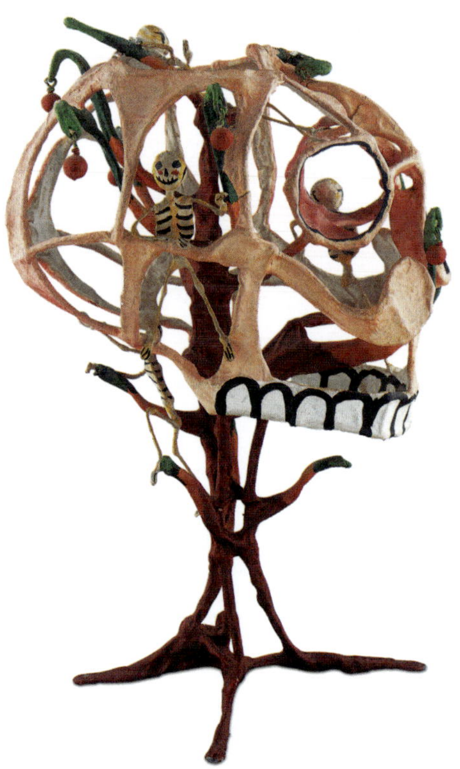

Saulo Moreno. Skull. Paper bound on a wire frame. Mexico City, 1960. Ruth D. Lechuga Collection of Popular Art / Franz Mayer Museum.

The families carried between them candles and black crêpe flowers, bouquets of fresh blossoms, evergreen and cypress crowns, baskets of food and fruit, and enormous pitchers of *pulque*.

Pulque wherever you looked. Sometimes a mule walking among the people, carrying two great wineskins of pulque, sometimes the driver carrying a demijohn full of the same liquor. Ancient women and children in party clothes or covered in rags, but always carrying the intoxicating liquid in their hands.

These were the people chattering, laughing, whistling, making a racket that smothered the distant notes of the city's tolling bells.

This was a pilgrimage of pain. At every step the path was blocked by a multitude of food and fruit stands, cantinas stocked with liquor, but with pulque always dominating.

Soon, a train twenty wagons long caught up to me. It was a curious sight: crammed with people in all their finery. The women sometimes had to go on foot because there was no room! They looked like herring in a barrel. They too were pilgrims of pain. And a hundred private coaches passed rapidly or slowly, blocking the road to La Piedad, full of mud puddles from the previous day's rain, pockmarked and crooked from lack of maintenance. In these carriages also rode the pilgrims of pain.

We arrived at La Piedad. The people swarmed; it was a carnival. We penetrated the sad little cemetery, the worst cared for of all. Though it could have been full of trees, it bristled with weeds. All classes of people are buried there, but above all the poor. The arriving pilgrims dispersed among the labyrinth of lanes that ran out to the fields of the lower classes. That was the final destination of the candles, the flowers, the baskets and the pulque.

At the entrance, some hundred Indians toiled at making and selling bouquets for the poor, because elegant bouquets are sold at elevated prices that day. I will not describe the tombs. Why bother? There are no works of art, nor even opulent sepulchers.

On the way out of the cemetery, I met a plump lady I know, accompanied by her gay young daughters who were all dressed up as if for a salon party.

"Sir," she said, addressing me, "Have you been to the French Cemetery?"

"No, ma'am, I am going there now." "Yes, you must go. How pretty it is! What elegant sepulchers! How rich and charming! And sir, you will see such beautifully attired people, for it is the most elegant cemetery in Mexico. True, some ladies look ridiculous, but others look quite fine."

"Ma'am," I replied, "I don't know a whit about clothes and fashion, but I will go to see the graves."

"Yes, yes, go see the graves. They are in good taste and very expensive. I believe that Mrs. What's-her-name's tomb must have cost at least 6 000 pesos, for if you take into account those thingumabobs, pure marble! bronze! and they have large urns worth 200 pesos! Go, you will have a wonderful time."

This is the general opinion that causes much pain to those who go to pray for their dead, as ordained by the Church.

I went to the French Cemetery and could hardly get in. Harassed by the people shoving, I made my retreat between the horses and the fifty carriages waiting there for the "elegant world," as my corpulent friend called it.

I returned to the city, but in the afternoon I went back out to La Piedad.

The cries that I heard upon arriving announced to me that the delirium between the sepulchers had turned to grief.

After praying, the crowd keeping vigil among the tombs had had to eat—nourishment was essential, the tears weakened one so. They had laid tablecloths beside the tombs or used the cemetery's own weeds as a table. Later they passed around jugs of pulque, and shed tears of pulque over the gravestones, and then the funereal orgy began.

The white liquor had exacerbated the sorrows; it talked vigorously, it sobbed, it damned, it swore, it was desperate. Physical love mocked death, and in the midst of this frenzy, rage, jealousy, desire, all the furies that can stir the human heart waved their red beacons, eclipsing the yellow light of the lilies and the graves.

The Sun was setting. The weeping willows and the poplars took on the opaline color of dusk. It was essential to bid farewell to the beloved ashes and make a final prayer and ingest a last libation. It was terrible.

Then the crowd began to leave, not as a beaten-down and sorrowful cortege, but like the unchained mobs of ancient Rome when from atop the temple steps was pronounced the sacramental word *Evohé* inaugurating the Saturnalia.

Groups of disheveled women sang bewildering songs and made frightening gestures. Violent feelings astir, men quarreled and came to blows, or staggered around until they fell. The 500 men that policed the avenue rode around on their horses with their swords drawn. Calzada de la Piedad was in complete pandemonium as the first shadows of nightfall crept across the last sacrifices of grief. And what was the Angel of Death doing in the meantime?

At night, all the city streets were alive with groups of animated mourners, singing and drinking until the wee hours.

A foreigner, witnessing this spectacle through his window, could only have concluded, "What drunks are the people of Mexico, and what awful voices they have!" ◆

—Translated by Jason Lange

Ignacio Manuel Altamirano. Born in Guerrero and deceased in Italy (1834–1893). He studied law at the Colegio de Letrán. He took part in the Ayutla revolution and fought the conservatives in the Reform War. As a critic and professor, he advocated an opening to universal literature. He published poetry (*Rimas* [*Rhymes*], 1871), stories, and novels, among which *Clemencia*, *Navidad en las montañas* (*Christmas in the Mountains*) and *El Zarco* stand out.

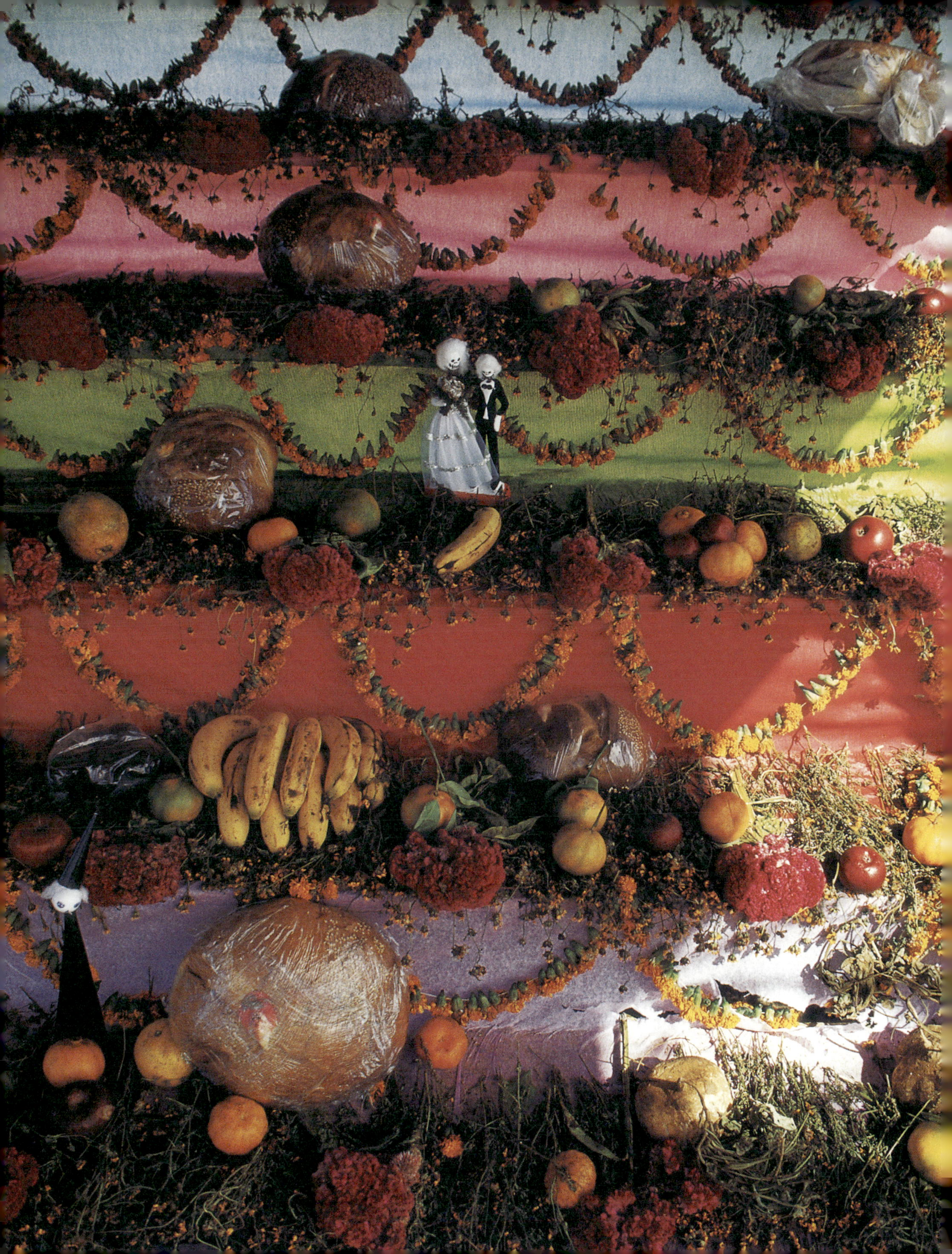

1882
DESPUÉS DE MUERTOS

José Tomás de Cuéllar

◆◆◆◆◆

From the most savage to the most civilized, all cultures divide their public ceremonies into two categories: rejoicing and funerals. No wonder it has been so since antiquity, given that these are the two phases of human life: one enjoys and suffers alternately, laughs and cries, is born and dies. By these two paths we humans have divided ourselves into two groups: the dead and the mourners; and into two cities: the silent cities called cemeteries and the happy cities where the survivors cry and laugh.

There are no darker hours in our life than those when we have mourned the loss of a loved one; and there is no idea more terrifying than that of our irremediable end.

Before the great mystery of death, human reason is annihilated and the manifestations of mourning have taken on more or less extravagant forms; but deep down there is always grief. Only Mexico could convert funereal pomp into rejoicing; only this country of sublime anomalies and contradictions could host the exaggerated, shameful wakes characteristic of uneducated, superstitious people.

It is easily understandable that Indians and uneducated Mestizos believe that, on the Day of the Dead, they have the unavoidable duty to buy the worst sweet rolls that are made in the entire year and the ugliest flowers with the worst fragrance on Earth—marigolds—to set up the offering accompanied by candles and incense fumigations. This custom is almost a rite, and from the allegorical point of view, it is not only forgivable but involves something like a badly expressed idea of immortality, given that food, the first priority of a living being and the price of life, is offered to the dead.

A taciturn Indian in front of a pile of marigolds, in front of sugar-coated buns, by the light of two candles and swathed in a cloud of incense, is a respectable mourner; he is an Egyptian from the time of Sesostris, in America, who is finding out that the road of progress is longer than it appeared at first glance.

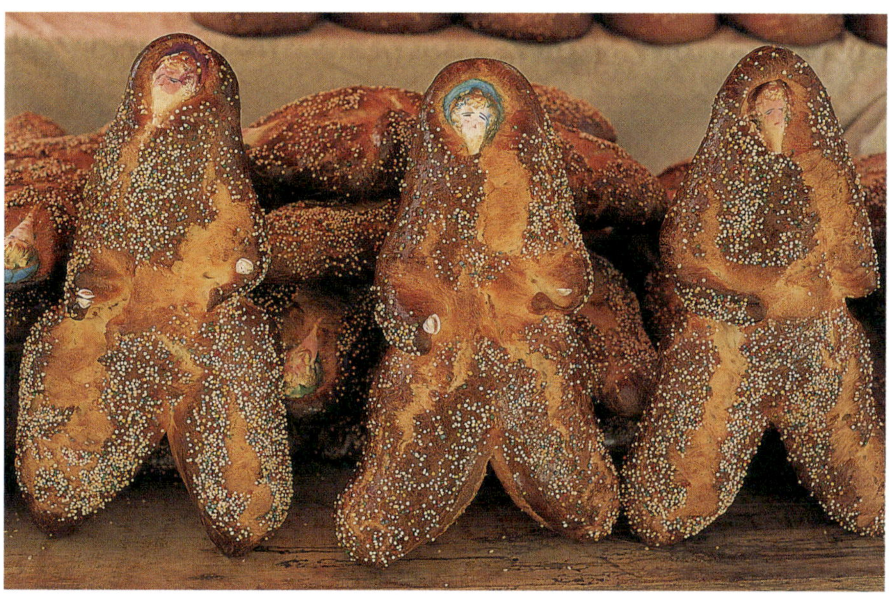

But the fact that the most illustrious members of Mexican society, in communion with the most abject of the populace, celebrate the commemoration of the Faithful Deceased with shouting and frolicking, seems to us, in the end, to have a highly distressing significance in terms of the moral order. And do not try to make us believe that this society divorced itself from the Catholic Church ever since the Reform, and that on the Day of the Dead, people do not follow the practices and rites of commemoration, but instead go to the Zócalo just because they feel like it—no, sir. People dress in black in the morning, cry in the cemetery in the afternoon, and flirt at night dressed in pink. Is it that the emotion, the grieving, and the sad memory of our loved ones who have died is also a lie? Who knows; but what is certain is that the current custom leads all of us to think the following: "When I die my people will mourn me seriously until November; and on the day consecrated by the Church for the remembrance of the dead, my wife and my children, my friends and family will participate in a festival created to make fun of the dead. Dressed in resplendent colors they will go around to the sound of the cancan inside a big tent and will dine lavishly and drown the last glimmer of sadness for my irreparable loss in champagne."

This terrible idea, which would make the stones tremble if they could be made to believe that they had to die, turns into a masquerade; and skulls and tombs become children's toys so the little ones can then merrily celebrate the death of their father.

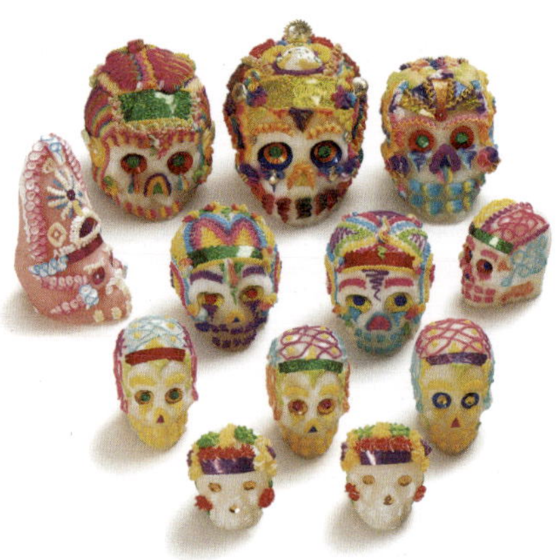

Or could it be that during the so-called Festivals of November, the Day of the Dead is of negligible importance compared to All Saint's Day? For me, the separation of Church and State began with the disrepute into which the saints had fallen in the eyes of a considerable majority of our society. The idea that people get excited by such an exceptionally Catholic memory does nothing to resolve my doubts.

Is it perchance the sad remembrance of a father, mother, brother, or dead child that consumes these tons of peanuts and dainties? Physiologically, great grief is incompatible with great appetite. What happens to this legitimate and serious grief so that it might be consumed with delight on November 2, and not only is consumed with delight, but consumes food and drink in excess?

Grief is logical, it is exhaled in tears and sobs and sighs. Our admirable organism contains no other juices nor nervous phenomena to express it. But the grief we are concerned with here, that grief of which people speak, the annual grief on a fixed date, is a strictly variegated, sweet-toothed grief and discourses more or less as follows: "Shall we commemorate our dead mother? Well then let's stuff ourselves; let's prescribe for ourselves an extraordinary dose of indigestible sweetmeats on this day, and may there be a lot of music and many amusements." And each family prepares itself for the festivals with the more or less direct intervention of the moneychanger, storing up the heterogeneous articles stated in this list we find in the Zócalo:

"Twenty-five yards of marvelous satin the color of egg yolks, and twenty yards of lace for Virginia; bismuth cream, aromatic bark of Havana, etc.; eighty yards of rose satin for Mother, matching shoes and sheer stockings; bonnets for the girls and blunt-toed boots; a ten-peso wreath for the

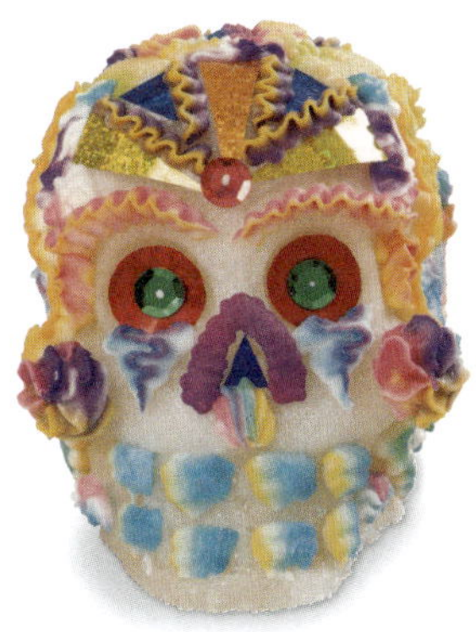

tomb of my godfather the general; a bouquet for my poor Aunt Charo; candles and candleholders for the family tomb in the Dolores Cemetery and a gratuity for the servant who keeps watch so nobody steals them; three mantilla veils; mole verde for the cook; a letter to cross the fence separating the public thoroughfare from Bejarano's enclosure; dinner in the Zócalo."

In this way and from aberration to aberration, Mexico these days presents a unique, truly idiosyncratic appearance to the eyes of the philosopher and the foreigner—one that may unfortunately lead them to emit rather unfavorable judgments about our culture.

The people conglomerate in the main square of the national capital to convert it, with social and municipal consent, into a popular market. To the detriment of education and decency, they improvise shelters out of bed sheets. They stretch out on the ground and spend the night on the stones; they set up their fruits and sweetmeats on the garbage, and improvise hearths and make bonfires and ply their wares until they are hoarse. They are the remnants of barbarity that make themselves at home in the heart of the city to celebrate the great wake as they have been doing for three centuries; but there is a relatively small group of civilized people who dress in satin the color of egg yolks and in French cashmere, who wear ostrich feathers and high heels. The yellow satin next to the sheets and mats of the shelters; the ostrich and white African stork feathers alongside straw hats; French cashmere beside the coarse cotton of the country—that is, the undergarments in which our people live—all make bad fellowship in appearance and protest at contact. The costumes are essentially different; but not so the sentiment for the dead.

The yellow satin eats truffles and the blanket eats peanuts, but satin and blanket alike eat twice as much these days to the honor and glory of the

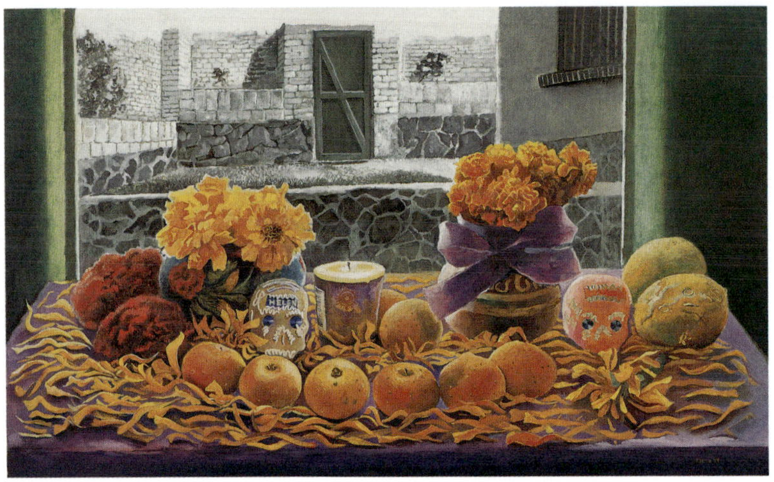

Elena Climent. *Altar de muertos con vista al jardín del recuerdo* (Altar of the Dead with a View of the Garden of Remembrance), 1999. Oil on canvas. 27.9 × 45.5 cm. Courtesy Mary Anne Martin Fine Art. **PAGE 168:** Mermaid. Bonded paper, molded and painted, on wood. Celaya, Guanajuato, 1990. Ruth D. Lechuga Collection of Popular Art / Franz Mayer Museum.

dead who no longer eat. Barbarity and refinement are in agreement on how they feel, they experience the same grief, the same pleasure, and the same appetite; but they do not like to join together, to rub elbows with each other. The yellow satin fears the fluff shed from coarse cotton fabric, blanket, and shawl. What can be done, then? To cry is requisite, to amuse oneself is requisite, marvelous satin is indispensable, the anniversary is getting close. From this emergency arises a clever savior, as in all difficult situations: Mr. Bejarano arrives and proposes to put up a wooden fence to make an enclosure that separates the yellow satin from the cheap, coarse cloth.

"Good idea!" shouts the yellow satin.

Bejarano adds, "This enclosure will belong to me for a few days."

"Excellent!" shout the ostrich feathers.

"But," continues Bejarano, "to get into my enclosure it will cost you four pesos."

"So what?" says the yellow satin disdainfully. "Don't you see we're all rich? Almost all of us are moneychangers."

Bejarano, satisfied with the reply, persuades City Hall, which of course is very easy to persuade, to loan him the Zócalo, and City Hall loans it. Mr. Fulcheri brings the equivalent of peanuts to the Zócalo and keeps his foodstuffs in booths from which they emerge at night as from a magician's hat, at prices that are deadly to any man.

Elegant Mexico begins a movement of separating the corn from the chaff that lasts four hours, during which everyone sees the satin of the others and remains persuaded of the utility of every class of clothing, that for four pesos they heard the same music they ordinarily have playing in the background, and that in the end they dined expensively. And the dead? No news to tell. What more could those poor cadavers ask for than their ten-peso wreath and their candles and their flowers? They've been given their offering but they haven't wanted to eat it. Might it be they do not have any appetite and know their condition?

And the mourners? All of them have lost one or more loved ones, all of them have cried and have open sores, badly healed wounds, and still bleeding, they present themselves on the solemn day of remembrance, on the official day, on the day of the Church, and what for? To enroll voluntarily in the list of those who pray and sob? No: To subscribe to Bejarano's enclosure and Fulcheri's menu.

And emotion, and grief, and mourning? Will all of these flowers of the soul go on joining the category of the marigold that is the most common and ugliest of flowers? Have luxury and pleasure robbed this generation's soul of spirituality and morality, gratitude and remembrance, sensitivity and logic? We do not know, but it is heartrending that there is something sadder than death: the happiness and indifference of the living. In any case, here we have a fact, on the basis of which we should not create any illusic for ourselves about the future, because *después de muertos*—after death, after the Day of the Dead—awaits us not only the tomb with all its hon but Bejarano's enclosure. ◆

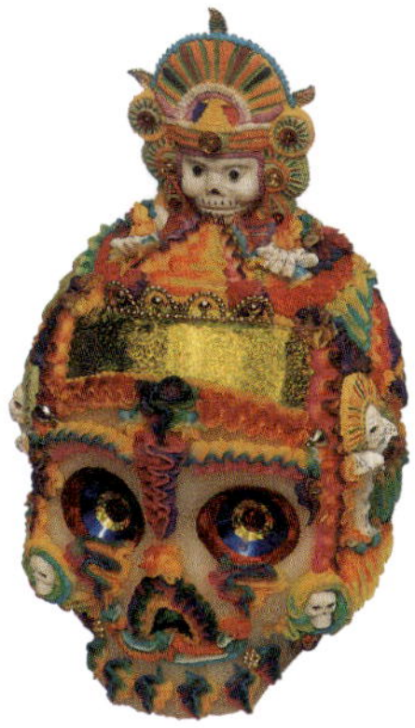

—Translated by Henry Munn

José Tomás de Cuéllar. Born and deceased in Mexico City (1830–1894). Cuéllar studied at the schools of San Gregorio, San Ildefonso, Militar, and at the Academy of San Carlos and was a journalist from the age of twenty. In 1868, he participated in the founding of La Bohemia Literaria, a group in which he worked as editor until 1872, when he joined the diplomatic corps in Washington, where he lived until 1882. In 1892 he was named a member of the Royal Spanish Academy. He was the author of several plays, including: *Deberes y sacrificios* (*Duties and Sacrifices*), *Natural y figura* (*Nature and Figure*), and *Cubrir las apariencias* (*Covering Appearances*); and poetry: *Obras poéticas* (*Poetic Works*) and *Versos* (*Verses*). His novels appeared as two series titled *La linterna mágica* (*The Magic Lantern*).

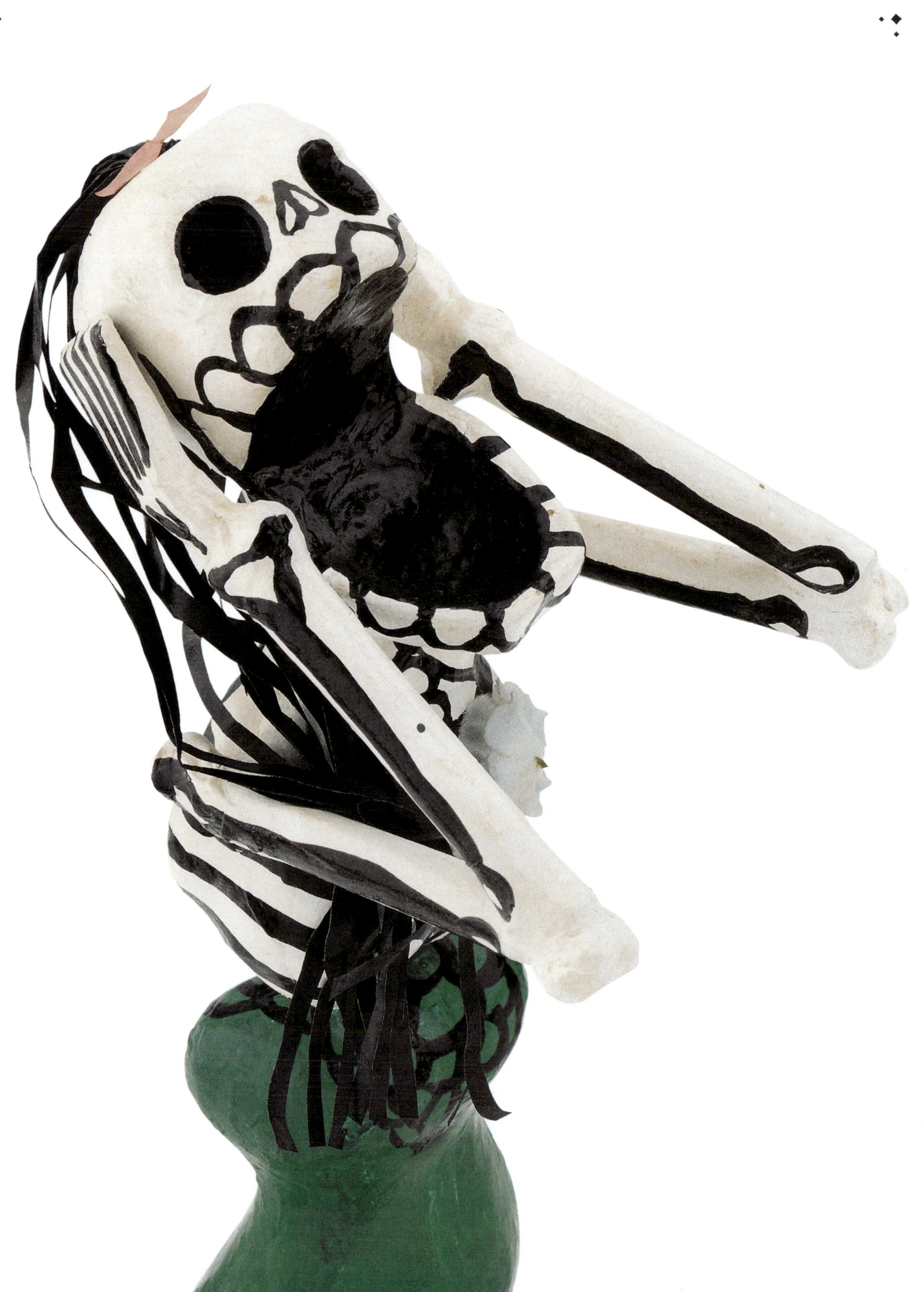

FEAR OF DEATH: ANGUISH IN LIFE

Paul Westheim

◆◆◆◆◆

Where, my dear, is my place in life?
Where is my one true home?
Where is the mansion I need?
I'm suffering here on Earth!

Cantares mexicanos

The skeleton as an artistic motif is nothing new. Popular Mexican imagery has delighted in representing death for millennia, just as Renaissance and baroque artists enjoyed painting angels and cupids. But this did come as a tremendous surprise—and perhaps even a traumatic experience—for visitors to the Exhibition of Mexican Art in Paris. They stood in front of a statue of Coatlicue, the goddess of life and of the Earth, who wears a death mask; they contemplated the skull that an Aztec artist carved out of rock crystal (one of the hardest minerals), investing in the creation long hours of work and his extraordinary skill in the craft; they looked at the etchings done by popular illustrators Manuel Alfonso Manilla and José Guadalupe Posada, who used skeletons to comment on social and political events at the time. They were informed that in Mexico, it is traditional on November 2 for parents to give their children skulls made of chocolate and sugar, each bearing the recipient's name on the forehead, and that the young people gleefully devour these macabre candies as if it were the most natural thing in the world. They were fascinated by the folk artists who used the humblest of materials—fabric, wood, clay and even gum—to create the skeleton dolls dressed in rags that are very common, well-loved toys among the Mexican people. Paul Rivet, in an account on the exhibition, spoke of unexpected designs, and asked, "What can be said about those dolls representing a bride and groom, but that are in fact skeletons?" This question reveals not only amazement but a hint of fear. For Europeans, the thought of death is a nightmare, and they hate to be reminded of the brevity of life; thus, to find themselves before a world that seems free of that anxiety, that plays with death and even mocks it, can only lead them to wonder about the strangeness of a place with such an inconceivable attitude.

Ancient Mexico did not possess the concept of Hell. It is possible and even probable that the obscure memory of an afterlife that is open to sinners lives on to this day in the people's subconscious (especially that of indigenous people). The image of the skeleton with the scythe and hourglass as the symbol of all things mortal was in fact imported into Mexico. On those occasions when it is used—for example, in representations of danse macabre—it is immediately adapted, acclimatized, Mexicanized, as in the case of Manilla and Posada. Xavier Villaurrutia, whose poetry revolves almost entirely around death, once wrote, "Here it is very easy to die, and the more Indian blood there is coursing through our veins, the more attractive death becomes. With more Spanish or Criollo blood, we fear death more, because that is what we are taught to do." The psychic burden that gives a tragic tone to the lives of Mexicans is not the fear of death, as it was two or three thousand years ago, but the anguish of life, the awareness of being exposed, and with insufficient means of defense, to a life plagued with danger, filled with the essence of evil.

The Indian's personal conviction that all life is suffering, that the submissive and the weak are the permanent victims of the strong—something that Rouault expressed when he included a quote from Plautus in one of his etchings from *Misery and War*: "Man is a wolf to man"—meant that the religious art of colonial Mexico passionately embraced the theme of Christ crucified in a thousand poignant variations, his body tortured by inhuman executioners, bleeding in a thousand terrifying ways. It is significant that such representations abounded in the eighteenth century, when Indian and Mestizo artists, nearly all of them anonymous, began to imprint their character and mentality on religious art. And the fact that these paintings and sculptures were found above all in simple village churches, in indigenous

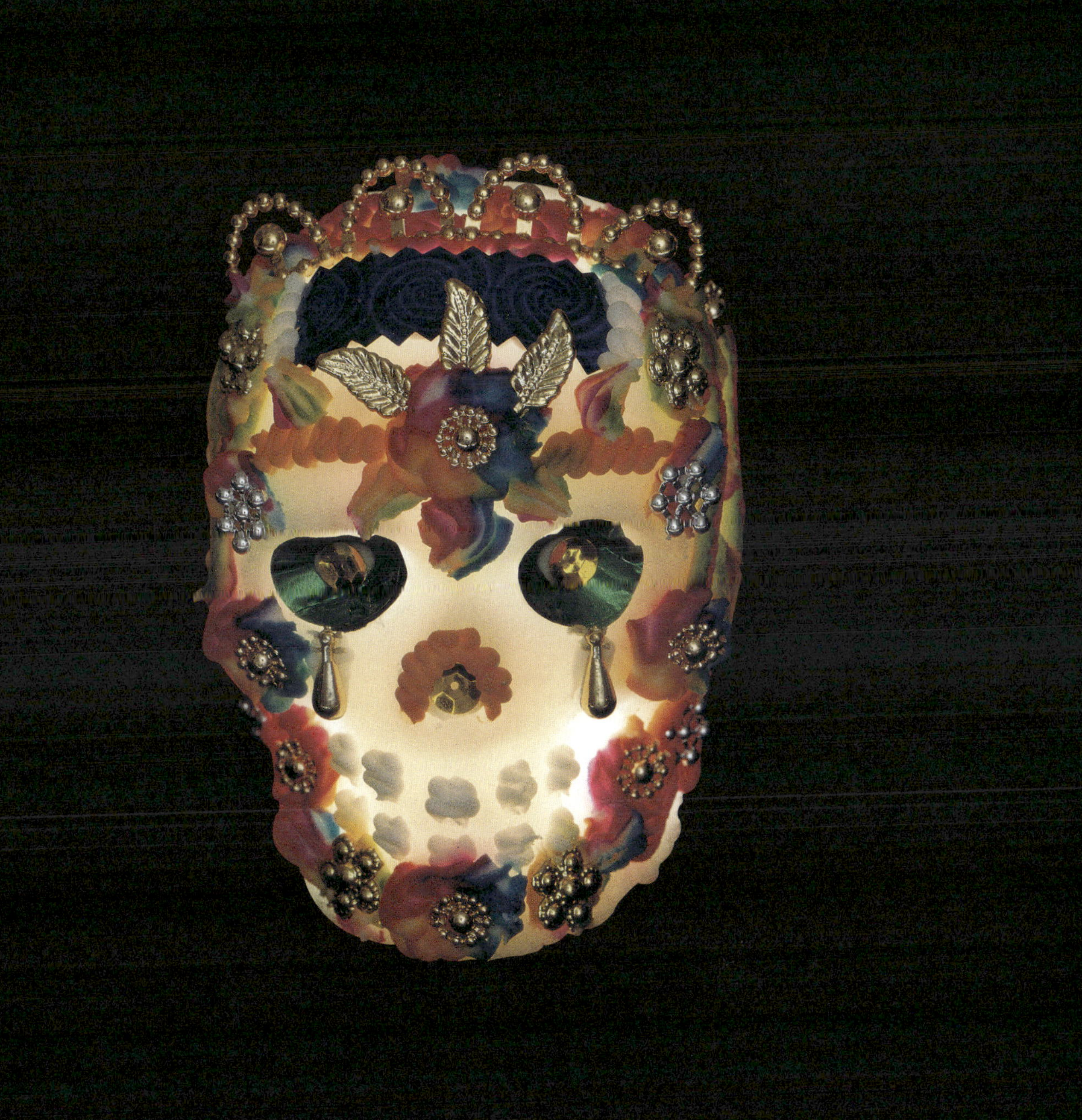

communities on the fringe of urban civilization, leads us to conclude that the martyrdom that man inflicts on man is a profound experience, primarily rooted in the Indian's sentimental world; and also that he is so drawn to the Christ figure because he feels torture as something very personal. Clearly, such a "pathos of material pain"—if I might cite Werner Weisbach's phrase in *The Art of the Baroque*—originates in Spanish realism, or more to the point, verism, which takes pleasure "in unbalancing the notion of life with bloody, terrible, frightening images." But it is also very clear that Mexico seized this theme with intense fervor—comparable to that with which it appropriated the churrigueresque style, providing it with all the pageantry and exuberance fitting to its particular idiosyncrasy—and that the colonial Nazarene is not simply a variation of the Spanish version, but an independent creation, the work of a specifically Mexican sensibility. "In those utterly wretched Christ figures of blood, sweat and tears, we find, with the infallible punctuality of the extraordinary, much of the dramatic indigenous mythology taking refuge, with forced comfort, in the meager and lamentable image of the village," writes Luis Cardoza y Aragón in his book, Pintura mexicana contemporánea (Contemporary Mexican Painting).

Anguish in life. Let us recall the words—written in the *Florentine Codex*—that the Nahua father said to his daughter when she reached the city at the age of six or seven: "Here on Earth, it is a place of much sorrow, a

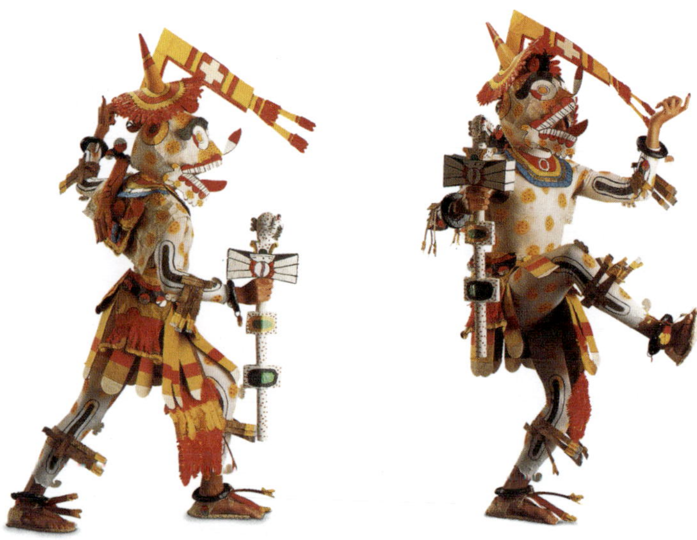

ABOVE AND OPPOSITE: Humberto Spíndola. Mictlantecuhtli performance, 1993. Costumes fashioned from tissue paper. Author's collection.

place where [. . .] bitterness and dejection are well known. A wind of obsidian blows and glides among us. [. . .] It is not a place of wellbeing here on Earth. There is no joy, there is no happiness."

Let us also recall a masterpiece by a painter from our days: *Tata Jesucristo* (Grandfather Jesus Christ) by Francisco Goitia, who, speaking of two women represented in his painting, said, "They are crying the tears of our race, our hardships—our tears, which are different from those of other people. All of Mexico's anguish is in them." The motive behind their sobbing is life, the pain of life, the uncertainty that is man's life on Earth.

Ancient Mexico did not tremble before Mictlantecuhtli, the god of death; it trembled before that uncertainty that is the life of men. They called it Tezcatlipoca. ◆

—Translated by Michelle Suderman

Paul Westheim. Historian born in Germany and deceased in Mexico City (1885–1963). Westheim was persecuted by the Nazis and went into exile in Paris. In 1940, he enlisted to fight the German invasion, and he arrived in Mexico in 1941. Among his works are *Pre-Hispanic Mexican Art*, *The Art of Ancient Mexico*, and *The Skull*, from which this fragment was taken.

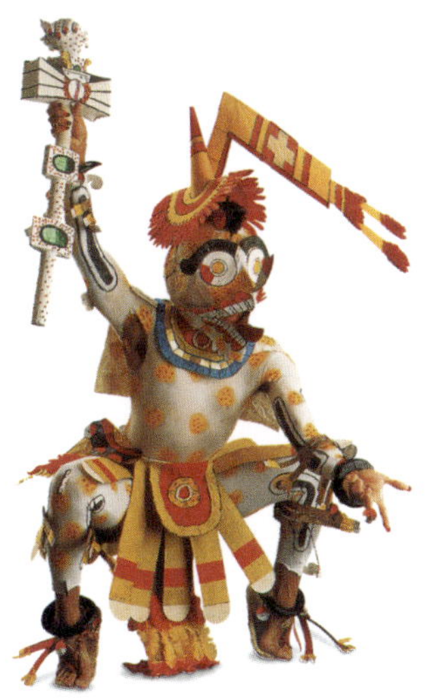

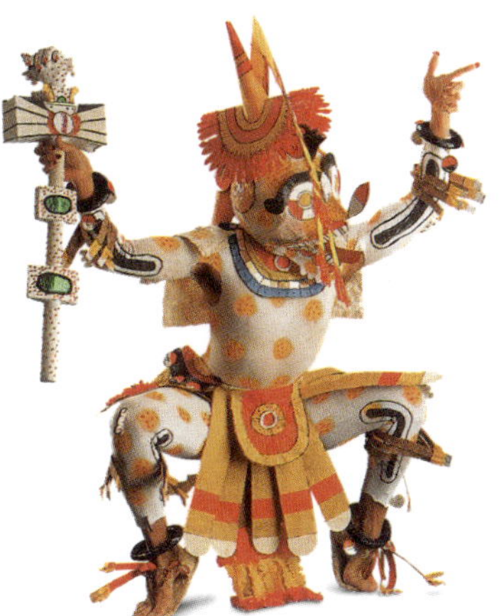

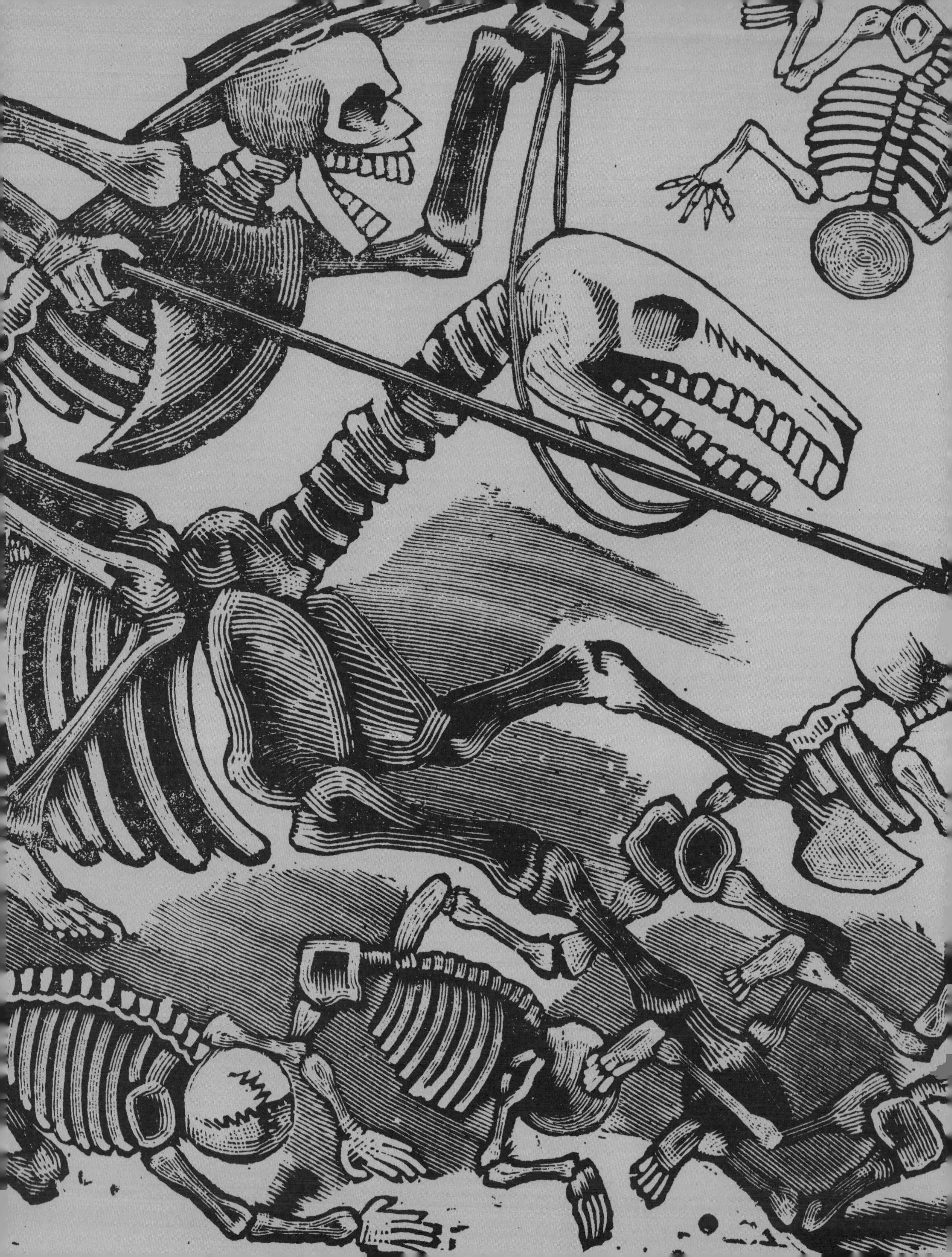

JOSÉ GUADALUPE POSADA'S *CALAVERAS*

Luis Cardoza y Aragón

◆◆◆◆◆

José Guadalupe Posada was born in Aguascalientes on February 2, 1851, when the enormous wound left by the American intervention of 1847 was still bleeding profusely: Mexico had lost over half its territory. In his childhood and adolescence he lived through the convulsions caused by the Laws of Reform, the French intervention and Juárez's battles; Porfirio Díaz's dictatorship and the gestation and initial triumph of the Revolution with Madero's entrance into Mexico City. Posada died in Mexico City on January 20, 1913, mere weeks before Huerta betrayed and murdered President Madero. He died as he had lived: virtually alone and poverty-stricken, after having worked for many different newspapers, as a book illustrator, making posters for bullfights, circuses, theaters, and so forth.

Posada was not an artist who got close to the people. To begin with, he was not even sure about considering himself an artist. He was unaware of his everyday state of grace. Let us not forget his kinship with the composer of the popular song known as the *corrido* (Constancio S. Suárez, and possibly others) and with the typographer's humor. They had a sense of who they were—working-class Mexicans—and the imagination, the sense of fancy, the genius or the cleverness to objectify that and give it shape with illustrations, words, and the tone and rhythm of popular songsters. That is, these men did not get close to the people, they weren't popular: they were the people.

Posada's *calavera* illustrations and poems not only had a critical or satirical connotation: they were also eulogistic or festive. Though *calaveras* were widespread in Mexico even before Posada, it is thanks to him and to the vast popularity he gave them that they became the deepest and most original trait of Mexican folk art—Juan Larrea called them "the national totem."

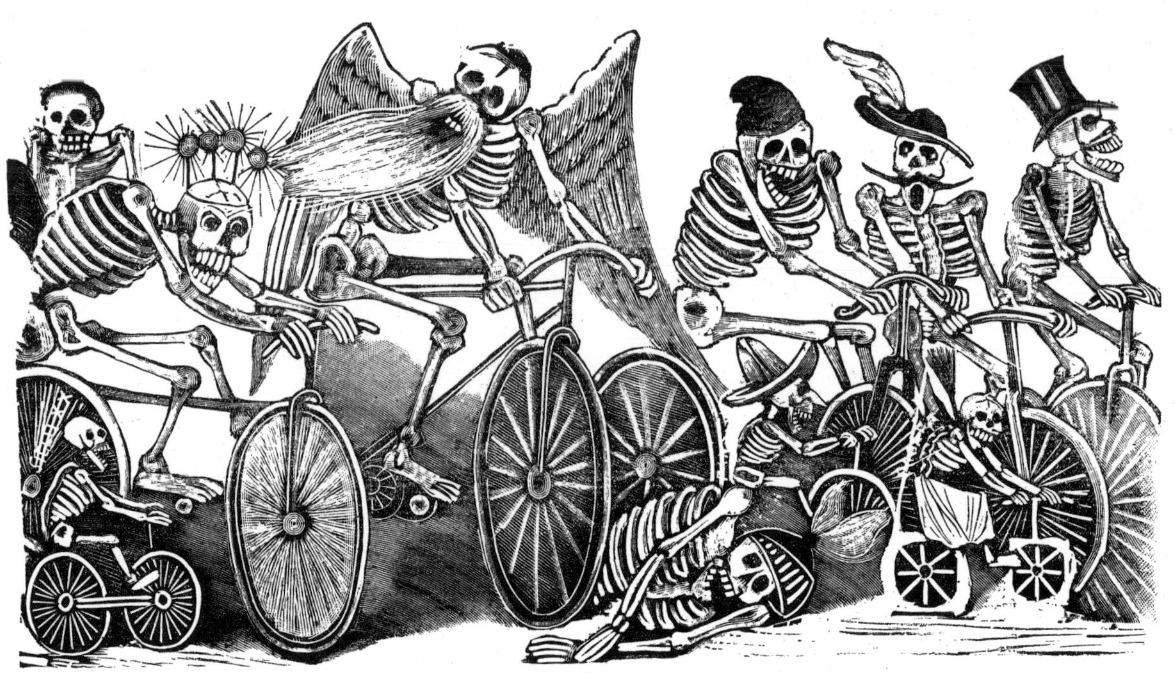

José Guadalupe Posada. *Calavera Las bicicletas* (Skull Bicycles).

Death is a universal theme of human expression. The way in which we care for it, the familiarity, the tenderness, the sensitivity with which Mexico regards death, its obsession that is neither tragic nor funereal but nuptial and festive, its immediate everyday nature, its imperious and serene visibility, its burbling laughter rather than a moan, contain the unlearned wisdom of a cosmic, playful conception. This conception that seems perpetually awestruck and so unique to Mexico harks back to pre-Columbian traditions interwoven with those of medieval Europe, with its *danses macabres* and Last Judgments. The Mexican version of the Grim Reaper, on the other hand—a vital one, a song of life, sublimated in sacrifice—did not treat us as men but as gods.

Posada's *calaveras*—threshed Coatlicues and *tzompantlis*—are the motif that reveals the most about his work and about himself. Today, foreigners appear more capable than Mexicans of detecting what lives behind that narcissism of death. The clarity of the intention exposes a secular hunger for the sacred, the stratification of myth, softened in what is reflexive and fantastic in the extreme. Before the absurdity of death, there is no place for tragedy, only for humor, and it answers its questions with joviality. Death responds to its own questions. Its answer: the certainty of it, of death, is forever. And a magical rebellion breaks out, one in which men and women and children and

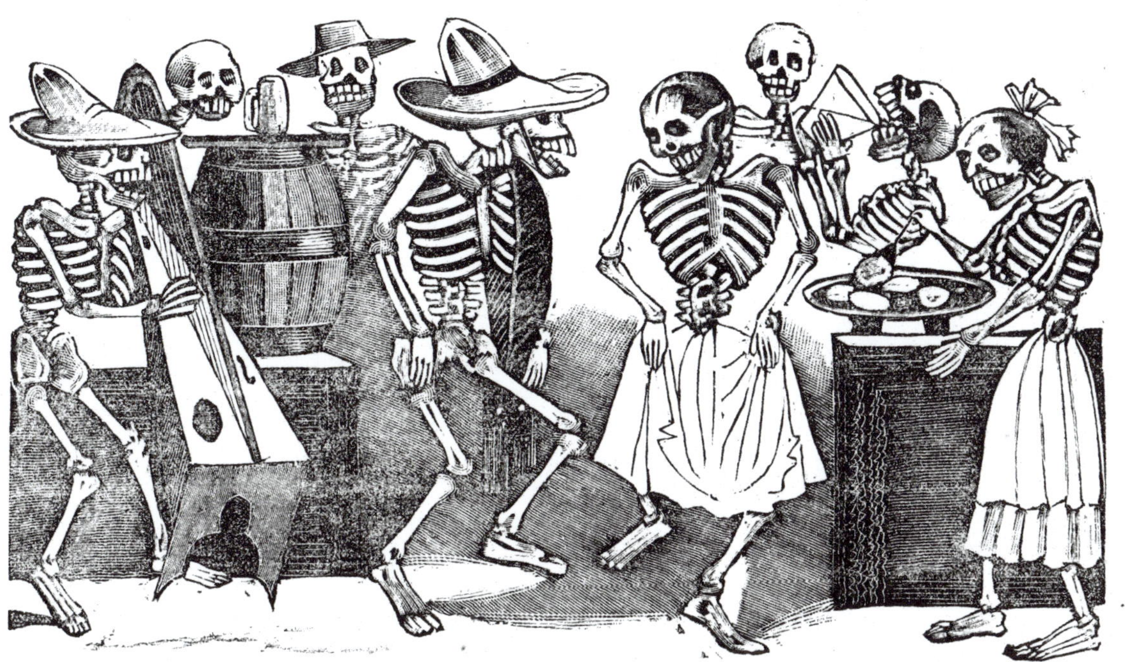

José Guadalupe Posada. *El jarabe en ultratumba* (Syrup in the Afterlife).

animals strip off not only their masks but also their flesh—they are no longer skinned but eaten away by a time that clocks do not even dream of. The definitive identity is reconquered; the ego becomes everyone, and not just the Other. This dawn foray toward the primeval is something that Posada does for us without suspecting it, like the magician at the fair who pulls real doves out of his handkerchief. Posada enjoyed himself so, reading all the tributes to his talent, visiting his own exhibitions in Mexico and abroad, bewildered like the magician at the fair whose occupation of illusionist is no longer mere façade. Posada does not realize that he remembers, and rises to his own level like water does, without ever obeying any mandate, within a concealed, personal resemblance that is not just a family likeness: it is absolute identicalness. This Posada—with his ear to the ground, listening to its pulse—is the one that most fascinates me. Here is the desire to be of stone and to not be: his doves are real. His excessive thirst from a distant and endless hangover. He does not know that he remembers. His *calaveras* are based on the incandescent syllables of an obscure language that all men have babbled about finiteness. There is a clouded liberating awareness of how man is enslaved to death, the creative obsession of a "heart that puts forth flowers in the middle of the night," hymns to the night of a death that is not mourned but rejoiced, flowered and

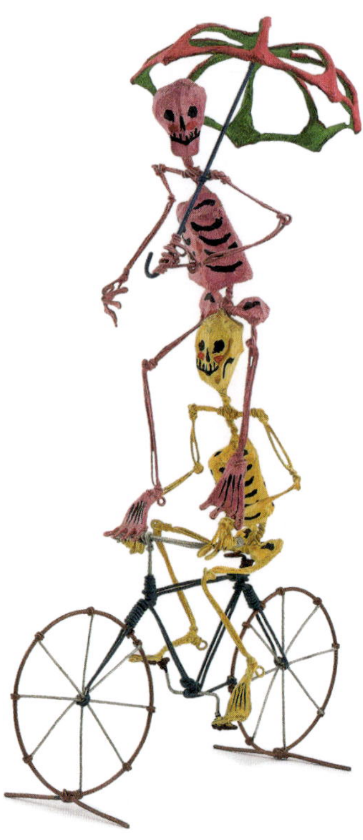

Saulo Moreno. *Ciclistas acróbatas* (Acrobat Cyclists). Bonded and painted paper, on a wire frame. Mexico City, 1970. Ruth D. Lechuga Collection of Popular Art / Franz Mayer Museum.

sung, with the Heraclitean lyre and bow. Communion, when we devour the sugar skull, is an unprepared ritual, scarcely transposed from the eroticism of sacrifice. We reach inside ourselves in search of an order required by the only absolute reality, the reality of death, or communion with it. In Mexico, death and life form such an immaterial coin that it only has one side. Holy water on the embers of Aztec passion lights a fire, and the cross on the forehead on Ash Wednesday mixes with the blood of the sacrificial victims: this is the kind of confluence that occurs in Posada's *calaveras*, with the naturalness of the ocean depths of innocence in the child's greedy bite out of a sugar skull.

Posada, in the first place, and later Orozco and the printmakers at the Taller de Gráfica Popular (Popular Graphics Studio) headed by Leopoldo Méndez, used calaveras in satire, in popular odes (*Corrido de Stalingrado* by Leopoldo Méndez, among others), with a range of emotions and thoughts. Here, the *calavera* was used not only for the date on which the Studio produced them and continues to produce them (November 2, the Day of the Dead), but

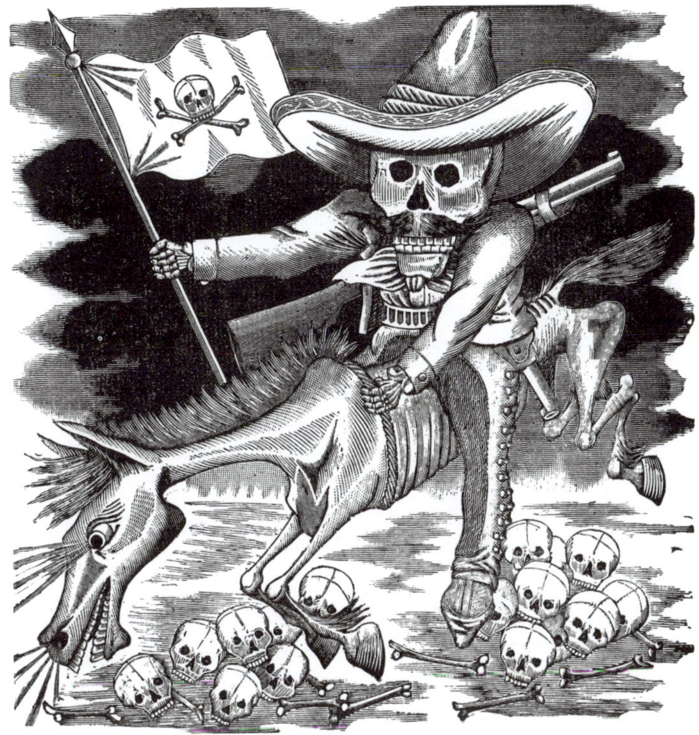

José Guadalupe Posada. *Calavera zapatista* (Zapatista Skull)

because they wield a fascination over the people's imaginary. The sugar skulls, the candy coffins, the caramel tibias and femurs, the Judases, the cardboard masks and dolls, and so forth, are not unbecoming topics of Mexican folk art, because of the power of the memory and the flavor of that universe. ◆

—Translated by Michelle Suderman

Luis Cardoza y Aragón. Born in Guatemala and deceased in Mexico City (1904–1992), Cardoza lived in Mexico starting in 1952. He collaborated in *Contemporáneos*. In 1979, his *Poesías completas y algunas prosas* (*Complete Poems and Some Prose*) was published. He was an art critic and wrote several books about Mexican art: *Rufino Tamayo, Pintura mexicana contemporánea* (*Contemporary Mexican Painting*), *Orozco, México: pintura active* (*Mexico: Active Painting*), *Arte mexicano de hoy* (*Mexican Art of Today*), and *José Guadalupe Posada*. In 1979, he received the Aztec Order of the Eagle. Doctor Honoris Causa for the University of San Carlos, in Guatemala.

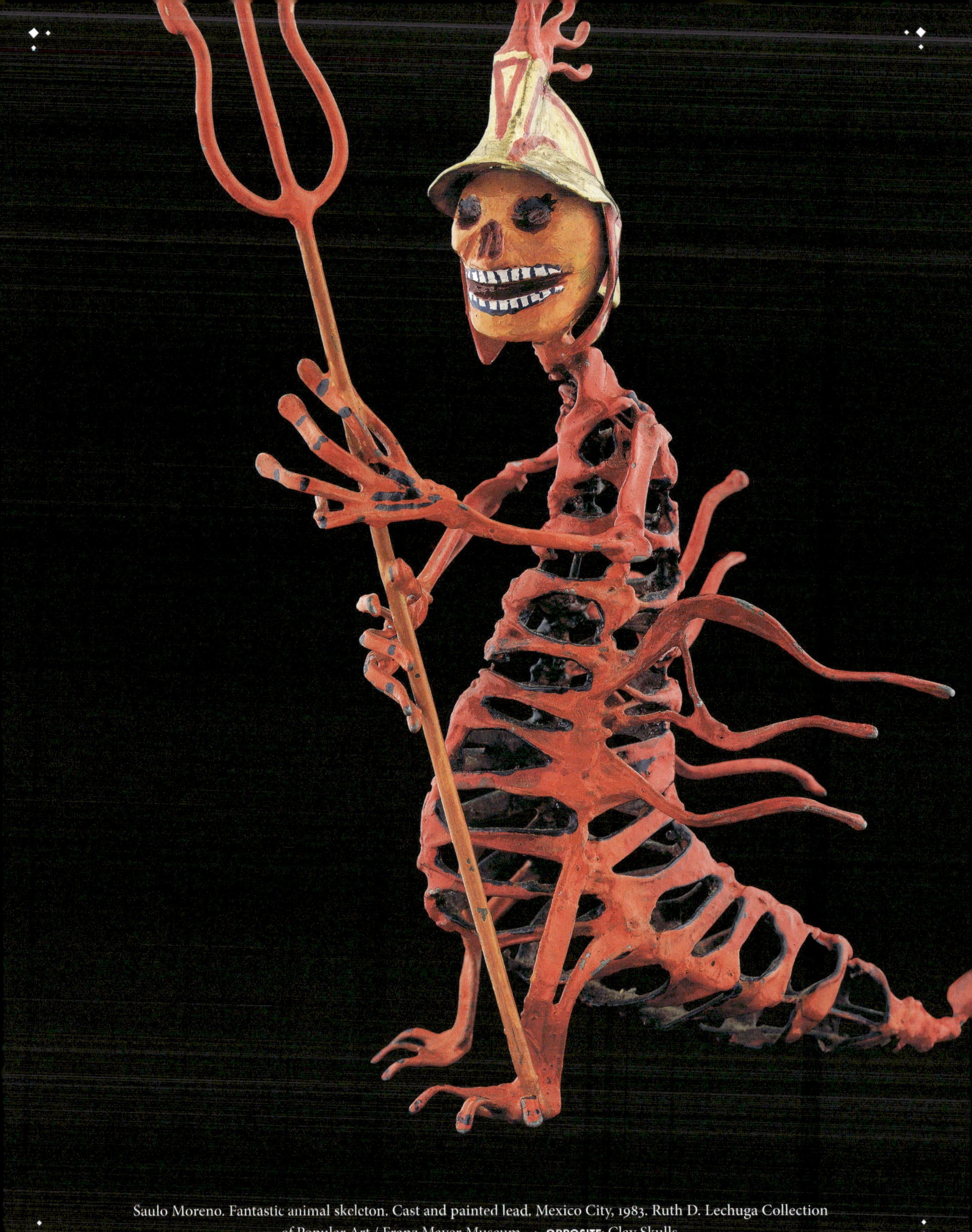

Saulo Moreno. Fantastic animal skeleton. Cast and painted lead. Mexico City, 1983. Ruth D. Lechuga Collection of Popular Art / Franz Mayer Museum. • **OPPOSITE:** Clay Skulls.

SKELETONS

Ruth D. Lechuga

◆◆◆◆◆

◆ PLAYING WITH DEATH ◆

It is not known when the tradition of making toys for the Day of the Dead first started. According to a detailed description by Antonio García Cubas, it already existed halfway through the nineteenth century. In all likelihood it is a more ancient custom.

Some toys are made to be placed in a Day of the Dead offering dedicated to deceased children so they can entertain themselves during their return visit

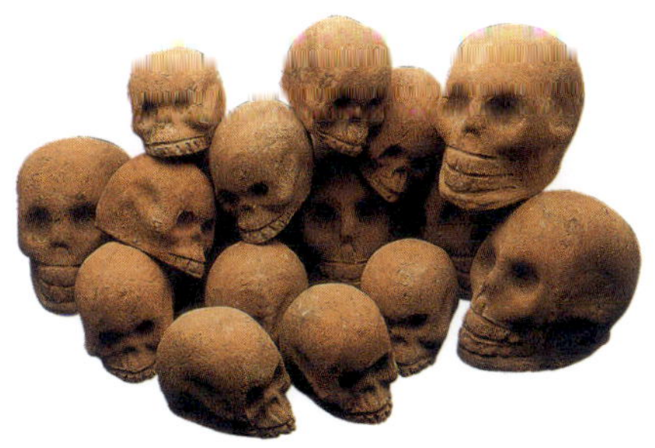

to Earth. But they are often made for living children, who love to play with the small multitiered tombs, miniature burial scenes, priests with chickpeas for heads, tiny offerings, and many other objects. Skeletons figure predominantly among these toys. They are frequently engaged in common mortal tasks: the typist hammering away at the keys of her typewriter, a woman grinding corn on her stone *metate*, another making tortillas, a writer filling page after page with his ideas. Other skeletons are vendors of all kinds of wares; or brides and grooms about to be wed. Some skeletons are seen enjoying a bubble bath, while others sport the headgear of different characters: chef, bullfighter, a dandy in a top hat, a woman with hair rolled up in big curlers . . . There are also skeletons lying in their coffins that sit up when a string is pulled.

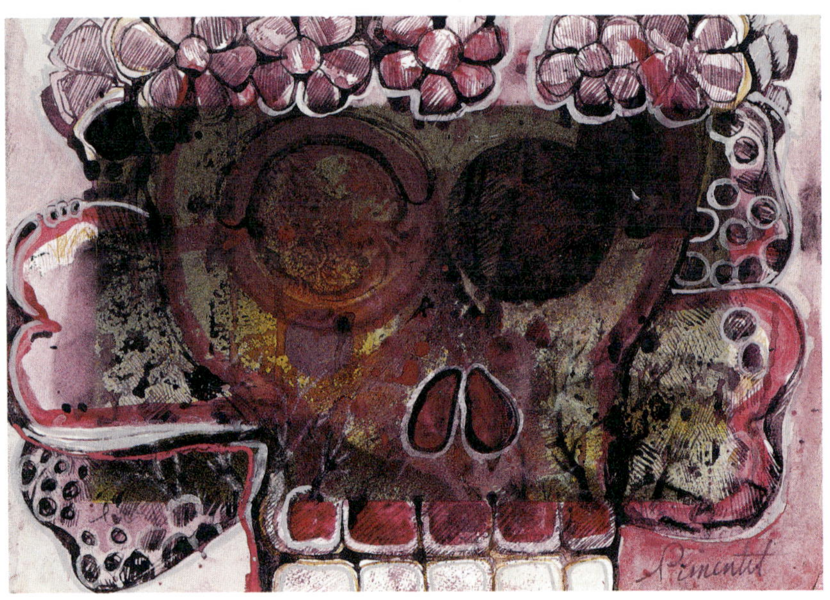

Rodrigo Pimentel. *Muerte hippy* (Hippy Death), 1968.
Ink on paper. 24.5 × 34.5 cm. Author's collection.

Another important tradition is the presentation of sugar skulls. They come in many sizes and are often decorated with a hat or flowers also made of sugar. These pieces are usually given away to friends or to courting couples, always with their names affixed. Aside from Mexico City, Toluca is a big production center for these pieces, as well as other places in the State of Mexico, such as Tenancingo.

The skeleton's popularity as a folk art motif spreads beyond that of objects made for the Day of the Dead. Skeletons appeared as papier-mâché Judases in a Holy Week tradition still very much observed in the 1960s. These huge figures measuring four or more meters in height were bought by large stores and decorated with gifts. At eleven in the morning on Holy Saturday, when church bells chimed to announce the Glory, these pieces were set off as fireworks. Smaller Judases were also made and continue to be, often as skeleton figures.

Several generations of the Linares family in Mexico City have been celebrated as manufacturers of Judases. But they also produce decorative sets of skeletons in different situations. For example, in 1986 the National Folk Art and Crafts Museum exhibited a tableau entitled *Death in Tremors*, created by artisans to commemorate the massive earthquake of the previous

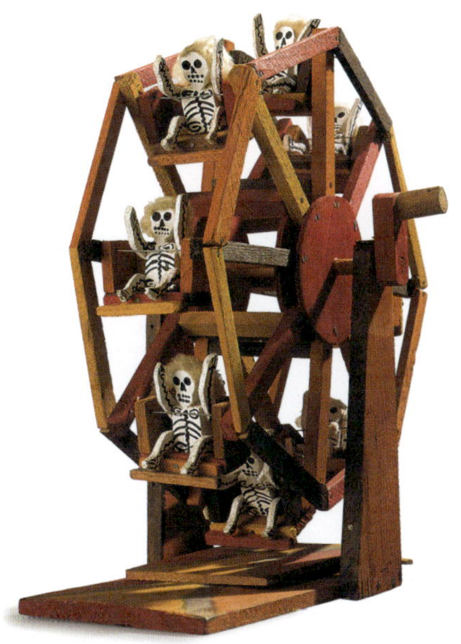

Wheel of Fortune. Painted wood. Private collection.

year. In this scenario the skeletons represented rescue workers in action, citizens anxious to help, the wounded they managed to pull out from some collapsed building, as well as the thieves that carried off televisions or other objects from amid the rubble.

Like the Linares, many folk artists make skeleton figures that change from year to year. In Metepec, in the State of Mexico, the customary "Trees of Life" metamorphose into "Trees of Death." Mexico City inhabitant Roberto Ruiz, who was awarded the National Arts and Science Prize in the Folk Arts and Traditions category, prefers the death theme for his miniatures. His pieces are carved out of bone in a mind-boggling variety of forms. Another artist who concentrates on the theme of death is Saulo Moreno, who makes his figures out of wire and paper.

• DANCING WITH DEATH •

Skeletons are not just confined to all kinds of street-art objects. They show up at some festivals as dancers wearing death's-head masks and black costumes painted with white bones.

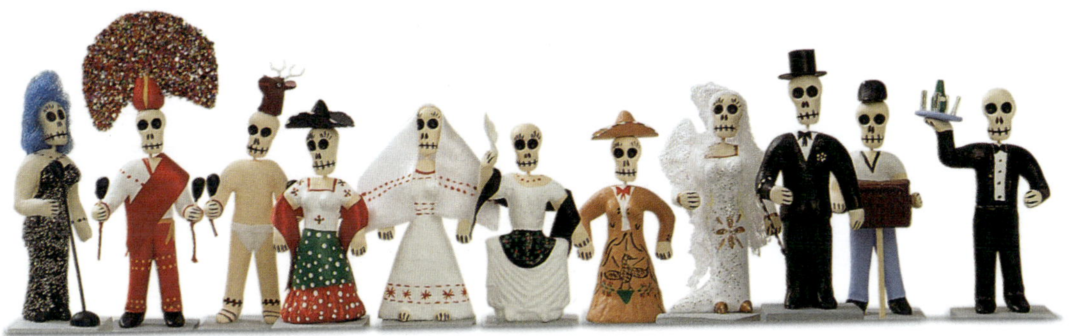

Skeletons dressed as characters from everyday life. Molded, fired, and painted clay.

Although dances are performed in some villages on November 1 and 2 to fête ancestors that are believed to pay a return visit on those days, they do not always feature a skeleton. But in Tepoztlán, Morelos, children dance with rod-and-paper skeletons that are often taller than their partners.

The main character in the Tecuán dance—which is performed on various occasions—is a tiger. In the version from Acatlán, Puebla, however, a skeleton is also present. The sky's the limit for dancing skeletons.

Not only the center of attention on All Soul's Day, skeletons are important figures at other fiestas, for instance, in the dances associated with moralizing plays that the missionaries used to teach religion to the Indians, namely *The Three Powers*, *The Mute People*, *The Seven Sins*, *The Saint Michaels*, *The Devils* and so forth. The state of Guerrero in particular has many such manifestations. For example, Tixtla's version of *The Devils*' dance portrays Lucifer's fall from Heaven, while a group of devils on the mountainside do battle with women and personifications of Death by turns. In Colima, for example, a Grim Reaper will occasionally appear in Nativity plays—another hand-me-down from the moralizing plays.

In a few Holy Week dances, the Jews or Pharisees who kill Jesus Christ wear masks, which in some villages symbolize the nocturnal forces that emerge at the end of every year to take possession of the Earth. On Holy Saturday, with Christ's resurrection, the danger implied by these forces vanishes. Among Jewish people, the personification of Death is common, albeit without any specific dancing role. Places where this takes place are El Doctor, Querétaro; Tanlajás, San Luis Potosí; San Bartolo Aguacaliente, Guanajuato; and Jesús María, Nayarit.

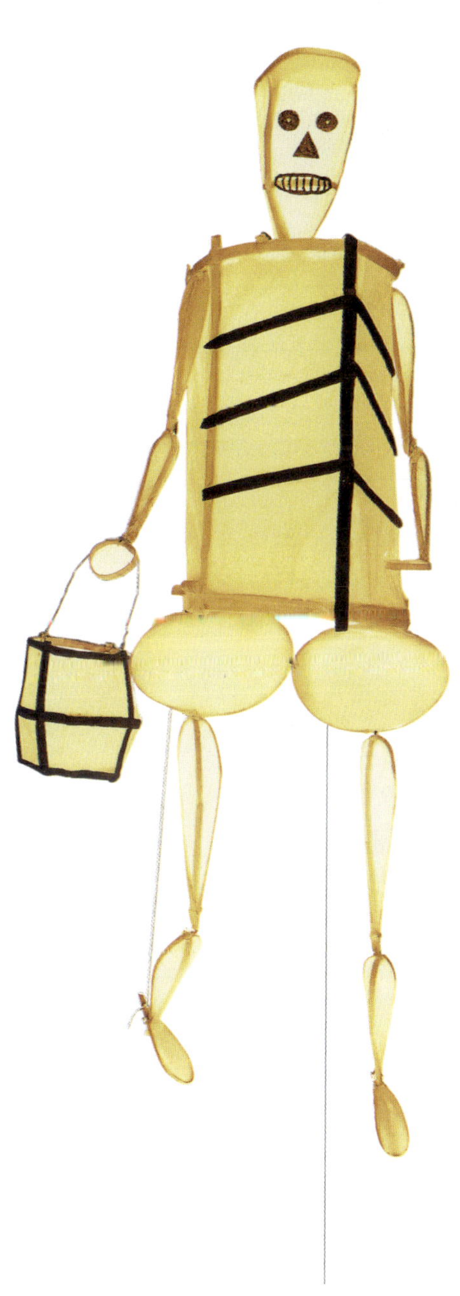

Skeleton for dance. Reed lined with tissue paper, attached with ties. Tepoztlán, Morelos, 1958.
Ruth D. Lechuga Collection of Popular Art / Franz Mayer Museum.

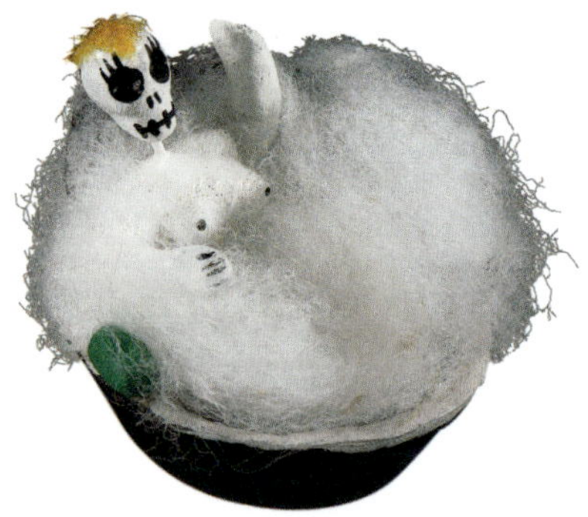

Death in a bathtub. Modeled, fired, and painted clay. Ruth D. Lechuga Collection of Popular Art / Franz Mayer Museum.
OPPOSITE: Luis Nishizawa. *Juderos*, n.d. Oil on wood. 60 × 45.5 cm. Courtesy Andrés Blaisten Foundation.

Mardi Gras or Carnival is another fiesta that might feature skeletons. The Tejorones dancers who perform at Carnival on the Mixtec coast of Oaxaca interpret many different scenes, such as a tiger hunt, childbirth, or a skirmish between an old man and a female skeleton, when the former is sometimes victorious. In Naolinco, Veracruz, one of the Moors in the Moors-and-Christians dance wears a skeleton mask. On the Tarascan plain of Michoacán a change of administration is accompanied by the dance of The Old Men, of which there are two versions: the Handsome Old Men and the Ugly Old Men, the latter making fun of the former. In San Juan Nuevo, the leader of the Ugly Old Men is a skeleton.

All these representations speak of the endless creativity of folk artists in making traditional and decorative objects alike, and assure us that the Mexican tradition of personifying Death, far from dying out, will continue to find fresh new artistic expressions every day. ◆

—Translated by Carole Castelli

Ruth D. Lechuga was a popular art researcher and photographer for more than fifty years. During that time, she created a museum of popular art with her collection, to which issue 42 of *Artes de México* was dedicated. She published *Indigenous Costuming of Mexico* and *Textile Techniques of Ancient Mexico*, among others. The collection Uso y Estilo, under the title *Ruth D. Lechuga: A Mexican Memory*, rescues the photographic work of this author, who, upon her death, donated her photographic archive with more than 20,000 negatives to *Artes de México*.

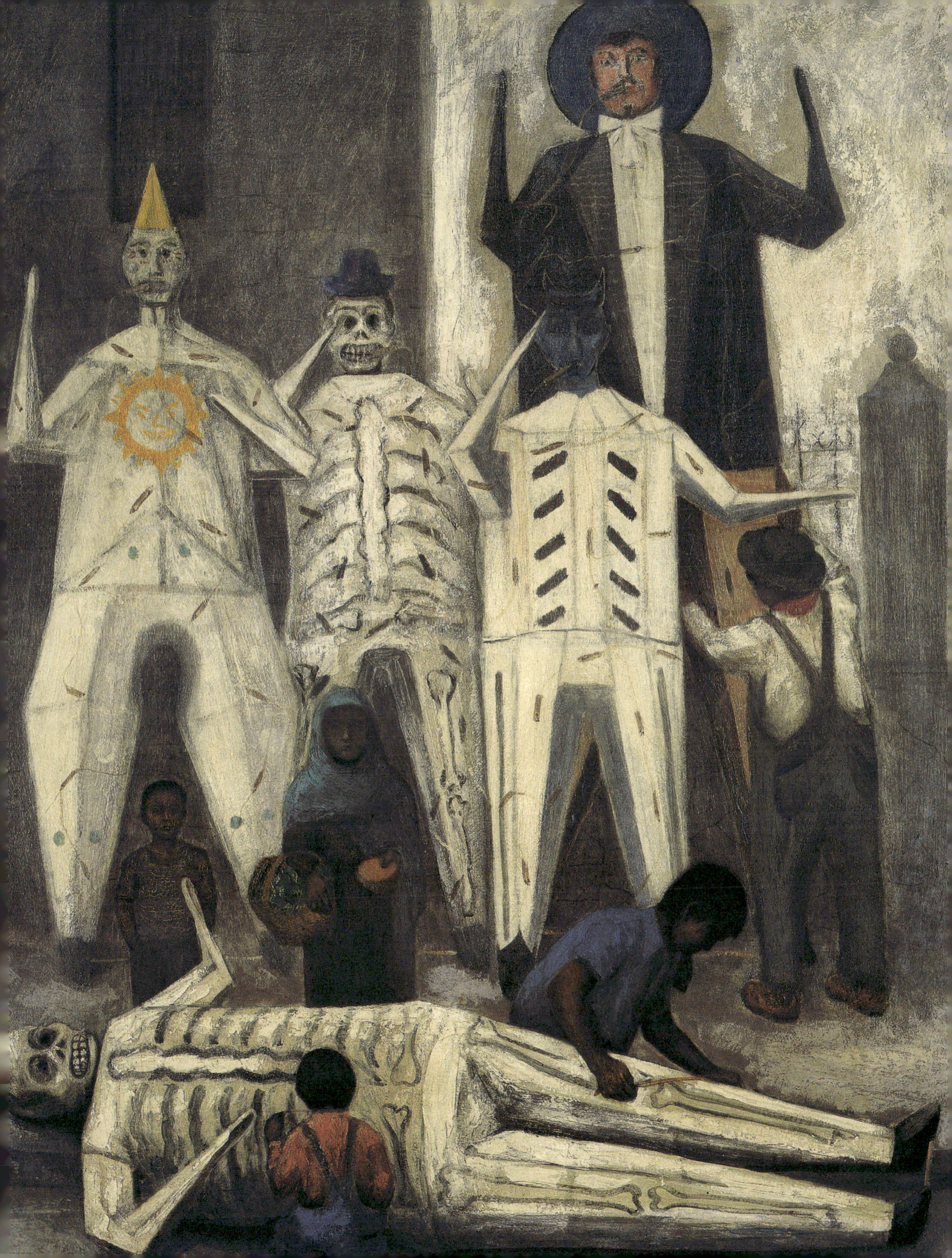

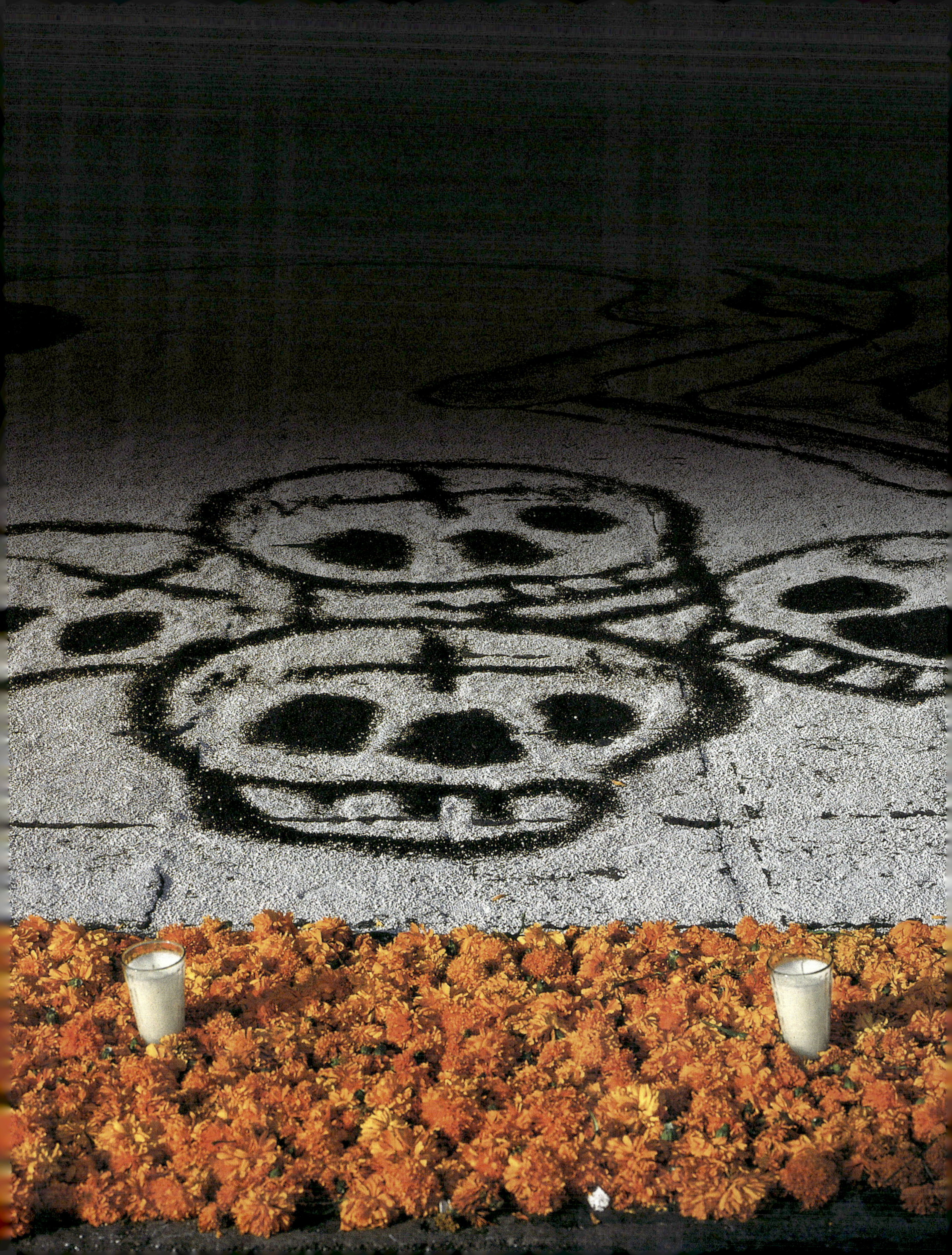

REMEMBRANCE, DISCOVERY, SELF-ASSERTION: CHICANO CUSTOMS ON THE DAY OF THE DEAD

Tomás Ybarra Frausto

◆◆◆◆◆

Mexicans in the United States maintain and transform ancestral culture in dynamic, fluid, and inventive ways. Patterns of culture manifest heterogeneity and variation within the Mexican community itself. Regional, class, gender, and historical factors influence cultural survival and change.

From ancient times to the present, Mexican culture has been anchored on the concept of duality, the eternal flow between opposites in the cycle of life and death. Commemorations of death are at once celebrations of life; rituals of remembrance, discovery and self-assertion. Chicano customs for the Day of the Dead reach back to millennial sources, incorporate present bicultural attitudes, and anticipate future cultural formations.

◆ REMEMBRANCE AND DISCOVERY ◆

The Day of the Dead is a time of remembrance where the living relate to their dead in direct and familiar ways.

The sociopolitical activism of Mexicans/Chicanos in the mid-1960s and the 1970s created a mass national movement of cultural regeneration, recovery, and reclamation. Mexican and Southwestern traditions were appropriated by community-based cultural workers and revitalized, given

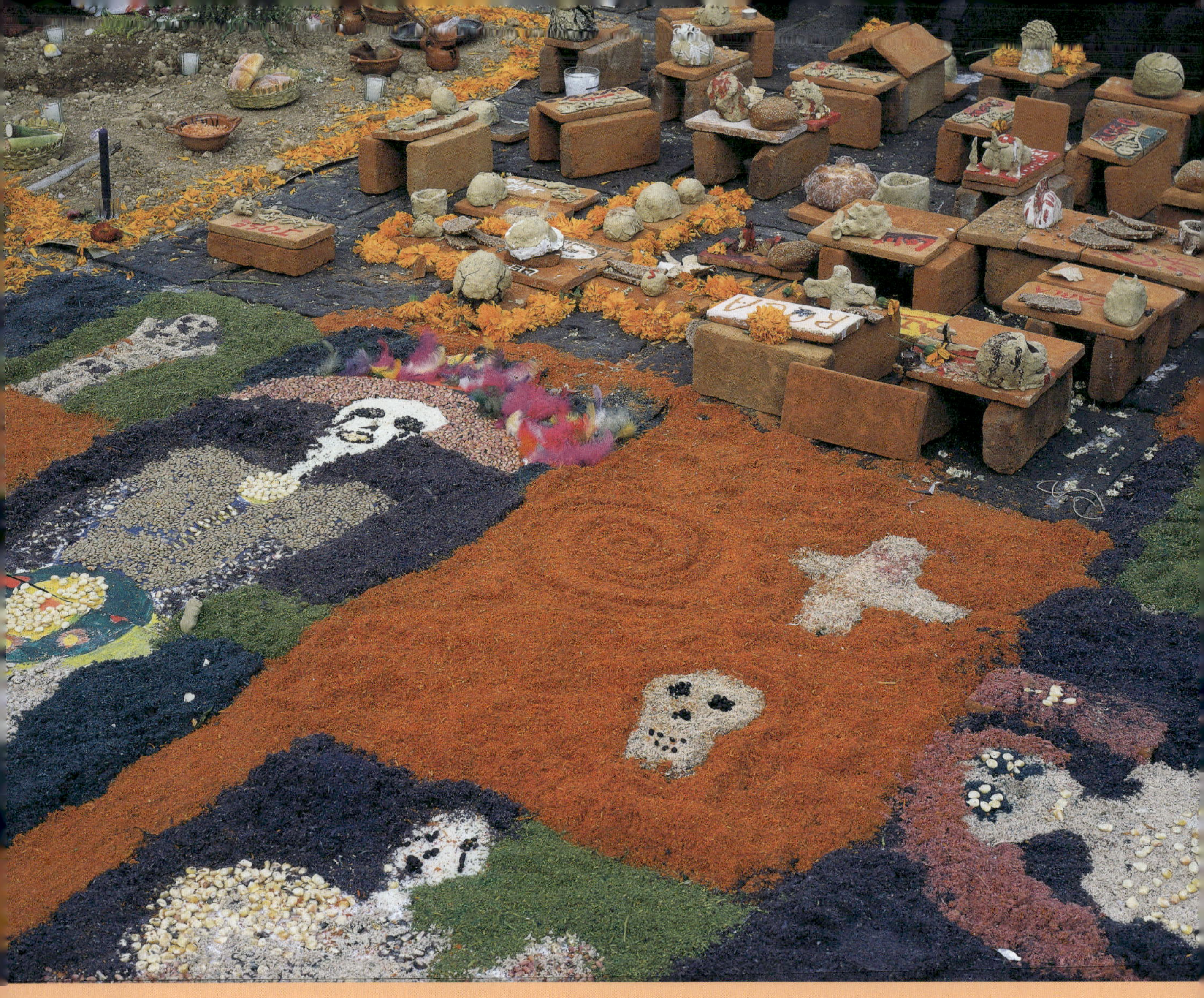

Offering in the Plaza de Santo Domingo. Mexico City, 2002. • **PAGE 188:** Painted sand offering.

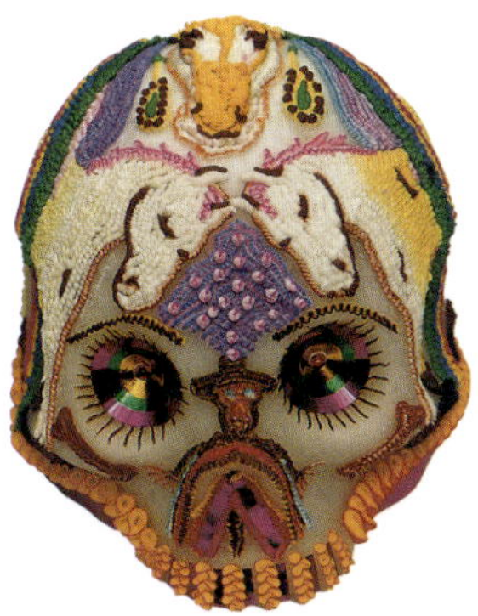

new meanings in diverse contexts. A spectacular example of this process of cultural transformation was the recovery and reinvention of the Day of the Dead by artists' groups and community art centers.

One of the initial resurrected traditions was the reintroduction of José Guadalupe Posada's iconography of *calaveras*. These humorous skeletal figures who mimic the foibles of humankind in the realm of the dead were rapidly incorporated into the Chicano visual vocabulary in posters, murals, and diverse forms of visual art.

Based on Posada's *calaveras,* the Teatro Campesino (Farmworkers' Theater) formed a *banda calavera*, a merry, boisterous band of musicians outfitted in skeleton costumes who paraded through the barrio announcing the theater's performances. Soon *calacas* (death figures) gamboled and pranced about the stage in many sketches created by the Teatro Campesino and subsequently in performances by countless theater groups throughout the country.

The full pantheon of Posada's *calaveras* soon began appearing as illustrations in community newspapers and student journals in colleges and universities. This tradition of print *calaveras* had been maintained in urban Chicano communities since the turn of the century and was now reinforced and expanded. Privately printed and financed by local business concerns, the print *calaveras* are broadsides or booklets with satirical verses lampooning notable community personalities. "*Calaveras*" in this case refer both to the witty, mocking poems and the skull and skeletal illustrations.

Another ancient Mexican tradition that was reinvented on this side of the border was that of the *ofrenda* (an altar or shrine made as an offering to the dead). In Mexican/Chicano communities, the ofrendas tend to

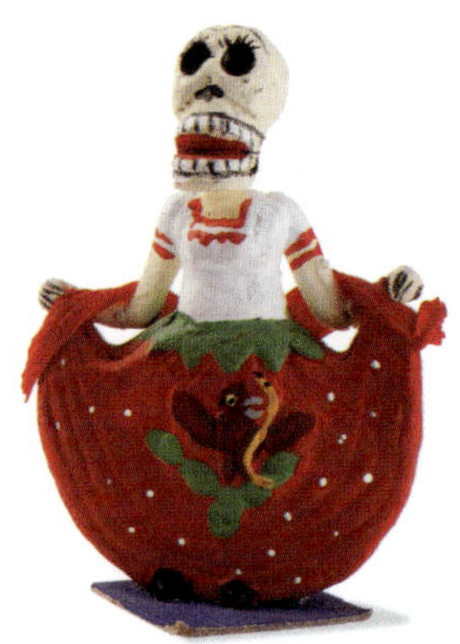

be collective commemorations created by artists in public spaces such as art centers, galleries, or museums. The individual aesthetics and skills of trained artists reinterpret the traditional ofrenda into fanciful, political, and personal visions. The altar form is retained not in its religious context but simply as a functional framework for the display of multilayered accumulations of objects. While traditional elements like candles, flowers, food, images of saints, and photographs of deceased persons remain, Mexican/Chicano ofrendas always include objects culled from a bicultural lived experience.

While the Chicano movement revitalized many Mexican "folk" and "high" art traditions, it also recovered cultural patterns and customs sedimented in the older Mexican settlements of the Southwestern United States. Through audacious and forceful new community rituals, parades and pageants, memorialization of death mixes the old and the new to underscore the eternal cycle of life and death.

• SELF-ASSERTION •

If the 1960s and 1970s were periods of cultural remembering and discovery, the millennium beyond the 1990s portends a phase of active self-assertion, a time of Mexican/Chicano political affiliation with other domestic Latino groups, and cultural connection with subaltern groups worldwide.

Within a new American landscape of multiculturalism, Chicanos will deepen their connections with ancestral Mexican culture engaging in a new and more mature cultural dialogue with contemporary Mexico. Tracings of

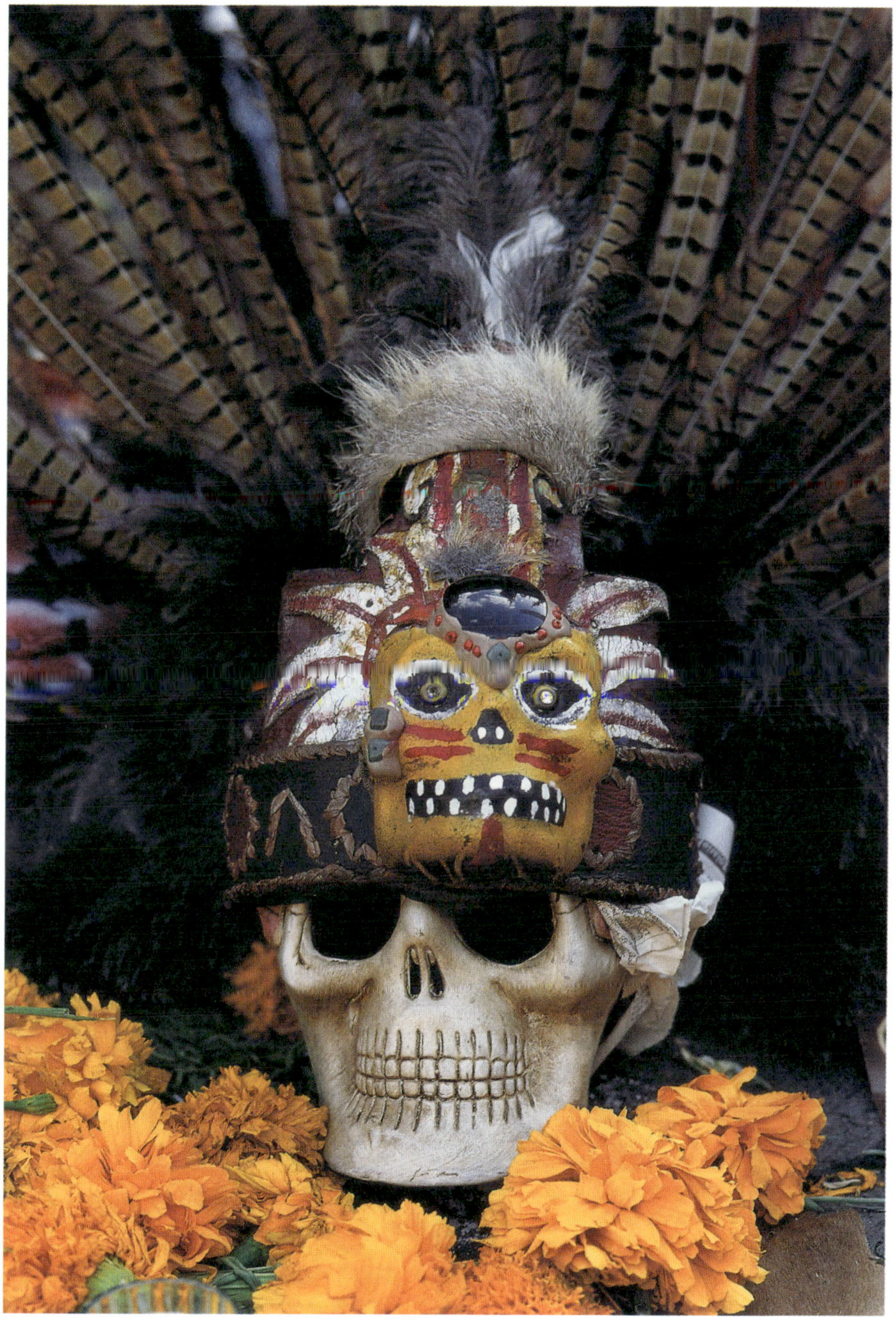

Offering in the Plaza de Santo Domingo. Mexico City, 2002. • **OPPOSITE:** Puebla china. Cooked and painted clay.

this new interface with Mexico are beautifully deployed in Lourdes Portillo's film *La ofrenda* (1989). Tracking traditions of the Day of the Dead on both sides of the border, the film is a powerful depiction of cultural retrieval and empowerment through the remaking of tradition. The following collage of voices from the film allows us to glean current Mexican/Chicano attitude toward the Day of the Dead.

Concha Saucedo: For us *Día de los Muertos* is the day on which our ancestors visit us, and it's the day that connects us to our cultural past. And for people who are separated from their homeland because they're in a foreign culture, and even for those of us who were born here, it becomes a central way of reinforcing [. . .] the community itself.

Amelia Mesa-Bains: Mexicans/Chicanos have revived and adapted Día de los Muertos. For us, the past is a never-ending source of active nostalgia. Here our celebrations may be different in form to those in Mexico, but the spirit of the tradition lives on. Art is about healing. When people participate in art, when they make it, when they view it, it's the same as making yourself well.

Concha Saucedo: La cultura cura means, if we were to translate literally, "culture heals," and essentially what it means is that there are elements in every culture that make people healthy—and particularly for Latinos. We have sometimes had to separate ourselves from that culture, and that separation, that dislocation, has created an imbalance, which in effect is unhealthy. And when we are saying "la cultura cura," we are saying "return to your culture," maintain your culture.

Our struggle is also a battle of memory against forgetting. We must redeem and reclaim the past in ways that transform present reality. ◆

Tomás Ybarra Frausto. Noted professor and essayist of Mexican-American culture. Frausto is currently Associate Director of Culture and Creativity at the Rockefeller Foundation in New York.

OPPOSITE: Humberto Spíndola. Performance as La Catrina, 1994. Tissue paper costume. Author's collection.

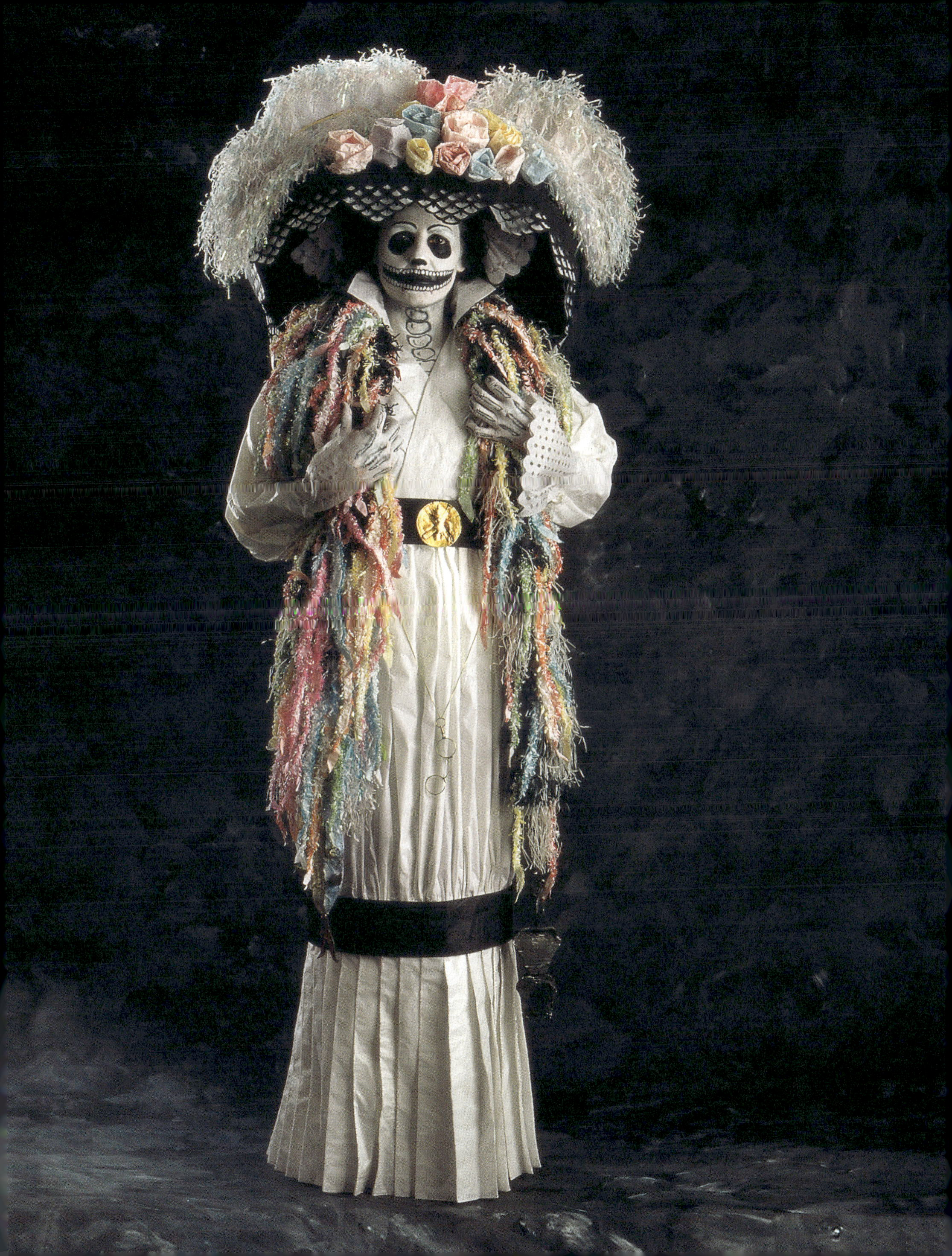

SUGAR BRIDE

Ana García Bergua

◆◆◆◆◆

I enticed Rosenda with some candles encircled by huge roses that I had placed on the altar for the Day of the Dead. That year I decided to decorate it without incense or skulls. My neighbors told me it looked more like a wedding arrangement, with the cake and the bottle of champagne instead of the classic tequila or beer. In the center I placed a portrait of Rosenda, yet another of those that I had found in my grandmother's trunk. I presumed she had been a relative of ours and would for some reason deserve to return.

I slipped into bed and pretended to sleep for several hours. Suddenly, in the wee hours, I heard mouselike noises. Beside the altar I found Rosenda wolfing down mouthfuls of the wedding cake. Her rather threadbare white frock, tied at the waist and with plunging décolletage in the fashion of her day, was getting spotted with cream and crumbs. No one had ever brought her back, she said, since her death; she felt she had spent centuries plunged in utter darkness that smelled of earth. How long has it been? she asked me in surprise. Not so long, I answered, without clarifying just how long. She was a very beautiful woman, voluptuous, yet with a look of fear in her eyes. Against her bosom she clutched a few chrysanthemums made of cloth. She was worried that this was the Final Judgment, that no one was going to forgive her for her many sins. Don't fret, I whispered, taking away her bouquet, I forgive you. I put my arm round her waist and we opened the champagne. In exchange for having her listen to me and being able to touch her, I offered to quench the thirst and hunger she had suffered for so many years. That's enough, she told me, feeling satisfied when, hours later, daylight began to creep in. She then made ready to return to her unknown land, but I locked her in the closet, paying no attention to her muffled cries and complaints. I will turn to dust, whether you like it or not, she sobbed. I let the whole day pass until the closet was silent once more. Meanwhile, I

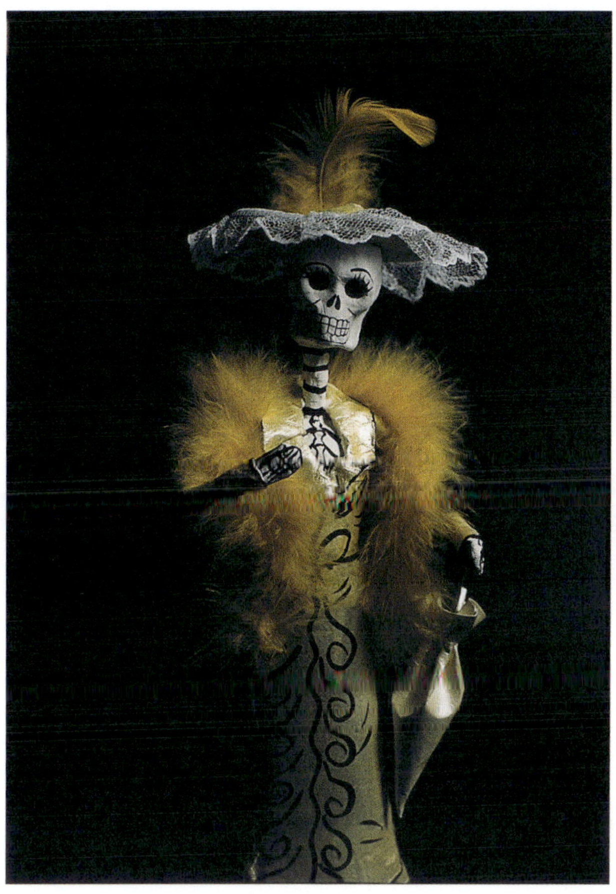

Catrina. Bonded and painted paper, on a wire frame. Private collection.

busied myself ceremoniously disassembling the altar. At twilight, having placed supper on the table and uncorked a bottle of red wine reminiscent of blood, I decided to take my dead woman out of the closet, with the certainty of finding her merely asleep but hungry. But to my great disappointment, among my grandmother's white silk shawls lay, as if blown in by the wind, a sugar skull bearing the name Rosenda on shiny paper on its forehead. It crumbled to dust in my fingers. ◆

—Translated by Carole Castelli

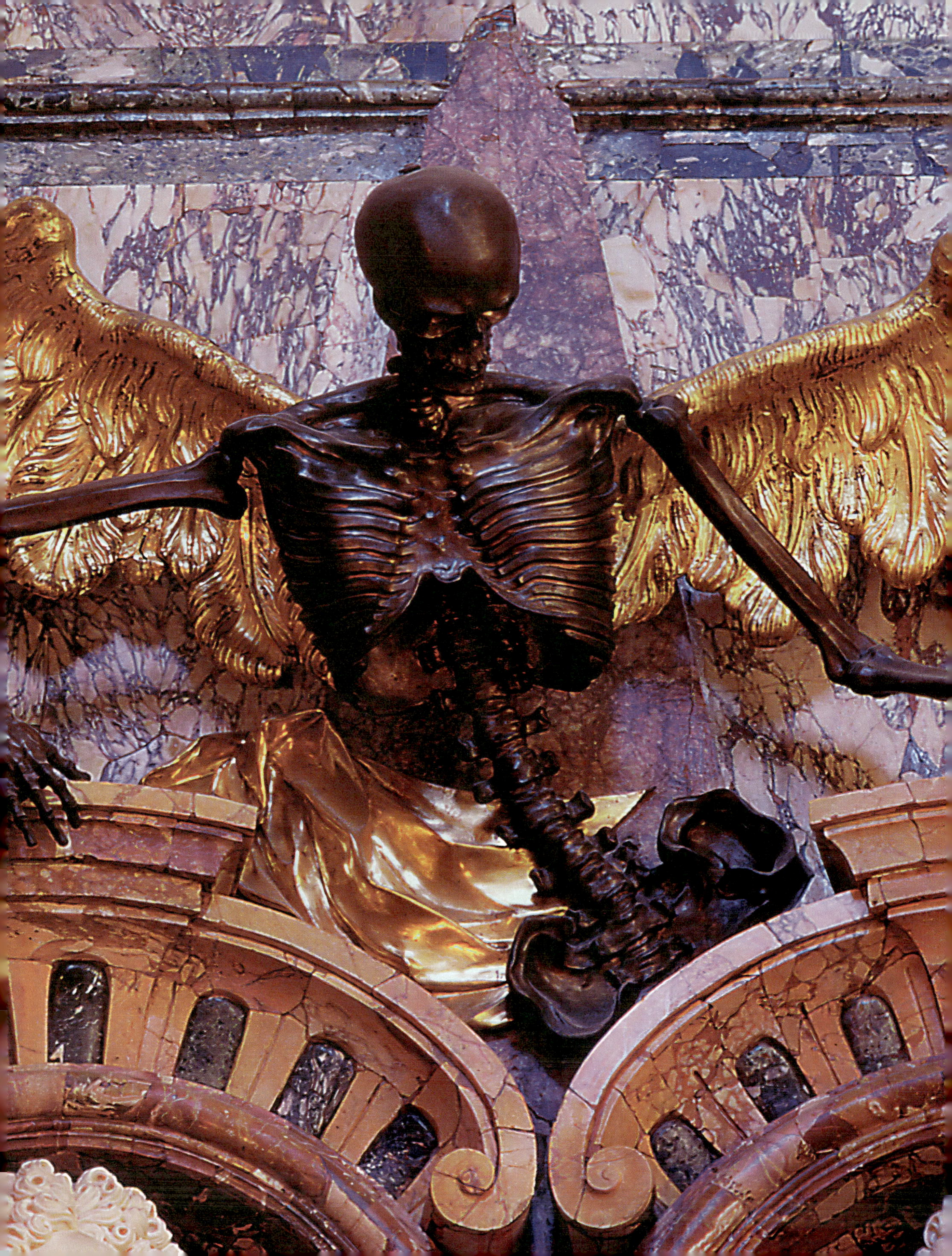

DEATH WITHOUT SKELETONS

Alfonso Alfaro

◆◆◆◆◆

We Mexicans like to feel different, special. This attitude is rooted in the idiosyncrasies of the country that our ancestors began building in the viceregal period. A society like this one that aspires to be a nation needs unifying feelings, converging references, elements identifying its tribe's members and distinguishing them from others: representations in which everyone can recognize his or her own features, no matter how fragmentarily.

Given the absence (fortunately enough) of a sacred, metahistorical association like those posited by collectivities united by blood ties or a common spirit, and also given the lack (unfortunately enough) of the kinds of bonds characteristic of societies founded around a common project, our ancestors and compatriots have had no other option but to create a communal identity which they have constructed over generations. This identity is based upon our history and its signs and thus belongs to the realm of symbols, representations, and culture.

In Mexico, the strength of these cultural ties (i.e., living imagery, complex recollections, community rituals) manages to counterbalance, to a degree, the serious fragmentation of social networks and the precarious nature of vaguely defined common goals.

◆ PATRIOTIC DEATH: THE GRINNING SKULL AND MESTIZO NATIONALISM ◆

A memory of historical cataclysms (the Conquest, invasions, revolutions) that naturally overlaps another, more deeply ingrained memory of earthquakes, added to a long list of thwarted dreams and dashed hopes, led Mexicans to construct one of our most popularly accepted myths: that we are a people with a special relationship with death. According to this collective fantasy, our familiarity with adversity allows us to laugh at it, and thus exact a subtle sort of revenge on our hard lives.

As matrilineal descendants of a people who made offerings of human hearts to Huitzilopochtli and as patrilineal descendants of the illuminati who stoked the Inquisition's bonfires, we could not be just like any other nation—at least, that's what twentieth-century Mexicans thought.

As a national identity took root during the post-revolutionary period, there also arose the fascinating image of a country whose inhabitants were treated in a peculiar way by the dead.

The founding myth of the "Mexican exception"—the alliance at Tepeyac Hill that turned this territory's scions into the chosen few—was thus officially sanctioned and ratified; at the same time, it acquired a different kind of sacredness that was acceptable to the heirs of both liberal and republican laicism. According to the theory that acquired increasing credibility over the twentieth century, we Mexicans have won a kind of poetic victory over that pale shadow which obliterates our hopes and loves at one fell stroke of its scythe: we have lost respect for it and are thus able to stare into its empty eyes, having turned this terrifying figure into something familiar and even ridiculous—nothing more than dry bones.

It goes without saying that this is not a true victory like the one that Christianity posits: evil (death being merely a natural consequence of it) defeated by a sacrifice that redeems us, symbolized by the resurrection of a divine being ("death, where is your victory?"); on the contrary, it is about the underdog challenging the powers that be (a defiant stance not unlike what the French call *pied de nez*) based on a realistic awareness of one's own limits—an attitude perhaps even distantly related to the stoic or Epicurean one.

Artists involved in the revolutionary nationalist movement (from José Guadalupe Posada to Diego Rivera) played a decisive role in sketching out this image of a people who could laugh at death and mitigate the species' unfortunate fate with a sharp, playful remark. They tried to endow the country with a new spirit and aesthetic language. They wanted it to be modern, progressive and for it to reach beyond the bounds of Catholic culture which they deemed "retrograde" and "obscurantist" and which bore a deep influence on both high art and folk art in those days.

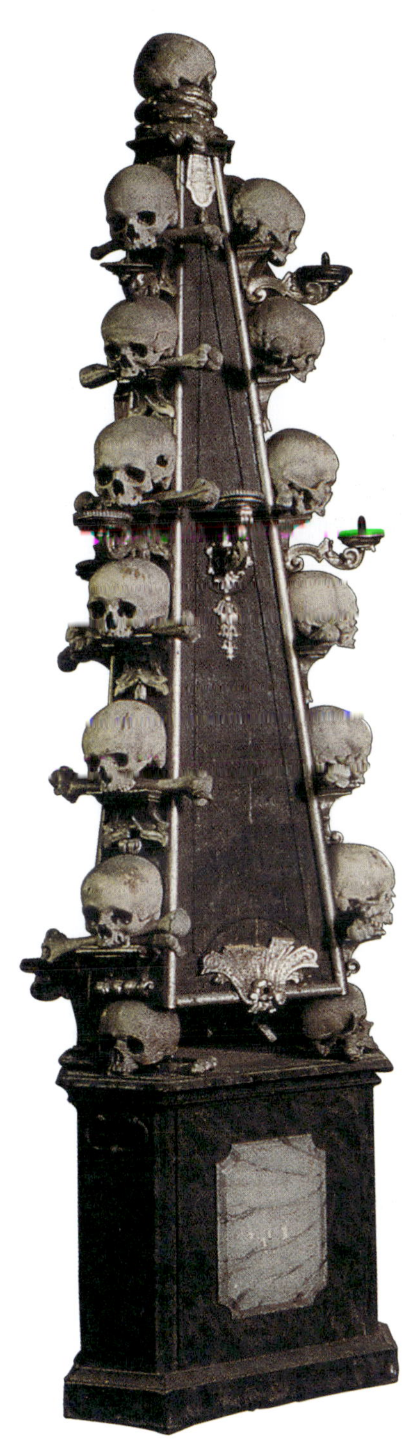

Jean-Blaise Santini Aichel. Ossuary in Sedlec. Bohemia, Czech Republic. • **PAGE 198:** Funerary monument in the chapel of San Francisco Aripa. Rome, Italy.

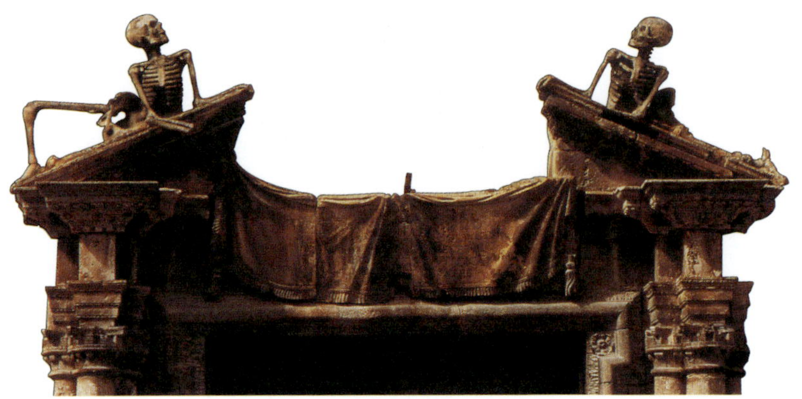

Facade of a church consecrated to the souls in purgatory. Gravina, Italy.

Paradoxically, the most Christian of European legacies—the medieval one—played a decisive role in the formation of this new image. The playful, mocking attitude toward death that revolutionary artists advocated as an idiosyncratic expression of the Mexican spirit bears an elemental kinship with the *danses macabres*. In them, Europeans of the late Middle Ages expressed their ambiguous relationship with the forces of the pre-Christian pantheon—still very much alive at that time—while experiencing a catharsis for the tensions arising from their conflicts with power and authority in a social system with firmly established, practically immutable hierarchies.

These manifestations—common to both folk and high art—reached their peak at the turn of the fifteenth century and pointed to the cracks in an infrastructure that was about to collapse. The eerie high jinks of dancing skeletons thus also echoed the revolts, hunger and plague announcing the Autumn of the Middle Ages, as evoked by Johan Huizinga.

The grotesque, frenzied imagery of European dances of death was used as a decorative motif on etching plates and cemetery walls alike. In them, worldly powerbrokers (wearing crowns, miters, or tiaras) were transformed into ridiculous, fleshless dancing skeletons and mingled with the

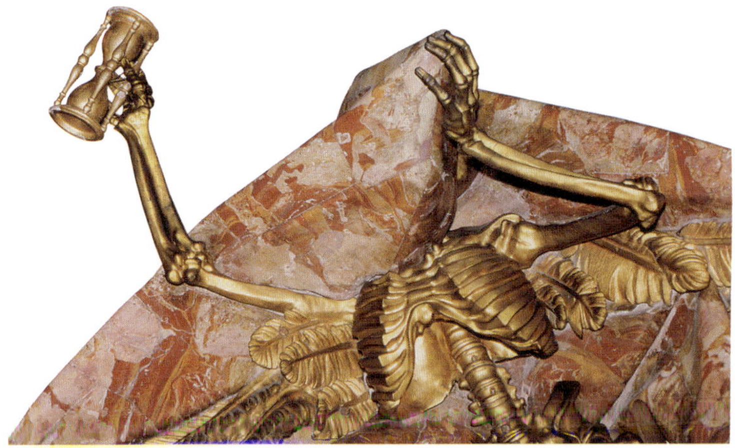

Gian Lorenzo Bernini. Detail from the tomb of Alexander VII. Transept of St. Peter's Basilica, Rome, Italy.

lowly masses—their subjects—who were reduced to the same condition. All the noble families and dignitaries in a society whose class structure (the hierarchical "orders") was practically set in stone were thus felled by the same definitive, inescapable sickle: a glimmer of wisdom proclaiming the human species' indivisibility (". . . *et in pulverim reverteris*") by lamenting life's brevity, by crying out in agony for the end of a troubled epoch, and by exacting a bitter revenge by laughing out loud at it.

In their attempt to purge from society everything that was Hispanic or Christian, the Mexican Revolution's heirs turned back to what they considered to be the other cradle of our cultural memory: the pre-Columbian world and twentieth-century indigenous societies. They believed there was a bountiful, autonomous substratum of culture which, in spite of its oppression by adverse powers, had managed to remain uncontaminated by European influences. They thought this spiritual wellspring still existed in rural communities—in the country folk who had given their blood to the revolution and aspired to once again take control of history. In the eyes of nationalist artists, the various manifestations of pre-Hispanic and folk art, grouped together as a single choir, were the complementary voices in the nation's song.

The recourse to this twofold inspiration, the fusing of these two forms of culture into a single image—as if twentieth-century rural societies were the direct, full-blooded descendants of native American civilizations, and as if the viceregal era had been but an ill-fated historical parenthesis rather than a period in history in which the foundations for a new society had been established—contributed in a powerful way to consolidating the cultural model of revolutionary Mexico.

Paul Westheim—who in 1953 began analyzing the disturbing affinity between formal expressions of the macabre medieval spirit and those that were becoming the norm among progressive sectors of Mexico City society—painted a much richer and more nuanced picture. Though he failed to question the budding myth, he observed the grave, tragic character of conceptions of death in pre-Hispanic societies (which naturally contrasts with the ecstatic spirit of revolutionary skeletons).

The dream was nonetheless beautiful as well as useful (it allowed Mexicans to create a deep, intangible cultural nexus and added to the collection of specific elements that they seemed to have in common) and it indeed followed its own course, its influence growing steadily as the Mexican Revolution itself became an object of patriotic worship.

The century's most notable intellectual, Octavio Paz, bore a decisive influence on the formation and consolidation of the image of our country as an exceptional place in terms of the way it dealt with death. In *The Labyrinth of Solitude*, Paz speaks of his own disenchanted outlook on life and history, characteristic of an individual who is the product of high Western culture and who identifies with Voltaire's and Kant's legacies, but also with Goya's. The book was written in Paris in 1950, coinciding with the time and place of birth of existentialism.

Paz's spirit of honesty—most likely that of an agnostic who was deeply aware of the transcendental dimension of both the human being and the universe—his objective, critical intellect—keeping him from falling under the spell of totalitarian illusions—his kindred sensibility with Lucretius and Petronius, making him wary of utopian dreams: all this allowed him to perceive the truly noble and yet tragic, Epicurean dimension in the aesthetic project of the generation of artists that preceded his own. As it is depicted in Paz's work, death is the end rather than salvation, since one is not redeemed through suffering—indeed, it is only art, work, and love that can save us (albeit provisionally).

The way in which revolutionary artists and popular culture in general within Mexico City's urban context faced death—hilarious and hurt, resigned and ironic, rebellious, despairing—was masterfully described in Paz's essay, leaving a deep mark on Mexican's self-awareness.

In his penetrating meditation on the reality and fate of his homeland, Paz gave life to a literary character who allowed him to exemplify the transformations of a youthful country still trying to figure out which course to follow at a time when its future remained undefined. This character's name had already appeared in Mexican literature, particularly in Samuel Ramos's work, but it is Paz who fleshed him out and turned him into a pillar of Mexican culture.

"The Mexican" of whom Paz speaks is not a prototype acting as a representative specimen of all the country's peoples (like a sociological or statistical example); rather, as the author of *The Labyrinth* explicitly states, his features are based on a single sector of the country's population: the man of the post-revolutionary age, aware of his society, striving to construct his own identity as a subject and committed to building a better Mexico.

Mestizo Mexicans—hungering for modernity but still living in a world permeated by the baroque spirit, recently deprived of the community references that had lent their lives harmony and security and thus impelled to search for symbolic points of reference, concerned with making their nation a respected one in keeping with the grand ideals of Criollos from the viceregal period—were singled out (among the country's wide spectrum of communities) as models based upon which the great poet and essayist would construct a wonderful literary persona: "the Mexican," the Malinche's bastard offspring who, sobbing and laughing at the same time, chokes on *pan de muerto* (bread traditionally made for the Day of the Dead), while his shattered soul explodes in the main square along with the fireworks after dusk on Independence Day.

Sketched out by Paz's talented hand, this image was the living portrait of certain sectors of the urban population (especially those living in Mexico City) whose features merged with those of an ideal subject seeking his roots in the cultures that are the product of the Enlightenment and Romanticism. *The Labyrinth*'s readers (a restless, erudite fringe of Mexican society: the spiritual offspring of nineteenth-century liberalism) were fascinated by the fact that they could identify with this character who, though his roots were immemorial, yearned for emancipation and the freedom to determine his own fate.

Swelling the ranks of the Mestizo cultural majority—over these years of accelerated social integration—many Mexicans came to accept as their own a poetic depiction that was a social project in and of itself. Individuals recently incorporated into nationalist culture finally knew what the features of their country's identity were—in lay or non-confessional terms—and what characteristic image of their nation they could present to a world whose acknowledgment was essential to them; thus, they enthusiastically adopted the new physiognomy depicted in this dazzling text, eventually turning it into a mirror.

Thanks to *The Labyrinth*, numerous inhabitants of the country's various regions learned what being Mexican meant and found out that one of the basic traits of their homeland's cultural identity was an ironic, playful, and defiant stance on death. They then began to slowly adopt an imagery, rituals, and opinions with which many of them had had no prior contact.

During the same epoch, other archetypes of the same nature were conceived, disseminated, and superimposed on the one we just described. In *Artes de México*'s issue on tequila (no. 21), we explored how this regional liquor's symbolic image was constructed and linked to the figures of the *charro* and the mariachi, and how this image reinforced the models needed by a society eager to adopt a consistent national identity.

Later, as revolutionary nationalism turned into an object of consensus, its models and aesthetic were disseminated more broadly, sometimes to the point of becoming cliché. There arose a Day of the Dead (based on the comic-macabre model described above), at first unofficially and then almost officially recognized by many branches of government. The aesthetic of the skeleton then spread to the realms of state-sponsored art and to more independent experimental practice, consumerism, and advertising.

"Skinny Death riding its scrawny mule" (cry the *lotería* callers at town fairs, to describe this figure on the game board), the disjointed, wisecracking figure of death that served as a model for Mestizo nationalism (and whose emblematic depictions are sugar skulls and the *Catrina*, or Death dressed as an elegant lady, as seen in one of Diego Rivera's murals) has spread, along with urban culture, practically across the whole country in less than a century, exemplifying the progress and consolidation of a communal identity. Today, even in regions where fifty years ago no one had heard of this image of death, funeral offerings imbued with an air of lightheartedness, humor, irony, and irreverence can be seen everywhere in late October and early November.

It is important to note that in Mexico—as in the European tradition—even the most conventional expressions of official folklore, colorfully decorated sugar skulls and dancing skeletons refer to the living rather than to the dead. The names written on skulls are our own (and those of our friends or of contemporaries blessed by power, fame, and fortune) rather than those of the dearly departed. This ritual is a playful way of expressing the message behind Ash Wednesday—that the sickle that cuts down everything in its path makes us equals, that hierarchies are merely provisional since there exists a deeper reality invisible to our worldly eyes.

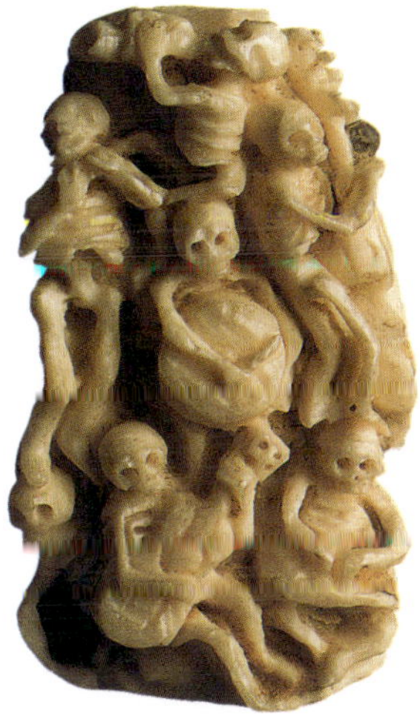

Roberto Ruiz. Miniature carved in bone. Mexico City, 1980s.
Ruth D. Lechuga Collection of Popular Art / Franz Mayer Museum.

The folklore surrounding death rites may be more rooted in the medieval European (and hence culturally Christian) tradition than our society would like to admit. It might be yet another manifestation of the fact that our cultures are firmly tied to the baroque world—a world where death never lies out of sight, or out of one's awareness.

The corrosively critical *calavera* (a poetic eulogy in life directed at the powers that be) thus coexists with an affectionate version of the same (in verses dedicated to our friends). The latter not only unites us by implying our kinship and common frailty: laughing with someone can also be a rudimentary and often clumsy way for shy individuals to express their affection for someone from a safe distance.

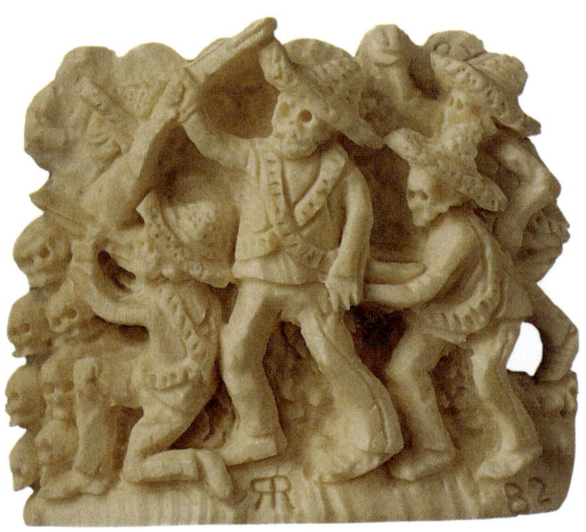

Roberto Ruiz. Miniatures carved in bone. Mexico City, 1980s.
Ruth D. Lechuga Collection of Popular Art / Franz Mayer Museum.

• DEATH WITHOUT THE GRIM REAPER: FILIAL TENDERNESS AND RESPECT •

The myth has proved to be effective because of its multiple meanings: in formal terms, the visual symbol for the new nationalist folklore is practically indistinguishable from and bears the same names as another object that functions on an entirely different symbolic level—the altar for the dead or offering. Viewing them superficially or from an outsider's perspective, one might think that these short-lived monuments that seem to abound in government buildings or Mexico City hotels and restaurants are identical to those that devout families in rural areas or residential neighborhoods use to decorate their homes or the graves of loved ones. In either case, we are dealing with compositions featuring flowers, candles, incense, food (most often bread and fruit), and evocative objects referring to a person or a theme and exhibiting varying degrees of fantasy (and sometimes true outbursts of creativity). But this is where similarities end: the home altar is always made for specific individuals and the mood of the ceremony is always serious, tender, imbued with respect and longing. There is no mockery or irony here.

Rural families from countless regions of Mexico—above all, those from predominantly indigenous cultural areas (as tradition is not as deep-rooted

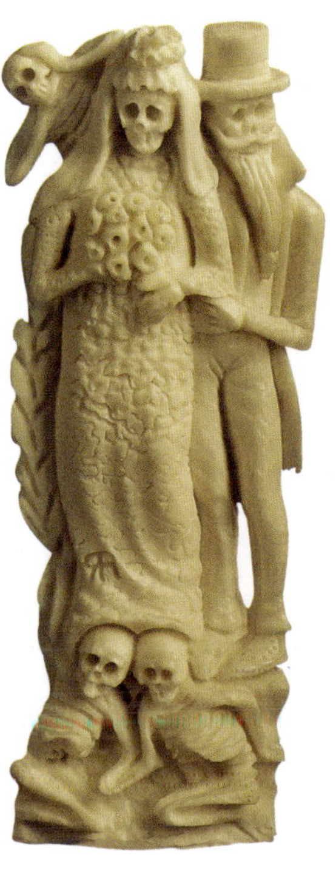

in places where Criollo culture is dominant)—have learned from elders that souls that have gone to Heaven as well as those lingering in Purgatory are only allowed to come and visit their relatives once a year when the Catholic Church's calendar commemorates All Saints' Day and All Souls' Day. That is why they carefully draw a path strewn with marigold petals that will guide the dead to the banquet table, set up in their home's main room; that is why, at least one day ahead of time, they begin cleaning and sprucing up their loved ones' graves. Preparing the feast requires the whole family's participation and considerable expense—the fact that it takes place at the height of harvest season is no coincidence. Putting the offering in place kindles intense emotions: the head of the family sometimes says a few words about those who are honored that day. In their respectful, heartfelt speeches, they place the emphasis on filial duties and deference, and explain to their children the values on which the cohesion of rural families is based: solidarity, respect, remembrance, and generosity.

This celebration is the most important event in the ceremonial life of millions of Mexicans. It is how they commemorate what they glean from their productive activities (agriculture) and strengthen the most important

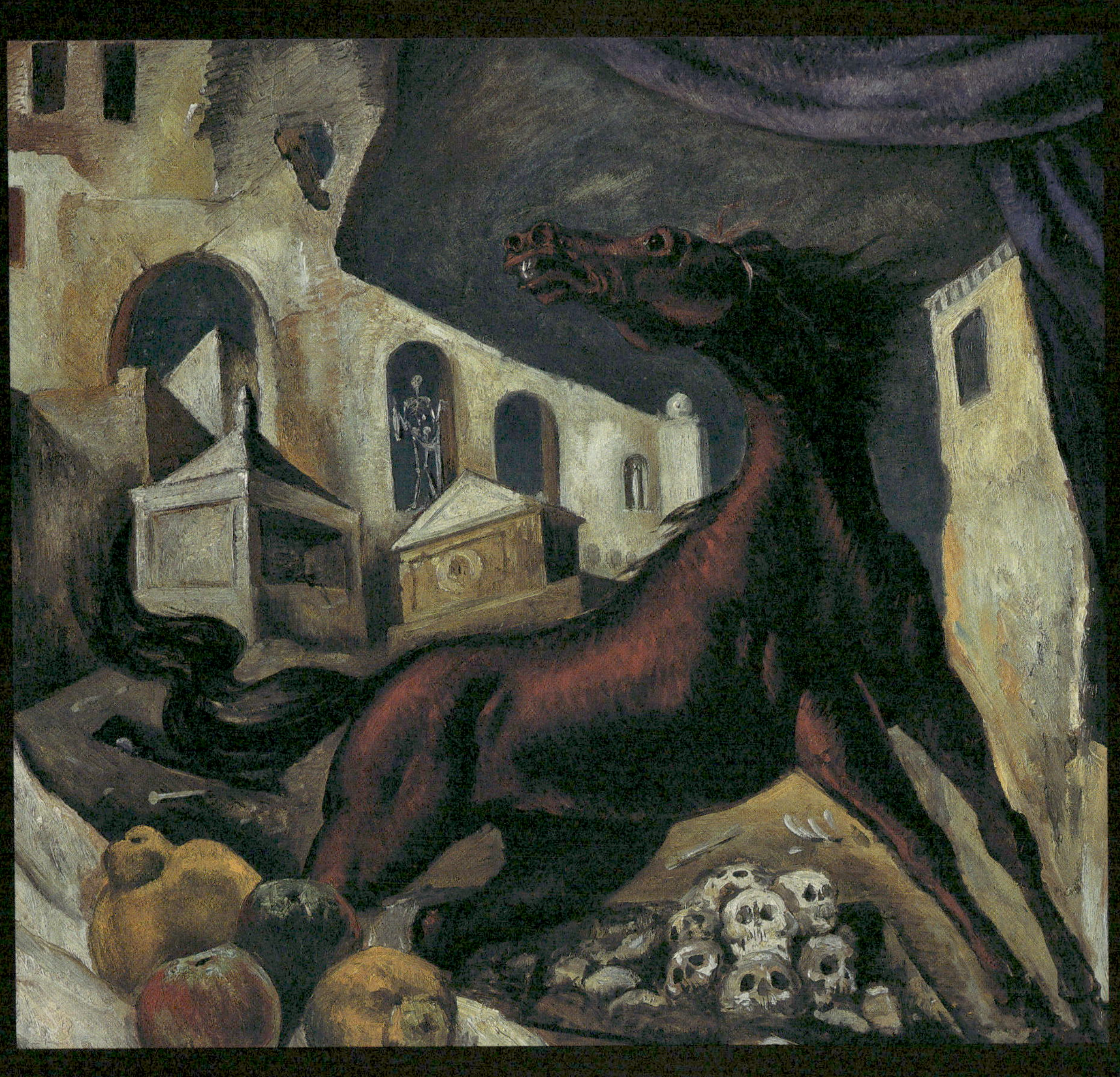

Roberto Montenegro. *Desesperación* (Desperation), 1949. Oil on masonite. 60 × 64 cm.
Courtesy Andrés Blaisten Foundation.

network in their social life—the family—while community ties are reaffirmed and reinforced in mutual visits, invitations, and hospitality. Paying homage to one's ancestors allows small children to clearly understand the responsibilities they will have as adults, deriving from a sense of gratitude: to be considerate of their parents and care for them not only through their senior years but also after death. Remembering is a way of prolonging life, of mitigating over generations the tragic effect brought on by the definitive annihilation of an individual, a consciousness or a hope. (Westheim notes that to ancient Mexicans, individual identity continued to exist over a span of several generations before it merged with an undifferentiated cosmic soul.)

The commemorative rituals that so many families from different states of Mexico carry out with such feeling—sparing, moreover, little time, effort, or expense—links them to other peoples around the globe (in Asia, for instance) where ancestor worship lies at the heart of ceremonial life and where the value system's most definitive reference is family unity.

In some cases, the banquet continues in the cemetery. Here families share fine foods with deceased relatives, as Romans did in the catacombs. Kith and kin converge by the grave and calmly chat with the decorum suited to a family gathering. As with any celebration, music often lends liveliness and warmth to the homage. *Norteño* bands, trios, or mariachis are sometimes overheard playing at different graves, while deceased parents' favorite songs bring a sweet sense of nostalgia to their children's hearts.

Given its ambiguous nature (at once valuable and detrimental) and the fact that it is a substance that can be made sacred, given its mysterious power to provoke both laughter and tears and to summon up at once dreams and nightmares, alcohol is an essential element of our rural world's celebrations and rituals, as it is in many other cultural regions around the globe. It is almost always a part of Day of the Dead festivities—in many places, it is the ceremonial offering *par excellence*—though its use varies according to local libation customs: though most often consumed in moderation, it is sometimes used in a violent and excessive manner. Hence the exalted character that certain funeral banquets adopt and that some hasty visitors mistake for an attitude akin to the jovial euphoria of altars inspired in the revolutionary tradition. In any case, these manifestations' general mood radically contrasts with the sentiment prevailing in official or secular folklore. There are no belly laughs here, no mockery of death, no boasting ("life is worth nothing"); on the contrary, these rites attempt to perpetuate the presence of loved ones by remembering them, extolling the value of life, and prolonging its pleasures as one enjoys the banquet, flowers, and music with one's senses.

These celebrations very rarely feature the distinctive signs of the first figure of death that we analyzed. The few images of skulls and bones we may see are related to the mortuary insignia of Catholic imagery (and are devoid of any sense of playfulness), though decorative elements derived from official altars have slowly begun to appear. These offerings bereft of dancing skeletons or sugar skulls allow us to see that many Mexicans (indeed, a majority of the rural population) have a different concept of the universe and a different understanding of fate; moreover, they shatter the homogenous image we have of a country united by a national essence characterized by a glorious rebel spirit that leads one to risk one's life and defy fate. By facing death in their own considerate, devout, characteristically simple and unaffected manner, these Mexicans have enriched our common motherland with the vigor of a distinct culture that bears a close resemblance to others flourishing throughout the world.

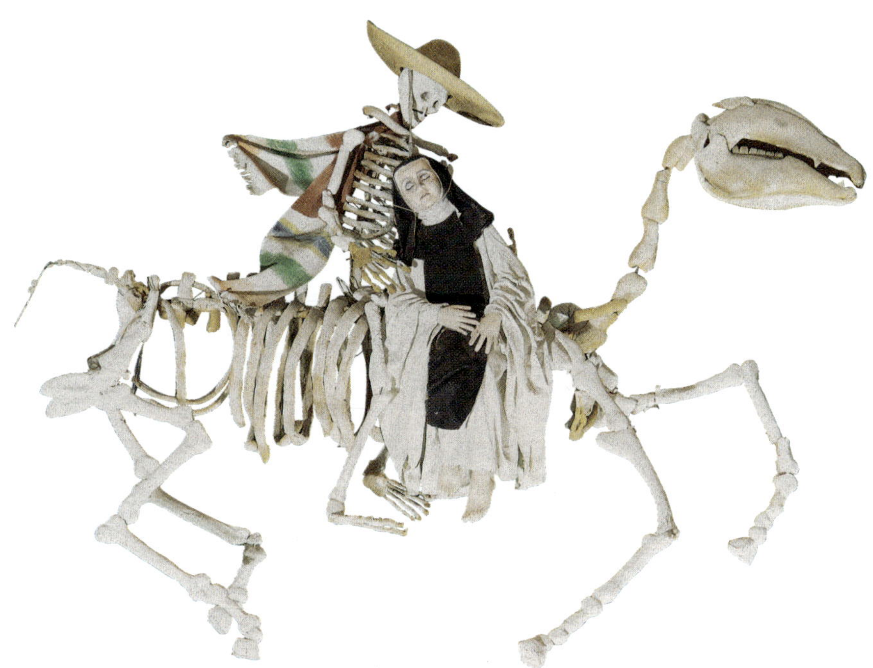

Central image of an altar of the dead dedicated to the Hieronymite nuns. University of the Cloister of Sor Juana.

We have seen that death has many faces in Mexico—not only that of the Catrina—and that this country is less magical and less homogenous than we like to think. In a country with so many different cultures, there are indeed many ways of dealing with pain, grief and the unknown.

• OTHER FACES OF DEATH: GHOSTS AND APPARITIONS •

In the rural world and its near neighbors, death may appear in many guises: in the beloved shape of parents, grandparents, or as the little angels personifying deceased infants—whose souls are only allowed to visit us when they are invited—but also as the terrifying grin of the wraiths who appear on dark and dismal nights or in deserted places. Ritual lends one the advantage of foresight. Beings from beyond the grave are always troubled and restless, no matter how much they were loved while they were alive. On the Day of the Dead, the gates to the world beyond can be opened and closed at determined hours (the same way that, in the modern world, psychoanalysis can open and shut the doors to the subconscious, the therapist's watch always as closely monitored as Death's hourglass).

In certain places, these ceremonies end with a fanfare, meant to remind beloved ancestors that their visit has ended and that they must return to their spectral abode. They must be discouraged from prolonging their stay among the living: their lingering presence always implies grief and great danger. Feeling the presence of souls furtively wandering among us along mountain trails or back alleys is likely to make one's skin crawl. In our country's rural folklore (as it happens throughout the world), tales abound concerning the sometimes protective and often perverse shadows of the dead mingling with the wild spirits of nature and creatures of the underworld.

In French, ghosts are called *revenants*—literally, "returners"—and in France as well as Mexico, no effort is spared to stop them from meandering about and to make sure that they remain on the other side of the chasm separating reality's different levels. In the same century as José Guadalupe Posada, Diego Rivera and Octavio Paz, another notable Mexican artist, Juan Rulfo, wrote a very important book that reveals the underlying structure of the visible and invisible realms in this rural world, where the boundaries between life and death are as tenuous as those separating reason from the subconscious in individuals who are either supremely gifted or disturbed. Thanks to *Pedro Páramo*, this dimension also came to form part of our high culture.

The silhouettes of death sketched out by these two new figures (that of folkloric ghost stories and the profound, refined persona depicted in Rulfo's texts) show us two other ways in which people still commonly face death in our country. It goes without saying that both of these are highly idiosyncratic and yet utterly universal since, in essence, they are similar to the characteristic ways that different peoples on other continents have of dealing with the phenomenon.

• METAPHYSICAL HELPLESSNESS •

In twentieth-century Mexico, it was not only the most eminent essays, novels, prints or murals that attempted to decipher our inseparable shadow's mysteries. Two of the epoch's most profound and powerful works of poetry also explore the issue, as is obvious from their titles: José Gorostiza's *Death Without End* and Xavier Villaurrutia's *Nostalgia for Death*. In spite of their profound differences, they both belong to the great Spanish literary

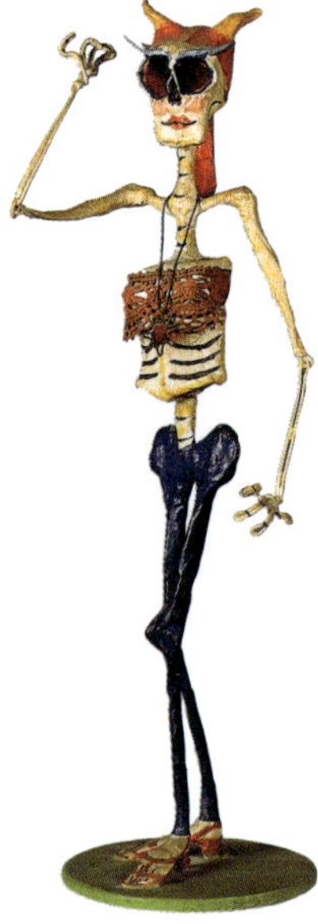

Saulo Moreno. Skeleton A-go-go. Bound and painted paper, on a wire frame. Mexico City, 1968. Ruth D. Lechuga Collection of Popular Art / Franz Mayer Museum.

tradition and broach the issues that have disturbed the Western conscience ever since Nietzsche and Heidegger.

Faced with a death without the promise of redemption and a life whose last frontier seems to be an empty sign, when one's existence becomes at once a fleeting paradise and an intermittent hell, to what may human beings resort besides the rebelliousness of art?

• THE MODERN WAY TO DIE: ASEPSIS AND DISCRETION •

Obviously, not all the spirits that Western ideology has adopted as fundamental references in our country share such a profound, refined vision imbued with both disillusionment and greatness.

In this respect, most upper-class urban Mexicans have an attitude similar to that of their European or American counterparts. We only need to observe the landscaped design of new graveyards (which go by different names now), the neutral atmosphere of funeral parlors, the increase in cremations, the sobriety of funeral services held in churches in residential neighborhoods. Here as in developed countries, death is an issue one

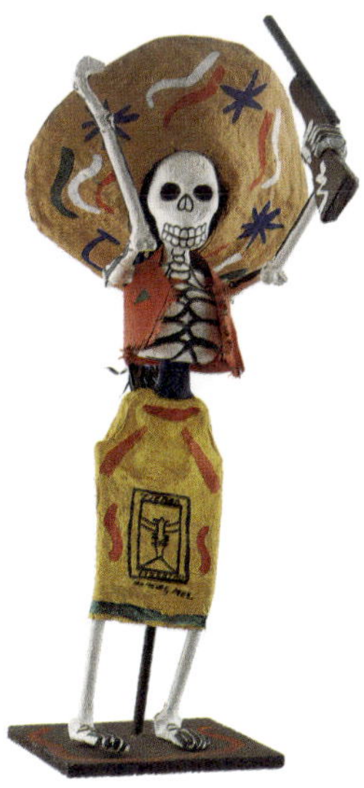

Zapatista Death. Bonded and painted paper, on a wire frame. Mexico City, 1989.

broaches with caution and decorum. Laughter is obviously out of the question. Members of these groups may occasionally take part in conventional manifestations of revolutionary folklore (which have been embraced by certain sectors of the middle class) though they will always maintain a safe distance and tend not to see any relation between the merrymaking skeletons and their own dead.

Death, in this cultural terrain, has undergone the same evolution as in post-Enlightenment Western societies, as Philippe Ariès and Louis-Vincent Thomas have pointed out. Some Mexicans living in the realm of modernity await resurrection while others observe with resignation the brevity of human life; a few of them still practice spiritualism, others pray for reincarnation, but practically no one makes a mortuary offering poking fun at his or her dead relatives.

Over recent decades, historians and anthropologists have taken a great interest in the study of attitudes toward death. Thanks to them, we are now aware of the huge transformations that Western societies have undergone, initially due to the extensive evangelization of European folk-cultures beginning in the seventeenth century and then, 100 years later, with the spread, no less importantly, of the Enlightenment's ideals and values (though this second process was more gradual and at first confined to elites).

These phenomena had a major influence on the beliefs and perceptions of both societies and individuals. The growth of the Catholic and Protestant Churches during the baroque period led to the gradual elimination of cultural expressions of a pre-Christian origin (still very much alive at this time, particularly among rural populations); the Enlightenment, for its part, encouraged the adoption of social models based on rational intelligence as their only guiding principle rather than on community and emotional ties.

As for the topic that concerns us here, these processes led to the supplanting of traditional attitudes and behavior while new northern European standards gradually gained acceptance. Throughout the Western world (including Mexico), people imbued with the spirit of modernity began to scorn ancient practices, qualifying them as superstitions. This category of course included offerings of foodstuffs and *agapes* (banquets held in cemeteries by the first Christians, after the fashion of the ancient Romans—a tradition Europeans had indeed conserved for millennia). In this regard, it is interesting to recall the reproving tone of José Tomás de Cuéllar's account of the Day of the Dead in Mexico City in 1882. What seems to most offend his sensibilities is the characteristic informality of family celebrations—an informality interpreted as irreverence by a man whose gaze had been molded by the modern's serious, distanced outlook upon things otherworldly.

In issue no. 43 of *Artes de México*, we broached in greater detail the transformation that affected Western societies' symbolic systems as a whole, as well as those of peripheral countries like our own in a less profound manner and at a later date. The progress of science, technical knowledge, medicine, and hygiene fueled the dream that reason and health could prevail. Any expression of what was considered to be related to evil or death was banished from sight and consciousness: madness and illness, extravagance and licentiousness, excess and death became indecent topics of conversation; boldly expressed emotions were also rejected as improper. Europeans—and cultures assimilated by their high culture—believed that everything could be (or had to be) clean and transparent. Depictions of *danses macabres* were destroyed and cemeteries were relegated to the outskirts of cities (following the example of the Cimetière des Innocents in Paris): new necropolises had to be built on the periphery, allegedly in order to prevent what was then commonly believed to be a risk of contagion, but more importantly, in order to eliminate depictions of death from the collective imagery.

Individuals whose cultural references are those of modernity have eradicated from their immediate environment practices that they consider archaic and a sensibility that they deem excessive. And they do not sublimate their grief with prints of laughing ghouls.

• FROM MACABRE DOLORISM TO A GENTLER KIND OF DEATH •

There is yet another face of death that enjoys a favored status in Mexico. In every corner of the country, one may encounter often splendid expressions of a tragic sort of pain: martyrs who have been dismembered or riddled with arrows, lost souls subjected to purification by fire, wretches enduring the most unlikely tortures, or bloody, mutilated and flayed Christs experiencing infinite suffering (in this regard, see *Artes de México* issue no. 10 and also the book *Corpus Aureum* in the Uso y Estilo collection).

Pious art of the baroque period flourished in our country and was indeed adopted as one of our culture's innate forms of expression.

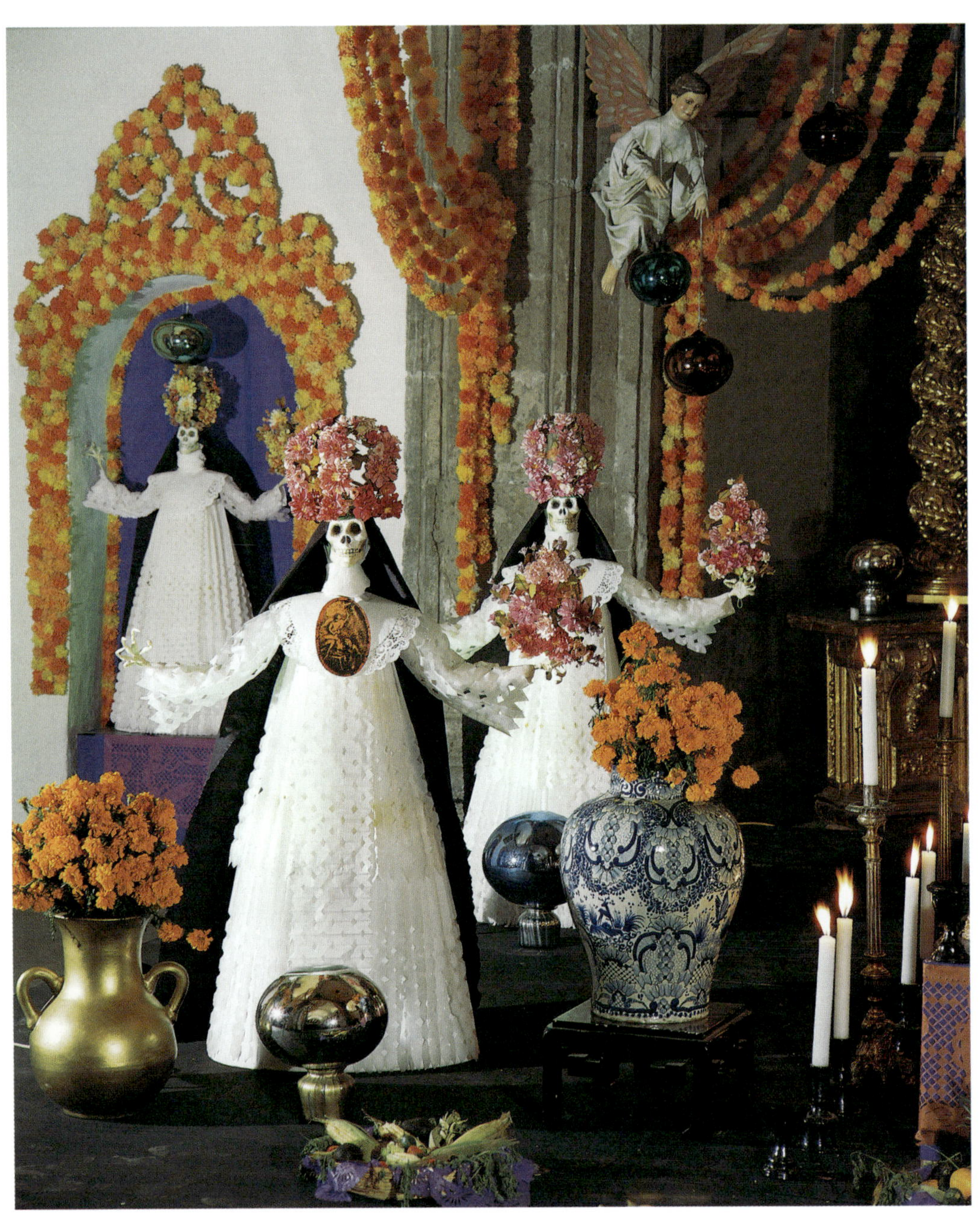

Altar of the Dead dedicated to the Hieronymite nuns. University of the Cloister of Sor Juana.

Spiritualities deriving from the concept of *De contemptu mundi*—a legacy of the monastic tradition—were reawakened by religious reform movements and bore a strong influence on art and forms of religious devotion in New Spain. The Catholic aesthetic of the baroque period, stemming from reforms implemented by the Council of Trent, created a religious culture that privileged sensory experience as a means of achieving transcendence. Consequently, often passionately executed poetic and artistic depictions of the mysteries of faith (and death in particular) were viewed with favor.

Moreover, the evolution of moral conscience (superseding ancient schema focusing on ritual purity) and the emphasis on freedom and each individual's responsibility in terms of his or her own salvation (derived from Catholic ideas about grace which, in those years, were perhaps the main point of theological contention) directed questions regarding the fate of human beings toward a truly crucial point: the moment of death. Indeed, eternal damnation or happiness could depend on the latter. To die well became these believers' main concern. St. Joseph's serene passing was the ideal model (though it is not described in the Gospels). Indeed, worship of this holy figure reached an unprecedented peak during these centuries (as he was named patron saint of the kingdom of New Spain).

Christianity posits that death can be overcome by the death of Christ and that we only have access to true (eternal) life thanks to his sacrifice. The semantic complexity of the sense of the macabre in baroque Catholicism—which drew extensively on medieval sources—owes much to this apparent paradox: only death can give life.

These theological and cultural questions were the inspiration for the production of truly outstanding art in New Spain.

A solid culture rooted in Catholic and Criollo traditions continues to thrive in many parts of Mexico (and is most prevalent, for instance, in areas where the Cristero revolutionary movement began). Here, death does not permit pranks or practical jokes. Indeed, it represents nothing less than the difference between eternal damnation and salvation.

Great literature—in this case, the work of Agustín Yañez—allows us to once again peer into a universe that remains as vital and intense as when *The Edge of the Storm* was written (though its inhabitants represent an ever-decreasing minority of the general population). Here, deceased ancestors are not embodied as playful skeletons but rather as glorious bodies deserving of worship or lost souls in need of prayers.

• ACROSS THE BORDER: THANKSGIVING AND HALLOWEEN •

Mexican cultures, like those of other countries, are constantly interacting with each other as well as with peoples abroad. For some generations now, the main point of reference here has been the United States (and not merely on a cultural level).

Millions of families (representing approximately a fifth of the country's total population) have taken local customs and flavors across our borders. Inversely, a growing number of Mexicans eagerly attempt to follow the ambitions, fashions, and even the heartbeat of this nation as consumer-society patterns continue to spread, given the extraordinary vigor of American pop culture and the fact that this power is a paradigm of modernity. But there also exists a phenomenon in the U.S. that could be compared to the rural Mexican family unit's most important ritual celebration: indeed, the closest American equivalent to the feast of the Day of the Dead—the kind that does not welcome mockery or jokes—is Thanksgiving dinner. Both of these traditions are related to the worship of corn and take place in November, the month of harvest; however, while the banquet here has a marked indigenous character, across the border it has become a transcultural celebration. In the U.S., only a small group of family members gather for a feast that was originally conceived to thank God, acknowledge each individual's effort in the harvest and the Earth's generous bestowing of its gifts; the ritual clearly attempts to integrate all communities under the ethical principles of the nation's founding fathers—industry and thrift. The evening spent at home is tranquil, intimate, and circumspect, and the menu features a healthful combination of bland, balanced flavors. In Mexico, on the contrary, the festivity summons a vast community of relatives, friends and neighbors, something that justifies the extravagant abundance of dishes offered: a feast for the poor, who can only binge once a year, and also a feast for the well-to-do, who can allow themselves the noble gesture of inviting a countless number of guests and then treating them like kings.

While the past is but a symbol and reminiscence at Thanksgiving (like the Holy Supper is in some Reform-inspired religious traditions), the Day of the Dead inscribes itself within a historical cycle based on a concept of time as endless and immobile: the guests of honor are deceased ancestors. This mnemonic ritual relates the Mexican families practicing it to Shintoist or Confucian families who know that there is no better way of ensuring social cohesion than cultivating love and respect for ancestors.

For the past century, Mexicans living in the U.S. have been concerned with the same search for an identity that has obsessed their kinsfolk who stayed behind on native soil. In their case, the phenomenon is intensified since they are immersed in a space of different signs and values. Moreover, their new homeland urges them to formulate in the most explicit way possible (and this is a trait of multicultural societies) the distinctive features and peculiarities of their own communal identity.

Under these conditions, it is normal that Mexicans "on the other side" and especially their children would most often resort to a nationalist cultural model (which includes the literary character created by Octavio Paz—"the Mexican"—and also Posada's and Rivera's depictions of skeletons). Moreover, those coming from rural areas where there is a tradition of family offerings (the sweetly nostalgic rather than mocking kind) attempted to mix two formulas—a serious, devout altar at home and a playful monument in schools and public buildings—like relatives of theirs moving to large Mexican cities had done.

On the other hand, among Mexicans living on this side of the U.S. border, the lay, republican representation of death, an image created in the

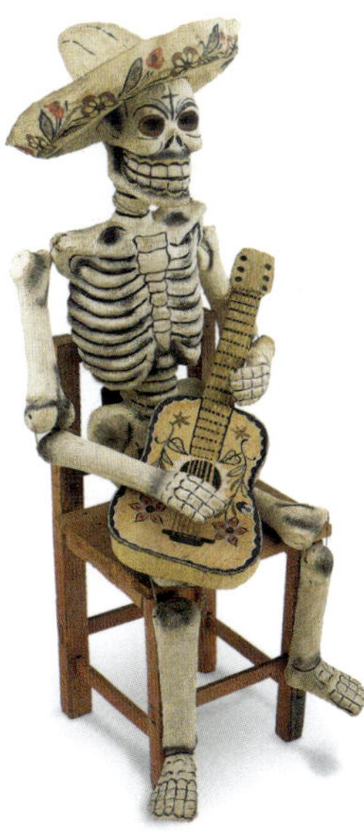

Charro musician. Bound, molded, and painted paper. Mexico City, 1975.
Ruth D. Lechuga Collection of Popular Art / Franz Mayer Museum.

early twentieth century, has experienced a rapid transformation in recent decades. By making All Saints' Day coincide with the Anglo-Saxon holiday of Halloween, the religious calendar caused these two forms of ceremony derived from European traditions (Mediterranean and baroque in Mexico, Nordic and Romantic in the U.S.) to begin mingling in terms of their forms and meanings, on city streets and in working-class homes.

The identity-based cultural model, tied to national borders, is being replaced by a new one which is still not well-defined.

These days, children in the streets of Mexico City are as likely to dress up as witches as they are skeletons, and many use a hybrid pumpkin and skull as a container for their treats ("Give me something for my skull," they say brandishing a plastic jack-o'-lantern).

Compared to witches' costumes and monsters on television, the traditional face of death loses power, becoming a mere mask, barely frightening in a playful, puerile way. This new phase of the process leads us a little closer to modernity, where the image of death must necessarily be banished, eliminated, or trivialized.

All invented traditions are subject to constant metamorphoses and this one is no exception to the rule. Today, the North American cultural space is still very much involved in its process of formation.

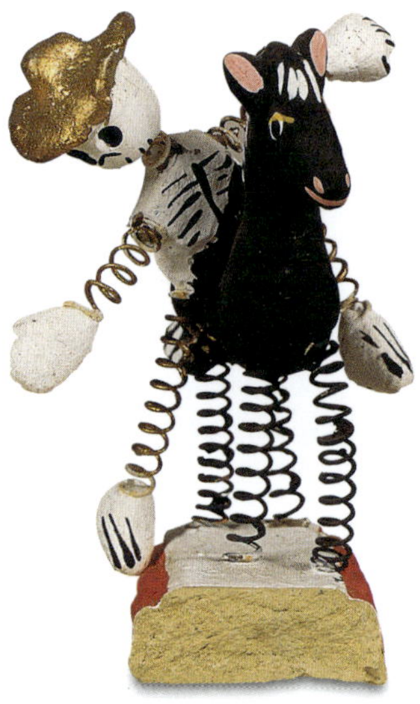

Horse rider. Modeled, fired, and painted clay. Juventino Rosas, Guanajuato, 1978.
Ruth D. Lechuga Collection of Popular Art / Franz Mayer Museum.

Societies, fortunately enough, do not have a fixed, immutable soul or a definitive idiosyncrasy common to all their members; they undergo transformations and even mutate.

We have seen that there are many different ways of dealing with life—and hence also with death—in Mexico, as everywhere else on the planet.

Some of the traditions that have taken root here are truly ancient and bear similarities to models that are extremely widespread throughout the world (i.e., rural customs), while the way others took hold seems to be the result of random historical accidents (i.e., post-revolutionary customs); finally, there are several traditions whose evolution we may trace back to the moment of their appearance (i.e., modern and baroque customs, etc.).

Furthermore, there exists in our country a particular image of death that was but a faded and almost imperceptible relic for some time, but which has acquired much greater visibility over the last few years and has even begun creating its own subculture.

The economic modernizations we have experienced—with no comparable phenomenon occurring in the social or cultural fields—dismantled the old state and corporate networks and yet failed to establish new ones that could both function as adequate replacements and be more consistent with the new economic models that the country has adopted. As a result, alternative networks have appeared, modeled on the former type and yet increasingly marginal, deviating further and further from the efforts required in the building of a democratic society. Moreover, with every new economic crisis, our country has seen the growth of a criminal fringe that has an aesthetic and a language of its own, expressed as an extraordinarily vital form of popular literature.

An heir of ancient medieval tradition, the noble old Mexican ballad known as the *corrido* has nowadays become the vent through which we can hear the breathing of a cultural sub-sector of Mexico which, while it stuffs its pockets with diamonds and "greenbacks," strays from the path of the communal project. In our literary world, a kind of folk poetry is blooming, singing passionately about the fleeting pleasures that easy money can buy, expressing, moreover, a familiarity with death that is far from humorous, the kind of death one meets in an ambush under the deafening fire of AK-47s.

In Colombia—a country that, tragically, has more experience in this field than we do—great writers living as expatriates have reflected upon

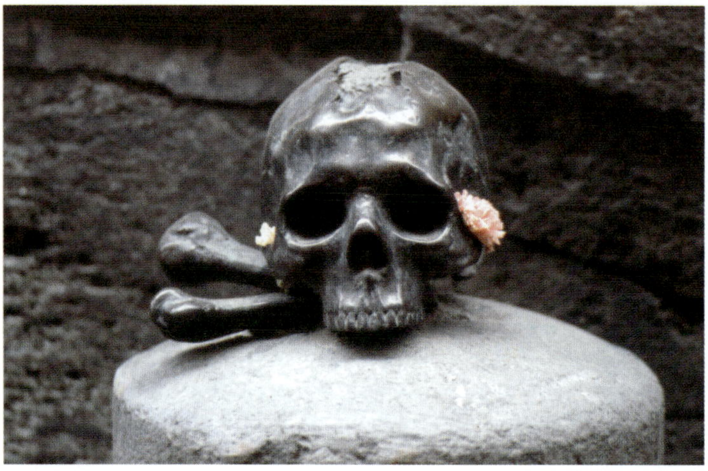

Skull located in front of a church consecrated to the souls in purgatory. Gravina, Italy.
OPPOSITE: Froylán Ruiz, *For María Cruz*, 1988, oil on canvas, 100 × 180 cm.

these worlds (Gabriel García Márquez in *News of a Kidnapping*, Fernando Vallejo in *Our Lady of the Assassins*). In Mexico, although Arturo Pérez-Reverte has set the tone with *La reina del sur* (Queen of the South), it has been the fringe community's own voice that we have heard over the past few years, sometimes expressing itself with striking honesty.

These moving, at times harsh, and often beautiful lyrics have found the guttural, visceral, and sensual strains of *norteña* music to be a fitting medium for singing to the youths who are being killed off in our streets.

This face of death that cuts lives short blindly, without hesitation, murdering more innocents than malefactors, is invoked daily by many people who have done everything possible to bring it upon themselves and yet attempt to ward it off with offerings, prayers, pilgrimages, gold medals, and diamonds. This figure of death is very much alive, and our country does not have the slightest idea what to do with it. ◆

—Translated by Richard Moszka

Alfonso Alfaro. Anthropologist and director of the research institute of *Artes de México*, where he has published various articles. This text is part of a series written under the auspices of the Alfonso Reyes chair of the University of Paris III—Sorbonne Nouvelle.

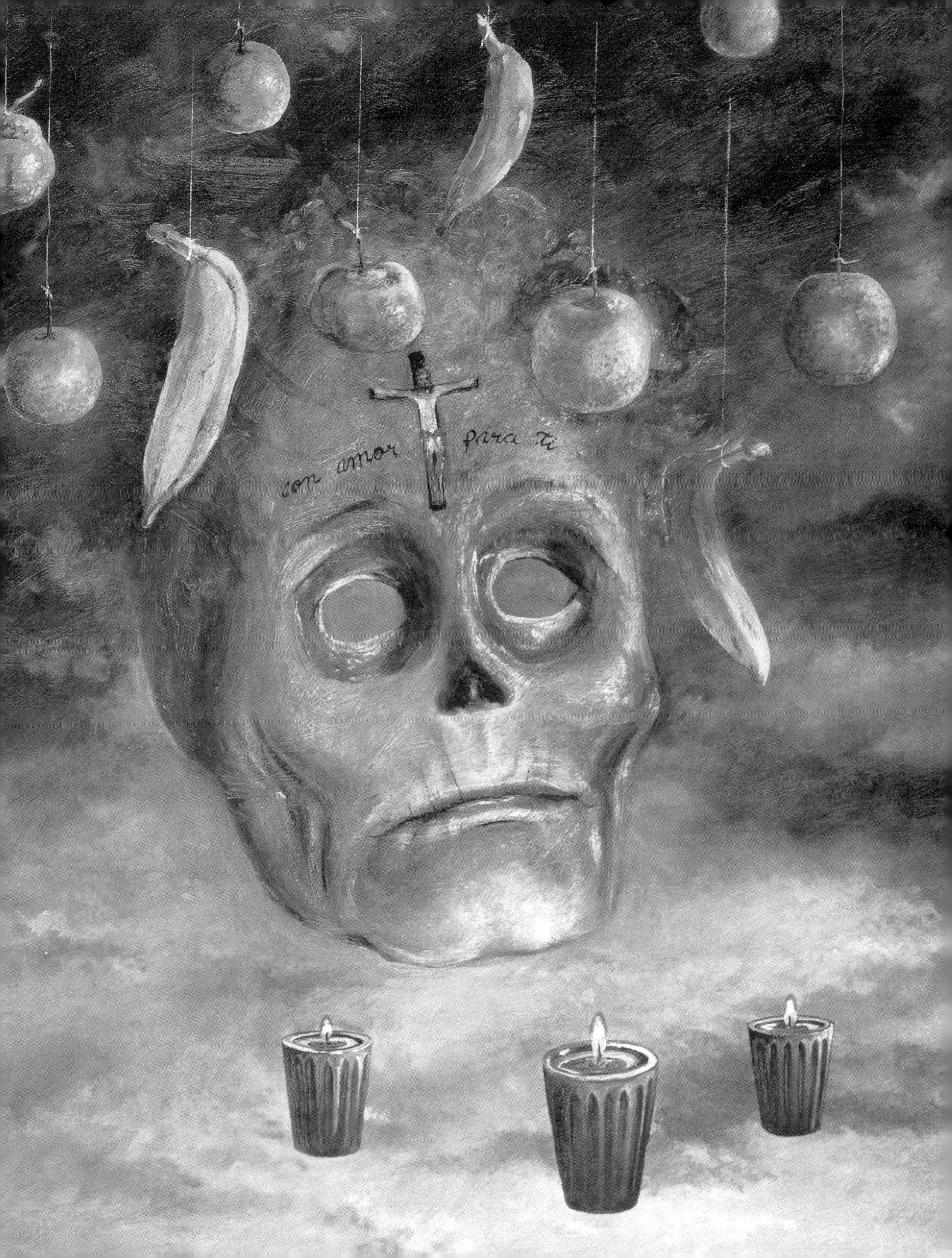
con amor para ti

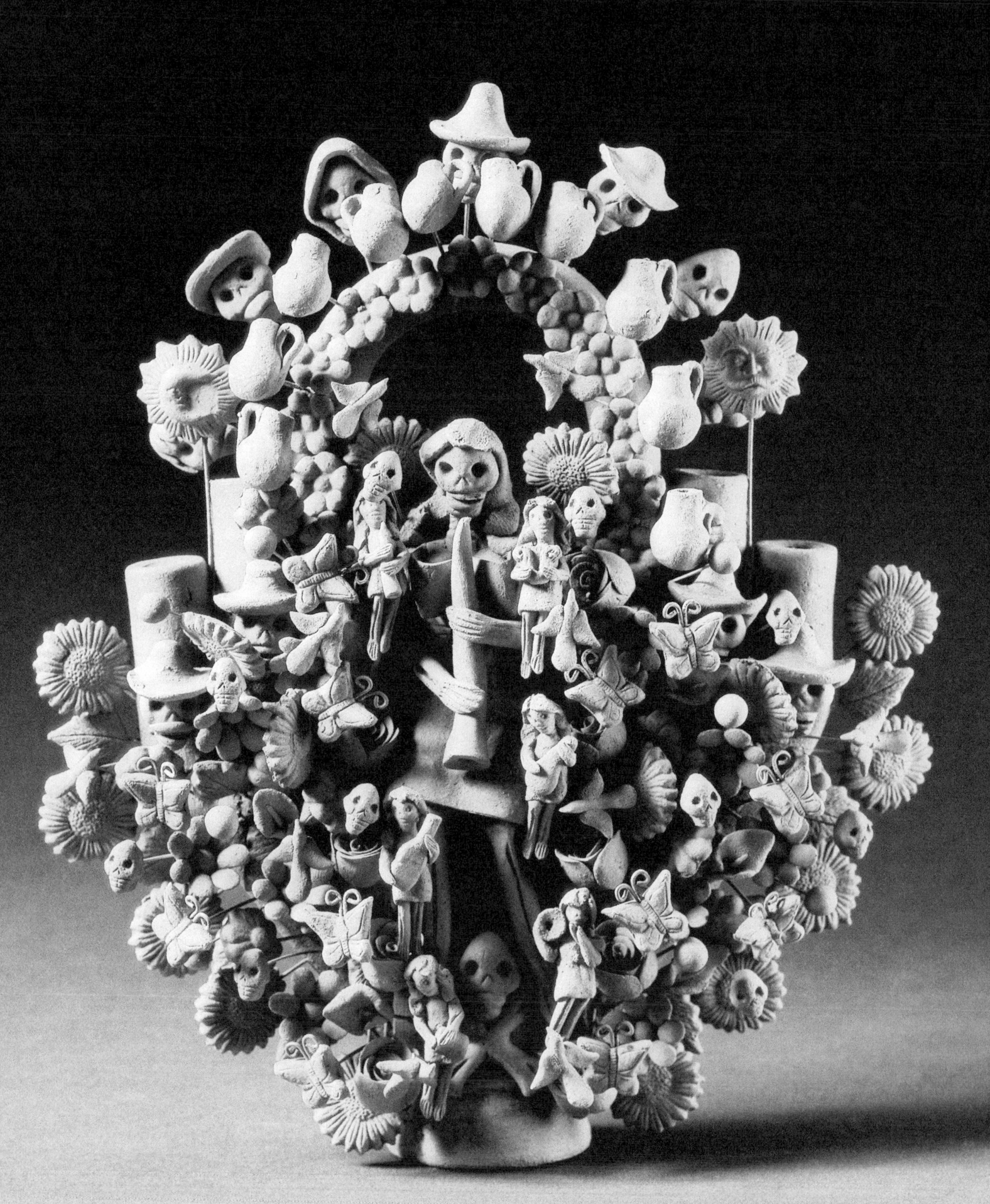

PARTE II

RISA Y CALAVERA

DESAFÍO TRANSFORMADO

Durante las últimas décadas del siglo XIX, la sociedad de la Ciudad de México celebraba el Día de Muertos de una manera distinta, y a veces distante, de la que se acostumbraba en el pasado. El sentido ritual cobraba, poco a poco, una forma festiva, más acorde con los tiempos modernos. Había quienes despreciaban la celebración tradicional por considerarla un atavismo; en cambio, otros más conservadores se lamentaban de los tintes frívolos que habían impregnado al Día de Muertos. La fiesta se secularizaba a medida que la sociedad se inscribía en los paradigmas de progreso de aquella época.

DESAFÍO TRANSFORMADO

DEL RITO A LA FIESTA

◆

EL DÍA DE MUERTOS EN EL SIGLO XIX

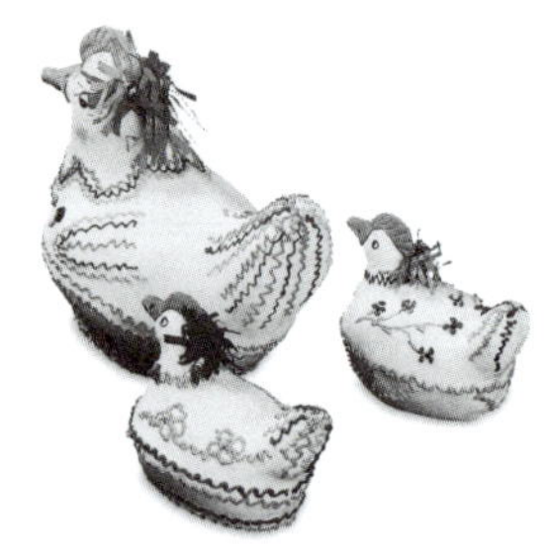

1763–1764 ALFEÑIQUE PARA TODOS SANTOS

Francisco de Ajofrín

◆

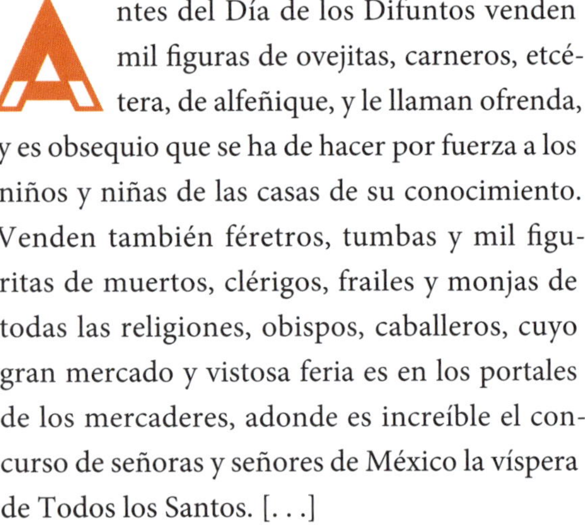

Antes del Día de los Difuntos venden mil figuras de ovejitas, carneros, etcétera, de alfeñique, y le llaman ofrenda, y es obsequio que se ha de hacer por fuerza a los niños y niñas de las casas de su conocimiento. Venden también féretros, tumbas y mil figuritas de muertos, clérigos, frailes y monjas de todas las religiones, obispos, caballeros, cuyo gran mercado y vistosa feria es en los portales de los mercaderes, adonde es increíble el concurso de señoras y señores de México la víspera de Todos los Santos. [. . .]

Todas estas figuras y monerías, y otras cosas de más entidad, las hacen los léperos con gran primor y por poco precio; y si esto mismo se les manda hacer, piden dinero adelantado (lo que es común a todo oficial en la América), y o no lo hacen, con lo que se pierde lo que se les da, o lo hacen mal, tarde y caro, con lo que se pierde la paciencia. ◆

1878 MUERTOS Y PANTEONES EN LA CIUDAD

Guillermo Prieto

◆

Recuerdo el clamoreo lúgubre que anunciaba desde el toque del alba el día consagrado a los recuerdos de la muerte, y a esos despojos que no tienen nombre especial y que vivieron con nuestra propia vida.

En muchas casas se encendían lámparas, velas y cirios como para revivir, en la intimidad del hogar, los más vivos recuerdos de las personas amadas.

Rompían por todas partes lamentaciones y lloros, la ternura y los diligentes cuidados se manifestaban en los adornos sepulcrales: cirios labrados, gasas, flores, coronas, abalorios y cuanto podía sugerir el cariño o la vanidad para honrar las tumbas.

Para el pópulo era un día de verdadero dolor y gozo.

Llorar al muerto, enterrar el hueso, comprar la fruta, disponer la ofrenda, pasear la plaza,

THIS PAGE: Sugar-paste figures; from Alfeñique Market, Toluca, State of Mexico. • **PAGE 226:** Tree of Death, baked painted clay, Metepec, State of Mexico.

estos eran muchos placeres y muchas seducciones para un día de lágrimas.

En las bizcocherías y panaderías se vendían y venden en cantidades fabulosas tortas de muerto con sus labores simétricas y su azúcar en polvo espolvoreada por encima; eran dulces de ordenanza el ponche, la sabrosísima jalea de tejocote y los alfeñiques que recorrían toda la escala social.

Para la jalea y para el alfeñique se celebraban verdaderas especialidades, y había tejocotes de particular nombradía; la gala de la jalea consistía en su transparencia y se hacía ostentación de aquella en que la tarjeta o dedicatoria se ponía en el fondo del platón leyéndose como a través de los cristales.

Los alfeñiques, especialmente los del convento de San Lorenzo, alcanzaron merecido renombre; eran pirámides y caprichos fantásticos, obeliscos, rocas, ríos y paisajes primorosos.

Pero el alfeñique constituía un ramo de cuantioso comercio que afectaba a la gente pobre.

Además, en las casas particulares, el alfeñique y las calaveras de azúcar suministraban pretexto y materiales para los regocijos del hogar.

De la clase media para abajo, era de verse a las muchachonas frescas, con los túnicos en holgura, las mangas remangadas, y listas para verter el almíbar sobre la fría losa que lo congelaba, arrancar trozos, golpear, pulir y sacar, como escultoras hábiles, gallinas y borregos, mulitas y juguetes en medio del ir y venir, los saltos y los hurtos de los chicos, que eran la vida y la sazón de la fiesta.

Los chicos, los criados, los conocidos, los infinitos devotos del préstamo forzoso creían cobrar derecho para pedir a todo el mundo su calavera y sus animitas, y ese contingente extraordinario caía sobre el mercado, para convertirse en entierritos de garbanzo, muertos, escribanos, tumbas, piras y ofrendas variadísimas.

La parte gastronómica tenía sus artículos de consumo de ordenanza, descollando para el populacho, en primer término, las "cabezas" calientes de horno, de las que se hacía fabuloso consumo, siendo los lugares más notables de expendio Necatitlán, La Retama, Nana Rosa, Don Toribio y las inmediaciones de las pulquerías de La Garrapata y de Tío Juan Aguirre, o las inmediaciones de Santiago Tlaltelolco, camposanto que revalidó su crédito en la primera invasión del cólera ocurrida en 1833.

Las personas más encopetadas recurrían al mole de guajolote para que los asistiese en sus tribulaciones, y los muertos de pan y de chacualole (calabaza cocida con miel de panocha) eran los manjares que se colocaban sobre los sepulcros, entre la cera, las abundantes frutas y las golosinas que constituían la ofrenda.

La ofrenda, particularmente en los pueblos de indígenas, era y suele considerarse como pingüe rendimiento de la Iglesia y de curas y sacristanes.

Pasados los llantos y el caer de las sombras, las lechuzas del templo se abalanzaban sobre las ofrendas de los difuntos, y aquel botín cuantioso regocijaba a los que quedaban con el alma en el cuerpo en este valle de lágrimas. [. . .]

La Iglesia no podía permanecer indiferente a las demostraciones de duelo; en cada templo, a las puertas y de trecho en trecho, en el interior de los cementerios, había una mesilla con su cubierta negra, sucia y con chorreones de cera; en ella una amarilla calavera, el acetre, el hisopo, y a la espalda la tosca silla del sacerdote y el característico tololoche alzando su cuello de rocín flaco sobre el aparato mortuorio-mercantil.

La tarifa de las pingües recaudaciones era sencilla: medio real por el responso rezado, y ciento por ciento más por el cantado, con el acompañamiento del desastrado tololoche.

La pitanza se depositaba en el acetre; bajo la mesa había uno o dos cántaros con agua para reponer la materia prima de las preces, y del canto y acetre había para que se llenara muchas veces y muchas se vaciara, recaudándose en algún camposanto popular, hasta seis y ocho mil pesos solo de responsos.

En esos grandes cementerios no aristocráticos, en las tardes y al caer la noche, eran las orgías, los desórdenes, las riñas espantosas y el llanto; el requiebro, la blasfemia y la sangre trazaban cuadros que por fortuna no alcanzamos ahora que se dice que tocamos en el último grado de la desmoralización. [. . .]

La noche era dedicada a los rosarios de ánimas o patrullas eclesiásticas con sus cantores y con su tololoche al frente, rezando y derramando responsos en las calles a diestra y siniestra.

El llamado de aquella comitiva era, por cuanto voz, como que se trataba de una serenata fúnebre, y el esmero y la vanidad se cifraba en que se proclamasen los nombres de los difuntos beneficiados y quedara entendido en el vecindario que no pasaban la noche aquellos pobres muertos sin un fandango a su manera.

Era muy frecuente que amantes desdeñados o matrimonios mal avenidos cohechasen a monigotes y cantantes para que proclamasen en su responso el nombre del petimetre veleidoso o de la querida infiel y entonces, si el aludido o alguno de sus deudos era de brío y alentaba coraje, sacudía trancazos, y aquellos gritos, y aquella zambra, y aquellas lágrimas calientes y genuinas, eran como quien dice el complemento y la gloria del día. [. . .]

Para este día se han multiplicado monumentos de exquisito gusto y aun de verdadera belleza artística. El culto de las flores es constante y complace ver a los padres de familia llevar a sus hijos a rendir homenaje a sus deudos queridos con esa ofrenda, símbolo de la plegaria y del amor [. . .]

El Panteón Francés es verdaderamente hermoso y digno de su objeto y de un pueblo civilizado: majestad, belleza, salubridad, grandeza religiosa, esmero y propiedad en el culto, todo se encuentra allí.

En cuanto a rosarios y fiestas nocturnas, han desaparecido, sin duda porque los interesados tuvieron presente el diálogo aquel que repetían en estos días los léperos:

—Comadre pelona, me alegro de verte.

—No andemos con chanzas, que yo soy la muerte.

O este otro, también leperocrático neto:

"Andando de vagamundo / me encontré una calavera, / y le dije en lo profundo: / A mí lo mismo me pega / más que sea del otro mundo". ◆

Guillermo Prieto. Nació y murió en la Ciudad de México (1818–1897). Estudió en el Colegio de San Juan de Letrán. Fue secretario particular de Valentín Gómez Farías y de Anastasio Bustamante. Fue profesor de Economía en el Colegio Militar. Combatió contra los estadounidenses en la guerra de 1847. Colaboró en la redacción de las leyes de Reforma. Fue diputado dieciocho veces y siete veces secretario de Hacienda. Inició su carrera periodística como redactor de *El Cosmopolita* y del *Diario Oficial*. En 1890 el diario *La República* lo nombró el poeta más popular del país. Perteneció a la Academia de Letrán y al Ateneo Mexicano.

1880
EL DÍA DE MUERTOS

Ignacio Manuel Altamirano

◆

En los antiguos tiempos, es decir, antes de la Reforma, México se despertaba el día 2 de noviembre al funeral clamor de la campana que doblaba en todas las iglesias, recordando que era el día de la conmemoración de los fieles difuntos.

¡Ah!, que tristeza y qué tedio causaba ese incesante y funeral clamoreo que comenzaba en la Catedral y que se repetía en los cien campanarios de los conventos y todas las iglesias, parroquias, capillas y ermitas que bordaban la ciudad de oriente a poniente, y de norte a sur! Era una incesante vibración acompasada, ronca, lúgubre, que daba origen a variados sentimientos, pero todos amargos. La tristeza, el pesar, el desaliento se apoderaban del corazón, como el cortejo pavoroso de los recuerdos del día. Porque ¿quién no había perdido a alguna persona amada, cuya memoria venía a evocar la voz de la campana?

Y los fieles conmovidos han obedecido hoy, lo mismo que en los antiguos tiempos, al mandato sagrado porque, aunque las campanas habían enmudecido por algunos años y se han disminuido en los presentes, la costumbre piadosa de conmemorar a los difuntos ha permanecido firme, mantenida por la tradición y por la ternura de las familias.

Así pues, aunque yo conocía ya las costumbres mexicanas en este día, y aunque venciendo la repugnancia que siento por los cementerios de las grandes ciudades—pues cuando quiero meditar sobre el gran problema de la muerte y envolverme en las sombras de la tumba para soñar en ellas, prefiero buscar, como el poeta inglés Gray, el cementerio de las aldeas—, me dirigí a visitar los panteones.

—¿Habrán cambiado algo las costumbres piadosas de los mexicanos en este día?—me pregunté—. ¿Serán otra cosa de lo que eran antes de la Reforma?

Y monté en un carruaje de alquiler que ese día, como todos los abominables vehículos de su especie, se pagan a peso y a dos pesos la hora. El que yo encontré por casualidad estaba arrastrado

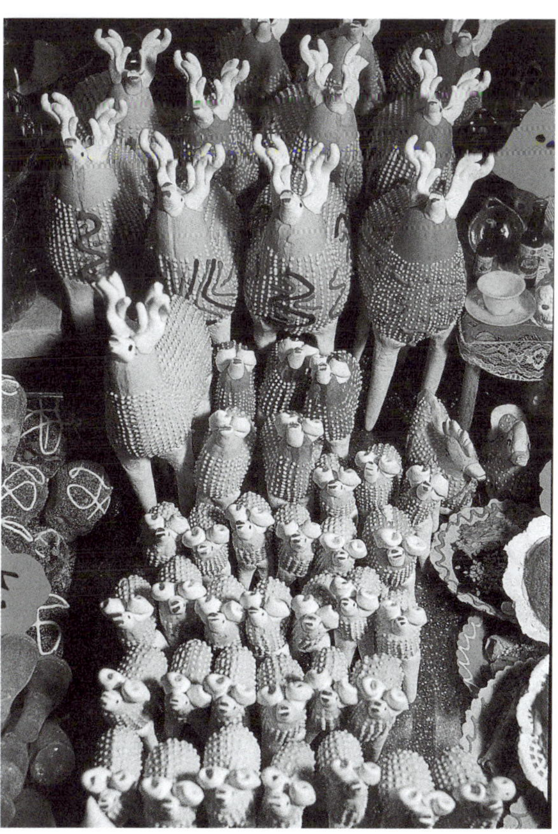

Alfeñique Market stand

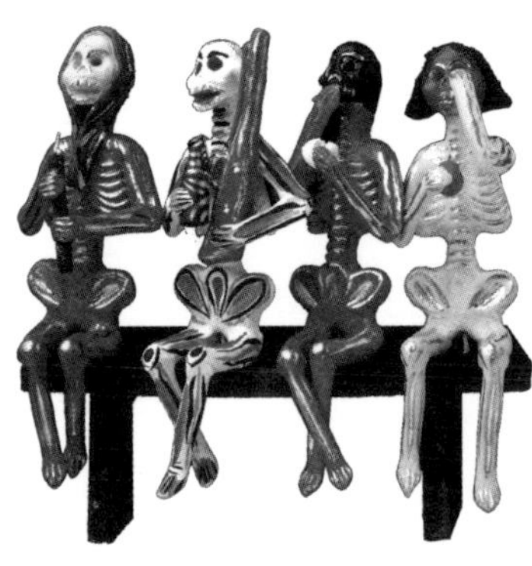

Pedro Soteno, Wake, baked painted clay, Metepec, State of Mexico, 1986, Ruth D. Lechuga Folk Art Museum.

por dos jamelgos amarillentos, desiguales y con un brío capaz de engañar al más listo.

Ya se sabe que en México hay ahora nuevos cementerios, y de diversa forma que la usada en otro tiempo. El Cementerio Francés, el de La Piedad en el mismo rumbo, el de Dolores en las colinas de Tacubaya, los dos de Guadalupe, el de San Fernando (cerrado ya para los nuevos pobladores), el del Campo Florido, al sur de la ciudad, y el de los Ángeles, al noroeste. Allí están sepultados los huesos de los muertos a quienes tienen que llorar los mexicanos.

Pero el de La Piedad y también el Francés son los más notables y concurridos.

Allá me dirigí triste, conmovido como debe estarlo todo el que hace una peregrinación a la morada de los muertos.

—¡Ah!—decía yo, olvidando por un momento que conocía las costumbres de esta noble ciudad—. ¡Cómo deben sonar en todo este camino los suspiros! ¡Cómo deben oscurecerse las frentes! ¡Cómo deben ir los ojos nublados por las lágrimas!

Es la vía sacra, la vía del dolor y de la ternura. Por aquí va el pesar silencioso, caminando a paso lento . . .

Interrumpió mi frase melancólica un concierto de alegres carcajadas y chillidos de regocijo.

Saqué la cabeza por la portezuela a fin de ver bien. Ya los jamelgos habían pasado la garita de Belén y trotaban en la calzada de La Piedad. A uno y otro lado de la carretera y del ferrocarril y bajo la sombra de los chopos y de los álamos que bordean la calzada, caminaba una procesión no interrumpida de personas alegres y turbulentas, divididas en grupos más o menos grandes. Era el pueblo pedestre de México, que presentaba un aspecto abigarrado y pintoresco. Las familias llevaban juntamente con algunos cirios y crespones o flores negras, ramos de flores naturales, coronas de siempreviva o de ciprés y cestos con comida, y frutas y enormes jarros de pulque.

Pulque por donde quiera. A veces era una mula mezclándose entre la gente y cargando dos grandes odres de pulque, a veces un cargador llevando una castaña con el mismo licor, y mujeres, ancianos y niños vestidos de fiesta o cubiertos de andrajos, pero siempre llevando en las manos el embriagante líquido.

Estas gentes eran las que parloteaban, reían, silbaban y formaban una algazara que dominaba las notas lejanas del doble que sonaba en la ciudad.

Aquella era la peregrinación del dolor. A cada paso interrumpían el camino multitud de puestos de comida y de frutas o cantinas surtidas de licores, pero dominando constantemente el pulque.

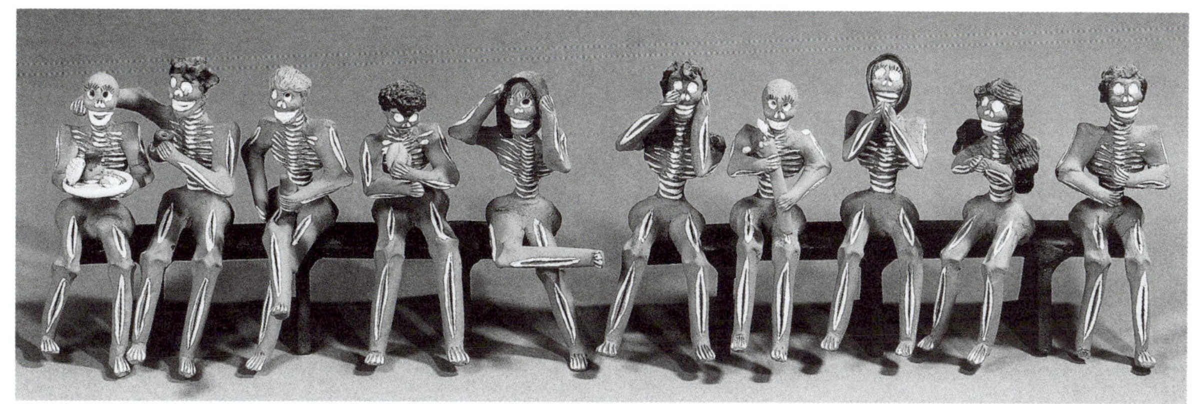

Mourners, baked painted clay, Metepec, State of Mexico.

A poco, alcanzome un largo tren compuesto de veinte vagones. Era curioso de ver. La gente bien vestida se apiñaba en ellos de un modo increíble. Las señoras iban de pie muchas veces; no cabían; eran un mundo. Parecían arenques en un barril. Aquellos también eran peregrinos del dolor. Y cien coches particulares de alquiler atravesaban rápida o lentamente, atascándose en el camino de La Piedad, lleno de charcos y de lodo, a causa de la lluvia del día anterior y de hoyancos y de sinuosidades, a causa del descuido. En esos carruajes también iban peregrinos del dolor.

Llegamos a La Piedad. Hormigueaba la gente; era una feria. Penetramos en el cementerio pobre y triste, el más mal cuidado de los cementerios, que podía estar lleno de árboles y que está erizado de yerba silvestre. Allí se entierra a toda clase de gente, pero con particularidad, a la pobre. Los peregrinos que venían se dispersaban en el laberinto de calles que conducen a los campos de las clases baratas. Allí iban a parar los cirios, las flores, los cestos y el pulque. En la entrada un centenar de indígenas se afanaba haciendo y vendiendo ramilletes de los pobres, porque los ramilletes elegantes se vendían ese día a precios subidos. No describiré las tumbas, ¿para qué? No hay obras de arte, ni siquiera sepulcros ricos.

Salimos de ese cementerio y encontré a una gruesa señora de mis conocidas, acompañada de sus jóvenes y pispiretas hijas que venían emperejiladas, como para una tertulia.

—¿Ha ido usted—me preguntó—al Panteón Francés?

—No, señora, allá voy en este momento.

—Sí, vaya usted, ¡qué lindo está!, ¡qué elegantes sepulcros!, ¡qué ricos y qué graciosos! Y verá usted muy hermosos trajes, porque allí está lo más elegante de México; es verdad que hay algunas señoras muy ridículas, pero en cambio otras van muy bien . . .

—Señora—repliqué—yo no entiendo una palabra de trajes y de modas, pero veré los sepulcros.

—Sí, sí: vea usted los sepulcros, son de muy buen gusto, muy costosos; yo creo que el de la señora fulana ha de haber costado lo menos 6,000 pesos; pues si el de los menganos . . . figúrese usted, puro mármol, bronce y tiene tibores de 200 pesos. Vaya usted, se divertirá usted mucho.

Este es el juicio general que arranca el dolor a los que van a orar por los muertos, según lo manda la Iglesia.

Fui al Panteón Francés, y casi no pude entrar. Me retiré acosado por los empellones del gentío y entre los caballos de los cincuenta carruajes que allí esperaban al mundo elegante, como le llamaba mi gruesa amiga.

Regresé a México, pero en la tarde volvía a La Piedad. La gritería que escuché al llegar al cementerio mexicano me anunció que el dolor había llegado al delirio entre los sepulcros.

En efecto, aquella muchedumbre que velaba junto a las tumbas, después de haber orado, había tenido que comer; era preciso comer, y las lágrimas se debilitan; se habían tendido manteles junto a las tumbas, o la misma yerba sepulcral había servido de mesa. Luego había circulado el jarro de pulque; después se habían derramado sobre las lápidas lágrimas de pulque, y luego comenzó la orgía funeral. El blanco licor había exacerbado los pesares; se hablaba recio, se sollozaba, se maldecía, se juraba, se desesperaba; el amor físico se burlaba de la muerte, y parece que, en medio de este frenesí, la cólera, los celos, los deseos, todas las furias que pueden agitar el corazón humano, agitaban sus rojas antorchas, eclipsando la tenue luz amarillenta de los lirios y de los sepulcros.

El sol se ponía. Los sauces llorones y los chopos se teñían con el color opalino de la luz de la tarde. Era preciso decir adiós a las cenizas amadas y hacer la última oración y la última libación. Esta fue terrible.

Después la muchedumbre comenzó a salir, pero no como sale una muchedumbre abatida y llorosa, sino como se desencadenaban las turbas de la antigua Roma, cuando el pontífice pronunciaba en lo alto de las gradas del templo la palabra sacramental *Evohé*, que inauguraba las Saturnales.

Los grupos de mujeres desmelenadas aturdían con sus cantares y espantaban con sus gestos; los hombres se agitaban con violencia, reñían o se daban de puñaladas o bamboleaban hasta caer. Los quinientos gendarmes que custodiaban la calzada corrían en sus caballos con el alfanje desnudo; la calzada de La Piedad era un inmenso *pandemonium* y las primeras sombras del crepúsculo envolvían los últimos sacrificios del dolor. ¿Y qué hacía entre tanto el ángel de las tumbas?

En la noche, por todas las calles de la ciudad, circulaban todavía a media noche los animados grupos de los afligidos, cantando y bebiendo.

El extranjero que, asomado a su ventana, hubiera presenciado este espectáculo, no habría podido menos que reasumir sus impresiones del día, diciendo:

—¡Qué borracho es el pueblo de México y qué mala voz tiene! ◆

Ignacio Manuel Altamirano. Nació en Guerrero y murió en Italia (1834–1893). Estudió Abogacía en el Colegio de Letrán. Tomó parte en la revolución de Ayutla y combatió a los conservadores en la guerra de Reforma. Como crítico y catedrático propugnó una apertura a la literatura universal. Publicó poesía (*Rimas*, 1871), cuentos y novelas, entre las que destacan *Clemencia*, *Navidad en las montañas* y *El Zarco*.

Aquí yacen mis bronces, mis laureles, mis discípulos todos, mis cabañas, mis libros, mis estatuas, mis pinceles, mi machete suriano, mis campanas, mis apuntes, mis notas, mis corceles, mis versos, mis praderas, mis montañas, mi mármol duro cual mi esfuerzo humano mis . . . ¡basta! . . . ¡que aquí yace Altamirano!

Calavera al autor publicada en *El Combate*, 2 de noviembre de 1887.

REFRANES POPULARES DEL DÍA DE MUERTOS

Al vivo todo le falta y al muerto todo le sobra.
A mí las calaveras me pelan los dientes.
No es mala la muerte cuando se lleva a quien debe.
Se hace pesado el muerto cuando siente que lo cargan.
Consejos y ejemplos que obligan, los que los muertos nos digan.
Cuando el tecolote canta, el indio muere . . . No es cierto, pero sucede.
Cuando estés muerto, todos dirán que fuiste bueno.
De aquí a cien años, todos seremos pelones.
De golosos y tragones están llenos los panteones.
Mala yerba nunca muere . . . y si muere, ni falta hace.
Al que por su gusto muere, la muerte le sabe a dulce.
Vámonos muriendo todos, que están enterrando gratis.
El muerto al pozo y el vivo al gozo.

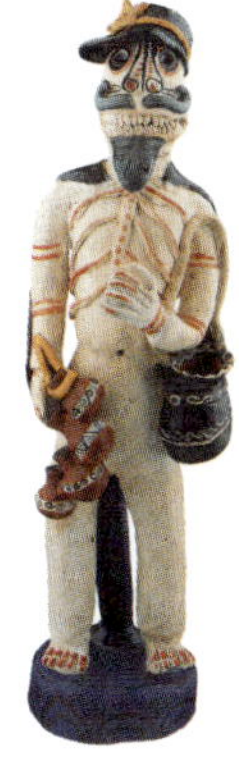

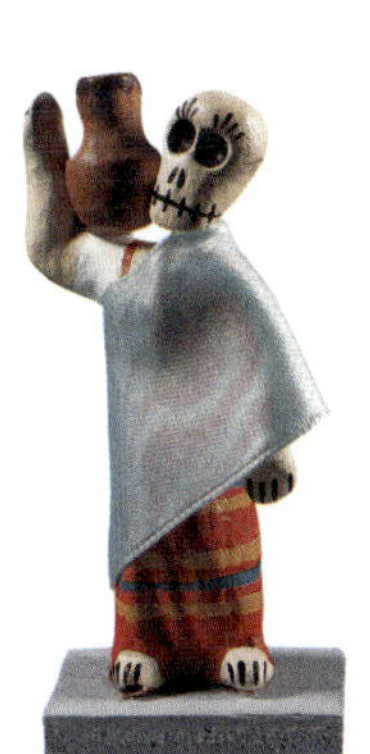

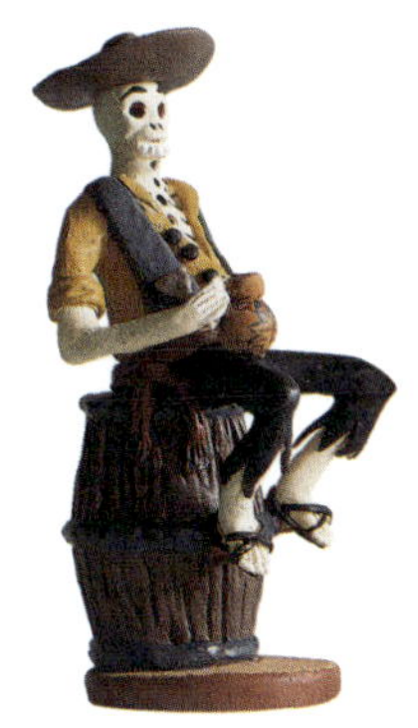

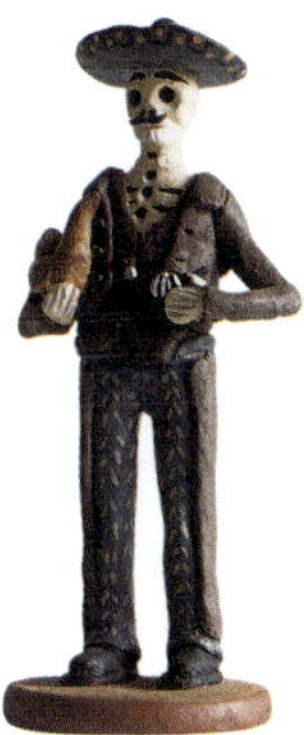

DE IZQUIERDA A DERECHA: Vendedor de ollas. Barro modelado y pintado. Ocumicho, Michoacán, 1990; Mujer con olla. Papel aglutinado y pintado, montado sobre triplay. Guanajuato, 1978. Both from Colección Ruth D. Lechuga de Arte Popular/Museo Franz Mayer; Muertes charras. Barro modelado, cocido y pintado. Metepec, Estado de México.

1882
DESPUÉS DE MUERTOS

José Tomás de Cuéllar

◆

Desde los salvajes hasta los más civilizados, todos los pueblos han dividido sus ceremonias públicas en dos categorías: los regocijos y las pompas fúnebres. Así ha sido desde la más remota antigüedad porque esas son las dos fases de la vida humana: se goza y se padece alternativamente; se ríe y se llora, se nace y se muere. Por estos dos caminos hemos llegado a dividirnos los humanos en dos secciones: los muertos y los dolientes; y a habitar en dos ciudades: en las ciudades silenciosas que se llaman cementerios o en las ciudades alegres donde lloran y ríen los que sobreviven.

Apenas hay horas más negras en nuestra vida que aquellas en que hemos llorado la pérdida de un ser querido; y apenas hay una idea más pavorosa que la de nuestro fin irremediable.

Ante el gran misterio de la muerte se anonada la razón humana y las manifestaciones del duelo han llegado a tomar formas más o menos extravagantes; pero en el fondo de todas ellas está siempre el dolor. Estaba reservado a México el convertir la pompa fúnebre en regocijo; estaba reservado a este país de anomalías y contradicciones hasta lo sublime, el decantado y oprobioso velorio de la gente inculta y supersticiosa.

Se comprende fácilmente que el indio y el mestizo inculto se crean en el deber ineludible de comprar el Día de Muertos los bizcochos más malos que se fabrican en todo el año, y las flores más feas y de peor aroma que produce la tierra, el cempasúchil, para poner la ofrenda, acompañada de velas de cera y de fumigaciones de incienso. Esta costumbre es casi un rito, y bajo el punto de vista alegórico, es no solo disculpable, sino que encierra como una idea mal expresada de la inmortalidad, puesto que el comer, la primera idea del ser viviente y el precio de la vida, se le ofrece al muerto.

Un indio taciturno y callado delante de un montón de cempasúchil, delante de bizcochos azucarados que respeta, y a la luz de dos velas de cera y envuelto en la nube del incienso es un doliente respetable, es un egipcio del tiempo de Sesostris, en América, que está probando que el camino del progreso es más largo que lo que parece a primera vista.

Pero que lo más granado de la sociedad de México, en unión de lo más abyecto de las masas populares, celebre la conmemoración de los fieles difuntos con gritos y vendimias tiene para nosotros en el fondo una significación altamente desconsoladora en el orden moral. Y no se nos quiera hacer creer que esta sociedad se divorció de la Iglesia católica desde la Reforma, y que en el Día de Muertos no se sujeta a las prácticas y ritos de la conmemoración, sino que la gente va al Zócalo porque le da la gana; no señor. La gente se viste de negro en la mañana, llora en el panteón en la tarde, y coquetea en la noche vestida de color rosa. ¿Es que el sentimiento y el duelo, y el recuerdo tristísimo de los que amamos y murieron es también mentira? No lo sabemos, pero lo cierto es que la actual costumbre nos lleva a cada quien a pensar de esta manera: "Cuando yo muera, me llorarán con seriedad los míos hasta noviembre; y en el día consagrado por la Iglesia al recuerdo de los muertos, mi mujer y mis hijos, mis amigos y mis deudos serán los actores de una fiesta inventada para burlarse de los muertos. Vestidos de colores relucientes se pasearán al son del cancán dentro de una gran barrada, y cenarán opíparamente para ahogar en *champagne* el último vislumbre de tristeza por mi irreparable pérdida".

Esta idea terrible que haría estremecer a las piedras si pudiera hacerles comprender que habían de morir, se torna en mojiganga; y del cráneo y de la tumba se hacen juguetes para los niños, para que más tarde puedan celebrar a carcajadas la muerte de su padre.

¡O será que, en lo que llamamos fiestas de noviembre, lo de los muertos es lo de menos, y de lo que se trata es del aniversario de Todos los Santos? Tengo para mí que el divorcio de la Iglesia y del Estado comenzó precisamente por el desprestigio en que habían ido cayendo los santos para una mayoría considerable de nuestra sociedad. No satisface mis dudas el imaginarme que la gente se entusiasma con ese recuerdo tan excepcionalmente católico.

¿Es acaso el doloroso recuerdo del padre, de la madre, del hermano, del hijo muerto, el que consume esas toneladas de cacahuates y de golosinas? Fisiológicamente los grandes dolores están en oposición con el apetito. ¿Qué le sucede a este dolor tan legítimo y tan serio, que se regodea de gusto el 2 de noviembre, y no solo se regodea de gusto, sino que se vuelve glotón en demasía?

El dolor es lógico; se exhala en lágrimas y en sollozos y suspiros. No hay en nuestro admirable organismo ni otros jugos, ni otros fenómenos nerviosos para expresarlo. Pero el dolor de que se trata, ese dolor que dice la gente, el dolor anual de fecha fija es un dolor estrictamente bejaranesco, abigarrado y goloso, y discurre poco más o menos de esta manera: ¿Conmemoramos a nuestra madre muerta?, pues hartémonos; propinémonos hoy una ración extraordinaria de golosinas indigestas, y que haya mucha música y muchas diversiones. Y cada familia se prepara a las fiestas, con la intervención más o menos directa del agiotista, acopiando los artículos heterogéneos que constan en esta lista que nos encontramos en el Zócalo.

"25 varas de raso maravilloso color de yema de huevo y 20 varas de encaje de a medio la vara para Virginia.

Crema de bismuto, cascarilla de La Habana, etcétera.

80 varas de raso color de rosa, para la mamá, zapatos del mismo color y medias de seda.

Gorros para las muchachas y botines despunteados.

Una corona de a diez pesos para la tumba de mi padrino, el general.

Un ramo de flores para la pobre de mi tía Charo.

Velas y candeleros para la tumba de la familia en Dolores y gratificación al criado que los cuida para que no se los roben.

Tres velomantillas.

Mole verde para la cocinera.

Suscripción para pasar a las tablas que separan el paseo público del erario de Bejarano.

Cena sobre el Zócalo".

De esta manera y de aberración en aberración, México presenta en estos días a los ojos del filósofo y del extranjero un aspecto *sui géneris*, enteramente nuestro, y que sugiere, por desgracia, no muy favorables calificaciones respecto a nuestra cultura.

El pueblo se aglomera en la plaza principal de la capital de la República para convertirla, con el beneplácito social y municipal, en tianguis de pueblo. Improvisa barracas, con detrimento de la educación y de la decencia, con las sábanas de la cama. Se echa en el suelo y pernocta sobre las piedras; coloca sus frutas y sus golosinas sobre la basura; improvisa fogones y hace lumbradas y se desgañita pregonando. Son los restos de la barbarie que vienen a sentar sus reales en el corazón de la ciudad para celebrar el gran velorio como lo ha estado haciendo hace tres siglos; pero se encuentra un grupo, relativamente corto, de gente culta, que se viste con raso color de yema de huevo y con casimir francés, que usa plumas de avestruz y tacones altos. El raso amarillo y las sábanas y petates de las barracas; las plumas de avestruz y de marabú y los sombreros de petate; el casimir francés y la manta del país, o sean los paños menores en que vive nuestro pueblo hacen un mal consorcio en la apariencia y protestan por el contacto. Los trajes difieren esencialmente; pero no así el sentimiento por los muertos.

El raso amarillo come trufas y la frazada cacahuates; pero raso y frazada comen doble esos días en honra y gloria de los muertos, que ya no comen. La barbarie y el refinamiento están de acuerdo con el modo de sentir; experimentan el mismo dolor, el mismo regocijo y el mismo apetito; pero les disgusta juntarse, rozarse. El raso amarillo teme la pelusilla que se desprende de la manta, de la frazada y del rebozo. ¿Qué hacer entonces? Llorar es preciso, divertirse es preciso, el raso maravilloso es indispensable, el aniversario se acerca. De esta emergencia brota un genio salvador, como en todas las situaciones difíciles; nace Bejarano, y propone poner unas tablas para hacer un redondel que divida al raso amarillo de la manta de a real.

—¡Buena idea!—grita el raso amarillo.

Bejarano agrega:

—Este redondel será mío por unos cuantos días.

—¡Excelente!—gritan las plumas de avestruz.

—Pero . . .—continúa Bejarano—para pasar a mi barraca se pagarán cuatro pesos.

—¿Y qué?—dice desdeñosamente el raso amarillo—. ¿No ve usted que todos somos ricos? Casi todos somos agiotistas.

Satisfecho Bejarano con la respuesta, persuade al ayuntamiento, que de por sí es tan fácil de persuadir, de que le preste el Zócalo, y el ayuntamiento se lo presta. Fulcheri lleva el equivalente de los cacahuates al Zócalo, y guarda sus comestibles en pequeños garitones, de donde salen en la noche como del sombrero maravilloso de Harman, a precios de muerto.

México elegante emprende un movimiento de trilla que dura cuatro horas, durante el cual cada quien se ha dado cuenta del raso de las otras, y queda persuadido de la utilidad de las prendas de todas clases, de que por cuatro pesos oyó la misma música que de ordinario oye de balde y de que cenó caro por final de cuentas.

¿Y los muertos? No tienen novedad. ¿Qué más pueden exigir esos pobres cadáveres que su corona de a diez pesos, y sus velas de cera y sus flores? Se les ha puesto su ofrenda, pero no han querido comérsela. ¿Será que no tienen apetito y ellos saben su cuento?

¿Y los dolientes? Todos ellos han perdido a uno o a muchos seres queridos, todos han llorado y tienen las llagas abiertas, las heridas mal cicatrizadas, y con ellas aún sangrando se presentan en el día solemne del recuerdo, en el día oficial, en el día de la Iglesia, a inscribirse voluntariamente ¿en el registro de los que rezan y los que lloran? No: a suscribirse en el redondel de Bejarano y en el menú de Fulcheri.

¿Y el sentimiento, y el pesar y el duelo? ¿Irán pasando todas estas flores del alma a la categoría del cempasúchil, que es la más ordinaria y fea de las flores? ¿El lujo y los placeres habrán acabado de robar al alma de esta generación el espiritualismo y la moral, la gratitud y el recuerdo, la sensibilidad y la lógica? No lo sabemos, pero es desgarrador que haya algo más triste que la muerte: la alegría y la indiferencia de los vivos. De todos modos, ya tenemos un dato para no hacernos ilusiones respecto al porvenir, porque después de muertos no solo nos espera la tumba con todos sus honores, sino el redondel de Bejarano. ◆

José Tomás de Cuéllar. Nació y murió en la Ciudad de México (1830–1894). Estudió en los colegios de San Gregorio, San Ildefonso, Militar y en la Academia de San Carlos. Fue periodista desde los veinte años. En 1868 participó en la fundación de La Bohemia Literaria, grupo en el que trabajó como editor hasta 1872, año en que se incorporó al cuerpo diplomático en Washington, donde vivió hasta 1882. En 1892 fue nombrado miembro de la Real Academia Española. Fue autor de varias piezas de teatro, entre ellas: *Deberes y sacrificios*, *Natural y figura* y *Cubrir las apariencias*; en poesía: *Obras poéticas* y *Versos*. Sus novelas aparecieron como dos series tituladas *La linterna mágica*.

DESAFÍO PERDIDO

TEMOR A LA MUERTE, ANGUSTIA DE VIVIR

Paul Westheim

◆

¿Qué es lo que ha llevado al mexicano a adoptar a la calavera como un motivo frecuente en la plástica y en el arte popular? Es importante su tradición mestiza—las representaciones tradicionales de la muerte se hallan a medio camino entre las danzas macabras europeas y el panteón prehispánico—, pero lo es más la angustia de confrontar lo irremediable. Desde esta perspectiva, este autor reflexiona en torno al esqueleto, ya no elemento distintivo de nuestra cultura, sino *leitmotiv* que nos ayuda a enfrentar la incertidumbre de la vida humana.

◆

¿Dónde es, corazón mío, el sitio de mi vida?
¿Dónde es mi verdadera casa?
¿Dó mi mansión precisa está?
¡Yo sufro aquí en la tierra!
Cantare mexicanos.

Traducción de Ángel María Garibay.

◆

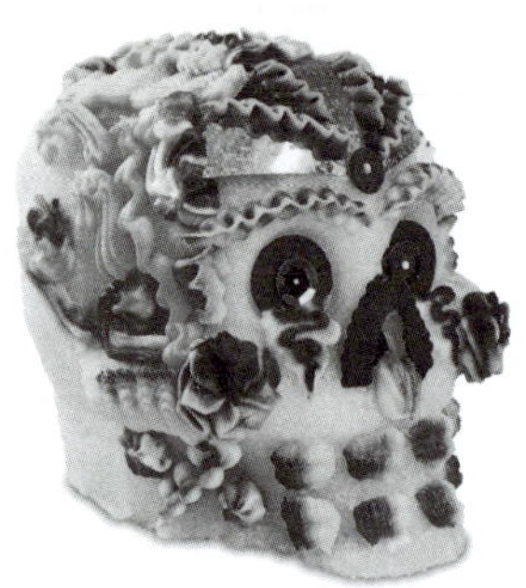

La calavera, como motivo plástico, es una fantasía popular que desde hace milenios se deleita en la representación de la muerte, como el Renacimiento y el Barroco en la de angelillos y cupidos: esto fue una tremenda sorpresa y casi un trauma para los visitantes de la Exposición de Arte Mexicano en París. Se paraban ante la estatua de Coatlicue, diosa de la tierra y de la vida, que lleva la máscara de la muerte; contemplaban el cráneo de cristal de roca—uno de los minerales más duros—, tallado por un artista azteca, en innumerables horas de trabajo, con asombroso dominio del oficio; miraban los grabados de los dibujantes populares, Manilla y Posada, que recurrían a esqueletos para comentar los sucesos sociales y políticos de su tiempo. Se enteraban de que en México hay padres que el 2 de noviembre regalan a sus hijos calaveras de azúcar y chocolate en las cuales está escrito el nombre de la criatura, y que esta se come encantada el dulce macabro, como si fuera la cosa más natural del mundo. Les fascinaba un arte popular que confecciona con materiales muy humildes—con tela, madera, barro y hasta con chicle—unos muñecos en forma de esqueletos, ataviados con abigarradas prendas, juguetes muy comunes y queridos por el pueblo . . . Paul Rivet, en una crónica sobre la exposición, habla de motivos inesperados y pregunta: "¿Qué decir de esos muñecos que representan una pareja en traje de boda, y son en realidad una pareja de esqueletos?". Pregunta en la que se vislumbra, además del asombro, un dejo de espanto. El europeo, para quien es una pesadilla pensar en la muerte y que no quiere que le recuerden la caducidad de la vida, se ve de pronto frente a un mundo que parece libre de esa angustia, que juega con la muerte y hasta se burla de ella . . . ¡Extraño mundo, actitud inconcebible!

El México antiguo no conocía el concepto de infierno. Es posible y hasta probable que en el inconsciente del pueblo, sobre todo del pueblo indígena, siga viviendo todavía el oscuro recuerdo de un más allá abierto aun al pecador. El hecho en sí es el mismo en todas partes, pero la concepción de la muerte es otra. La imagen del esqueleto con la guadaña y el reloj de arena, símbolo de lo perecedero, es en México de importación; en los casos en que se la acoge—por ejemplo, en las representaciones de la danza macabra—se adapta enseguida, se aclimata, se mexicaniza, como lo vemos en Manilla y Posada. Xavier Villaurrutia, cuya poesía gira, casi enteramente, en torno a la muerte, escribió alguna vez: "Aquí se tiene una gran facilidad para morir, es más fuerte su atracción conforme mayor cantidad de sangre india tenemos en las venas. Mientras más criollo se es, mayor temor por la muerte, puesto que eso es lo que se nos enseña". La carga psíquica que da un tinte trágico a la existencia del mexicano, hoy, como hace dos y tres mil años, no es el temor a la muerte, sino la angustia de la vida, la conciencia de estar expuesto, y con insuficientes medios de defensa, a una vida llena de peligros, llena de esencia demoniaca.

La íntima convicción del indio de que la vida es sufrimiento, de que el sumiso y débil es víctima de la brutalidad del fuerte—aquello que Rouault expresó al poner en uno de sus grabados de *Miserere et Guerre*, la sentencia de Plauto "El hombre es el lobo del hombre"—hizo que el arte religioso del México colonial adoptara con verdadera pasión y tratara con mil conmovedoras variantes el tema del Cristo martirizado, cuyo cuerpo, fustigado por inhumanos verdugos, chorrea sangre de mil pavorosas maneras. Es significativo que estas representaciones abunden en el siglo XVIII, siglo en que el indio y el mestizo, ejecutantes casi siempre anónimos, empiezan a imprimir al arte religioso su carácter y mentalidad. Y el hecho de encontrarse esas pinturas y esculturas sobre todo en las humildes iglesias pueblerinas, en aldeas de población indígena al margen de la civilización urbana, admite la conclusión de que el martirio que el hombre inflige al hombre es una experiencia honda y primordialmente arraigada en el mundo sentimental del indio; y que el Cristo es tan particularmente adorable para él porque siente la tortura como algo muy suyo. No cabe duda de que tal "patetismo del dolor material"—permítaseme citar esta frase de Werner Weisbach en el libro *El arte del barroco*—procede del realismo o, más bien, del verismo español, que se complace "en recargar la idea de la vida con imágenes de lo sangriento, lo terrible y espantoso". Pero tampoco hay duda de que México se apoderó del tema con intenso fervor—comparable al fervor con el que se adueñó del estilo churrigueresco para dotarlo de la pompa y exuberancia que corresponde a su propia idiosincrasia—y que el Nazareno colonial no es una simple variante del español, sino una creación independiente, obra de una sensibilidad específicamente mexicana. "En los Cristos misérrimos de aullidos, de sudor y de sangre, encontramos, con la puntualidad infalible de lo extraordinario, gran parte de la dramática mitología indígena anidando, con forzado confort, en la exigua y lamentable imagen de la aldea", dice Cardoza y Aragón en su libro *Pintura mexicana contemporánea*.

Angustia de vivir. Recordemos las palabras—escritas en el *Códice florentino*—que el padre nahua decía a su hijita cuando esta llegaba a la edad de seis o siete años: "Aquí en la tierra es lugar de mucho llanto, lugar donde . . . es bien conocida la amargura y el abatimiento. Un viento como de obsidianas sopla y se desliza sobre nosotros . . . no es lugar de bienestar aquí en la tierra, no hay alegría, no hay felicidad".

Y recordemos también la obra maestra de un pintor de nuestros días, *Tata Jesucristo* de Francisco Goitia, quien, hablando de las dos mujeres representadas en su cuadro, dice: "Están llorando lágrimas de nuestra raza, penas y lágrimas nuestras, diferentes a las de los otros. Toda la congoja de México está en ellas". Lo que las hace sollozar es la vida, el dolor de la vida, la incertidumbre que es la vida del hombre en la tierra.

El México antiguo no temblaba ante Mictlantecuhtli, el dios de la muerte; temblaba ante esa incertidumbre que es la vida del hombre. La llamaban Tezcatlipoca. ◆

Paul Westheim. Historiador nacido en Alemania (1885) y muerto en la Ciudad de México (1963). Fue perseguido por los nazis y se exilió en París. En 1940 se alistó para combatir la invasión alemana. Llegó a México en 1941. Entre sus obras se encuentran *Arte antiguo de México*, *Ideas fundamentales del arte prehispánico en México*, *Obras maestras del México antiguo* y *La calavera*, de donde fue extraído este fragmento.

DESAFÍO PLÁSTICO

LAS CALAVERAS DE JOSÉ GUADALUPE POSADA

Luis Cardoza y Aragón

◆

Imposible entender la estética mexicana de la calavera sin la obra del grabador decimonónico José Guadalupe Posada. Sus esqueletos ejercen una especial fascinación en quien los contempla, pues, al aproximarse a la muerte desde una perspectiva lejana a la religiosidad, nos ofrecen una visión de esta resignada e irónica. En este ensayo, el autor explora las posibles fuentes de las que abrevan estas calacas, y reflexiona en torno a dichas obras, en las que muerte y vida se expresan en el lenguaje popular.

◆

José Guadalupe Posada (Aguascalientes, 2 de febrero de 1851) nació cuando la tremenda herida de la intervención norteamericana de 1847 sangraba a borbotones: México había perdido más de la mitad de su territorio; vivió en su niñez y adolescencia las convulsiones causadas por las leyes de Reforma, la Intervención francesa y las luchas de Juárez; la dictadura de Porfirio Díaz, y la gestación y el triunfo inicial de la Revolución con la entrada de Madero a México. Cuando Huerta traiciona y asesina al presidente Madero, Posada había muerto semanas antes (Ciudad de México, 20 de enero de 1913) como había vivido: casi solo y pobremente, después de haber trabajado en numerosos periódicos, en ilustración de libros, carteles de corridas de toros, circos, teatros, etcétera.

Posada no era un artista que se acercaba al pueblo. Para empezar, seguramente no se creía artista. Ignoraba su estado de gracia cotidiano. No olvidemos la integración—perdón por la palabra—con el autor del "corrido" (Constancio S. Suárez, y otros, posiblemente) y con la gracia del tipógrafo. Tenían la sensibilidad de lo que eran: pueblo mexicano; la imaginación, el sentido de su fabulación, el genio o la inteligencia de objetivar, de darle forma con las ilustraciones, las palabras, el tono, el ritmo de los cantadores populares. Es decir, estos hombres no se acercaban al pueblo, no eran populares: eran pueblo. [. . .]

Sus calaveras no solo tienen connotación crítica o satírica; tienen también connotación elogiosa o festiva: su aprovechamiento común en México antes de Posada y después de él, por la gran popularidad que les dio—"el tótem nacional", escribió Juan Larrea—alcanzó a ser la característica más honda y original del arte popular mexicano.

La muerte es tema universal de la expresión humana. El sentido con que se la cuida, la familiaridad, la ternura, la sencillez con que México considera la muerte, su obsesión que, no siendo trágica ni fúnebre, sino nupcial y natal, su cotidianidad inmediata, su visibilidad imperiosa y serena, su risa manante más que un gemido, encierran la sabiduría no aprendida de

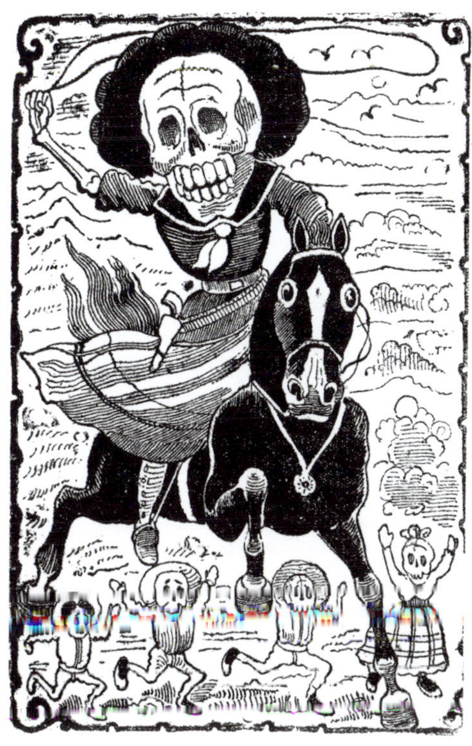

José Guadalupe Posada, *Don Juan Tenorio.*

una concepción cósmica y lúdica, como perpetuamente maravillada, peculiarísima de México y que proviene de tradiciones precortesianas entretejidas con las del medievo europeo, con sus danzas macabras y juicios finales; pero la muerte mexicana, una muerte vital, un canto a la vida, sublimada en los sacrificios, no nos trataba como hombres, sino como dioses.

Las calaveras de Posada—*tzompantlis*, *coatlicues* desgranadas—son el motivo más profundo y revelador de su obra y de sí. El extranjero parece escuchar hoy, mejor que el mexicano, lo que vive detrás de ese narcisismo de la muerte. La claridad de la intención evidencia un hambre secular de lo sagrado, la estratificación del mito, macerado en lo reflexivo y en lo más fantástico. Ante el absurdo de la muerte no cabe la tragedia, sino el humor, y a sus preguntas responde con jovialidad. La muerte se responde sus propias preguntas. Su respuesta: la certidumbre de que ella, la muerte, es para siempre. Y estalla una rebelión mágica en la cual hombres y mujeres y niños y animales se despojan no solo de sus máscaras, también de sus carnes; ya no desollados, sino roídos por un tiempo que los relojes no pueden ni soñar. Se reconquista la identidad definitiva; el yo se vuelve todos, y no solo el otro. Esta salida matinal hacia lo primigenio, Posada la hace para nosotros sin sospecharlo, como el mago de feria que saca del pañuelo palomas de verdad. ¡Cuánto se divertía Posada leyendo los homenajes, visitando sus exposiciones nacionales e internacionales, alelado como el mago de feria cuya suerte de ilusionista dejó de ser apariencia! Posada ignora que se acuerda, y busca su nivel como el agua, sin escuchar mandato alguno, dentro de una semejanza íntima y oculta que no es un aire de familia: es un huracán de familia. Este Posada—con la oreja puesta sobre la tierra, oyendo su latido—, es el que más me emociona. Aquí está la sed de ser piedra y de no serlo: sus palomas reales. Sed desmesurada de una "cruda" remotísima y sin término. No sabe que se acuerda. Sus calaveras se apoyan en las incandescentes sílabas erguidas de un lenguaje oscuro que sobre la finitud han balbuceado todos los hombres. Hay una nublada conciencia libertadora de la servidumbre del hombre a la muerte, la obsesión creativa de un "corazón que está brotando flores en la mitad de la noche", himnos a la noche de una muerte no llorada sino sonreída, florida y cantada, con la lira y el arco heraclitanos. La comunión, cuando

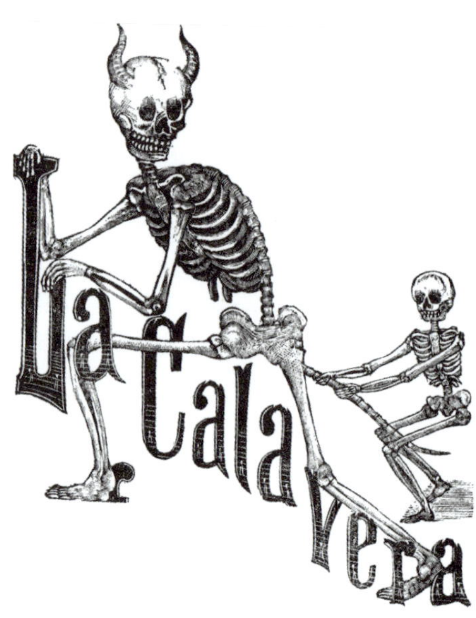

José Guadalupe Posada, *The Skeleton*.

devoramos el cráneo de azúcar, es un ritual desprevenido, apenas transpuesto, del erotismo de los sacrificios. Nos penetramos en busca de un orden que requiere la única realidad pura, la realidad de la muerte, o la comunión con ella. La muerte y la vida son en México una medalla tan tenue que solo una cara tiene. El agua bendita sobre el ascua de la pasión azteca alumbra, llama, y la cruz en la frente del miércoles de ceniza mézclase con la sangre de los sacrificios: tal confluencia ocurre en las calaveras de Posada, con la naturalidad del mar de fondo de la inocencia, en la golosa tarascada del niño a la calavera de azúcar.

Posada, en primer término, después Orozco y los grabadores del Taller de Gráfica Popular, con Leopoldo Méndez a la cabeza, se valieron de las calaveras en las sátiras, en las odas populares (*Corrido de Stalingrado*, de Leopoldo Méndez, por ejemplo), con una amplitud de sentimientos y pensamientos en que la calavera se empleó no solo por la fecha en que el Taller las hacía y las sigue haciendo (2 de noviembre, Día de Muertos), sino porque ejercen una gran fascinación sobre la fantasía popular. No son temas peyorativos del arte popular mexicano—las calaveras de azúcar, los féretros de dulce, las tibias y los fémures de caramelo, los judas, las máscaras, los muñecos de cartón, etcétera—, por la vehemencia del recuerdo y por el sabor de tal orientación. ◆

Luis Cardoza y Aragón. Nació en Guatemala y murió en la Ciudad de México (1904–1992). Vivió en México desde 1952. Colaboró en *Contemporáneos*. En 1979 se publicaron sus *Poesías completas y algunas prosas*. Fue crítico de arte y sobre arte mexicano escribió: *Rufino Tamayo*, *Pintura mexicana contemporánea*, *Orozco*, *México: pintura activa*, *Arte mexicano de hoy* y *José Guadalupe Posada*. En 1979 recibió la Orden del Águila Azteca. Doctor Honoris Causa por la Universidad de San Carlos, en Guatemala.

Por las orillas de Cuautla
flota una horrible bandera,
que empuña la calavera
del aguerrido Zapata.

Al sonar las doce en punto
monta en un brioso corcel,
ese indomable difunto,
sale cruzando con él.

Y atraviesa al trote brusco,
esas bastas serranías
y se llega hasta el Ajusco,
centro de sus correrías.

y allí parte para el cerro
donde su tesoro guarda,
que es llamado del jilguero,
y allí del cuaco se baja.

Dobla su negra bandera
que es signo de muerte airada,
pues tiene en medio pintada
una horrenda calavera.

Y dice: —Paciente aguardo
el comerme ese pollito
con mi buen cuate guajardo,
y así lo haremos en molito.

Guisado con las canillas
que a docenas resultaron
en los trenes que asaltaron
mis valerosas gavillas.

¡Tiempos felices aquellos
en que gozaba de veras!
¡Cuántos montones con ellos
hicimos de calaveras!

DESAFÍO POPULAR

LA CALACA

Ruth D. Lechuga

◆

La importancia de la calaca como motivo del arte popular mexicano trasciende la fiesta del Día de muertos. En este artículo, la autora nos ofrece un recorrido por las más diversas manifestaciones artesanales de las calaveras—relacionadas o no con la celebración de los primeros días de noviembre—y nos da cuenta de una interesante paradoja: en México, la muerte es un personaje vital que se reinventa día con día.

◆

JUGAR CON LA MUERTE

No se sabe cuándo se originó la tradición de hacer juguetes de muertos. Desde luego ya existía a mediados del siglo XIX, según da cuenta la detallada descripción de Antonio García Cubas, por lo que es probable que sea una costumbre más antigua.

Algunos se destinan a la ofrenda del Día de Muertos dedicada a los niños que han fallecido, con el fin de que los pequeños tengan con qué jugar durante su visita a la tierra. Pero en muchas otras ocasiones se hacen para los niños vivos, quienes juegan encantados con las tumbitas de varios pisos, los entierritos, los padrecitos con cabeza de garbanzo, las ofrenditas y con muchos otros objetos más de esta índole.

Los esqueletos ocupan un lugar importante entre estos juguetes. Las calacas hacen frecuentemente tareas que acostumbran realizar los vivos: la mecanógrafa teclea afanosamente en su máquina de escribir, una señora muele el nixtamal en su metate, otra hace tortillas, un escritor llena página tras página con sus ideas, otros venden toda clase de artículos, unos novios están a punto de casarse; hay algunas calacas que toman encantadas un baño de espuma, y otras que lucen diferentes tocados en la cabeza: como de cocinero, de torero, de catrín con gran chistera, de mujer con el pelo enrollado sobre grandes tubos . . . También dentro de estos esqueletos hay los que yacen dentro de su tumba y se asoman al jalar un hilo.

Otra importante tradición son las calaveras de azúcar. Las hay de muchos tamaños y frecuentemente están decoradas con algún sombrero o con muchas flores del mismo material. Estas piezas suelen regalarse a los amigos, o a los novios, y llevar pegado en la frente el nombre de quien la recibirá. Además de la Ciudad de México, un centro importante para la elaboración de estas piezas es Toluca, aunque otros lugares del Estado de México, como Tenancingo, también las producen.

Pero la importancia de la calaca como motivo de arte popular trasciende los objetos creados para el Día de Muertos. El esqueleto es motivo usual en los Judas de papel aglutinado, tradición de Semana Santa aún importante en la década de 1960. Aquellas figuras enormes, de cuatro metros o más de altura, eran compradas por las grandes tiendas y decoradas con algunos regalos. A las 11 de la mañana del Sábado Santo y cuando las campanas de la iglesia tocaban para anunciar la gloria, estas piezas eran estalladas como juegos pirotécnicos, y los espectadores se abalanzaban para tratar de adueñarse de algunos objetos. También se hacían y todavía se hacen Judas más pequeños, muchos de los cuales tienen forma de esqueleto.

Varias generaciones de la familia Linares en el Distrito Federal son importantes juderos. Pero también hacen conjuntos decorativos de calacas en diferentes situaciones. Por ejemplo, en 1986, en el Museo Nacional de Artes e Industrias Populares, se podía apreciar una escena llamada "La muerte temblorosa", ejecutada por estos artesanos en recuerdo del gran temblor del año anterior. En aquella representación los esqueletos simulaban ser "los topos" en acción, los ciudadanos que ofrecieron su valiosa ayuda para salvar a los heridos que lograron sacar de algún edificio caído, pero también simulaban a los ladrones que aprovecharon la situación para llevarse alguna televisión u otros objetos de entre los escombros.

Al igual que los Linares, muchos otros artistas populares hacen figuras de calacas que, aunque ya no forman parte de la tradición del Día de Muertos, aún nos hablan del desafío plástico que el motivo del esqueleto ha suscitado entre los creadores mexicanos. En Metepec, Estado de México, los habituales árboles de la vida se transforman en árboles de la muerte. Habitante de la Ciudad de México, Roberto Ruiz, quien es Premio Nacional de Ciencias y Artes en la rama de Artes y Tradiciones Populares, prefiere para sus miniaturas el tema de la muerte. Sus piezas son

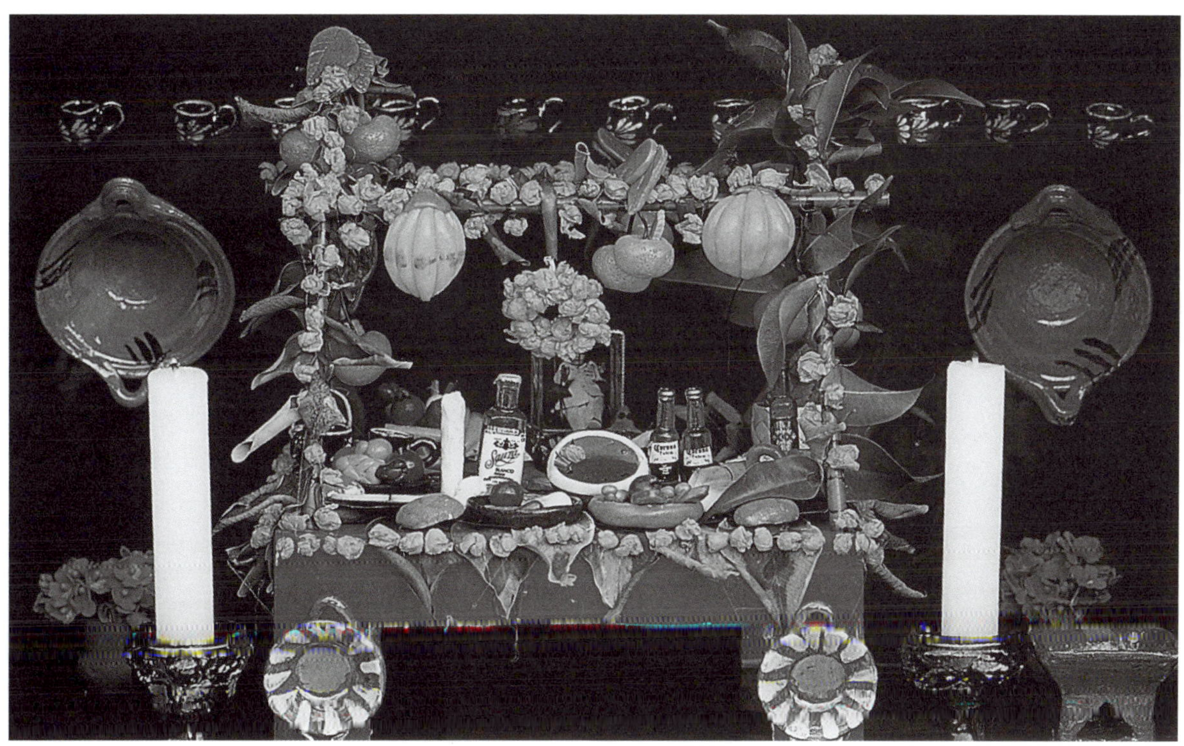

Miniature offering inspired by altars in Oaxaca, Mexico City, 2000.

talladas en hueso con una inacabable variedad de formas. Otro artista que se dedica al tema de la muerte es Saulo Moreno, quien elabora sus figuras con alambre y papel.

DANZAR CON LA MUERTE

Pero la calaca no solo ha dado pie a infinidad de objetos de arte popular. En algunas festividades cobra vida en danzantes vestidos de negro, con los huesos pintados en blanco y una máscara de calavera.

Aunque durante el 1 y 2 de noviembre se danza en algunos pueblos, las danzas celebradas en estas fechas no siempre tienen como personaje a una calaca. Sin embargo, en Tepoztlán, Morelos, los niños bailan con su esqueleto de vara y papel de china que a menudo es más alto que su acompañante.

El personaje principal de la danza del "Tecuán"—que se baila en distintas ocasiones—es el tigre; sin embargo, en Acatlán, Puebla, también existe un esqueleto. De hecho, no hay límite para que la calaca participe en una danza.

El esqueleto es un personaje importante en algunas danzas derivadas de los autos moralizantes con los que los misioneros enseñaban la religión a los indígenas. Entre estas danzas podemos citar "Las tres potencias", "Los mudos", "Los siete vicios", "Los san Miguelitos", "Los diablos", y otras. El estado de Guerrero es especialmente rico en estas manifestaciones. En la versión de Tixtla de la danza de "Los diablos", por ejemplo, se escenifica la caída de Lucifer del cielo, mientras que en la montaña un grupo de diablos pelea alternativamente con mujeres y con muertes. También vemos a la calaca en pastorelas, otro tipo de auto moralizante. Esto sucede por ejemplo en Colima.

En algunas danzas de Semana Santa, los judíos o fariseos que matan a Jesucristo usan máscaras, que en algunos pueblos aluden a las fuerzas nocturnas que cada fin de año salen para apropiarse de la tierra. El Sábado de Gloria, con la resurrección de Cristo, se liquidaba el peligro que estas fuerzas representan. Entre los judíos, la muerte es un personaje muy frecuente, aunque no tiene un papel específico en la danza. Algunos lugares en donde esto sucede son El Doctor, Querétaro; Tanlajás, San Luis Potosí; San Bartolo Aguacaliente, Guanajuato, y Jesús María, en Nayarit.

El Carnaval es otra fiesta en la que es común apreciar calacas. Los tejorones, que danzan en esta fiesta en la costa mixteca de Oaxaca, interpretan diferentes escenas, como la cacería de un tigre, el nacimiento de un niño o las peleas entre un viejo y una muerta, donde a veces gana el viejo.

En Naolinco, Veracruz, uno de los moros de la danza de "Moros y cristianos" usa máscara de calaca. En la meseta tarasca de Michoacán el cambio de mayordomía se acompaña con la danza de los "Viejitos", que tiene dos versiones: los "Viejitos bonitos" y los "Viejitos feos", que son una burla de los primeros. La maringuilla—el personaje femenino que deriva de La Malinche—de estos últimos, en San Juan Nuevo, es una calavera.

Todas estas representaciones del esqueleto dan cuenta de la inagotable creatividad de los artistas populares, tanto para los objetos tradicionales como para los decorativos, y aseguran que la tradición mexicana de las representaciones de la muerte, lejos de extinguirse, encuentre cada día nuevas y valiosas expresiones plásticas. ◆

Ruth D. Lechuga fue investigadora de arte popular y fotógrafa por más de cincuenta años. Durante ese tiempo creó un museo de arte popular con su colección, al que está dedicado el número 42 de *Artes de México*. Publicó *Traje indígena de México* y *Las técnicas textiles del México antiguo*, entre otros. En la colección Uso y Estilo, el título *Ruth D. Lechuga, una memoria mexicana* rescata la obra fotográfica de esta autora. A su muerte, donó a *Artes de México* su archivo fotográfico con más de 20 000 negativos.

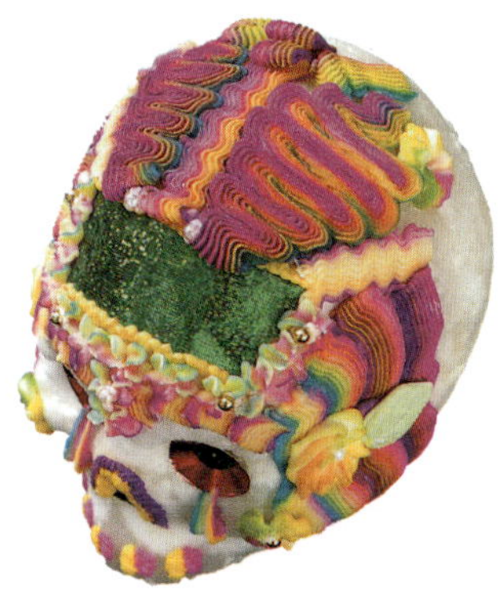

DESAFÍO RECREADO

RECUERDO, DESCUBRIMIENTO Y VOLUNTAD: COSTUMBRES CHICANAS DEL DÍA DE MUERTOS

Tomás Ybarra Frausto

◆

¿Cómo se transforman las tradiciones al confrontar una nueva realidad? ¿Qué rasgos nuevos adquirió la celebración del Día de Muertos al otro lado de la frontera norte? ¿Qué significa para los migrantes continuar con esta entrañable tradición? En estas páginas, el autor nos plantea varias respuestas para estas interrogantes.

◆

Los mexicanos que viven en Estados Unidos mantienen y transforman su cultura ancestral de manera dinámica, fluida y creativa. Dentro de la comunidad mexicana los patrones culturales se manifiestan con heterogeneidad y diversidad; existen factores regionales, de clase y género, así como históricos, que influyen en la supervivencia y el cambio cultural.

Las costumbres mexicanochicanas del Día de Muertos se remontan a orígenes milenarios, a la vez que incorporan actitudes biculturales contemporáneas, y vaticinan formaciones culturales venideras. Son, al mismo tiempo, celebraciones de vida y rituales de recuerdo, descubrimiento y voluntad.

EL RECUERDO

El Día de Muertos es la fecha del recuerdo, cuando los vivos se relacionan con sus muertos de manera directa y familiar.

El activismo sociopolítico de los chicanos durante las décadas de 1960 y 1970 creó un movimiento masivo de regeneración nacionalista, de recuperación y reclamación cultural. Las tradiciones mexicanas y del suroeste de Estados Unidos fueron incorporadas por los obreros de las comunidades, quienes las revitalizaron y les dieron nuevos significados dentro de diversos contextos. Un ejemplo espectacular de este proceso de transformación cultural fue la recuperación y reinvención del Día de Muertos por grupos de artistas y centros artísticos comunitarios. Una de las primeras tradiciones en ser resucitada fue la de las calaveras creadas por José Guadalupe Posada. Estas figuras esqueléticas y cómicas pasaron a ser parte del vocabulario visual de los chicanos en sus carteles, murales y otras formas de expresión plástica.

Inspirándose en estas calaveras, el Teatro Campesino formó una Banda Calavera: un alegre y ruidoso conjunto musical disfrazado de calaveras, que recorría el barrio anunciando las funciones de los teatros. Pronto, en muchos de los actos creados por el Teatro Campesino, aparecieron las calacas brincando y haciendo maromas en los escenarios, y posteriormente en las funciones de muchos otros grupos de teatro por todo el país.

El panteón de las calaveras de Posada tampoco tardó en hacer su aparición en las ilustraciones de los periódicos de la comunidad y en las revistas de los estudiantes en los colegios y universidades. La tradición de imprimir las calaveras, tanto de versos satíricos y burlones como de ilustraciones, que se había mantenido en las comunidades mexicanochicanas de las urbes desde la vuelta del siglo XX, se vio así reforzada y expandida. La impresión por lo general corre a cargo de particulares, y es financiada por los comerciantes locales.

Otra tradición mexicana antigua que se reinventó de este lado de la frontera es la de la ofrenda. En las comunidades mexicanochicanas las ofrendas tienden a ser celebraciones colectivas creadas por artistas en espacios públicos, tales como centros culturales, galerías o museos. La estética individual y el oficio de los artistas profesionales han dado como resultado la reinterpretación de la tradicional ofrenda, y la han vuelto una visión fantasiosa, política y personal. La forma del altar se mantiene no tanto por su contexto religioso, sino simplemente como un marco de referencia funcional para exhibir la acumulación de múltiples capas de objetos. Aunque aún se utilizan elementos tradicionales tales como velas, flores, comida, imágenes de santos y fotografías de los fallecidos, las ofrendas de los chicanos siempre incluyen objetos extraídos de su experiencia bicultural.

Mientras que el movimiento chicano revitalizó muchas tradiciones mexicanas tanto folclóricas como artísticas, también rescató patrones y costumbres culturales sedimentadas en los viejos asentamientos mexicanos del suroeste de Estados Unidos. Mediante nuevos, audaces y fuertes rituales comunitarios, así como por desfiles y festivales que recuerdan la muerte, lo viejo y lo nuevo se mezclan para destacar el eterno ciclo de la vida y la muerte.

LA VOLUNTAD

Si las décadas de 1960 y 1970 fueron periodos de recuerdo y descubrimientos culturales, la de 1990 fue una época de afiliación política para los mexicanochicanos, así como para otros grupos latinos de Estados Unidos, y de conexiones culturales con otros grupos subalternos de todo el mundo.

Dentro del panorama multicultural de este país, los mexicanochicanos pudieron profundizar sus vínculos con la cultura mexicana ancestral y establecer un diálogo cultural nuevo y más maduro con el México actual. La película *La ofrenda*, de Lourdes Portillo, representa con gran belleza algunos de los indicios de esta nueva interrelación con México. Esta cinta, que traza las tradiciones del Día de Muertos en ambos lados de la frontera, es un retrato de la recuperación cultural y de la habilitación de su poder mediante la recreación de esta tradición. *El collage* de voces de la pista de sonido de la película nos permite enterarnos de las actitudes actuales de los mexicanochicanos con respecto al Día de Muertos:

Concha Saucedo: Para nosotros, el Día de Muertos es cuando nuestros ancestros nos visitan, y es la fecha que nos conecta con nuestro pasado cultural . . . Y para la gente que está separada de su país—porque estamos en una cultura ajena, aun para los que nacimos

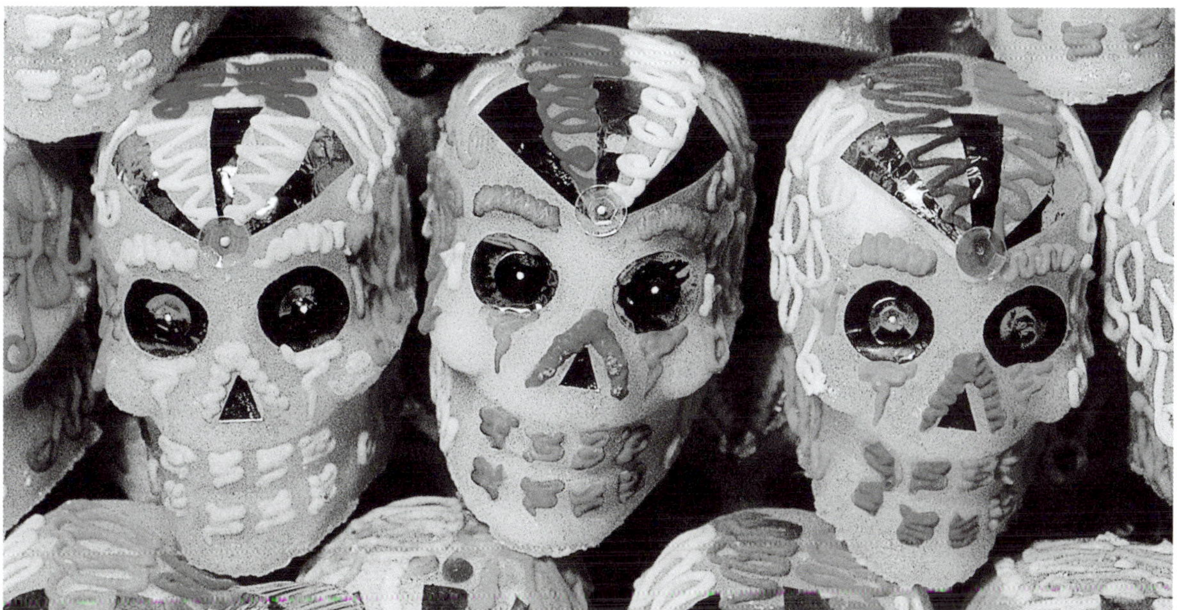

aquí—se vuelve una forma muy importante de la comunidad misma.

Amelia Mesa-Bains: Los chicanos hemos revivido y adoptado el Día de Muertos. El pasado es una fuente inagotable de nostalgia activa. Nuestras celebraciones pueden tener diferente forma que las de México; pero el espíritu de la tradición pervive. El arte tiene que ver con curar: cuando la gente participa en una expresión artística como esta, cuando la hace y la ve, es como si se curara de algo.

Concha Saucedo: Decir que "la cultura cura" significa que la cultura nos alivia. Esencialmente esto quiere decir que hay elementos en todas las culturas que, si se les preserva, dan salud a la gente, en particular a los latinos. Nosotros nos hemos tenido que separar de esa cultura, y esa separación ha creado un desequilibrio que es, en efecto, una "mala salud". Y cuando decimos que "la cultura cura", estamos diciendo "regresa a tu cultura", mantenla.

Nuestra lucha es también una batalla de la memoria contra el olvido. Debemos redimir y reclamar el pasado de manera que transforme la realidad actual. ◆

Tomás Ybarra Frausto. Connotado catedrático y ensayista de la cultura mexicanoamericana. Actualmente es director asociado de cultura y creatividad de la Rockefeller Foundation en Nueva York.

DESAFÍO LITERARIO

NOVIA DE AZÚCAR

Ana García Bergua

◆

A Rosenda la atraje con unos cirios rodeados de grandes rosas que había colocado en el altar de muertos. Ese año se me ocurrió adornarlo sin incienso ni calaveras; más bien parecía, me dijeron los vecinos, un arreglo de boda, debido al pastel y a la botella de champán, en vez del clásico tequila o la cerveza. En medio acomodé el retrato de Rosenda y otro más que encontré en el baúl de mi abuela. Supuse que había sido pariente nuestra y que por algo merecería regresar.

Me metí a la cama y fingí dormir durante varias horas. De repente, en la madrugada, escuché ruidos como de ratón. Junto al altar me encontré a Rosenda comiendo con glotonería el pastel de bodas. Su sayo blanco, algo raído ya, ceñido a la cintura y escotado de acuerdo con la moda que le tocó vivir, estaba manchado de crema y migajas. Nadie la había traído jamás, me dijo, desde su muerte; siglos creía llevar sumida en una oscuridad con olor a tierra. ¿Cuánto tiempo ha pasado?, me preguntó sorprendida. No demasiado, le respondí, sin aclararle cuánto. Era una mujer bella, de carne generosa, con una llama de temor en la pupila. Contra su pecho estrujaba unos crisantemos de tela. Le preocupaba que este fuera el Juicio Final, que nadie la fuera a perdonar por sus muchos pecados. No te apures, susurré, quitándole el ramo, yo te perdono. La ceñí por la cintura y descorchamos champán. A cambio de que me escuchara y de poder tocarla, le ofrecí saciar la sed y el hambre de tantos años. Con eso basta, me dijo ahíta, cuando pasadas las horas empezó a clarear el día. Luego se dispuso a regresar a su tierra ignota, pero yo la encerré con llave en el armario, sin hacer caso de sus gritos y sus lamentos. Me convertiré en polvo, lo queramos o no, gritaba entre sollozos.

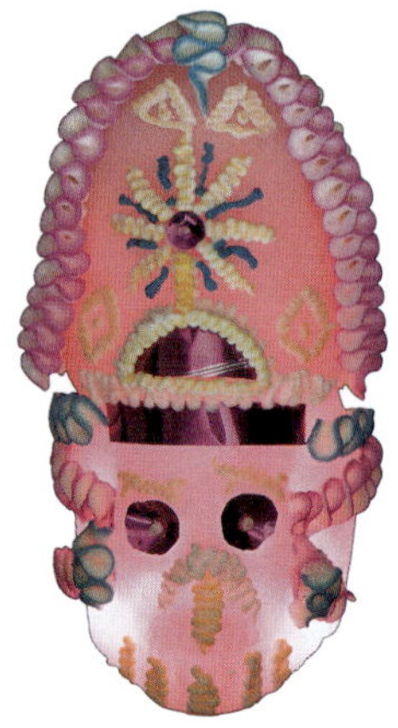

Dejé pasar el día completo hasta que el armario quedó en silencio otra vez. Mientras, me ocupé de desmontar el altar con cierta ceremonia. Al ocaso, dispuesta ya la cena en la mesa y descorchado un tinto que recordaba la sangre, decidí sacar a mi muerta del armario, seguro de encontrarla dormida y hambrienta. Pero cuál no fue mi decepción: entre los chales de seda blanca de mi abuela yacía tirada, como empujada por el aire, una calavera de azúcar que llevaba en la frente el nombre de Rosenda de papel plateado, y que se me deshizo en polvo entre los dedos. ◆

Tomado de *La confianza en los extraños*, Plaza y Janés, 2002.

DESAFÍO REVISADO

LA MUERTE SIN CALAVERAS: LOS MEXICANOS Y "EL MEXICANO"

Alfonso Alfaro

◆

Este país es, quizá, menos mágico y menos homogéneo de lo que quiere la leyenda. Como corresponde a una sociedad de tantas culturas, hay aquí múltiples formas de hacer frente a la pérdida de los seres queridos, al sufrimiento de la agonía, al vértigo de lo desconocido. ¿De qué manera se convirtieron las huesudas y las calacas en signos del nacionalismo mestizo? ¿Cómo llegaron los mexicanos a persuadirse a sí mismos de que tenían con la muerte una relación de privilegio?

◆

A los mexicanos nos gusta sentirnos distintos, peculiares. Esta actitud no es ajena a las características del país que nuestros antepasados comenzaron a edificar desde la época virreinal. Una sociedad como esta, que aspira a construirse como nación, necesita afectos que unan, referencias que confluyan, elementos que identifiquen a los miembros de la tribu y los distingan de los demás: retratos donde cada uno pueda reconocer, aunque sea de manera fragmentaria, rasgos de su propia imagen.

A falta (por fortuna) de un vínculo sacralizado y metahistórico semejante a los que postulan las colectividades que creen en las razas o los pueblos que se sienten unidos por la sangre o por un alma común, a falta (desgraciadamente) de lazos como los que aglutinan a las sociedades fundadas en torno a un proyecto, nuestros ancestros y nuestros compatriotas han tenido que dar forma a una identidad compartida, y la han ido fabricando a lo largo de generaciones. Esa identidad se ha edificado sobre nuestra historia y sus signos, y pertenece, por tanto, a la órbita de los símbolos, las representaciones, la cultura. En México, la solidez de estos nexos de carácter cultural (imágenes vivas, recuerdos elaborados, ritos comunitarios) logra, hasta cierto punto, compensar la grave fragmentación de las redes sociales y el carácter precario y nebuloso de los objetivos comunes.

LA MUERTE PATRIÓTICA: LA CALAVERITA Y EL NACIONALISMO MESTIZO

Una memoria de cataclismos históricos (Conquista, invasiones, revoluciones) que se empalma naturalmente sobre otra, más honda, de sacudidas telúricas, aunada a una acumulación de sueños frustrados, de ilusiones desvanecidas, alentó a nuestros coterráneos a erigir uno de nuestros mitos más florecientes: el de que somos un pueblo que guarda con la muerte una relación de privilegio. Según esta fantasía colectiva, nuestra familiaridad con el infortunio nos permite obtener una secreta revancha sobre la adversidad: la carcajada.

Un linaje descendiente por línea materna de un pueblo que ofrendaba corazones a

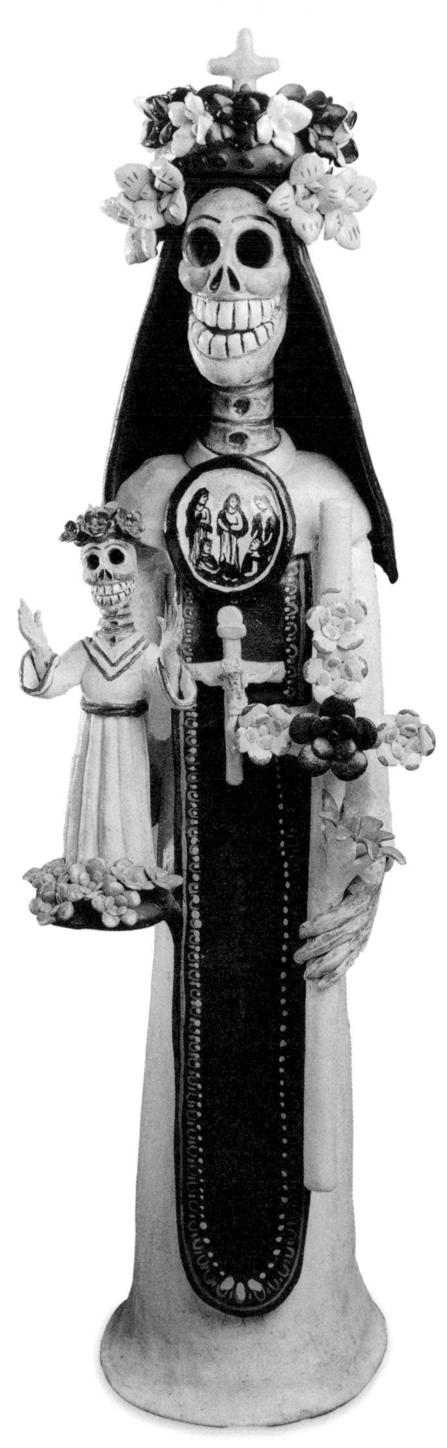

Hieronymite nun, unbaked painted clay, Metepec, State of Mexico.

Huitzilopochtli y, por vía paterna, de los iluminados que encendían las hogueras de la Inquisición, no podía ser igual a todos, pensaron los mexicanos del siglo XX.

Al tiempo que se fortalecía una identidad nacional a lo largo de los "regímenes emanados de la Revolución" se fue bosquejando la fascinante imagen de un país cuyos habitantes habían recibido un trato particular por parte de los pobladores de las mansiones oscuras.

El antiguo vínculo fundador de la "excepción mexicana", la alianza del Tepeyac, que hacía a los hijos de este territorio una estirpe elegida, se veía de esta manera refrendado y confirmado, y adquiría, al mismo tiempo, una sacralidad distinta, aceptable también para los herederos del laicismo liberal y republicano. Los mexicanos, según la tesis que se fue consolidando a lo largo del siglo XX, hemos obtenido sobre la sombra blanquecina que va segando, al filo de su guadaña, las esperanzas y los amores, una suerte de victoria poética: le hemos perdido el respeto y podemos mirar fijamente sus ojos vacíos, hemos convertido a la dama terrible en un personaje familiar y ridículo: una simple calaca.

No se trata, por supuesto, de un verdadero triunfo como el que postula el cristianismo: el mal (del que la muerte es solo un corolario) derrotado por un sacrificio que redime y cuyo signo es la resurrección de una persona divina ("muerte, ¿dónde está tu victoria?") sino, por el contrario, de un gesto de desafío del pequeño sobre el poderoso (un desplante parecido al gesto que los franceses llaman *pied de nez*), basado en una conciencia realista de los propios límites, un impulso lejanamente emparentado, quizá, con la actitud de estoicos y epicúreos.

En el trazo de esa imagen de un pueblo capaz de burlarse de la muerte, de paliar el adverso destino de la especie con un regocijado exabrupto, tuvieron una participación decisiva los artistas afines al nacionalismo revolucionario (de Posada a Rivera). Ellos intentaban dotar al país de un nuevo espíritu y de un nuevo lenguaje estético. Querían que fuera moderno y progresista, exterior al horizonte de la cultura católica, que había llegado a impregnar en profundidad las expresiones del arte culto y de las tradiciones populares, y que en esa época se consideraba "retrógrada" y "oscurantista".

De manera paradójica, una influencia determinante para la formación de esta nueva imagen vino en línea recta de la más cristiana de las herencias europeas: la medieval. La actitud lúdica y burlesca ante la muerte que los artistas revolucionarios preconizaron como expresión idiosincrática del alma mexicana manifiesta afinidades esenciales con las *danses macabres*. En ellas, los europeos de la Edad Media tardía expresaban a un tiempo la ambigüedad de sus relaciones con las fuerzas del panteón precristiano, todavía sumamente vivas, y aligeraban, de manera catártica, las tensiones surgidas de sus conflictos con el poder y la autoridad, en un sistema social de jerarquías fijas y casi inmutables.

Estas manifestaciones, hijas a un tiempo del arte culto y del popular, tuvieron su momento de auge entre los siglos XIV y XV para dar cuenta de los crujidos de un andamiaje que iba a desplomarse. El jolgorio escalofriante de las calaveras danzantes era, pues, también el eco de las rebeliones, del hambre y de la peste que anunciaban ese otoño de la Edad Media evocado por Huizinga.

Las danzas de la muerte europeas, con su iconografía grotesca y delirante, decoraban las planchas de los grabadores y los muros de los cementerios. En ellas los grandes de la tierra (tocados de corona, mitra o tiara), convertidos en descarnada osamenta ridícula y saltarina, se mezclaban con la baja plebe de sus súbditos reducidos también a la misma condición. Todas las alcurnias y dignidades de una sociedad de estamentos casi congelados (los "órdenes") se veían así allanadas por el rasero definitivo e ineludible: un destello de sabiduría que afirmaba la unicidad de la especie humana ("*. . . et in pulverim reverteris*"); expresión de angustia por la brevedad de la vida, gemido desgarrador producido por las zozobras de una época turbulenta, amarga revancha que estalla en risotada.

Los hijos de la Revolución mexicana, en su intento por dejar atrás todo lo que fuera hispánico o cristiano, habían decidido volver sus ojos hacia lo que parecían ser las matrices alternativas de nuestra memoria cultural: el mundo precolombino y las sociedades indígenas del siglo XX. Existía un opulento sustrato cultural autónomo, que, pensaban, a pesar de las fuerzas adversas, había logrado mantenerse libre de la contaminación de las influencias europeas. Esa reserva espiritual, postulaban, se encontraba viva en las comunidades rurales, en ese pueblo campesino que había vertido su sangre en la Revolución y que aspiraba a retomar la historia en sus manos. En la óptica del arte nacionalista, las expresiones plásticas de la arqueología prehispánica y de las artes populares eran, unidas en una sola polifonía, las voces complementarias de ese canto común.

El recurso a esa doble inspiración, la amalgama entre esas dos formaciones culturales en una sola imagen—como si las sociedades campesinas del siglo xx fueran herederas directas, intocadas, de las civilizaciones autóctonas; como si el pasado virreinal no hubiera sido más que un aciago paréntesis y no una experiencia fundacional de la nueva sociedad—, contribuyó poderosamente a consolidar el modelo simbólico del México revolucionario.

Paul Westheim, al analizar ya desde 1953 la inquietante afinidad entre las expresiones formales del espíritu macabro medieval con las que comenzaban a convertirse en norma canónica entre los sectores progresistas de la Ciudad de México, propuso una visión mucho más rica y matizada. Él recordó también—aunque sin poner en cuestión el mito naciente—el carácter grave y trágico de las concepciones de la muerte en las sociedades prehispánicas (que contrasta, naturalmente, con el ánimo bullanguero de las calacas revolucionarias).

El sueño, sin embargo, era hermoso y útil (permitía a los mexicanos crear un hondo e intangible vínculo cultural, acrecentar el acervo de los elementos que parecían serles comunes y específicos) y continuó su camino haciéndose cada vez más fuerte a medida que la Revolución se convertía en objeto de culto patriótico.

La principal figura intelectual mexicana del siglo xx, Octavio Paz, tuvo una influencia decisiva en la formación y consolidación de la imagen de nuestro país como un territorio de excepción en sus tratos con la muerte. En *El laberinto de la soledad*, el poeta da cuenta de su propia visión desencantada de la vida y de la historia, característica de un hijo de la alta cultura de Occidente que se reconoce en el legado de Voltaire y de Kant, pero también en el de Goya. El libro fue escrito en el lugar y la época de la eclosión del espíritu existencialista (París, 1950).

Su espíritu, que era probablemente el de un agnóstico sincero y profundamente atento a la dimensión trascendente del hombre y del universo, su inteligencia reticente y crítica que lo alejó de las ilusiones totalitarias, su sensibilidad afín a la de Lucrecio y Petronio, que lo precavió de las ilusiones y las utopías, le permitieron percibir en el proyecto estético de los artistas de la generación que lo precedía una dimensión de gran nobleza, al mismo tiempo trágica y epicúrea. La muerte que aparece en la obra de Paz no es promesa de vida eterna, sino final: el sufrimiento no redime; solo salvan—provisionalmente—el arte, el trabajo, el amor.

La manera de encarar la muerte (hilarante y herida, resignada e irónica, rebelde, desesperanzada) que habían llegado a formular los artistas revolucionarios y las expresiones populares del mundo urbano de la Ciudad de México fue descrita por su pluma magistral en ese ensayo que marcó profundamente la conciencia que los habitantes del país tenían de sí mismos.

En su penetrante meditación sobre la realidad y el devenir de su patria, Paz dio vida a un personaje literario que le permitió ejemplificar las transformaciones de un país joven que buscaba su rumbo en esa época de futuro abierto. El nombre de este personaje había ya aparecido en nuestras letras, en particular en la obra de Samuel Ramos, pero es Paz quien le da su plena configuración y lo convierte en un hito fundamental de nuestra cultura.

"El Mexicano" de quien habla el autor de *El laberinto de la soledad* no es un prototipo que tenga funciones de muestra representativa de todas las poblaciones del país (semejante a los que podrían proponer la sociología o la estadística) sino, por el contrario, como él lo declara explícitamente, es un rostro inspirado en uno solo de los grupos humanos que lo habitan: el hombre perteneciente a las generaciones posrevolucionarias, consciente de su sociedad, empeñado en construirse como sujeto, comprometido con la edificación de México.

Los mexicanos mestizos, todavía impregnados del espíritu barroco, pero ansiosos de modernidad, recientemente despojados de sus horizontes comunitarios armónicos y secularizantes y, por lo tanto, empeñados en la búsqueda de referencias simbólicas, preocupados por dar a su patria un lugar digno, acorde con los ideales de grandeza heredados de los criollos del Virreinato, fueron escogidos (entre la enorme variedad de pobladores del país) para servir como modelos a partir de los cuales el gran poeta y ensayista construiría un espléndido personaje literario: "El Mexicano", ese hijo bastardo de la Malinche cuya alma desgarrada estalla en el Zócalo con los fuegos de artificio la noche del 15 de septiembre y que se atraganta, entre sollozos y carcajadas, con el pan de muerto.

Esa imagen era el retrato vivo, trazado por un artista egregio, de ciertos sectores urbanos y específicamente capitalinos, cuyos rasgos se mezclaban con los de un sujeto ideal en busca de anclaje entre las culturas herederas de las Luces y el Romanticismo. Los lectores de *El laberinto de la soledad* (pertenecientes a la franja inquieta y culta de la población e hijos espirituales del liberalismo del siglo XIX) se reconocieron fascinados en ese personaje de arraigos inmemoriales, pero urgido de emancipación y de un destino de libertad.

Muchos mexicanos, en la medida que engrosaban—a lo largo de esos años de acelerada integración social—los sectores de la cultura mestiza mayoritaria, iban aceptando como propio un retrato poético que era en sí mismo un proyecto de sociedad. Los individuos recién incorporados a la cultura nacional sabían por fin cuáles eran, en términos de una definición laica, no confesional, los rasgos de identidad de su nación, cuál era la imagen distintiva que podían presentar ante un mundo cuyo reconocimiento les era indispensable, y fueron adoptando, entusiasmados, el nuevo rostro que percibían en ese texto deslumbrante que llegaron a convertir en un espejo.

Numerosos habitantes de las variadas comarcas del país aprendieron (gracias a *El laberinto de la soledad*) qué quería decir ser mexicano, y supieron que una de las características fundamentales de la identidad cultural de su patria era un desplante irónico y juguetón ante la muerte: comenzaron entonces a hacer suyos, poco a poco, una actitud, un ceremonial y una iconografía que para muchos habían sido totalmente desconocidos.

Por los mismos años se fraguaron y consolidaron otros arquetipos de la misma naturaleza, sobrepuestos a este. (En el número de *Artes de México* consagrado al tequila—número 27—hemos explorado la manera como se construyó la imagen simbólica de un licor regional que, asociado a las figuras del charro y el mariachi, contribuyó a sustentar los modelos que necesitaba una sociedad ansiosa de darse a sí misma una identidad nacional consistente.)

Más tarde, a medida que el nacionalismo revolucionario se fue convirtiendo en un objeto de consenso, sus modelos y su estética aumentaron su difusión e incluso han llegado en ocasiones a banalizarse. Comenzó a haber un Día de Muertos (basado en este modelo lúdico-macabro) primero oficioso y luego casi oficial en numerosas dependencias públicas. La estética de la calaverita penetró luego en los territorios del arte patrocinado por el Estado y de la experimentación libre, en los del consumo y de la publicidad.

"La muerte ciriquiciaca montada en su mula flaca" de los gritones de las loterías de feria, la muerte descoyuntada y chacotera que sirve de modelo al nacionalismo mestizo—y cuyos signos emblemáticos son la Catrina del mural de Rivera y la calavera de azúcar—ha llegado ya, en menos de un siglo, a casi todo el territorio nacional de la mano de la cultura urbana, en una muestra del avance y la consolidación de una identidad compartida. Hoy, incluso en regiones donde hace medio siglo nadie había oído hablar de esa imagen de la muerte, proliferan entre los últimos días de octubre y los primeros de noviembre las ofrendas fúnebres impregnadas de un aire ligero y jocoso, irónico e irreverente.

Es importante señalar que, como en la tradición europea, en México, aun en las expresiones más convencionales del folclor oficial, los coloridos cráneos de azúcar y las huesudas descoyuntadas hacen referencia a los vivos, no a los muertos. Los nombres que se inscriben en las calaveritas son los nuestros (y los de nuestros amigos y contemporáneos bendecidos por el poder, la fama o la fortuna), no los de las ánimas benditas. Este es un ritual que expresa de manera lúdica el mensaje del Miércoles de Ceniza (el filo que todo lo allana nos iguala, las jerarquías son solo temporales, existe una realidad más honda, distinta de la que aparece a nuestros ojos).

Muchas expresiones macabras de la tradición popular mexicana tienen su origen directo en las vertientes europeas de nuestra cultura: la muerte era en esos horizontes familiar y visible. Sus saltos descoyuntados suprimían las jerarquías. Su guadaña nivelaba segando las cabezas, pero ofrecía una esperanza sin límites.

Estas manifestaciones del talante carnavalesco son quizá más medievales y europeas (y, culturalmente, cristianas) de lo que a nuestra sociedad le gusta admitir. Se trata, tal vez, de una expresión más del firme anclaje de nuestras culturas en el horizonte del barroco vivo, un territorio donde la muerte no desaparece de la visión ni de la conciencia.

La calavera corrosiva y crítica (dirigida a los poderosos) coexiste así con la entrañable (en los versos dedicados a los amigos). En esta última no solo nos hermana la certidumbre de nuestra semejanza, de nuestra común fragilidad: la risa compartida puede ser también una forma rudimentaria, a veces torpe, de acariciar desde lejos, la manera que tienen los tímidos de expresar el afecto.

LA MUERTE SIN CALAVERAS: TERNURA Y PIEDAD FILIAL

El mito ha podido ser eficaz porque reposa en un formidable efecto polisémico: el signo plástico del nuevo folclor nacionalista es formalmente casi indistinguible y lleva los mismos nombres (altar de muertos, ofrenda) de otro objeto cuyo funcionamiento simbólico es totalmente distinto. Si se mira apresuradamente o desde fuera, es posible pensar que los monumentos efímeros que se erigen en un recinto oficial o que proliferan en los hoteles y restaurantes de la Ciudad de México son idénticos a los que las familias del mundo rural o barriero aderezan devotamente en sus hogares o en los camposantos. En ambos casos se trata, con menor o mayor fantasía—a veces con un verdadero derroche de creatividad—, de composiciones a base de flores y velas, incienso, alimentos (donde abundan el pan y las frutas) y objetos evocadores que hacen referencia a una persona o un tema. Pero aquí comienzan a aparecer las diferencias esenciales: el altar doméstico está siempre destinado a personas concretas y el talante de los actos ceremoniales es siempre grave, tierno, impregnado de respeto y añoranza. No hay en él burla ni ironía.

Las familias campesinas de numerosas regiones del país, sobre todo en aquellas zonas donde predomina la herencia indígena (la tradición está menos arraigada en los territorios influidos por la cultura criolla), han aprendido de sus antepasados que tanto las ánimas del purgatorio como aquellas que se encuentran ya en la gloria tienen permiso de venir a visitar a sus deudos una sola vez al año, cuando el calendario litúrgico de la Iglesia católica conmemora las festividades de Todos los Santos y los Fieles Difuntos. Por eso preparan con esmero el camino de cempasúchil que habrá de guiarlas hasta la mesa del banquete, instalada en el recinto principal de la casa; por eso han ido, por lo menos desde la víspera, a limpiar y embellecer las tumbas donde reposan los restos de los seres queridos. La preparación del festín ha exigido la movilización de toda la familia y un gasto considerable (el momento, en pleno periodo de cosecha, no es fruto del azar). La instalación de la ofrenda es ocasión de una intensa actividad emotiva: los jefes de familia pronuncian a veces pequeñas alocuciones dirigidas a los homenajeados. En sus palabras llenas de afecto y reverencia subrayan los deberes de la piedad filial y hacen explícitos ante sus hijos los valores que fundamentan la cohesión del grupo doméstico campesino: solidaridad, respeto, memoria, generosidad.

Esta fiesta es el hito mayor en la vida ceremonial de millones de mexicanos. En ella celebran a un tiempo los fastos del ciclo de su actividad productiva (la agricultura) y fortalecen la red más importante de su vida social (la familia), los nexos comunitarios se reafirman y consolidan por las visitas, invitaciones y agasajos mutuos. El homenaje rendido a los ancestros permite a los hijos menores conocer con absoluta claridad las responsabilidades que la gratitud exigirá de ellos cuando sean adultos: atención y cuidado de los padres no solo a lo largo de la vejez desvalida, sino más allá. La memoria es una manera de prolongar la vida, de atenuar, a lo largo de las generaciones, el efecto trágico de la aniquilación definitiva de un nombre, una conciencia, una esperanza.

(Westheim recuerda que para los antiguos mexicanos la supervivencia de la identidad individual se prolongaba a lo largo de unas cuantas generaciones antes de fundirse en un alma cósmica indiferenciada.)

Esta conmemoración, que muchas familias de distintos estados realizan con tanto afecto y a la que consagran recursos cuantiosos, las emparenta con poblaciones análogas de otras latitudes donde el culto a los ancestros es el eje estructurante de la vida ceremonial y donde la unidad doméstica es la referencia decisiva del sistema de valores.

En algunos casos, el banquete se prolonga en el cementerio. Ahí los deudos, como hacían ya los romanos, comparten las viandas de lujo con sus amados visitantes. Los parientes se instalan alrededor de la sepultura y departen tranquilamente con la etiqueta habitual de una celebración doméstica. Como en cualquier festejo, la música viene con frecuencia a dar intensidad y calor al homenaje. Conjuntos norteños, bandas, tríos, mariachis pueden llegar a mezclar sus notas de una tumba a otra, mientras las piezas preferidas de los padres difuntos hacen aflorar en el corazón de los hijos una dulce añoranza.

El alcohol, por su carácter de sustancia sacralizable, por su naturaleza ambigua (bienhechora y nefasta), por su misterioso poder de provocar la risa y el llanto, de suscitar sin transición tanto el ensueño como la pesadilla, es en nuestro mundo rural, como en muchas regiones culturales del mundo, un elemento esencial de celebraciones y ritos. En muchos sitios es la ofrenda ceremonial por excelencia, y en estos festejos suele estar presente de manera casi general, pero su uso varía de una región a otra siguiendo los patrones locales de libación: moderado y sereno en muchos casos, puede llegar a ser vehemente y excesivo. De ahí el carácter exaltado que adoptan ciertos banquetes fúnebres, y que algunos visitantes apresurados confunden con una actitud semejante a la euforia jolgoriosa de los altares inspirados en la tradición revolucionaria. De cualquier manera, la tónica general de estas manifestaciones es radicalmente distinta de las que predominan

Los abuelos difuntos no son, en el México indígena, héroes ni santos: lo más hermoso que se recuerda de ellos son sus debilidades, sus antojos. Por eso se ofrece a cada uno según la propia inclinación—según el propio gusto—su pepián preferido, su copita de Zacualpan, su guitarra, sus cigarritos. "Antes has de dispensar, Vicenta Marcela, que este año no te estamos atendiendo como te mereces y como nos acordamos de ti. Ya ves cómo se ha puesto todo, y luego con lo de la graduación de Gerardo, que con el favor de Dios se le hizo salir de su secundaria, quedamos desbarajustados, pero aquí te hicimos tu molito como a ti te gustaba y que tus nietas se vayan enseñando para que luego te lo sigan haciendo ya que se casen. El champurrado ya te lo hizo la mayora, a ver cómo le quedó".

Alfonso Alfaro. *Los espacios del sazón.*

en el folclor laico y oficial. No hay aquí ninguna carcajada, ninguna burla de la muerte, ningún desplante ("la vida no vale nada"); estos ritos, al contrario, intentan prolongar la presencia de los seres amados a través de la memoria, enaltecer el valor de la vida, alargando sus gozos a través del disfrute sensorial del banquete, las flores, la música.

En estas celebraciones es muy raro encontrar los signos distintivos de la primera figura de la muerte que hemos analizado. Las pocas imágenes de cráneos y osamentas que están presentes se encuentran relacionadas con las insignias mortuorias de la iconografía católica (y no están revestidas de elemento lúdico alguno), aunque han comenzado a aparecer poco a poco elementos decorativos provenientes de los altares oficiales. En estas ofrendas sin huesudas gesticulantes ni calaveras de dulce, muchos mexicanos (mayoritarios entre las poblaciones de raigambre campesina) nos permiten entrever otra concepción del cosmos y otra idea del destino, al tiempo que fracturan la imagen homogénea de un país unido por un alma nacional marcada por una magnífica rebeldía del espíritu, capaz de jugarse la vida y desafiar la fatalidad. Con su manera tierna y devota de encarar la muerte, una manera marcada por la sencillez, ausente de aspavientos, esta tradición enriquece a esta patria común con el vigor de una cultura distinta, tan semejante a las que florecen en otros continentes.

Hemos visto que en México la muerte no adopta un solo rostro—el de la calavera Catrina—y que este país es menos mágico y menos homogéneo de lo que nos gusta creer. En realidad, hay múltiples maneras de asumir el sufrimiento y las angustias e inquietudes de lo desconocido, como corresponde a un país de tantas culturas.

OTROS ROSTROS DE LA MUERTE: FANTASMAS Y APARECIDOS

Además de los rasgos entrañables de los padres, los abuelos o los angelitos fallecidos en la infancia—cuyas almas tienen permiso de venir de visita cuando son esperadas—, en el mundo rural y sus prolongaciones, la muerte reviste también a veces el rictus aterrador de los difuntos que pueden irrumpir en mitad de una noche lúgubre o de un paraje desierto. El rito tiene la ventaja de la previsión. Los seres de ultratumba son siempre desasosegantes, no importa cuán amados hayan sido en vida. El Día de Muertos permite abrir y cerrar, a hora fija, las puertas del más allá (como en el mundo moderno el psicoanálisis permite controlar, reloj en mano, las del subconsciente).

En algunos sitios, estas ceremonias terminan con algarabía y ruidos estruendosos destinados a recordar a las ánimas (especialmente las desconocidas) que la visita ha terminado y que están obligadas a retornar a su fantasmática morada. Hay que evitar el riesgo de que alguna decida prolongar su estancia entre los vivos: su presencia no podría dejar de acarrear desazón y graves peligros. Su deambulación por callejas y cañadas, su presencia sigilosa entre nosotros, suele provocar escalofrío. En nuestro folclor rural (como en el del mundo entero) abundan los relatos donde las sombras protectoras o perversas de los difuntos se mezclan con las de los genios de la naturaleza y las criaturas de los inframundos.

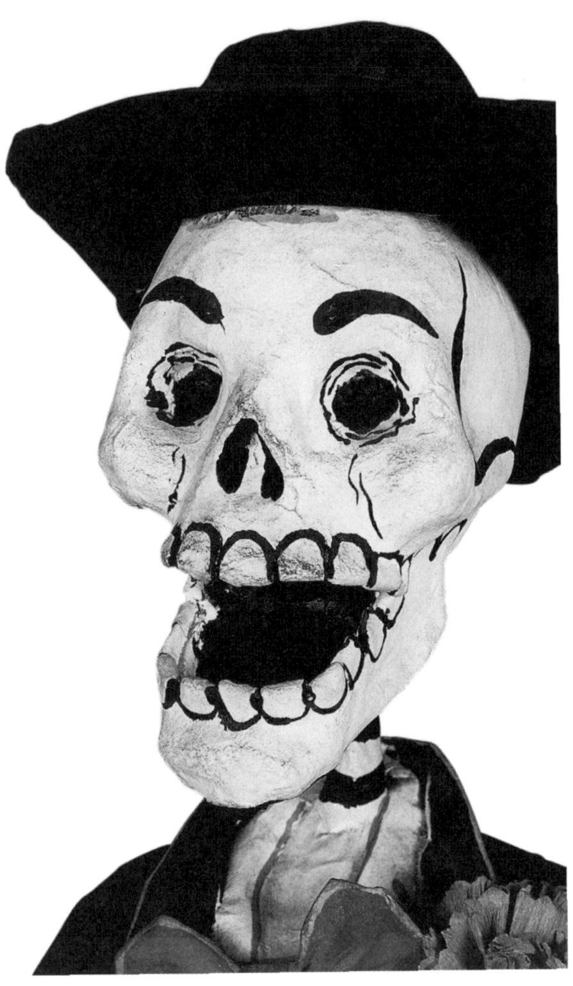

Groom (detail), painted paper-mâché on wire frame, Mexico City, 1988, Ruth D. Lechuga Folk Art Museum.

En francés, los aparecidos se llaman *revenants*, los que regresan. Allá como aquí es necesario hacer todo lo posible para evitar sus errancias y procurar que permanezcan del otro lado de la frontera que separa los niveles de la realidad. En el mismo siglo de Posada, Rivera y Paz, otro de los artistas mayores de México, Juan Rulfo, produjo una obra capital donde aflora la configuración que adquieren los reinos de lo visible y lo invisible en ese mundo rural, donde las fronteras entre la vida y la muerte son tan tenues como las que separan la racionalidad del inconsciente en los espíritus geniales o turbados. Gracias a *Pedro Páramo*, también esta dimensión tiene cabida en los territorios de nuestra alta cultura.

Las siluetas de la muerte que estas dos nuevas figuras nos presentan (la popular de los relatos de aparecidos, la honda y refinada de los textos rulfianos) nos ofrecen otras dos maneras de encararla plenamente vigentes en nuestro país, totalmente mexicanas, por supuesto, pero también totalmente universales, porque ambas tienen afinidades esenciales con las que reconocen como propias otros pueblos tan distintos del nuestro.

EL DESAMPARO METAFÍSICO

En el siglo XX mexicano, no solo el grabado y el muralismo, no solo el ensayo y la novela, intentaron escudriñar, en sus obras más ilustres, los misterios de nuestra sombra inseparable. Dos de las más profundas y vigorosas creaciones poéticas llevan también la huella de su nombre: *Muerte sin fin* de José Gorostiza, y *Nostalgia de la muerte* de Xavier Villaurrutia. A pesar de sus diferencias, ambas pertenecen a la gran tradición literaria de nuestra lengua y hacen eco a la inquietud que perturba a la conciencia occidental posterior a Nietzsche y a Heidegger.

Frente a una muerte sin promesa de redención, ante una vida cuya última frontera parece ser un signo vacío, cuando la existencia se convierte al mismo tiempo en un paraíso efímero y un infierno intermitente, ¿qué queda a los hombres sino la rebeldía del arte?

LA MUERTE DE LOS MODERNOS: ASEPSIA Y DISCRECIÓN

Obviamente, no todos los espíritus que en nuestro país han adoptado como referencias fundadoras los cánones occidentales comparten una visión tan profunda y refinada, teñida, al mismo tiempo, de desencanto y grandeza.

La mayoría de nuestros compatriotas que pertenecen a las clases acomodadas urbanas tienen, a este respecto, una actitud semejante a la de sus homólogos europeos o estadounidenses. Basta observar el diseño ajardinado de los nuevos panteones (que ya nunca se llaman así), la atmósfera neutra de los velatorios, el auge de las cremaciones, la sobriedad de los ritos funerarios que se celebran en las iglesias de las colonias residenciales. Ahí la muerte es, como en los países desarrollados, algo que se aborda con reserva y pudor. Obviamente sin carcajadas. Los miembros de estos grupos pueden a veces participar, con cierto desapego, en las manifestaciones convencionales del folclor revolucionario (que ha llegado a arraigar en algunos sectores de las clases medias), pero no suelen establecer correspondencia alguna entre sus propios muertos y las calaveritas jolgoriosas.

La muerte, en estos territorios culturales, ha experimentado la misma evolución que Philippe Ariès y Louis-Vincent Thomas han señalado para las sociedades occidentales después de la ilustración. Entre los mexicanos inscritos en la órbita de la modernidad hay los que esperan la resurrección, otros constatan, resignados, la brevedad de las horas humanas, unos pocos practican todavía el espiritismo, otros anhelan la reencarnación, pero casi nadie pone una ofrenda mortuoria para reírse de sus familiares difuntos.

El estudio de las actitudes ante la muerte ha despertado en las últimas décadas un gran interés entre historiadores y antropólogos. Gracias a unos y otros, ahora conocemos las enormes transformaciones que experimentaron las sociedades occidentales, en primer lugar a causa de la profunda evangelización de que fueron objeto las culturas populares europeas particularmente a partir del siglo XVII, y luego cien años más tarde, con la no menos importante difusión de los ideales y valores ilustrados (aunque este segundo proceso fue más paulatino y estuvo inicialmente reservado a las elites).

Estos fenómenos tuvieron una influencia capital en las percepciones y en las creencias tanto de los individuos como de las sociedades. La expansión de las Iglesias (tanto de la católica como de las protestantes) que tuvo lugar durante los siglos barrocos fue relegando cada vez más las expresiones culturales de origen precristiano (entonces sumamente vivas, en particular entre las poblaciones rurales); la ilustración aceleró la adopción de modelos sociales cada vez menos comunitarios, menos emotivos, más ansiosos de proponer como única guía a la inteligencia racional.

Para el tema que nos ocupa, el resultado fue que mientras los nuevos patrones noreuropeos ganaban terreno, las actitudes y comportamientos tradicionales se iban debilitando. En todo el mundo occidental (incluyendo nuestro país), las personas imbuidas del espíritu moderno comenzaron a mirar las antiguas prácticas por encima del hombro, y a calificarlas de "supersticiones". Por supuesto, las ofrendas de alimentos, los ágapes en los cementerios (que eran habituales entre los primeros cristianos, como entre los romanos antiguos y que muchos europeos conservaron por milenios) entraban en esa categoría. Es interesante recordar, a este respecto, la narración, imbuida de un aire reprobatorio que hace José Tomás de Cuéllar del Día de Muertos de 1882 en la Ciudad de México. Lo que más parece irritar su sensibilidad es el ánimo distendido propio de las celebraciones familiares, que parece irreverente a un hombre cuya mirada ha sido ya modelada por la gravedad y la distancia con que los modernos consideran las cosas de ultratumba.

En el número 43 de *Artes de México* hemos abordado con más detenimiento esa transformación que afectó al conjunto de los sistemas simbólicos de las sociedades occidentales, y que, en los países periféricos como el nuestro, fue menos profunda y más tardía. Los progresos de la ciencia y la técnica, los avances de la medicina y de la higiene alentaron el sueño de un triunfo posible de la razón y de la salud. Todas las expresiones de lo que se consideraba el mal o la muerte fueron arrinconadas al exterior de la visión y de la conciencia: tanto la locura como la enfermedad, tanto el despilfarro como el desenfreno, tanto el exceso como la muerte se convirtieron en temas impropios; la vehemencia en la expresión de los sentimientos sufrió el mismo tipo de rechazo. Los europeos—y las poblaciones asimiladas a su alta cultura—creyeron que todo podía—y debía—ser limpio y transparente. Las representaciones de las *danses macabres* fueron destruidas y los cementerios (siguiendo el ejemplo del de los inocentes, en París) expulsados del corazón de las ciudades: las nuevas necrópolis debían ubicarse en las periferias para impedir (se creía entonces) las posibilidades de contagio, pero sobre todo para alejar la imagen de la muerte.

Los individuos cuyas referencias culturales son las de esa modernidad, han erradicado de su entorno unas prácticas que consideran arcaicas y una sensibilidad que les parece excesiva. Tampoco ellos subliman la pena con estampas de parcas rijosas.

DEL DOLORISMO MACABRO AL BIEN MORIR

Otro más de los rostros de la muerte tiene en México un lugar de predilección. En todos sus rincones es posible encontrar expresiones, a menudo espléndidas, de un trágico dolorismo: mártires asaeteados, descuartizados, ánimas benditas sometidas a la purificación de las llamas, condenados que son objeto de las más inverosímiles torturas, Cristos sanguinolentos, lacerados, desollados, traspasados de un sufrimiento infinito (ver, a este respecto, el número 37 de *Artes de México* y el libro *Corpus Aureum* de la colección Uso y Estilo).

El arte de la piedad barroca pudo florecer aquí en terreno fértil y llegó a convertirse en uno de los lenguajes expresivos connaturales a nuestras culturas. Las espiritualidades *De contemptu mundi*, heredadas de la tradición monacal y reactivadas por los movimientos de reforma de la vida religiosa, estuvieron sumamente presentes en el arte y las formas de devoción en la Nueva España. La renovación tridentina y los impulsos estéticos del catolicismo barroco, orgánicamente ligado a ella, conformaron una cultura religiosa que concedía un lugar privilegiado a las experiencias sensibles como vía de acceso a la trascendencia. De esa manera se vieron favorecidas las expresiones plásticas y poéticas—con frecuencia vehementes—en torno a los misterios de la fe y en particular de las postrimerías.

Además, el desarrollo de la conciencia moral (sobre los antiguos esquemas centrados en la pureza ritual) y el énfasis en la libertad y en la responsabilidad de cada individuo en su propia salvación (derivada de las posiciones católicas sobre la gracia, que en esos años eran tal vez el objeto principal de controversia teológica) orientaban la disyuntiva capital del destino humano hacia un punto verdaderamente crucial: el instante de la muerte. De él podía depender la felicidad o la condenación eterna. Lograr una buena muerte se convirtió en la principal preocupación de estos creyentes. El sereno tránsito de san José—aunque no aparece descrito en los evangelios—era el modelo ideal. Su devoción alcanzó en esos siglos un auge sin precedentes (el reino de la Nueva España le fue especialmente consagrado).

El cristianismo postula que la muerte puede ser vencida por la muerte (de Cristo), que la vida verdadera (la eterna) solo nos es accesible gracias a su sacrificio. La complejidad semántica del sentido macabro en el catolicismo barroco—que abrevaba con entusiasmo en las fuentes medievales—debe mucho a esta aparente paradoja: solo la muerte puede dar la vida.

El arte novohispano generó, gracias a esos impulsos teológicos y culturales, una valiosa producción.

Una cultura popular de inspiración católica y de raigambre criolla continúa palpitando en varias regiones del país (y es sobresaliente, por ejemplo, en las zonas donde hizo explosión el movimiento cristero). En ellas, la muerte no permite bromas, ni jugarretas. Lo que en ella se dirime es nada menos que la salvación o la condenación eternas.

De nuevo la gran literatura, en este caso Agustín Yáñez, nos permite asomarnos a un universo que sigue siendo tan intenso y vital (aunque, sin duda, cada vez más minoritario) como en los años en que se escribió *Al filo del agua*. En él, los difuntos no son calacas catrinas, sino espíritus gloriosos dignos de veneración o ánimas benditas necesitadas de sufragios.

EN EL OTRO LADO: *THANKSGIVING, HALLOWEEN*

Las culturas mexicanas, como las de todos los países, se encuentran en continua interacción entre sí y con las del mundo. Aquí, desde hace varias generaciones, el principal polo de referencia (no solo cultural) está representado por los Estados Unidos.

Millones de familias (alrededor de la quinta parte de nuestra población) han llevado allende las fronteras los sabores y las usanzas de estas tierras y, en sentido inverso, cada vez son más numerosos los mexicanos que, a causa de la expansión de los patrones de la sociedad de consumo y al formidable vigor de la cultura popular de los Estados Unidos, una potencia que es paradigma de la deseada modernidad, se esfuerzan en seguir con entusiasmo sus impulsos, sus modas y hasta el ritmo de su respiración. Los Estados Unidos conocen también un fenómeno que podría ser equiparado a la gran

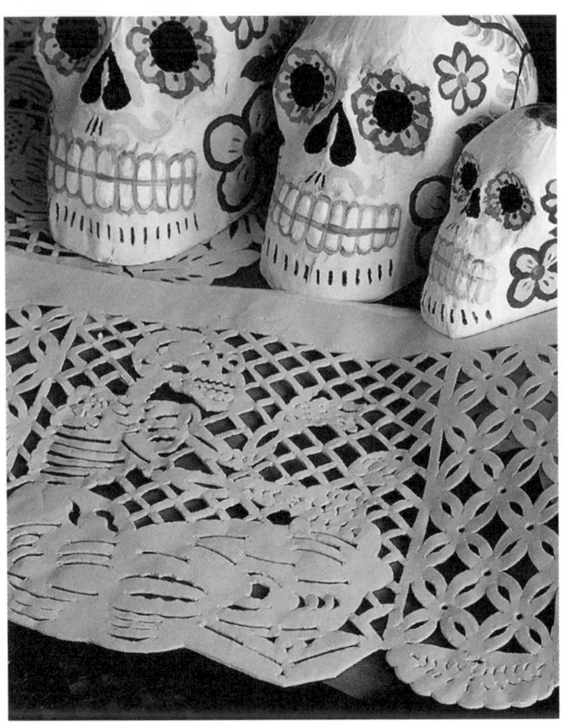

Cut-out tissue-paper skeleton and paper-mâché skulls.

celebración ritual del grupo doméstico (que en México sólo sobrevive en el espacio rural y sus prolongaciones): el más próximo equivalente estadounidense del banquete familiar del altar de muertos (el que se realiza sin chistes ni juegos) es la cena del día de Acción de Gracias. Ambos están ligados al culto del maíz y tienen lugar en noviembre, mes de cosecha, pero mientras aquí tiene un marcado carácter indígena, allá se ha convertido en una celebración transcultural. En los Estados Unidos reúne a los miembros de un grupo reducido, la familia, y está en su origen destinada a agradecer a Dios y a reconocer la contribución del propio esfuerzo en la generosidad con que la tierra puede prodigar sus dones; es el ritual que pone de manifiesto la integración de todas las comunidades en torno a los principios éticos de los padres fundadores: la laboriosidad, el ahorro. La velada es hogareña y serena, íntima y discreta, y su menú es una saludable composición de sabores neutros y equilibrados. En México, por el contrario, el festejo convoca a la comunidad sin número de los parientes, amigos y vecinos, y esto justifica la extravagante desmesura en la cantidad y en la abundancia de los platos: fiesta de pobres que se atiborran una vez al año, fiesta de príncipes que pueden permitirse el gesto señorial de invitar sin tener en cuenta el número y el tratar a cada uno por todo lo alto.

Mientras en *Thanksgiving* el pasado es solo símbolo y reminiscencia (como en la Santa Cena en algunas tradiciones religiosas de origen reformado), el Día de Muertos se inscribe en un ciclo histórico arraigado en un tiempo infinito e inmóvil: los comensales de honor son los ancestros desaparecidos. Este rito de la memoria emparenta a las familias mexicanas que lo practican con los grupos domésticos shintoístas y confucianos, que saben que nada hay tan sólido para ligar a una sociedad consigo misma como el cultivo del cariño y el respeto por los antepasados.

Los mexicanos de los Estados Unidos han estado preocupados durante el último siglo por la misma búsqueda de una imagen identitaria que ha obsesionado a sus hermanos y primos que se quedaron en el terruño. En su caso, el fenómeno se ha acentuado por estar inmersos en un espacio diferente de signos y valores. Además, su nueva patria los insta a que formulen, de la manera más explícita posible (es una característica de las sociedades multiculturales), los rasgos distintivos y las peculiaridades de su propia identidad comunitaria.

Es natural que, en estas condiciones, los mexicanos "del otro lado" y sus hijos (sobre todo estos últimos) hayan recurrido con frecuencia al modelo cultural nacionalista (que incluía al personaje literario creado por Octavio Paz—El Mexicano—, y también a los esqueletos de Posada y Rivera). Aquellos que, además, provenían de regiones rurales donde la tradición de la ofrenda familiar (la suave añoranza sin calacas, ni exabruptos) intentaban, quizá, como muchos recién llegados a las grandes ciudades mexicanas, integrar ambas fórmulas (altar devoto en la casa, monumento jocoso en la escuela, la asociación o el recinto público). O, por otra parte, entre los mexicanos "de acá, de este lado", la parca laica y republicana, una imagen moldeada en la primera mitad del siglo xx ha sufrido en las últimas décadas una rápida transformación. El calendario litúrgico, al hacer coincidir su día con la festividad anglosajona de *Halloween* (dos formas ceremoniales heredadas de la tradición medieval europea: mediterránea y barroca en el caso mexicano, nórdica y romántica en el estadounidense), hace que ahora, en las calles de las ciudades y en los hogares de las clases populares y medias, comiencen a entreverar sus formas y sus significados.

El modelo cultural identitario, de horizontes nacionales, va siendo reemplazado por otro, todavía insuficientemente definido.

La mayoría de los niños que uno puede encontrar esos días deambulando por la capital mezclan brujas y calacas, y muchos arman, para construir una alcancía, un objeto híbrido que es al mismo tiempo cráneo y calabaza ("¿me da mi calaverita?", dicen esgrimiendo una *jack-o'-lantern*).

Equiparado a los disfraces de brujas y a los monstruos de la televisión, el rostro de la muerte se va diluyendo, transformándose en una simple máscara capaz de producir apenas un leve escalofrío lúdico y pueril. Este peldaño nos acerca un poco más a esta modernidad donde su imagen debe forzosamente alejarse, desvanecerse, trivializarse.

Todas las *invented traditions* están sujetas a una incesante metamorfosis y esta no podía escapar a la regla. Hoy, el espacio cultural norteamericano se encuentra en plena formación.

LA *SANTA MUERTE* Y EL *CUERNO DE CHIVO*

Las sociedades, felizmente, no tienen un alma fija e invariable, una idiosincrasia definitiva y común a todos sus miembros; van transformándose, mutando incluso. Hemos visto que, en México, como en todas partes, existen maneras muy distintas de asumir la vida y, por lo tanto, de hacer frente a su término.

Algunas de las que aquí han llegado a arraigarse son muy antiguas y tienen correspondencias con modelos sumamente extendidos por todo el planeta (la campesina), otras parecen obedecer en su configuración a los azares de nuestra historia (la revolucionaria), de varias podemos seguir la traza desde el momento de su aparición (la moderna, la barroca . . .).

Existe en nuestro país una imagen de la muerte que, descolorida y casi imperceptible durante mucho tiempo, ha adquirido en los últimos años una gran visibilidad y comienza a producir su propia subcultura.

Las modernizaciones económicas que hemos padecido—desconectadas de un acompañamiento adecuado en los terrenos de la sociedad y la cultura—desarticularon las antiguas tramas de tipo patrimonial y corporativo sin alcanzar a sustituirlas por otras, más acordes con los nuevos modelos que ha adoptado el país. El resultado fue el surgimiento de redes de pertenencia calcadas sobre el antiguo formato, cada vez más marginales, más divergentes de los esfuerzos que requiere la construcción de una sociedad democrática. El aumento de la marginalidad delincuente, que nuestro país ha visto crecer acompañando a cada crisis de la economía, tiene también su expresión estética. Hay ahora una literatura popular, extraordinariamente viva, que se ha convertido en su lenguaje.

El viejo y nobilísimo corrido, heredero de una antigua tradición medieval, es ahora la rendija por la que podemos escuchar la respiración de ese México que se cubre de esmeraldas y "billetes verdes", mientras se aleja de las rutas del proyecto común. Florece en nuestras letras una poesía popular que canta la llama de los placeres efímeros atizada por el dinero fácil, y que expresa la familiaridad con una muerte que no tiene nada de risible: es la que se da y se recibe en cualquier emboscada cuando retumban los cuernos de chivo.

En Colombia, un país que nos lleva en este terreno una trágica ventaja, esos mundos han sido abordados por grandes plumas, pero desde el exterior (Gabriel García Márquez en *Noticia de un secuestro*, Fernando Vallejo en *La Virgen de los sicarios*). Aquí, Arturo Pérez-Reverte, en *La reina del sur*, acaba de abrir esa compuerta, pero desde hace algunos años es la propia voz de esa marginalidad la que se expresa, a veces con una descarnada sinceridad.

Esos versos profundamente emotivos, a veces duros, con frecuencia hermosos, han encontrado en la música norteña los acordes (guturales, viscerales, carnales) que necesitaba para cantar a una juventud que se desangra.

Esa muerte ciega que troncha sin titubeos, destripando a más inocentes que culpables, es diariamente invocada por muchos que hicieron todo lo posible por atraerla, y que intentan, sin embargo, alejarla con ofrendas, plegarias, peregrinaciones, medallas de oro y diamantes. Esa muerte no es jocosa y está viva, y nuestro país no tiene la menor idea de qué hacer con ella. ◆

Alfonso Alfaro. Antropólogo. Director del Instituto de Investigaciones de *Artes de México*. En esta editorial ha publicado varios libros y artículos. Este texto forma parte de una serie escrita bajo los auspicios de la cátedra Alfonso Reyes de la Universidad de París III-Sorbonne Nouvelle.

OPPOSITE: Muerte florida. Papel aglutinado y pintado, sobre armazón de alambre. Ciudad de México.

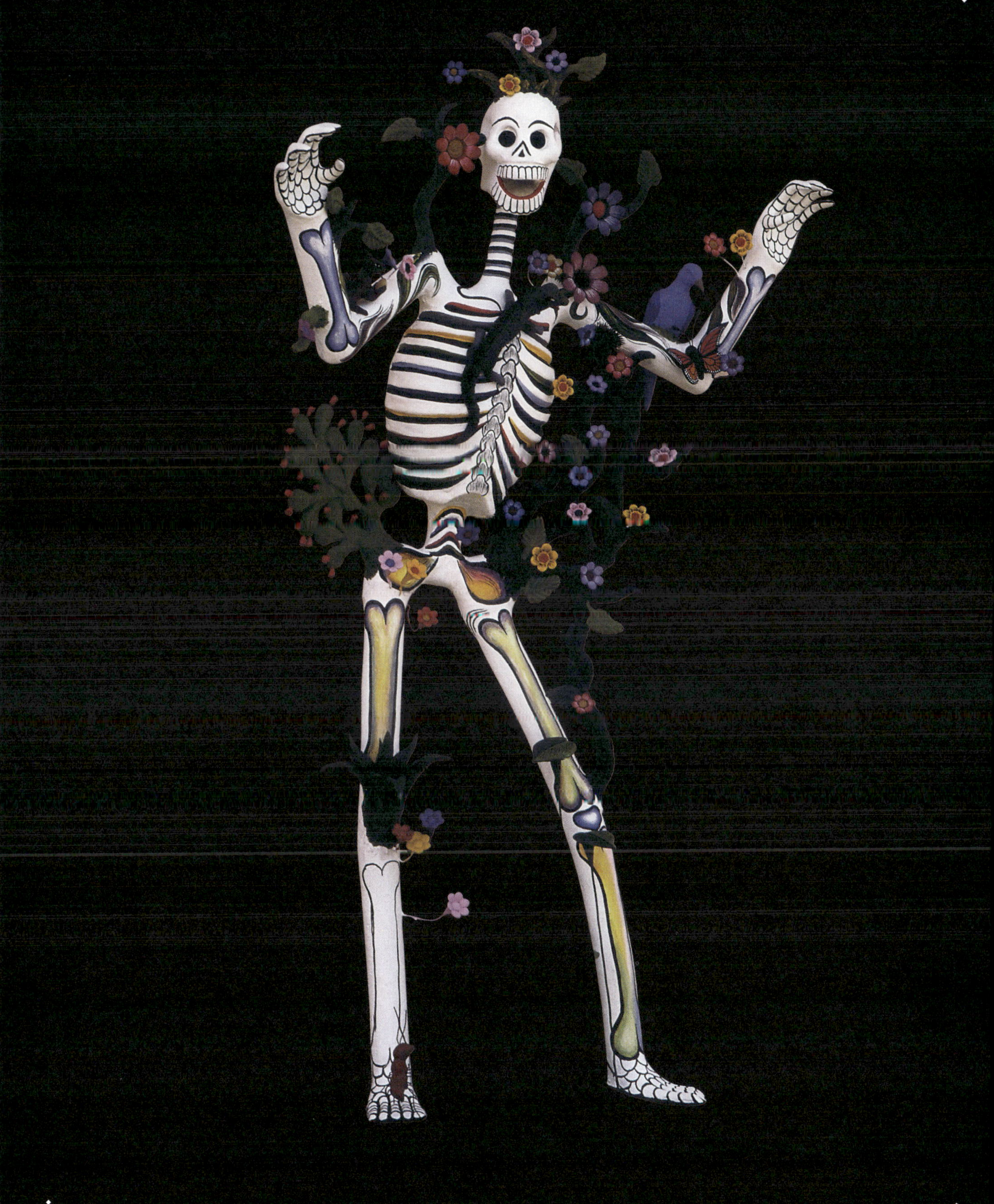

BIBLIOGRAPHY

◆◆◆◆◆

Ajofrín, Francisco de, *Diario del viaje que por orden de la sagrada Congregación de Propaganda Fide hizo a la América Septentrional en el siglo XVIII.* [1740], ed. Vicente Castañeda and Alcover, Real Academia de la Historia, Madrid, 1958, t. xii, vol. 1.

Anguiano, Marina, *et al.*, *Las tradiciones de días de Muertos en México*, México, Dirección General de Culturas Populares, SEP, 1987.

Arzate, María Celia, and Marisa Casillas, "El retorno de las ánimas", en *México Indígena*, núm. 7, México, INI, 1985.

Bartolomé, Miguel, and Alicia Barabas, *Tierra de la palabra: historia y etnografía de los chatinos de Oaxaca*, Oaxaca, Instituto Oaxaqueño de las Culturas-Fondo Estatal para la Cultura y las Artes-INAH, 1996.

Benítez, Fernando, *Los indios de México*, México, Era, 1977.

——, *Viaje al centro de México*, Fondo de Cultura Económica, México, 1995.

Cardoza and Aragón, Luis, *José Guadalupe Posada*, Universidad Nacional Autónoma de México, Dirección General de Publicaciones, México, 1963.

Carmichael, Elizabeth, and Chloë Sayer, *The Skeleton at the Feast: The Day of the Dead in Mexico*, Texas, University of Texas Press, 1991.

Childs, Robert V., and Patricia B. Altman, *Vive tu recuerdo. Living Tradition in the Mexican Days of the Dead*, Los Ángeles, Universidad de California, 1982.

Clark de Lara, Belem (comp.), *José T. de Cuéllar*, Cal y Arena (Los imprescindibles), México, 1999.

Díaz Cíntora, Salvador, *Meses y cielos*, México, UNAM, 1994.

Durán, Fray Diego, *Historia de las indias de Nueva España e islas de tierra firme*, México, Editora Nacional, 1967.

El Colegio del Idioma Totonaco, "Los muertos entre los totonacas", en *México Indígena*, núm 7, México, INI, 1985.

Eliade, Mircea, *Tratado de historia de las religiones*, México, Era, 1992.

Fernández Ledesma, Gabriel, "El triunfo de la muerte", *México en el arte*, México, noviembre de 1948.

Galinier, Jacques, *La mitad del mundo*, México, UNAM-CEM-CA-INI, 1990.

Gamboa, Fernando, "Calaveras". *México en el arte*, México, noviembre de 1948.

García Bergua, Ana, *La confianza en los extraños*, Plaza y Janés (Debate), México, 2002.
Garibay, Ángel María, *La literatura de los aztecas*, México, Joaquín Mortiz, 1979.
——, *Poesía indígena*, México, UNAM, 1962.
Gómez Atzin, Simón, *La ofrenda totonaca de Todos Santos de Papantla*, Veracruz, México, Cuadernos de trabajo MNAIP, 1979.
Guiteras, Calixta, *Los peligros del alma*, México, FCE, 1965.
Hernández Arias, José Rafael, and Erika Saric Gordillo, *La muerte. Una antología*, Valdemar, Madrid, 2000.
Lechuga, Ruth D., *Máscaras tradicionales de México*, México, Banobras, 1991.
Morales Viramontes, María Cristina, "Día de Muertos en la Huasteca de Hidalgo", en *Boletín del INAH*, núm. 6, México, 1985.
Morera, Jaime, *Pinturas coloniales de las ánimas del purgatorio*, Universidad Nacional Autónoma de México, México, 2001.
Navarrete, Carlos, *San Pascualito rey y el culto a la muerte en Chiapas*, México, UNAM, 1982.
Palacios Albiñana, Joaquín (ed.), *Antología de la poesía macabra española e hispanoamericana*, Valdemar, Madrid, 2001.
Paz, Octavio, *El laberinto de la soledad*, Fondo de Cultura Económica, México, 1995.
Poniatowska, Elena, Tomás Ybarra Frausto, *et al.*, *Día de Muertos: A Celebration of this Great Mexican Tradition Featuring Articles, Artwork and Documentation from Mexico Across the United States*, Mexican Fine Arts Center, Texas, 1995.
Prieto, Guillermo, *Crónicas escogidas*, comp. Juan Domingo Argüelles, Océano, México, 2004.
Quirarte, Vicente (comp.), *Ignacio Manuel Altamirano*, Cal y Arena (Los imprescindibles), México, 1999.
Rodríguez Álvarez, María de los Ángeles, *Usos y costumbres funerarias en la Nueva España*, El Colegio de Michoacán-El Colegio Mexiquense, México, 2001.
Sayer, Chlöe, *Skeleton at Fest*, Thames & Hudson, Londres, 1985.
Séjourné, Laurette, *Supervivencias de un mundo mágico*, México, FCE, 1996.
Villaurrutia, Xavier, *Nostalgia de la muerte*, Ediciones Coyoacán, México, 2001.
Westheim, Paul, *La calavera*, Fondo de Cultura Económica (Breviarios), México, 1996.

DAY OF THE DEAD

Artes de México

Library of Congress Control Number: 2023930348

ISBN: 978-1-4197-6754-8
eISBN: 979-8-88707-529-7

Book design by Priscila Vanneuville

Published in 2024 by Cernunnos, an imprint of ABRAMS.

Printed and bound in China
10 9 8 7 6 5 4 3 2 1

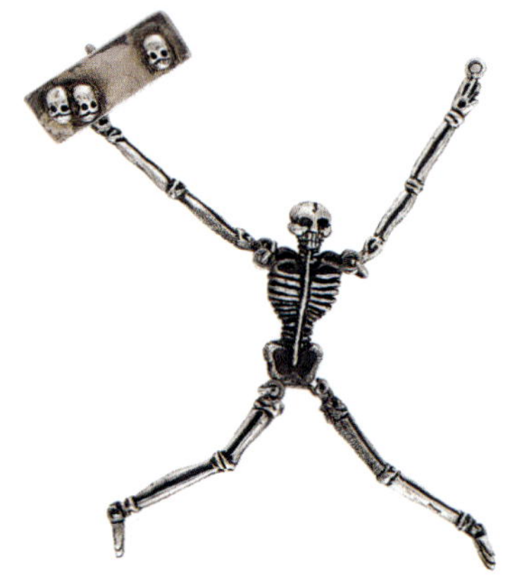

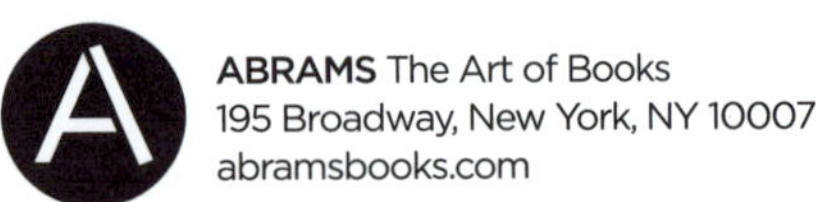

ABRAMS The Art of Books
195 Broadway, New York, NY 10007
abramsbooks.com